ENCLOSURE ACTS

ENCLOSURE ACTS

Sexuality, Property, and Culture in Early Modern England

EDITED BY

RICHARD BURT AND

JOHN MICHAEL ARCHER

Cornell University Press

ITHACA AND LONDON

First published 1994 by Cornell University Press.

Printed in the United States of America

∞The paper in this book meets the minimum requirements of the
American National Standard for Information Sciences—Permanence
of Paper for Printed Library Materials, ANSI Z39.48-1984.

Library of Congress Cataloging-in-Publication Data

Enclosure acts : sexuality, property, and culture in early modern
  England / edited by Richard Burt and John Michael Archer.
    p.   cm.
  Includes bibliographical references and index.
  ISBN 0-8014-2745-2 (alk. paper). — ISBN 0-8014-8024-8 (pbk. :
alk. paper)
    1. English literature—Early modern, 1500–1700—History and
criticism.   2. Literature and society—England—History—16th
century.   3. Literature and society—England—History—17th century.
4. Women and literature—England—History—16th century.   5. Women
and literature—England—History—17th century.   6. Shakespeare,
William, 1564–1616—Political and social views.   7. Shakespeare,
William, 1564–1616—Characters—Women.   8. Social problems in
literature.   9. Property in literature.   10. Renaissance—England.
11. Sex in literature.   I. Burt, Richard, 1954– .   II. Archer,
John Michael.
PR418.S64E53   1994
820.9'003—dc20   93-33886

For Nora Claire Brannen-Burt
and in memory of
Rosena Terrance Archer

Contents

ENCLOSURE ACTS

Introduction

RICHARD BURT AND
JOHN MICHAEL ARCHER

The essays in this volume represent two ways in which critics of early modern English culture currently employ the discourse of enclosure, closure, and containment in their work on the sixteenth and seventeenth centuries. We have included essays on the enclosure and consolidation of land, which constituted an important stage in the transition from feudalism to capitalism, and on the redefinition and enclosure of sexuality and the body within the symbolic order which accompanied this process. The first, perhaps more familiar type of enclosure has lent itself to Marxist and New Historicist approaches; feminists and other critics concerned with gender and sexuality have addressed the second. By reevaluating enclosure as an object of both feminist and historicist analysis, we hope to add a new dimension to the ongoing critique of early modern symbolic practices.

We acknowledge at the outset the uneven development within Renaissance studies which makes for differences in the way our contributors position themselves within the topic. This book is an intervention in Renaissance studies, in where it has been and where it seems to be going. Owing in part to the persuasiveness of the New Historicism, the study of Renaissance culture has secured an ascendancy within literary studies in general at a time when political criticism has achieved a similar hegemony within literary theory. Renaissance studies and political criticism of one sort or another often intersect; feminist analysis of the construction of gender in early modern times, New Historicist sampling of power relations in court society, and cultural materialist genealogies of class and nationality all come to mind.

Much of the recent work on property and the body in early modern culture is concerned to relate gender and class, or, in the familiar phraseology of current criticism, to historicize gender and to engender history.[1] This work has led to a series of theoretical debates between cultural materialists and New Historicists on the one hand, and between both of these schools and feminists on the other.[2] A degree of consensus has emerged, but it has done little to break down an unprofitable division in which each kind of criticism insists on the priority of its categories over those of the others. More crucially, critical debates over the competing claims of history, class, and gender have constructed a relationship between orthodoxy and heterodoxy which distorts both, situating the heterodox as subversion and the orthodox as its containment, fatalistically underwritten or morally denounced by the theorist. Enclosure strikes us as a paradigmatic case because it seemingly sets up the spatial metaphorics that our postmodern categories perpetuate.[3] Yet it is clearly insufficient to condemn enclosure as a version of containment while celebrating the transgression of bodily and territorial boundaries as a form of pure subversion or resistance in early modern England.

Political criticism may be hegemonic, but it is hardly uniform; within Renaissance studies itself different methods and interests are related as much by antagonism as by consensus. The essays in our collection, which deal variously with bodily enclosure and the enclosure of property, exemplify this uneven hegemony. In this introduction we likewise refuse to attempt a synthesis of these divergent approaches. We wish instead to emphasize the figure of enclosure itself as the uneven ground on which sexuality and politics meet in the cultural study of early modern England. We feel that the mutual implication of sexuality and politics within current assumptions about oppositional criticism calls for a reconsideration of the way sexuality and politics have been thought through the body in spatial terms: notions such as displacement, center, margin, and so on. Above all, we wish to question the spatial model of subversion and containment in which the early modern enclosure of property and the body seems to participate.

To a great extent, the containment model can be traced back to Michel Foucault's critique of the traditional definition of power as repression, a force that comes from above to threaten the individual with rules and prohibitions. In *Discipline and Punish* he argues that power does not "repress," "mask," or "conceal", rather, it produces, and what it produces is a visible domain of individuals and objects arranged in space.[4] Vision had figured in the ancien régime only as an absence, as darkness or a screen effect behind which power hides. Foucault traces the replacement of this repressive model with a spatial and visual one in which the Panopticon, Jeremy Bentham's centralized prison where inmates were both contained and kept under constant surveillance, serves as the locus classicus.[5] Foucault shifts the conceptualization of power, in both his mapping of its actual workings and the metaphors he uses to describe them, from the axis of liberty and repression to that of light and darkness. But in some ways the "new" alignment of power relations in *Discipline and Punish* reflects notions about power as traditional as the repressive hypothesis. It still stages power in spatial terms, for the visibility of the individual enclosed within the field of surveillance takes the place occupied by repression in the old arrangement. Furthermore, the containment of the individual within surveillance presupposes the individual's containment *of* surveillance, "a gaze which each individual under its weight will end by interiorising to the point that he is his own overseer."[6]

In the first volume of his *History of Sexuality,* Foucault opposes his productive politics to the repressive hypothesis. Far from repressing sexuality from early modern times to the present, power has incited discourse about it, creating through its censorships and clinical categories the selfsame subversive identities that eventually claim to resist power.[7] "Where there is power, there is resistance," Foucault asserts; "and yet, or rather consequently, this resistance is never in a position of exteriority in relation to power." He goes on to claim that resistance is not "within" power either, but his antirepressive hypothesis perpetuates the traditional theory's spatial vocabulary: "The points, knots, or focuses of resistance are spread over time and space at varying densities, at times mobilizing groups or individuals in a definitive way, inflaming certain points of the body, certain moments in life, certain types of behavior."[8] The locus of containment, however, has switched from surveillance and internalization to the production of individuals as effects of power.

In rehearsing the different positions in the theoretical debate over Foucault's legacy, we aim not to adjudicate between them but to point out a contradiction within current critical practice which springs in part from a problem in Foucault's conception of power itself. Critics of the New Historicism have related this movement's elision of resistance to its interpretation of Foucault's theory of power as a theory of monolithic containment, in which subversion is elicited only to confirm the necessity of domination.[9] The work of the anthropologist Mary Douglas suggests a different view of subversion by placing the body and its role as an image of society at center stage. Anxiety over bodily boundaries incorporates fears of social subversion, for "all margins are dangerous. If they are pulled this way or that the shape of fundamental experience is altered. Any structure of ideas is vulnerable at its margins. We should expect the orifices of the body to symbolise its specially vulnerable points."[10] Julia Kristeva has taken up Douglas's ideas to argue that bodily boundaries are established through the rejection, or abjection, of part of what identity was originally founded on.[11] Boundaries are made possible by the very things they exclude; what we retrospectively call subversion founds a fragile process of containment. Gender and sexuality are instrumental in this feminist revision of the model of resistance or transgression in which, as Luce Irigaray describes it, "the body's pleasure always results from a forced entry—preferably bloody—into an *enclosure*. A *property*? By whom, for whom, is that property constituted?"[12] Judith Butler has proposed that "the critical inquiry that traces the regulatory practices within which bodily contours are constructed constitutes precisely the genealogy of 'the body' in its discreteness that might further radicalize Foucault's theory."[13]

The work of Mikhail Bakhtin on corporeal boundaries has already exerted a substantial influence on critics of the Foucauldian paradigm as it relates to the early modern period.[14] Bakhtin's thematization of the grotesque body suggests ways in which figures such as the outspoken woman, the cross-dresser, and the peasant during carnival or in revolt all incarnate a subversive licentiousness that escapes the license of authority. This list of subversive figures can be expanded, and it makes an interesting catalogue: the scold, the whore, the witch, the sodomite, the beggar, the impoverished city dweller, and the ranters, Levellers, and women preachers who, in the seventeenth century, came to embody the utopian demands of the lower orders. The adoption of Bakhtin entails a critical practice in which the critic searches out a moment of transgression in the text (figured, for example, in something as material as bodily incontinence) at which all forms of containment fail.[15]

Another, more sympathetic response to Foucault draws on Bakhtin as well, but with some second thoughts. These critics set themselves the task of writing a history of subjectivity focused on multiple forms of domination and resistance operating through internalized thresholds of constraint. Bakhtin is stripped of his utopian and liberatory elements, for Foucault's attack on the repressive hypothesis in *The History of Sexuality* is taken at its word, and the carnivalesque is cast as the regulated release of social pressure on which authority depends. Norbert Elias's history of the civilizing process has also been influential here.[16] In an essay on city comedy, Gail Kern Paster has brought Bakhtin and Elias together to argue that gender was constructed along with class when the grotesque or leaky body was specifically attributed to women by a patriarchal culture anxious to police their supposedly free-flowing speech and behavior.[17] Francis Barker has traced the emergence of modern subjectivity out of the theatrical display of the body on the Renaissance stage; inwardness in his account was constructed through a play of surfaces in the public realm.[18] And as Peter Stallybrass and Allon White have shown, the grotesque body has been recoded as an obscene body in the public sphere of bourgeois culture.[19] Yet the carnivalesque is not some moment of pure liberation in their account. Instead it betokens the emergence of phobic and hysterical reactions within bourgeois culture and society to the repressions of society itself.

Jonathan Dollimore has followed the implications of much of this work to some possible conclusions.[20] Early modern attacks on crossdressing and sodomy, he maintains, embody a perverse dynamic in which the socially marginal figure of the deviant becomes discursively central. The turn toward discourse which accompanies Dollimore's rehabilitation of perversity suggests that the questions that have led us into the dead end of subversion's enclosure and attenuation can be reformulated. "By moving away from the misleading language of entities towards that of social process and representation," Dollimore writes, "there emerge different conceptions of domination and dissidence."[21] The uncertain status of the word *sodomy* in early modern England is his prime example. Sodomy signified a generalized evil figured as diverse and outside the social order rather than perverse and peculiar to deviant subjects within it. The accusation of sodomy was the vehicle for two processes: displacement, in which an array of subaltern figures— witches, rebels, papists—were linked through a chain of corruption and otherness, and condensation, whereby one figure is made to stand in for the entire chain.[22] Displacement and condensation are spatial terms, but they also refer to syntagmatic movements between psyche and society which ultimately cut across the barrier between them. As Judith Butler remarks, "The spatial distinctions of inner and outer . . . remain linguistic terms that facilitate and articulate a set of fantasies, feared and desired."[23]

The spatial vocabulary of enclosure and containment may be part of an ingrained opposition in our thought about the past which can only be critiqued from within rather than cast completely aside. Writings by Alan Bray and Jonathan Goldberg on the relationship between sodomy and the institution of patronage in early modern aristocratic culture show how such a critique might be effected. If sexual activity between men, signified if not yet "identified" by the term *sodomy,* was recognized principally in the figure of the "other" at the limit of society, it was also enclosed within the heart of the social hierarchy itself, occluded and misrecognized even by its participants in the patronage bond.[24] Patronage, we would add, neither subverts the dominant sexual order nor contains sexual dissidence; it is a social process, and thus a discursive one, which oxymoronically perpetuates and erases the "perversity" that constitutes society.

It makes little sense to regard such perversity as a heterodoxy contained or repressed within the enclosure of the orthodox. The perverse is closer, in fact, to what Pierre Bourdieu calls "doxa," the universe of all that is taken for granted in a society, all that is constantly spoken but never spoken about.[25] "Practical belief is not a 'state of mind,' " Bourdieu writes, "but rather a state of the body. Doxa is . . . the pre-verbal taking-for-granted of the world that flows from practical sense."[26] Orthodoxy and heterodoxy play out their struggle within the narrow zone of opinion superimposed on a body of misrecognized and unarticulated practices and predispositions. The real dialectic, however, takes place not between the orthodox and the heterodox but between the heterodox and the unspeakable itself. Proponents of heterodoxy constantly try to bring the open secrets of doxa within the enclosure of opinion. The orthodox, by contrast, wish to keep the field of opinion small; they serve as a diversion, a second front that lures heterodoxy into a constricted antinomy of left and right which actually maintains the boundary between the recognized and the misrecognized. It is doxa, the practice of the body, that encloses both heterodoxy and orthodoxy: Bourdieu even provides a diagram in which the oval representing orthodox and heterodox opinion is contained or enclosed within a frame he labels the "universe of the undiscussed."[27] Yet the unavoidable spatial metaphor collapses once we recognize that all three categories are best thought of as different ways of relating, or not relating, speech and action. "If one accepts the equation by Marx in *The German Ideology,* that 'language is real, practical consciousness,' it can be seen that the boundary between the universe of (orthodox or heterodox) discourse and . . . what cannot be said for lack of an available discourse, represents the dividing-line between the most radical form of misrecognition and the awakening of political consciousness."[28]

Attention to discourse and the heterodox in the Renaissance suggests new points of departure for the study of both sexuality and property during the period. The essays of *Enclosure Acts* take up this opportunity in differing but related ways. The book is arranged in two parts. The first, under the heading "Common Grounds: Sexual and Economic Demarcations," concerns the setting of territorial and sexual boundaries; the second, "Boundary Disputes: Consequences of Consolidation," deals with what happened *within* and *between* boundaries, from disputes over the management of water to the Civil War and its aftermath. The essays in both sections also trace the gradual formation of English literary culture during the later sixteenth and seventeenth centuries. Since the setting and upsetting of boundaries were enacted through action and language, it is not surprising that the popular theater of Marlowe and Shakespeare played a key role in the representation of enclosure and containment. The enclosed world of pastoral and topographical poetry in the seventeenth century responds to anxieties about an unstable public life by turning to private languages which nevertheless remain unsettling; the consolidation of a gendered and sexually regulated public sphere through devices such as "dictionary English" is yet another response.

Part I opens with three essays that address the issue of agricultural enclosure; each offers its own perspective on Jack Cade's fatal invasion of Alexander Iden's garden in 2 *Henry VI,* perhaps the period's most memorable staging of claims for and against property. After evoking Thomas More's influential indictment of enclosure in *Utopia,* James Siemon, in "Landlord Not King: Agrarian Change and Interarticulation," reads the Iden scene along with literary and nonliterary texts through Bakhtin's concept of heteroglossia, arguing that enclosure was less an economic reality than a symbolic weapon in contemporary polemics. William Carroll's essay, " 'The Nursery of Beggary': Enclosure, Vagrancy, and Sedition in the Tudor-Stuart Period," is a latter-day coney-catcher's guide to the class of vagabonds and beggars attributed to enclosure and reflected in Shakespeare's starving rebel, who is given all the marks of the rural "masterless man." In "Jack Cade in the Garden: Class Consciousness and Class Conflict in 2 *Henry VI,*" Thomas Cartelli looks at how Cade articulates an emerging consciousness of social status and the antagonisms to which it gave rise. These three essays ground our collection by examining the encounter of Iden and Cade through the progressively focused lenses of economy, society, and class while refusing to simplify the relationship between history and discourse.

The three chapters that follow also have in common texts by Shakespeare, but they shift the focus of the collection from the historical enclosure of property to enclosure as a trope for the ways in which the body was marked and bounded by gender and sexuality in the period. In "Foreign Country: The Place of Women and Sexuality in Shakespeare's Historical World," Phyllis Rackin examines how strategies of gender division operated both spatially, marked on the landscape itself, and discursively, through the moral language that constructed gender as a structure of exclusion and inclusion. Beginning with *1 Henry VI,* in which all the female characters are French, Rackin notes that women in the history plays are typically represented as inhabitants of foreign territories, while foreign territories are depicted as feminine. The essays by Deborah Willis and Richard Wilson ground gender firmly in the body, particularly the female body and the operations through which it was sexed, aged, and finally enclosed in both public and private discourse. In "Shakespeare and the English

Witch-Hunts: Enclosing the Maternal Body," her discussion of Shakespeare and the politics of witchcraft, Willis adopts a psychoanalytic approach, reading the first tetralogy's representations of Joan of Arc and Margaret of Anjou in terms of the witchcraft trials and the stigmatization of motherhood and its secret power which they enacted. In "Observations on English Bodies: Licensing Maternity in Shakespeare's Late Plays," Wilson looks at the figure of the mother from a different viewpoint, combining Foucault with the diaries of Shakespeare's son-in-law John Hall to illuminate the romances. Here the woman's body is an enclosed maternal space that nevertheless cannot be looked into, penetrated, or rendered stable; paradoxically, it is at once contained and unbounded.

The final three essays in this section are concerned with the policing of behavior and the containment of sexuality. In examining the problems of these strategies, they move us into the concerns of the second part of the collection. In "The Poetry of Conduct: Accommodation and Transgression in *The Faerie Queene*, Book 6," Michael Schoenfeldt employs Bourdieu's notion of symbolic violence in examining the literature of courtesy and Spenser's own efforts to break into the closed circle of the court by reinscribing its class exclusions through his poetry. Social control in both the symbolic and physical realms sometimes established new identities as sites of resistance to the very authority that delimited identity. Thus, Judith Haber attributes the early modern discourse of sodomy to its tentative enclosure by the construction of the social in her essay "Submitting to History: Marlowe's *Edward II*." Taking up critical interpretations of the "unpointed," or unpunctuated, letter from Mortimer which ambiguously sentences Edward to death, Haber maintains that the dialectic between readings that celebrate the king's sexuality and those that problematize it is subsumed in an aporia between socially constructed meaning and the complete failure of meaning, between "point" and "pointlessness." But in "The 1599 Bishops' Ban, Elizabethan Pornography, and the Sexualization of the Jacobean Stage," Lynda Boose shows how censorship, a radical intervention in the construction of meaning, could backfire. The Bishops' Ban of 1599, which silenced some of London's most prominent writers, has usually been read as an attempt to quell satire pure and simple. In Boose's view, however, the bishops' action was equally an attempt to suppress a newly salacious tone, heard initially in John Marston's writings, which culminated in a peculiarly English combination of Juvenalian satire with the obscenity of Pietro Aretino. The ban led writers such as Marston and Thomas Middleton to desert print for the stage, thus contributing to the sensational and highly sexualized theater of the early seventeenth century, despite the increased centralization of stage censorship under the Master of the Revels.

Part II opens with Jonathan Gil Harris's essay, "This Is Not a Pipe: Water Supply, Incontinent Sources, and the Leaky Body Politic," which further complicates the notion of securely bounded identities and territories. Harris draws on Bakhtin to analyze the failure to enclose and manage water in civic and literary discourse. His interest in the archaeology of urban spaces takes up where the essays about agricultural enclosure in the first section leave off. In moving from country to city, however, he shows how anxieties about property were compounded by an imagery of the grotesque, often female, body within in the urban scene.

The "boundary disputes" to which Harris alludes establish the keynote for the other essays in this section. The enclosure riots of the 1630s, millenarian ideas about sexuality, and the Civil War found a common, if detached and indirect, expositor in Andrew Marvell. Taken together, the essays on Marvell, by John Rogers, Cristina Malcolmson, and Jonathan Crewe, powerfully represent the aims of this collection in exploring how spatial enclosure was linked to exclusion and containment within the discourses of gender and sexuality. Rogers's essay, "The Enclosure of Virginity: The Poetics of Sexual Abstinence in the English Revolution," relates the poet's obsession with sexual "retirement" or self-exclusion to the millenarian thought of the 1640s and 1650s, in which the dialectic between private and public, between the contemplative and active lives was worked out. In "The Garden Enclosed/The Woman Enclosed: Marvell and the Cavalier Poets," Malcolmson addresses agricultural enclosure and its relation to women and landscape. She shows how enclosure in the work of mid-century poets and pamphleteers functions both to sequester the contemplative soul from civil unrest and as an artificial imposition that uneasily regulates the potentially destructive forces of nature. Malcolmson argues that Marvell and the Cavaliers blend the female body with an eroticized landscape of garden or field to constitute the ground on which male aristocratic control over the property of England is tested and, in most cases, justified.

Crewe's essay "The Garden State: Marvell's Poetics of Enclosure," the final one in the Marvell group, offers a careful consideration of the garden poems and "Upon Appleton House." Renaissance pastoral, Crewe asserts, acknowledged paradisal origins in a lost past, but Marvell's verse reveals the perversity of these origins in the biblical and classical traditions. The "garden state" of Eden and the Ovidian state of nature were both characterized by tales of gender conflict and sexual transgression, and both intimate the instability of the political state that would contain these violent origins. In "Upon Appleton House," the Fairfax estate similarly originates in William Fairfax's seizure of the person of Isabel Thwaites and the property of Nun Appleton, a *hortus*

conclusus harboring prelapsarian lesbian sexuality. Crewe demonstrates
that Marvell's renewal of pastoral depends on a return to such perverse
beginnings and their amplification in "hypernatural" phenomena such
as the creation of hybrid tulips or the discovery of New World flora.
The risk for Marvell's poetics was the loss of linguistic control to powerful female figures such as the prioress and the rebellious Thestylus.
The three Marvell essays account in complementary ways for this poet's complex response to the crisis of the mid-seventeenth century, the
threatened disruption of necessary limits to land and identity which he
nevertheless recognized to be heterodox in themselves.

Our collection ends with Juliet Fleming's essay "Dictionary English
and the Female Tongue," which signals another response to that crisis.
Language itself, as Crewe suggests, is a means of containing people and
their property; in the later seventeenth century its role became particularly evident in the positioning of women within the rapid standardization of English. Fleming maintains that the first English lexicographers divided the linguistic community into those whose speech was
"correct" and those, such as women and other "unskillful persons,"
who were outside the linguistic "pale" (an analogy drawn from the borders of the English colony in Ireland) and therefore in need of instruction. Although early dictionaries ostensibly catered to the needs of
women, Fleming shows that they excluded the women readers they
were supposed to educate. English became an enclosed, socially encoded, and metropolitan language, authorized by a manufactured consensus as to what was "common" usage.

The essays in this volume show that there was no simple opposition
between enclosing orthodoxy and transgressive heterodoxy during the
English Renaissance. Together they challenge the conventional ways in
which early modern culture is delimited without and divided up
within, suggesting that discourse itself breaks down the notion of
power as enclosure or containment. A similar shift from spatial to discursive ways of thinking about the historical representation of enclosure takes place within Foucault's work, and (more compellingly)
between Foucault's work and that of contemporary critics who have
taken up the exploration of gender and sexuality in the early modern
period. The turn toward the enclosing and disclosing acts of language
itself is anything but a turn away from politics and the body. For example, it might involve the discursive constitution of the grotesque
body, the "loud word spoken in the open," in aristocratic as well as
peasant or middle-class culture, and among women as well as men.[29]
Bakhtin's work on invective, billingsgate, and what we now call hate
speech has been largely ignored, but it opens up new paths for the
study of antagonism among various groups in early modern society, an

antagonism that includes high culture and its satiric traditions. The drive for common ground entails endless border disputes, both in the early modern texts our contributors discuss and among the various schools of thought intent on practicing political criticism within Renaissance cultural studies. Yet a more productive division of labor may lie beyond, or rather among, the restricted and restricting enclosures of current critical practice.

N O T E S

1. The work of Peter Stallybrass has been very important here: see "Patriarchal Territories: The Body Enclosed," *Rewriting the Renaissance: The Discourses of Sexual Difference in Early Modern Europe*, ed. Margaret W. Ferguson, Maureen Quilligan, and Nancy J. Vickers (Chicago: University of Chicago Press, 1986), pp. 123–44, and Stallybrass and Allon White, *The Poetics and Politics of Transgression* (Ithaca: Cornell University Press, 1986). Another influential reading is provided by Gail Kern Paster, "Leaky Vessels: The Incontinent Women of Jacobean City Comedy," *Renaissance Drama*, n.s., 18 (1987), 43–65. Among related approaches, see Karen Newman, "Renaissance Family Politics and Shakespeare's *The Taming of the Shrew*," *English Literary Renaissance* 16 (1986), 131–45; Frank Whigham, "Reading Social Conflict in the Alimentary Tract," *ELH* 55 (1988), 333–50; and Lynda E. Boose, "Scolding Brides and Bridling Scolds: Taming the Woman's Unruly Member," *Shakespeare Quarterly* 42, 2 (1991), 179–213. Historians and critics have long debated the role of the enclosure of land in early modern England. In addition to the works cited in James Siemon's essay in this volume, see Richard Lachmann, *From Manor to Market* (Madison: University of Wisconsin Press, 1987), and Richard Halpern, *The Poetics of Primitive Accumulation* (Ithaca: Cornell University Press, 1991).

2. The founding texts of these debates include Jean E. Howard, "The New Historicism and Renaissance Studies," *English Literary Renaissance* 16, 1 (1986), 26–46; Carol T. Neely, "Constructing the Subject: Feminist Practice and the New Renaissance Discourses," *English Literary Renaissance* 18, 3 (1987), 3–19; Lynda Boose, "The Family in Shakespeare Studies; or—Studies in the Family of Shakespeareans; or—The Politics of Politics," *Renaissance Quarterly* 60 (1987), 707–42; Marguerite Waller, "Academic Tootsie: The Denial of Difference and the Difference It Makes," *Diacritics* 17 (1987), 2–20; and James Holstun, "Ranting at the New Historicism," *English Literary Renaissance* 19, 2 (1989), 189–225.

3. We wish to acknowledge Lynda Boose's lead here. The present collection emerged from a series of panels she organized for a conference on Renaissance national traditions held at Glasgow in August 1990. She generously allowed us to borrow her term "enclosure acts" for the title of our volume.

4. Michel Foucault, *Discipline and Punish: The Birth of the Prison*, trans. Alan Sheridan (New York: Vintage, 1979), p. 194.

5. Foucault, *Discipline and Punish*, pp. 195–228, and "The Eye of Power," in *Power/Knowledge: Selected Interviews and Other Writings*, ed. Colin Gordon (New York: Pantheon, 1980), pp. 146–65.

6. Foucault, "The Eye of Power," p. 155.

7. Michel Foucault, *History of Sexuality*, vol. 1, *An Introduction*, trans. Robert Hurley (New York: Vintage Books, 1980), pp. 17–35.

8. Ibid., pp. 95, 96.

9. See, for instance, Holstun, "Ranting at the New Historicism."

10. Mary Douglas, *Purity and Danger: An Analysis of the Concepts of Pollution and Taboo* (London: Ark Paperbacks, 1984), p. 121.

11. Julia Kristeva, *Powers of Horror: An Essay on Abjection*, trans. Leon Roudiez (New York: Columbia University Press, 1982).

12. Luce Irigaray, *This Sex Which Is Not One*, trans. Catherine Porter, with Carolyn Burke (Ithaca: Cornell University Press, 1985), p. 201.

13. Judith Butler, *Gender Trouble: Feminism and the Subversion of Identity* (New York: Routledge, 1990), p. 133.

14. See especially Mikhail Bakhtin, *Rabelais and His World*, trans. Helene Iswolsky (Bloomington: Indiana University Press, 1984), and *The Dialogic Imagination*, ed. Michael Holquist, trans. Caryl Emerson and Michael Holquist (Austin: University of Texas Press, 1981).

15. See Michael Bristol, *Carnival and Theater: Plebeian Culture and Renaissance Authority* (New York: Methuen, 1985), and "In Search of the Bear: Spatio-Temporal Form and the Heterogeneity of Economies in *The Winter's Tale*," *Shakespeare Quarterly* 42, 2 (1991), 145–67. Notions about the grotesque body have accompanied a renewed attention to the popular in political studies of Renaissance drama. See Robert Weiman, *Shakespeare and the Popular Tradition: Essays on the Social Function of Shakespeare's Dramatic Form*, trans. Robert Schwartz (Baltimore: Johns Hopkins University Press, 1978); Walter Cohen, *Drama of a Nation: Public Theater in Renaissance England and Spain* (Ithaca: Cornell University Press, 1985), and, in a non-Marxist vein, Annabel Patterson, *Shakespeare and the Popular Voice* (London: Basil Blackwell, 1989), which draws on Bakhtin.

16. Norbert Elias, *The Civilizing Process*, vol. 1, *The History of Manners*, and vol. 2, *Power and Civility*, trans. Edmund Jephcott (New York: Pantheon, 1982).

17. Paster, "Leaky Vessels," pp. 44–45, 63.

18. Francis Barker, *The Tremulous Private Body: Essays on Subjection* (New York: Methuen, 1984).

19. See Stallybrass and White, *Poetics and Politics of Transgression*.

20. Jonathan Dollimore, *Sexual Dissidence: Augustine to Wilde, Freud to Foucault* (Oxford: Clarendon, 1991).

21. Ibid., p. 27. Once again, Foucault's influence is felt in the turn toward perversion; see *History of Sexuality*, esp. pp. 36–49.

22. Dollimore, *Sexual Dissidence*, pp. 239–40.

23. Butler, *Gender Trouble*, p. 134.

24. Alan Bray, "Homosexuality and the Signs of Male Friendship in Elizabethan England," *History Workshop* 29 (1990), 1–15; see also his *Homosexuality in Renaissance England* (London: Gay Men's Press, 1982). Jonathan Goldberg, "Colin to Hobbinol: Spenser's Familiar Letters," in *Displacing Homophobia: Gay Male Perspectives in Literature and Culture* (Durham, N.C.: Duke University Press, 1989), pp. 107–26. Valerie Traub asserts that "if male homoeroticism was officially invisible unless associated with other transgressions, then female homoeroticism was even more so," in "Desire and the Difference it Makes," in Wayne, *The Matter of Difference*, p. 95. She locates two areas for investigation—female friendship (related to patronage in our sense) and cross-dressed comedic heroines—but chooses the second path in this essay.

25. Pierre Bourdieu, *Outline of a Theory of Practice*, trans. Richard Nice (Cambridge: Cambridge University Press, 1977), pp. 164–66; see also his *Logic of Practice*, trans. Richard Nice (Stanford: Stanford University Press, 1990), p. 68.

26. Bourdieu, *Logic of Practice*, p. 68. Unfortunately, the relationship between doxa and the body in Bourdieu's own practice soon resolves itself into a familiar mechanism for the determination of sexual difference according to gendered "spaces," at once "symbolic" (p. 78) and "biologically preconstructed" (p. 71).

27. Bourdieu, *Outline*, p. 168.

28. Ibid., p. 170; on the struggle between heterodoxy and orthodoxy, see pp. 168–70.

29. The phrase is from Bakhtin, *Rabelais*, p. 182. This chapter, "The Language of the Marketplace," contains Bakhtin's most suggestive work on billingsgate and invective.

PART I

COMMON GROUNDS:

SEXUAL AND ECONOMIC

DEMARCATIONS

1. Landlord Not King: Agrarian Change and Interarticulation

James R. Siemon

The long-running debate over the agrarian origins of capitalism in early modern England has been usefully reconceptualized by John E. Martin in terms of a transitional social formation characterized by an "articulated combination" of feudalism and capitalism rather than their linear succession.[1] Central to this articulated combination is the complex encounter of feudalism's "parcellised sovereignty" or "juridical-conditional ownership" with changing conditions that facilitated the emergence of "capitalist" landowning, "because through them land was released for the market, absolute property was consolidated, rents became subject to market forces, and the traditional constraints on agricultural development were removed by the destruction of the peasant economy. Land was freed and made available for new forms of management and usage."[2]

Accounts of agrarian change from the sixteenth century to the present have considered enclosure a key element in each of these developments. Although intense debate surrounds everything about enclosure—its extent, occasions, conditions, chronology, and effects—two broad notions of its agents have emerged. On the one hand, there is the long-standing awareness of the aggression of landlords seeking to convert peasant holdings to pasture; on the other are arguments emphasizing internal economic differentiation within the peasant community itself, which left land-holding polarized between large tenants interested in specialized land use and poor tenants struggling to retain the means of survival represented by common rights and open fields.[3] In this essay I assume that outright eviction and internal differentiation are, in Martin's phrase, "two faces of a changing agrarian structure," and attempt to locate aspects of these changes in a discursive context.

17

The key terms in Martin's structural articulation—land, market, absolute property, rent, traditional constraint, management, and development—represent for early modern England a field of discursive *interarticulation,* of that struggle, qualification, and implicature that the Bakhtin circle calls social-heteroglossia, and which it finds enacted around, about, and within utterances employed by agents and ideologies.[4] Through a survey of polemical usage and an analysis of three Shakespearean "garden" scenes and Burgundy's lament for the "best garden of the world," I attempt to reconstruct aspects of discursive interarticulation through which agents in this transitional social structure addressed changing conditions, encountered one another, and, most crucially though no less dialogically, voiced themselves.

I

When the Oxford *Henry V* comes to the Duke of Burgundy's lament for war's devastation of "this best garden of the world," the editor's notes refer to the "rather peculiar inclusion of hedges" and suggest, despite an acknowledgment of hedges as "the most normal species of agricultural fence or boundary" in England, that their presence might originate in Virgilian accounts of beekeeping.[5] Although there may be little to encourage such strained explanation, familiarity with English attacks on enclosure—a tradition of remarkable durability from the late Middle Ages to the present—renders Burgundy's speech "peculiar" enough:

> . . . all her husbandry doth lie on heaps,
> Corrupting in it own fertility.
> Her vine, the merry cheerer of the heart,
> Unpruned dies; her hedges even-plashed,
> Like prisoners wildly overgrown with hair,
> Put forth disorder'd twigs; her fallow leas
> The darnel, hemlock, and rank fumitory
> Doth root upon, while that the coulter rusts
> That should deracinate such savagery.
> The even mead—that erst brought sweetly forth
> The freckled cowslip, burnet, and green clover—
> Wanting the scythe, withal uncorrected, rank,
> Conceives by idleness, and nothing teems
> But hateful docks, rough thistles, kecksies, burs,
> Losing both beauty and utility.
> And all our vineyards, fallows, meads, and hedges,
> Defective in their natures, grow to wildness.

> Even so our houses and ourselves and children
> Have lost, or do not learn for want of time,
> The sciences that should become our country,
> But grow like savages—as soldiers will
> That nothing do but meditate on blood . . .
>
> (5.2.39–60)

The assumed values here obviously belong to an ideology of improvement, of "sciences" exercised upon a fallen world where the natural and the human are both "defective in their natures." The "wildness" of this "uncorrected" nature is to be tamed for "utility," and its "idleness" is to be governed according to the management of "time." Above all, boundaries and distinctions demand maintenance: "hedges" to return order to a husbandry now in disordered "heaps." This element, of course, might awaken attention insofar as it represents quickset hedges—the very symbol of "capitalist" landowning, pursuit of profit, exploitation of rural labor, expropriation of land, and the development of absolute private property—as the martyred prisoners of disorder.

One might argue that this acclamation of order and distinction is authorial, expressing class-oriented values akin to those evident in Montjoy's horrified reaction to boundary violation among the unsorted dead, who lie in anarchic confusion of nobility with commons, masters with subjects, men with beasts, agents of savage rage or hired servitude with chivalric combatants:

> To sort our nobles from our common men—
> For many of our princes, woe the while,
> Lie drowned and soaked in mercenary blood.
> So do our vulgar drench their peasant limbs
> In blood of princes, and our wounded steeds
> Fret fetlock-deep in gore, and with wild rage
> Jerk our their armed heels at their dead masters . . .
>
> (4.7.69–75)

The implied social threat registered in this reaction to proximity and confusion is most clearly oriented in reference to economically occasioned "mercenary blood" drowning princes. The attitude toward distinction in class here, as toward division of land in Burgundy's speech, might appear symptomatic of a Shakespearean complicity with values of power and blood.

But there is another possibility. The association of "common," "vulgar," and "peasant" with "mercenary" and its opposition to "noble," "princes," and "masters" epitomize a traditional view of French society as bipolar, that is, lacking the English yeomanry, the "free," land-holding peasant of median wealth and glorious *voluntary* military capacity.[6] In fact, and despite apparent similarities of orientation, the values expressed by Burgundy and Montjoy are—in certain specific, conditionally significant aspects—at potential odds. This disagreement may be highlighted by juxtaposing Burgundy's speech and the "garden" scenes of *The Contention, 2 Henry VI*, and *Richard II* with the conditions, arguments, and values associated with enclosure.

II

In the wake of the French Revolution, the English traveler and agricultural writer Arthur Young noted that as of 1794 the French had no equivalent for the English enclosure by act and expressed doubts that such "progress" could ever be made, since in France it was now "the will of *the people* that is to govern; and I know of no country where the people are not against inclosures."[7] "*The people*" oppose "inclosures": whatever the limitations of Young's qualification to pronounce in such global terms, there can be no question that his assessment is supported by the evidence concerning England. Commentary on enclosure, whether derived from the testimony of "the people" in court or through petition, or from the official proceedings and polemic of those making assertions in their behalf, is overwhelmingly negative—and remarkably consistent.

Despite the extreme variety of what modern analysis, with its attentiveness to localization, has described as the causes, origins, and formal articulations of enclosure, there is a striking discursive consistency in expressions of opposition to it. J. A. Yelling may remind us that enclosure, to take only a few examples, has been "attributed in particular cases to population growth, to population decline, to the presence of soils favourable or unfavourable to arable, to industrial and urban growth, to remoteness from markets, to the dominance of manorial lords, to the absence of strict manorial control, to increased flexibility in the common-field system, and to the absence of such flexibility."[8] But always and almost everywhere one encounters variations on the themes of nostalgia and loss concerning the human costs of agricultural change. In this chain of utterances stretching from the sixteenth century to the present, from Sir Thomas More to modern historians, Marx's own discourse (which itself takes account of earlier polemic) may furnish a useful compendium: from the later fifteenth century the "free peasant proprietors" (or their usual embodiment, "the yeomanry, the class of independent peasants") lose feudal rights to communal property as a result of the "usurpation of the common lands" by enclosure, and are thereby "precipitated without any transitional stages from [their] golden age to [their] iron age":

> The place of the independent yeoman was taken by tenants at will, small farmers on yearly leases, a servile rabble dependent on the arbitrary will of the landlords, the systematic theft of communal property was of great assistance, alongside the theft of the state domains, in swelling those large farms which were called in the eighteenth century capital farms, or merchant farms, and in "setting free" the agricultural population as a proletariat for the needs of industry.[9]

Similar views are found in earlier commentators on the Tudor years, such as John Aubrey, who looked back from the post-Restoration period to a "Golden Age" when men lived in feudalism's "Nest of Boxes: for Copy-holders (who till then, were Villaines) held of the Lords of the Manor, who held of a superior Lord, who held perhaps of another superior Lord or Duke, who held of the King," and contrasted this past with a present in which the "lovely campania" of feudal land-holding has been replaced by property enclosed "for the private, not the public good," and has thereby come to "[swarm] with poore people."[10] Contemporary commentary strikes similar notes. Writer after writer laments the passing of the moral economy: Francis Trigge (1604) evokes a "merie England" transformed by "covetous Inclosures [that] have taken this ioy and mirth away," destroying "communitie of feeding," "communitie of dwelling," and the "Yeomanrie . . . the ancient glory of England."[11] William Harrison (1587) decries "the universality of this evil" of imparking for hunting or cattle keeping as "not sparing the very commons whereupon many townships now and then do live" and deems it a species of the rich man's "laying of house to house and land to land."[12] "These inclosures," writes Philip Stubbes (1583), "be the causes why rich men eat vp poore men, as beasts doo eat grasse."[13] "The landlord who "incloseth commons . . . is an vsurer," writes William Vaughan (1600), and those landlords who "doe leave no ground for tillage, but doe enclose for pasture many thousand acres of ground within one hedge" despoil the yeomanry of independence and the poor of their "tenements."[14]

Despite their ubiquity, consistency, and sympathy-evoking rhetoric, such complaints—with their lamentation over the conditions and values of a communal past undergoing brutal violation as greedy enclosers take away "the common field," which as John Stow maintains "ought to be open and free for all men"—neither accurately defined the facts or the timing of enclosing nor, more crucially, succeeded in halting it.[15] Modern estimates suggest that the major portion of enclosing took place before the sixteenth century—as many contemporary writers knew and sometimes acknowledged—and just after it.[16] Nevertheless, there were factors at work in the latter part of the sixteenth and early seventeenth centuries that kept enclosure a vexed and highly symbolic topic. There was dearth, of course: particularly devastating was the conjunction of the repeal of previous antienclosure legislation in 1593 with the generally bad harvest years of 1593–97. There was the combination of the dearth that hit the Midlands in 1607–8 with particularly concentrated and offensive local instances of enclosing and conversion of land to grazing. And there was attendant governmental activity in the antienclosure statutes of 1597 and the enclosure commission of 1607, the last large-scale inquiry.[17] Why, then, despite its demonstrable capacity to awaken outrage; despite condemnations from the first official statute against depopulation in 1489 through seven royal commissions, twelve statutes, and numerous proclamations; despite decisions by the Privy Council, Star Chamber, and Court of Requests; despite countless tracts, sermons, debates, and petitions, did enclosing become not only widespread but, by the mid-seventeenth century, publicly defensible?[18] Certain aspects of the complex factors involved in this phenomenon and their relationship to the emergent values of a nascent capitalism deserve attention.

For one thing, considerable evidence suggests that the very "people" who were attacking enclosure or being defended against it were often themselves engaged in acts of "enclosure" and in defending enclosures. So, for example, the first item included in the demands of the Kett rebellion in 1549—a rebellion that had as one of its stated goals rights of common for freeholders and copyholders—was a request that "where it is enacted for enclosing that it be not hurtful to such as have enclosed saffron grounds for they be greatly chargeable to them, and that from henceforth noman shall enclose any more."[19] And, in the seventeenth century, the Levellers, who took their name from the leveling of quickset hedges and park palings, exempted from their objections such enclosures as are "only or chiefly for the benefit of the poor."[20] Such apparent contradictions can and should be localized: the cultivation of saffron was an important industry in Robert Kett's Norfolk, for example, and the reference to the defense of enclosure may be attributable to the East Anglian farming custom of foldcourse, which entitled the manorial lord to pasture sheep as he pleased on tenants' lands and was thus "liable precisely to reverse the attitude of manorial lord and tenant toward enclosing."[21] But however resistant such local instances are to generalization, and however challenging the individuating factors involved—such as Kett's having his own fences destroyed in the rising he later headed, or Lord Protector Somerset's privately being a rack-renter and encloser—there are larger, less local and personal issues and trends at work.[22]

In fact, the word *enclosure,* like the hedges that embody it, functions during the period as an exemplary instance of the heteroglossic—an arena for the criss-crossing of disputed and competing values and orientations.[23] So, for example, one senses the social cross fire when the Doctor of the *Discourse of the Commonweal of This Realm of England* by Sir Thomas Smith is compelled to defend the common field system not only against the arguments of the landed knight—"That which is possessed of many in common is neglected of all"—but also against the general will attributed to those actually working the land.[24] The Husbandman of the *Discourse* maintains, "Everyday some of us encloses a [plot] of his ground to pasture, and were it not that our ground lies in the common fields intermingled one with another, I think also our fields had been enclosed of common agreement of all the township long ere this time" (p. 57). Under such pressure from so many fronts, the Doctor strategically delimits a definition of enclosure that typifies the multivocality of the era's discourse:

> I mean not of all enclosures, nor yet all commons, but only of such enclosures as turn common arable fields into pastures, and violent enclosures of commons without just recompense of them that have right to common therein. For if land were severally enclosed to the intent to continue husbandry thereon and every man that had right to common had for his portion a piece of the same to himself enclosed, I think no harm but rather good should come thereof, if every man did agree thereto. (p. 50)

Of course, every man would not and did not agree thereto. Nonetheless, individuals of virtually every stratum of tenancy and ownership apparently came to agree with the Doctor that enclosure of arable land for improvement—if not for conversion to pasture—was "good," or, to employ a term with which the Doctor has considerable difficulty, that the enclosure of arable land was *profitable.* The process by which profit—the immoral cause of multiplying pastures and enclosures, according to the *Discourse* (p. 51)—becomes synonymous with "advancement," that which "nourishes every faculty" (p. 58), and becomes thereby a proper end of *property* rather than a synonym for appropriation and violation of the moral economy, may be indexed in contemporary utterances.

If, as Maurice Beresford argues, the problem presented by enclosure and its attendant depopulation was generally articulated in the public debate and legislation of the late fifteenth and early sixteenth centuries in terms of the profit incentive driving deliberate action by landlords who bring about the extinction of still viable common field communities, there are nevertheless indications that by the latter part of the sixteenth century this polemical discourse hardly fits the facts, and that, in E. C. K. Gonner's assessment, a "new period in the history of inclosure begins, marked by the steady growth of farming improvement as an active motive."[25] Instead of enclosure by the manorial lord for pastoral use, enclosure by agreement became dominant during the period, according to J. A. Yelling.[26] Agreement, of course, should not be taken to rule out force or even violence as a factor in tenurial and agricultural change. But there is evidence that in the mid-sixteenth century enclosure began to be associated with—and thus to be defensible in terms of—"more intensive economies, requiring a less drastic reorganisation of farm structures and providing more employment."[27] So, for example, the tenants of Mudford and Hinton proposed to divide up the common fields in 1554 because "every man will use a further trayvale and dylygence with his londe to converte yt to the best use and purpose."[28] And even as the Justices of Nottinghamshire complained that enclosure was driving people into the towns, they exempted from their criticism enclosures under five acres on the grounds that such enclosures actually improved agriculture without causing depopulation.[29] Such arguments characterize the frequently reprinted improvement literature of John Norden and Sir Anthony Fitzherbert, who both denounce forced enclosure by lords seeking to rack-rent or depopulate, but assert that arable land enclosed by agreement may prove "halfe as good agayne in all maner of profytes to the tenantes as it was before."[30] This improving literature is permeated, furthermore, with values of industry, thrift, individual discretion, efficiency, and private property rights. Thus, when Thomas Tusser contrasts the wealth and efficiency of land held in "severall" with the poverty and disorder of land commoned in "Champion countrie," he not only employs the language of Tudor-Stuart authority on behalf of enclosure—"Where champions ruleth the rost, / there daily disorder is most"—but also maintains:

> More profite is quieter founde,
> (where pastures in severall be:)
> Of one sillie aker of ground,
> than Champion maketh of three.
> Againe what a ioy it is knowne,
> when men may be bold with their own?[31]

Against the threat of both "lordes of the soile" and the "commoners" who "for commons . . . crie" and "count it their owne they can get,"

Tusser defends the enclosed farm as not only efficient but also right, original, proper to individual possession and use—one's "own" to "be bold" with—rather than itself a usurpation of the juridical-conditional rights of community, lord, or crown.[32] Furthermore, such values are not particular to express defenders of enclosure itself but are instead part of a larger rationalization of property and labor informing utterances in realms as diverse as theology and theater.

Employing a discursive arsenal of terms and assumptions concerning real property throughout his theological writings, William Perkins writes against the notion of grace available without the church:

> It puls downe the pale of the Church, and laies it waste as every common field: it breeds carelessness in the use of means of grace, the word and Sacraments; when as man shall be perswaded, that grace shall be offered to every one effectually, whether hee be of the Church or not, at one time or other; whersoever or howsoever he live: as in the like case, if men shall be tolde that whether they live in the market towne or no, there shall be sufficient provision brought them, if they will but receive it and accept of it, who would then come to the market?[33]

Here, the pale of the enclosed field is assumed to predate the common, the common itself to be equated with inevitable "waste" ("as every common field"), and the ills of Arminianism to be epitomized in "carelessness"—about uses and means, about time, space, and style of life, about property and propriety. The ills Perkins invokes, of course, are antithetical to the classical values of rationalized production, whereas the assumed primacy of the market itself and *its* demands on human space, time, and labor in the final lines are more than predictive of social-economic hegemonies to come. Perkins's metaphoric usage—untroubled by that need for self-explanation and localization found in Norden and Fitzherbert—registers assumed sympathy with values that radically oppose the culturally dominant antienclosure discourse.

These conflicting values and orientations can be found variously conjoined in *The Contention, 2 Henry VI*, and *Richard II*. In them we find the two faces of agrarian change: the polarization of a peasantry already internally differentiated in values as well as wealth, and the aggression of landlord against feudal tenant. But we also find a remarkable conception of labor and property which bids to cast both in a different light.

III

In both the 1590s *Contention* and the 1623 *2 Henry VI*, Alexander Iden's encounter with John Cade is represented as the confrontation of

a Kentish smallholder with an intruding Kentish commoner.[34] The Alexander Iden of 2 *Henry VI* expresses pride in the double sufficiency of
his brick-walled garden *and* his own hospitality, which renounces a
competitive economy that seeks "to wax great by others' waning, / Or
gather wealth . . . with what envy" (4.10.20–21). To Iden, inheritor of
a garden "worth a monarchy" (4.10.19), Cade's intrusion—coming
"like a thief to rob my grounds / Climbing the walls in spite of me the
owner" (4.10.33–34)—appears not only theft and an insult to his authority of ownership but as an affront to his capacity to "[send] the
poor well pleased from my gate" (4.10.23). By contrast, the Eyden of
the *Contention* claims neither his namesake's hospitality, nor his lack of
interest in competition, nor his garden, nor quite the same possession.
Content with his "land" because its "pleasure" equals that of the court,
Eyden spends no pity on the poor. Cade seems to him not a thief but a
trespasser. Furthermore, his boundaries, though inherited, are not the
brick walls of Iden's "fee simple" garden but the very emblems of enclosed arable: "Ist not inough," Eyden demands, "that thou hast broke
my hedges, / And enterd into my ground without the leaue of me the
owner" (G4ʳ). In the *Contention,* the relation of property to appropriating enclosure appears uncompromised by the temporal continuity
embodied in Iden's brick, by the comparatively innocuous status of a
garden plot, by the absolute heritability of fee-simple ownership without feudal entail, by the threat of robbery, or by a rhetoric of hospitality. Thus, the Folio palliates the potential identification of Iden with
possessive accumulation, effectively increasing the difference in values
distinguishing the Kentish landowner from the ambitious, hungry
Kentish clothier.

     Between the publication of these two texts, in the years in which the
rescinding of previous antienclosure legislation coincided with the
dearth of 1594–97, Shakespeare wrote the garden scene of *Richard
II*.[35] The gardener is neither the possessive individualist of *The Contention* nor the socially conscious owner of 2 *Henry VI.* His land-holding
status is left totally undetermined, but the values he embodies and the
attitudes he expresses concerning enclosure, as well as other aspects of
the changing agrarian economy, are pronounced, and they intersect
remarkably with elements of feudalism elsewhere in the play. In pursuit of stated aims of "profit," the gardener—unlike either Eyden or
Iden—labors rather than owns. He is represented not as "lord of the
soil," not as a lesser embodiment modeled on the sovereign as preem-
inent possessor of land, but as himself a "modle" for the *occupation* of
monarchy. His authority derives specifically from "skill," from efficient
management rather than from title of land or birth—the mainstays of
feudalism's juridical-conditional structure. Nor is he called upon, as are

the others, to enact yeomanry's mythic service as armed defender of
that structure in order to participate in the political nation. His activities of political and agricultural critique are represented as instances
of independent discrimination and evaluation occasioned by occupa-
tional needs meeting specific circumstances: he must actively intervene
by excluding, restraining, measuring, and developing according to
"time of yeare" and the ever evolving conditions presented by "newes."
The values he articulates are those of a rationalized economic production concerned with profit, number, condition, and efficiency rather
than with land and deference. These values constitute an ideal of propriety exercised within the enclosed "compas of a pale" which are extended to the "sea-walled garden," the disorder of which is defined as
occasioned by a "wastefull king" and epitomized in the violated boundaries of England's "knots disordered" and "hedges ruinde" (G3^r–G3^v).
And such evaluations comment powerfully on the feudal values elsewhere assumed, invoked, and conflicted in the heteroglot encounter of
monarch and Lancastrians.

What the gardener actually possesses is neither capitalism's absolute
property in land nor feudalism's conditional right to land but the capital of skill in his occupation. The seriousness with which this idealization of labor is taken is evident in the fact that his status by virtue of this
possession is represented as manifestly more secure than that entailed
in the inherited land of the House of Lancaster or in the heritable title
of the monarch himself. This surprising security, most vividly indexed
in his cogent resistance to the Queen's degrading attacks, corresponds
to emergent values registered in Perkins's account of occupation: "an
occupation is as good as land, because land may be lost; but skill and
labour in a good occupation is profitable to the end, because it will
help at neede, when land and all things faile."[36] Profitable skill and labor: if the actions and pronouncements embodying these values in
early modern England often appear pitiless toward the poor and displaced, as Perkins himself frequently seems to be, that harshness could
justify itself in the presumptive universality of its measure. It even applies to King Richard—and to his successors. Most clearly this is true in
the case of Hal, whose gratuitous fall seems contrived to necessitate his
"redemption" through an otherwise unnecessary labor of statecraft
and management. It is the case of his father, his grandfather, and their
king, however, that makes the relation of these values to changing
agrarian conditions most clear.

From the perspective of feudalism, Richard is guilty of two related
innovations against juridical-conditional ownership which render him
no longer England's supreme lord—in Gaunt's phrase not king but
"landlord" (C4^v). Both these violations of tradition represent promi-

nent aspects of early modern England's transitional articulation. First, Richard is represented as doing what Elizabethan lords are so frequently criticized for doing: violating customary tenurial relations by converting his own demesne lands to leasehold property for the use of exploitive middlemen—"farmers" in contemporary usage—rendering it to Gaunt's feudal perspective "leasde out . . . Like to a tenement or pelting Farme" rather than preserving it as the Edenic mutual right of England's chivalric "breede of men" (C3^v).[37] Second, Richard intervenes in Bolingbroke's own case at precisely the point where large numbers of English landholders proved vulnerable to much-denounced seigneurial aggression: entry into inheritance.[38] In both cases Richard represents versions of popular agrarian villainy—the greedy evicting or rack-renting landlord, who contributed to the emergence of capitalist absolute property by treating land as an estate for profit rather than a conditional tenure held in feudalism's "nest of boxes." But he is not an encloser.

In fact, his managerial middlemen—those who Bolingbroke claims have broken the ties of feudal allegiance between his lord and himself—are represented as violating Bolingbroke's enclosures. With his "disparkt . . . parkes" (E4^r), Bolingbroke claims sympathy as the victim of seigneurial antienclosure violence which has reduced him to that prototypical figure of agrarian displacement, the "wandering vagabond" (E3^r).[39] Thereby we may be reminded of the fact that enclosing could be articulated during this period as an innocent, proper means of agricultural management, as well as of the fact that antienclosure violence was frequently—sometimes with help commissioned from commoners—the expression of landlord aggression against enclosing tenants or against other landlords rather than the simple expression of popular outrage or class antagonism.[40]

In the complex though necessarily provisional context I have constructed, it may appear significant that Bolingbroke's rising downplays patriotic disinterestedness while both protesting feudal allegiance ("true service" [G2^r]) and articulating claims of absolute property independent of feudal conditionalities of grant, tenure, or holding; or that Bolingbroke's coming for "his owne" (G2^r) is coupled with the repeated invocation of economic profit which his adherents—including the gardener himself—may pursue.[41] Furthermore, Bolingbroke's strategic interarticulation of feudal and capitalist values should be contrasted with the uncompromising feudal values embodied in Gaunt's elegiac vision of England's garden as "this other Eden, demy Paradice" undergoing wrenching transition from the hierarchic solidarity of "christian seruice and true chiualry" (C3^v) to leasehold contractuality—a vision remarkably closely related to that of Cade in 2 Henry VI and powerfully countered by the gardener. Whatever the disjunct situations of Cade's utopian vision of himself as warrior aristocrat in a society "all in one livery, that they may agree like brothers, and worship me their lord" (2 *Henry VI* 4.2.71–72) and a fallen present constituted by "parchment" bondage—in which to "but seal once to a thing" has meant being "never mine own man since" (4.2.76–80)—with Gaunt's elegy for a king epitomizing a whole "breede of men" dis-identified by "parchment bonds" (*Richard II* C4ʳ), the voice of an old order and a new disorder are represented as fundamentally related in professed values. Neither recognizes the complicity of his feudal values and an emergent absolutism which would use them, perhaps even believe them—as does Richard—when possible.[42] By contrast the gardener's response to the queen's attempt to cast him into a similarly disjunct identity as "old Adams likeness," new-fallen as "cursed man" (G3ᵛ) by virtue of his socially inappropriate attainment of political consciousness, professes an awareness, which by virtue of its capacity for both socioeconomic rationalization of the "newes"—of changing conditions of class and politics—and personal regret for the costs of change—to Richard and his queen—appears designed to measure precisely the degree to which he is constructed as "his owne" but also a man of the times, neither an unconstrained subjectivity nor a tool, but capable precisely of the conditional freedom of agency.[43] His enclosed garden, like that of England, is not Eden, nor can it be Edenic, but it may be managed. In this, too, his garden agrees with the speech of Burgundy and the polemic of Norden, which identifies weeds as inevitable "markes of the first curse," but the earth as capable of being "reformed" by "Industry," "thryft," and enclosure, "praise worthy and profitable to the planter, and to the common wealth."[44]

If, as Joyce Oldham Appleby maintains (following Michael Polanyi), market values can become pervasive only when the pursuit of profit is a socially accepted goal, then these plays and the discourses that surround enclosure—however variously and discrepantly—would appear to participate in the formulation of that goal.[45] Enclosing is an element in this formulation, and, as I hope to have suggested by now, "enclosing" should be not only localized but contextualized in the heteroglot conditionality of its feudal-capitalist interarticulation. Whether Shakespeare, when it came to William Combe's attempted enclosure of his Welcombe tithe holdings in 1614–15, could not "help" the enclosure of his moiety, as Thomas Greene seems to consider writing in his diary, or, whether, as Greene actually does write, he could not "beare" it, Combe could defend his—violently and legally resisted—action in terms of absolute rights to his own ("there was never psident seene that a man seised of an absolute and ffree estate should deprive himself of that libertie and be bound to husband his land to the Contente of a Third Pson"); in terms of improvement ("ye tents and freeholders Comon will be rather much bettered than Impayred by this Inclosure"); and in terms of hospitality and profitable management ("for necessarye mainteynance of hospetallitie & good husbandrie").[46] Combe was blocked—by communal violence and legal resistance, and by Chief Justice Coke's intervention—but the Stratford Corporation's defense of its source of funds for the poor dependents on the tithes was only one such encounter among countless others. Elsewhere arguments and force, coercion and agreement, internal differentiation and landlord eviction contended in a discursive interarticulation accompanying the encounter of changing values and conditions. Thus, for a final example, Stow's account of enclosing in the London suburbs betrays a certain opening for the inevitable. The antienclosure violence on the suburban commons in 1515 has given way to change, Stow writes,

> after which time (saith Hall) these fields were never hedged, but now we see the thing in worse case than ever, by means of inclosure for gardens, wherein are built many fair summer-houses; and, as in other places of the suburbs, some of them like Midsummer pageants, with towers, turrets, and chimney-tops, not so much for use of profit as for show and pleasure, betraying the vanity of men's minds, much unlike to the disposition of the ancient citizens, who delighted in the building of hospitals and alms-houses for the poor, and therein both employed their wits, and spent their wealths in preferment of the common commodity of this our city.[47]

Available in Stow's denunciation of enclosure is one crucially important qualification of disapproval: the relative superiority of "use of profit" is allowed over show, pleasure, and vanity. The problem of the displaced poor, moreover, is conceded to be an "ancient" concern of hospital and almshouse, of charitable institutions and individuals, as if the manorial economy, with its agricultural system of mutually interdependent conditional owner-tenants, had never existed.

NOTES

1. John E. Martin, *Feudalism to Capitalism: Peasant and Landlord in English Agrarian Development* (Atlantic Highlands, N.J.: Humanities Press, 1983). For a range of recent representative opinions in this perennial debate, see esp. R. H. Hilton, *The Transition from Feudalism to Capitalism* (London: NLB, 1976); Eugene Kamenka and R. S. Neale, eds., *Feudalism, Capitalism, and Beyond* (New

York: St. Martin's Press, 1976); R. A. Butlin, *The Transformation of Rural England c. 1580–1800: A Study in Historical Geography* (Oxford: Oxford University Press, 1982); R. J. Holton, *The Transition from Feudalism to Capitalism* (New York: St. Martin's Press, 1975); Richard Lachmann, *From Manor to Market: Structural Change in England, 1536–1640* (Madison: University of Wisconsin Press, 1987); and essays by and about Robert Brenner in T. H. Aston and C. H. E. Philpin, eds., *The Brenner Debate: Agrarian Class Structure and Economic Development in Pre-Industrial Europe* (Cambridge: Cambridge University Press, 1985). R. H. Tawney, *The Agrarian Problem in the Sixteenth Century* (1912; reprint New York: Burt Franklin, n.d.), remains valuable.

2. Martin, *Feudalism* p. 103.

3. Ibid., p. 123, following R. H. Hilton, "A Study in the Pre-History of English Enclosure in the Fifteenth Century," in *The English Peasantry in the Later Middle Ages* (Oxford: Clarendon Press, 1975); see also Paul Glennie, "In Search of Agrarian Capitalism: Manorial Land Markets and the Acquisition of Land in the Lea Valley, c. 1450–c. 1560," *Continuity and Change* 3 (1988), 11–40.

4. For a representative discussion of heteroglossia, see M. M. Bakhtin, *The Dialogic Imagination* trans. Caryl Emerson and Michael Holquist (Austin: University of Texas Press, 1981), pp. 284–316. For a provocative account of enclosure as awakening a "clash of voices," see Maurice Beresford, "Habitation versus Improvement: The Debate on Enclosure by Agreement," in *Essays in the Economic and Social History of Tudor and Stuart England,* ed. F. J. Fisher (Cambridge: Cambridge University Press, 1961), pp. 40–69.

5. William Shakespeare, *Henry V,* ed. Gary Taylor (Oxford: Clarendon Press, 1982), 5.2.36n. Further references to *Henry V* are cited from this edition.

6. On the English yeomanry, see Francis Bacon, *History of King Henry VII,* in *The Works of Francis Bacon,* ed. James Spedding, Robert Leslie Ellis, and Douglas Denon Heath, vol. 11 (Boston: Taggard and Thompson, 1865), pp. 142–46.

7. Arthur Young, *Travels during 1787, 1788, and 1789 in the Kingdom of France* (1794), abridged ed., ed. Jeffrey Kaplow (New York: Anchor Books, 1969), pp. 300–301.

8. J. A. Yelling, *Common Field and Enclosure in England, 1450–1850* (London: Macmillan, 1977), p. 3.

9. Karl Marx, *Capital,* trans. Ben Fowkes (New York: Random House, 1976), 1:877–95; quotation from p. 886. On Marx's reading, see J. P. Cooper, "In Search of Agrarian Capitalism," *Past and Present* 80 (1978), 27–28. The best account of early polemic is Joan Thirsk, *The Agrarian History of England and Wales,* vol. 4, *1500–1640* (Cambridge: Cambridge University Press, 1967), pp. 213–39. Yelling offers useful remarks on contemporary assessments; see *Common Field,* esp. pp. 214–17.

10. John Aubrey, *Wiltshire: The Topographical Collections* (London: Longman, 1862), pp. 7–13.

11. Francis Trigge, *The Humble Petition of Two Sisters* (1604: STC 24280), sigs. D3–D4v.

12. William Harrison, *The Description of England,* ed. Georges Edelen (Ithaca: Cornell University Press, 1968), pp. 256–57.

13. Philip Stubbes, *Anatomy of the Abuses in England,* ed. F. J. Furnival (London: New Shakespeare Society, 1877–79), p. 117.

14. William Vaughan, *The Golden Grove* (1600: STC 24610), pt. 2, chap. 23; pt. 3, chap. 22.

15. John Stow, *Stow's Survey of London*, ed. Henry B. Wheatley (London: J. M. Dent, 1912), p. 376.

16. On the chronology, see J. R. Wordie's important article, "The Chronology of English Enclosure, 1500–1914," *Economic History Review*, 2d ser., 36 (1983), 483–505. Wordie finds England 45 percent enclosed by 1550 with 2 percent additional enclosure to 1599 and 24 percent more enclosed in 1600–1699 (p. 502).

17. On these conjunctions, see Thirsk, *Agrarian History*, pp. 226–36.

18. For a suggestive account of this complicated change and the role of changing land use in the eventual toleration of enclosure, see Beresford, "Habitation versus Improvement," and C. G. A. Clay, *Economic Expansion and Social Change: England 1500–1700* (Cambridge: Cambridge University Press, 1984), esp. pp. 79–80.

19. B. M. Harleian Mss. 304, fol. 75.

20. Bodleian Pamphlets, 1648, c. 15, 3, Linc., as quoted in Tawney, *Agrarian Problem*, pp. 149–50; on the Levellers and hedges, see p. 338.

21. Diarmaid MacCulloch, "Kett's Rebellion in Context," *Past and Present* 84 (1979), 51. On saffron, see Stephen K. Land, *Kett's Rebellion: The Norfolk Rising of 1549* (Totowa, N.J.: Rowman and Littlefield, 1977), p. 71.

22. On Kett's fences, see Land, *Kett's Rebellion*, pp. 42–43; on Somerset, see M. L. Bush, *The Government Policy of Protector Somerset* (Montreal: McGill-Queen's University Press, 1975), pp. 57, 63.

23. For conflicting uses of "enclosure," see Tawney, *Agrarian Problem*, pp. 149–50. Roger Manning points out concurrent meanings of the word *hedges*— "imposition of order upon disorderly and seditious persons, or the abridgement of freedom and economic independence"—a formulation which omits the fact that hedges could imply the *constitution* of freedom and economic independence. Roger B. Manning, *Village Revolts: Social Protest and Popular Disturbances in England, 1509–1640* (Oxford: Clarendon Press, 1988), pp. 29–30.

24. Sir Thomas Smith, *A Discourse of the Commonweal of This Realm of England*, ed. Mary Dewar (Charlottesville: University Press of Virginia, 1969), p. 50. Further references are cited by page in the text.

25. Maurice Beresford, *The Lost Villages of England* (London: Lutterworth, 1954), pp. 178–82; E. C. K. Gonner, *Common Land and Inclosure* (1912), 2d ed. (New York: A. M. Kelley, 1966), p. 137; more recent support of Gonner's view is provided in Clay, *Economic Expansion*, p. 79.

26. Yelling, *Common Field*, p. 22.

27. Ibid., p. 23.

28. R. H. Tawney and Eileen Power, eds., *Tudor Economic Documents*, 3 vols. (London: Longmans Green, 1924), 1:61–62.

29. William Page, ed., *The Victoria History of the County of Nottinghamshire* (London: Constable, 1910), 2:282.

30. Sir Anthony Fitzherbert, *The Boke of Surueyinge and Improvements* (London: 1548?), STC 11012, fol. 50; compare John Norden, *The Surveyors Dialogue* (London: 1606), STC 18639, p. 97.

31. Thomas Tusser, *Five Hundred Points of Good Husbandry*, expanded ed. (London: 1593), STC 24384, chap. 52, Stanza 22.

32. Ibid., sts. 11–17.

33. *The Works of William Perkins* (Cambridge, 1609–13), STC 19650, 1:295.

34. Quotations are from 1594 Q1 of *The Contention*, in *Shakespeare's Plays in Quarto*, ed. Michael J. B. Allen and Kenneth Muir (Berkeley: University of Cal-

ifornia Press, 1981); 2 *Henry VI* quoted from Andrew S. Cairncross's Arden edition (1962; reprint London: Methuen, 1985). Citations from 2 *Henry VI* are
given in the text. The lines from *Contention* are taken from G4^r.

35. Quotations from 1597 Q1 of *Richard II*, in Allen and Muir, *Shakespeare's
Plays.* The garden scene occupies G3^r–G3^v.

36. Perkins, *Works*, 1:752. Compare Christopher Hill's account of Perkins in
"Puritans and the Poor," *Past and Present* 2 (1952), 32–50.

37. On the importance of conversion of tenancy to market-adjustable leasehold, see Eric Kerridge, "The Movement of Rent, 1540–1640," *Economic History Review,* 2d ser., 6 (1953), 16–34; Butlin, *Transformation,* pp. 35–37. On
farmers, see Kerridge, "Movement," pp. 31–33.

38. See Tawney, *Agrarian Problem,* pp. 297–310; see also Robert Brenner's
analysis in Aston and Philpin, *The Brenner Debate.*

39. On the language of vagabondage and poverty, see William C. Carroll,
"Language, Politics, and Poverty in Shakespearian Drama," *Shakespeare Survey*
44 (1992), 17–24.

40. In the reigns of Edward VI and Henry VIII, according to Manning, "enclosure riots were merely one species of violence employed by the gentry in
pursuing quarrels with rival gentry or enforcing uniformity of agricultural usage upon their tenants" (*Village Revolts,* p. 39; also pp. 40, 53). Later violence
in the 1590s also included, though apparently to a lesser degree, such gentry
quarrel (pp. 79–81).

41. On the downplaying of patriotism in Bolingbroke's case, see J. H. Hex-
ter, "Property, Monopoly, and Shakespeare's *Richard II,*" in *Culture and Politics
from Puritanism to the Enlightenment,* ed. Perez Zagorin (Berkeley: University of
California Press, 1980), pp. 1–24.

42. On the heteroglot encounters of feudalism, absolutism, and Bolingbroke's economics, see James R. Siemon," 'Subjected Thus': Utterance, Character, and *Richard II,*" *Shakespeare Jahrbuch* (Weimar) 126 (1990), 65–80.
Compare Martin's analysis of absolutism in *Feudalism.*

43. "Agency" is used here as in the analyses of Pierre Bourdieu; see, e.g., *In
Other Words: Essays Towards a Reflexive Sociology,* trans. Matthew Adamson (Stanford: Stanford University Press, 1990).

44. Norden, *Surveyors Dialogue,* pp. 242, 225, 208.

45. Joyce Oldham Appleby, *Economic Thought and Ideology in Seventeenth-
Century England* (Princeton: Princeton University Press, 1978),pp. 15–16.

46. Thomas Greene's diary entries concerning Shakespeare and the Welcombe enclosure include this entry for August 14, 1615: "Sept W Shakespeares
tellyng J Greene that I was not able to ħé beare the enclosinge of welcombe."
The diary (Stratford-upon-Avon, Miscellaneous Documents, vol. 13 [BRU 15/
13]) is reprinted in C. M. Ingleby, *Shakespeare and the Enclosure of Common Fields
at Welcombe* (Birmingham: Robert Birbeck, 1885), p. 11. Combe's letter
(Stratford-upon-Avon, BRU 15/1, item 107) is reprinted in B. Roland Lewis,
The Shakespeare Documents (1941; reprint Westport, Conn.: Greenwood Press,
1969), 2:463–64. For a vivid account of Shakespearean records in this and
other relevant areas, see Robert Bearman's forthcoming work, *Shakespeare in
the Stratford Public Records Office* (Stratford-upon-Avon: Shakespeare Birthplace
Trust).

47. Stow, *Survey,* 381–82.

2. "The Nursery of Beggary": Enclosure, Vagrancy, and Sedition in the Tudor-Stuart Period

WILLIAM C. CARROLL

The central interpretive paradigm of the sixteenth-century movement of enclosure was lucidly set forth in 1516 by Sir Thomas More. In the famous account in Book 1 of *Utopia*, Hythloday describes the sheep "that used to be so meek and eat so little. Now they are becoming so greedy and wild that they devour men themselves." Parasitical land-owners have enclosed "every acre for pasture," leaving "no land free for the plow." A single "greedy, insatiable glutton . . . may enclose many thousand acres of land within a single hedge. The tenants are dismissed and . . . forced to move out." When their pittance of money is gone, he continues, "what remains for them but to steal, and so be hanged . . . or to wander and beg? And yet if they go tramping, they are jailed as sturdy beggars. They would be glad to work, but they can find no one who will hire them." What can such displaced men do, Hythloday asks, "but rob or beg? And a man of courage is more likely to rob than to beg." Thus a generation of thieves and beggars is created. The English lawyer is preparing a response to these accusations and promises, "I will demolish all your arguments and reduce them to rubble," when the Cardinal interrupts him.[1] This might be the only instance in literature, or life, when we would have wished to hear a lawyer speak more.

I would emphasize here these primary elements of More's, or Hythloday's, analysis:

1. Enclosures are initiated by "the nobility and gentry, yes, and even some abbots."
2. Their intention, spurred by parasitical greed, is to replace arable land with pasture for sheep.
3. Their tenants are always victimized by enclosure and cast into poverty.

34

4. The formerly honest and hardworking peasants are turned into thieves or sturdy beggars wandering the countryside.

These four assertions in More's paradigm inevitably lead to some version of a pastoral communism as an eminently reasonable response to an intolerable economic and political situation. Economic historians have described any number of individual case histories that fit More's paradigm exactly, Sir Thomas Tresham being one of the more notorious.[2] More's paradigm, moreover, is quoted approvingly and taken over in all its essentials by Marx in *Capital,* where this social upheaval is analyzed as an element of the transition to capitalist production: "Thus were the agricultural people, first forcibly expropriated from the soil, driven from their homes, turned into vagabonds, and then whipped, branded, tortured by laws grotesquely terrible, into the discipline necessary for the wage system."[3]

We should remind ourselves, however, that each generalization in More's paradigm is contradicted, or at least complicated, by considerable historical evidence:

1. Enclosures were not always initiated by the nobility, gentry or church; indeed, in 1549 even the rebel Robert Kett proclaimed a wish to preserve some long-standing enclosures in the first article of his demands ("We pray your grace that where it is enacted for inclosyng that it be not hurtfull to suche as have enclosed saffren grounds for they be gretly chargeablye to them, and that from hensforth noman shall enclose any more").[4]

2. The reason for enclosure was often technical agricultural innovation and improved efficiency of tillage rather than the wish to pasture sheep; and some acts of enclosure, as Roger B. Manning has shown, were initiated by gentry against other gentry as part of more complex political, religious, or personal feuds.[5]

3. Tenants were not always victimized; indeed, many formally agreed to enclosure.[6]

4. Not all displaced tenants turned into thieves or beggars. Moreover, enclosure was far from the only cause of vagrancy, even in rural areas, but was rather one of several complex social conditions that led to vagrancy.

What continues to stand out nearly five centuries later is not the historical accuracy of More's paradigm, though his account certainly was frequently if not always the case, but rather the interpretive power of that paradigm, its nostalgic vision—one might almost say fantasy—of an always already lost communal perfection. This power derives in part from the fact that the very term *enclosure* is so unstable in the period, used as an all-purpose signifier for virtually every negative socioagricultural development, "at once too broad and too narrow," as R. H. Tawney once noted.[7] As a metaphor in other discourses, enclosure was invariably negative; as Flamineo cynically notes in *The White Devil*, to take but one example, locking up one's wife is futile: "These politic enclosures for paltry mutton makes more rebellion in the flesh than all the provocative electuaries [aphrodisiacs] doctors have uttered since last Jubilee."[8] Yet recent work in economic history has complicated every historical generalization about the enclosure movement in this period; indeed, "all attempts at generalization about the movement are hazardous," Joan Thirsk notes.[9] An apparent consensus among literary scholars that enclosure is *invariably* a negative needs to be contested, then, and the existence of a counterdiscourse, arguing the benefits of enclosure, needs to be reacknowledged. After briefly describing some of the contemporary arguments for and against enclosure, I will narrow my focus to one surprising point of agreement between these oppositional discourses, and then follow that point into several dramatic representations of the 1590s, particularly Shakespeare's *2 Henry VI*. The point of agreement in the counterarguments involves the creation of "sturdy beggars," an epidemic of masterless men which seemed to many an uncontrollable, chaotic energy threatening the entire social order of both country and city.[10]

I

The Thomas More paradigm held that enclosure creates vagrancy through depopulation. One opponent of enclosure a century and a half later put the case exactly as More had seen it: "When these enclosures have made farmers cottagers, and cottagers beggars, no way of livelihood being left them, these poor with their families are forced into market towns and open fielded towns, hoping they may find some employment there." But the process merely snowballs, for the newly poor "lay such burthens upon open fields that they are not able to bear them," and so yet more wandering poor are created.[11] In addition to outright expulsion from newly enclosed commons, rising prices led to higher rents for the legitimate tenants, with the same results—the expulsion from the land of those who had always worked it. The hypocrisy and cruelty of the landowners is perfectly captured in John Taylor's 1621 vision of the country Lord who

Ignobly did oppresse
His Tenants, raising Rents to such excesse:
That they their states not able to maintaine,
They turn'd starke beggers in a yeare or twaine.
Yet though this Lord were too too miserable,
He in his House kept a well furnish'd Table:
Great store of Beggers dayly at his Gate,
Which he did feed, and much Compassionate.
(For 'tis within the power of mighty men
To make five hundred Beggers, and feed ten.)[12]

Taylor's description of rising rents leading to impoverishment and beggary reflects hundreds of archival depositions. John Bayker's well-known letter to Henry VIII, nearly a century earlier, told exactly the same story: "Ys yt not a petyfull cays: to come in to a lytyll vylage or towne wer that thayre haythe beyne twentye or thyrty howses and now are halfe off thayme nothynge but bayre walls standing: ys yt not a petyfull cays to se one man have yt in hys hands wyche dyd suffyse ij or iij men wen the habytatyons were standynge."[13] The consummate dramatic exemplar of the type is no doubt Philip Massinger's Sir Giles Overreach (c. 1624), who shrugs off accusations that he is a "grand encloser / Of what was common, to my private use," his ears "pierced with widow's cries," while "undone orphans wash with tears" his threshold. Overreach also unfolds plans of Machiavellian cleverness "to hedge in the manor / Of [his] neighbor, Master Frugal."[14] The enclosing landlord, as one writer in 1632 ironically put it, "loves to see the bounds of his boundlesse desires; hee is like the Divell, for they both compasse the earth about."[15]

The painful economic realities of depopulating enclosure eventually produced two stereotypical dramatic figures of oppression. First, as we have seen, is "the grand encloser of the commons, for / His private profit or delight," as Massinger terms the type in another play, The Guardian (c. 1633).[16] A second type of oppressor is the greedy farmer, much lower on the socioeconomic scale, as in A Knack to Know a Knave (c. 1592), who has "raised the markets and oppress'd the poor, / And made a thousand go from door to door."[17]

In the counterdiscourse of enclosure in this period, arguments were made against excessive common waste ground, and for enclosures because they were for "the general good of the commonwealth," as Sir Thomas Smyth said, "both in the breed of serviceable men and subjects, and of answerable estates and abilities."[18] Sir Anthony Fitzherbert argued for enclosures in 1539 because the value of any piece of land would be increased "by reason of the compostyng and dongyng of the catell, that shall go and lye upon it both day and nighte," and because enclosure would create "as many newe occupations that were not used before" as were lost.[19] In 1573 Thomas Tusser asked in rhyme,

> More plentie of mutton and biefe,
>   corne, butter, and cheese of the best,
> More wealth any where (to be briefe)
>   more people, more handsome and prest,
> Where find ye (go search any coast)
>   than there, where enclosure is most?
>   (*TED* 3:64)

An anonymous pamphleteer in the 1650s argued more philosophically on behalf of enclosure, in part because "husbandry is the fundamental prop and nutriment of the Commonwealth," and, less convincingly, because there was "no example of common fields in all the divine word, nor in any skilful author writing of husbandry, as Virgil, Tully, etc" (*SCED*, p. 146). More mystically, he announced, "God is the God of order, and order is the soul of things, the life of a Commonwealth; but common fields are the seat of disorder, the seed plot of contention, the nursery of beggary" (*SCED*, p. 144).

In More's paradigm, then, enclosure *causes* beggars, but in the counterdiscourse it is the *failure* to enclose that causes beggars. In the aftermath of the Midlands revolt of 1607, one member of the House of Lords argued, using a familiar metaphor, that "the nurseries of beggars are commons as appeareth by fens and forests," whereas "wealthy people [live in] the enclosed countries as Essex, Somerset, Devon, etc" (*SCED*, p. 107). The anonymous pamphleteer quoted earlier argued that "common fields are the seedplots of contention" because "there is much unrighteous dealing," and "every man being for himself, he that thrives on his farm thriveth commonly by hurting his neighbor, and by his loss," because "trespasses are very frequent" (*SCED*, p. 145). "Common of pasture," argued one Elizabethan surveyor, was a "maintaining of the idlers and beggary of the cottagers," and King James proposed in 1610 that the House of Commons move against the numerous cottages on commons and in forests which were "nurseries and receptacles of thieves, rogues and beggars."[20] Enclosure, as always, was in the eye of the copyholder.

Whether one argued for or against enclosures as state policy, however, the common specter of social discord was the nightmarish vision of a new-created race of masterless men, of beggars and vagabonds wandering the roads, homesteading on the dwindling common wastes, poaching and fence breaking at will; ironically, vagabonds had even been hired to participate in local enclosure riots by the disputants.[21] As More noted, "A man of courage is more likely to rob than to beg." One antienclosure writer put it in 1550: "And now they have nothynge, but goeth about in England from dore to dore, and axe theyr almose for Goddes sake. And because they will not begge, some of them doeth steale, and then they be hanged, and thus the Realme doeth decay" (*TED* 3:56). It was exactly this state of affairs that concerned government authorities, for the swarms (in the usual dehumanizing metaphor) of masterless men were, like their city cousins, also thought to be ready material for riot and insurrection. Enclosure, or the lack of enclosure, led to beggars and masterless men, and *they* certainly led to sedition.[22] And sedition could never be tolerated. In a telling analogy, the parliamentary speaker of 1607 quoted earlier wondered whether the alleged causes of the Midlands revolt—depopulating enclosures— ought to be redressed immediately, lest encouragement be given to such rebellion, and he reminded his listeners that "in Edward the sixth his time the remedy was not pursued until two years after the rebellion of Kett" (*SCED*, p. 107).

II

Although no large-scale political rebellion occurred in this period, at least after 1549, nevertheless there were frequent eruptions of civil disorder, particularly in the 1590s, both in the country, with the abortive Oxfordshire rising of 1596 as perhaps the most notorious act of sedition, and in London—where an "epidemic of disorder," as one historian describes it, disrupted life between 1581 and 1602.[23] Public and private rhetoric in this period was often highly inflammatory; memories of Kett or Jack Cade were frequently recalled, particularly in connection with enclosure riots and related acts of sedition. In Thomas Lodge's *Wits Miseries and the Worlds Madnesse* (1596), the personification "Sedition, the Trouble worlde," is active in religion and politics, both in the city and "in the countrie, [where] hee stormes, and railes, against inclosures, telling the husbandmen that the pleasures of their Lords, eates away the fat from their fingers; and these rackt rents . . . are the utter ruine of the yeomanrie of England: the conclusion of his talke alwaies is insurrection, and commotion. . . . This is hee that saith that warre is a good tree, and bringeth forth good fruit, namelie store of good crownes: and it is a paradox of his, That it is better [to] live a Rebell then die a begger."[24]

Such voices were heard frequently during the disastrous harvest failures of the mid-1590s, particularly in Oxfordshire. In the ringleader of the Oxfordshire rising, Bartholomew Steer, Tudor authorities found exactly the threat to political and social order they had always imagined. A group of poor petitioners there was reported to have said "that yf they Could not have remedie, they would seek remedie themselves, and Cast down hedges and dytches, and knocke down gentlemen." Steer told his interrogators "the poore did once Rise in Spaine and Cutt down the gentlemen, and sithens that tyme they have lyved merily there." In England, he believed, "there would be somewhat adoe shortlie in this Countrie, more then had beene seene a greate while, ffor that manie would Rise. . . . Yt was but a monthes work to overrun England." Steer's ultimate vision of a national rising, though it would turn out to be only a hallucination, involved leveling the "hedges and ditches" of local enclosures, then marching on London itself, as Wat Tyler, Jack Straw, and Jack Cade once had done, and joining up with the mobs who had recently rioted in the city: "When the prentices heare that wee bee upp, they will Come and Joine with us. . . . He was rather induced to thinck the same," his interrogator reported, "by reason of the late intended insurrection in London, and that certain Prentices were then hanged."[25]

Steer's dream of a rural-urban proletarian solidarity was a hopeless one, in the view of the anonymous author of *A Students Lamentation* (1596), a supposed insider's account of the apprentices' riots, though from a counterrevolutionary perspective. Even princes have failed in acts of sedition, the author notes, "and shall vulgar people, nay inconsiderate boys have any hope to prosper in tumultuous riots? No assuredly, for as the great escape not, the baser cannot choose but perish. Of Jacke Straw, Will Waw, Wat Tiler, Tom Miller, Hob Carter and a number more such seditious inferiour ringleaders to seditions and conspiracies most notable, what hath been the end? Misery, destruction, and shame."[26]

The association of masterless men and certain forms of sedition was quite close, then, particularly when enclosure was an issue. The rebel Falconbridge in Thomas Heywood's *1 King Edward IV* (c. 1599), to take an example from the drama, is at some pains to distinguish himself from the usual kind of sedition, invoking a social class contempt which demonstrates the allegedly "natural" association of the poor with rebellion, but distinguishes theirs from his own:

> We do not rise like *Tyler, Cade,* and *Straw,*
> *Bluebeard,* and other of that rascal rout,
> Basely like tinkers or such muddy slaves
> For mending measures or the price of corne,
> Or for some common in the wield of Kent

Thats by some greedy cormorant enclos'd,
But in the true and antient lawfull right
Of the redoubted house of *Lancaster.*[27]

The litany of economic injustices, particularly enclosure, which might justify rebellion, and have done so in the past, is not relevant; rather, like most actual risings in the period, this one is led not by the peasantry but by a discontented nobleman.

Both dramatists and civil authorities nevertheless accepted the equation between masterless men and sedition, as Shakespeare's Henry IV articulates it:

And never yet did insurrection want
Such water colors to impaint his cause,
Nor moody beggars, starving for a time
Of pell-mell havoc and confusion.[28]

The inherent lawlessness of the masterless men of the countryside is dramatized in several plays of the 1590s, such as *Woodstock* (c. 1591–94), and especially *The Life and Death of Jack Straw* (c. 1593), in which Straw asks Wat Tyler, "Who would live like a beggar, and may be in this estate[?]"[29] Jack Cade's revolt in Shakespeare's 2 *Henry VI*, however, is perhaps the most directly connected to the issues of vagabondage and enclosure. Edward Hall's *Union of the Two Noble and Illustre Famelies of Lancastre and Yorke* (1548) makes Cade's ancestry plain: on Cade's return to London, "divers idle and vacabonde persons resorted to him from Sussex and Surrey, and from other partes to a great number. Thus this glorious Capitayn, compassed about, and environed with a multitude of evil rude and rusticall persones, came agayn to the playn of Blackeheath."[30] Moreover, in one of the rogue pamphlets of the period, *Martin Mark-all* (c. 1608), Cade is in fact said to be the "originall and beginning" of the Regiment of Rogues of the kingdom—more or less the Ur-vagabond. Cade's rebellion and march on London are joined, in this version, by the "Rakehels and Vagabonds . . . [and] masterlesse men" of Kent.[31] In another rogue pamphlet, Thomas Dekker's *O per se O* (1612), contemporary rogues and beggars are said to be like "Jack Cade and his rebellious ragamuffins."[32] So, too, Shakespeare's Cade, in 2 *Henry VI,* is followed by an army of vagabonds, "a ragged multitude / Of hinds and peasants, rude and merciless" (4.4.31–32). Cade himself is said, in the comic asides of Dick Butcher and Smith the Weaver, to have all the hallmarks of a vagabond: he was "born under a hedge," his father's house was "but the cage," and he is himself a "valiant" beggar, who has been "whipp'd three market-days together," and been "burnt i' th' hand for stealing of sheep" (4.2.49–60). In elaborating the fantasy that he is the son of Edmund Mortimer, finally, Cade himself offers that he is the older, hitherto unknown child, who, "being put to nurse, / Was by a beggar-woman stol'n away" (4.2.135–36).

Cade's genealogy is clear enough, and his political platform, though lunatic in some of its details, is also familiar in its claims. His assertions that "seven half-penny loaves [shall be] sold for a penny" and that he will "make it felony to drink small beer" are meant to be comical, but he also demands that "all the realm shall be in common" (4.2.65–66), which he repeats later, even more generally: "And henceforward all things shall be in common" (4.7.17). Here Cade sounds like his fellow rural rabble-rouser, the infamous Parson Ball, who, in *The Life and Death of Jack Straw*, argued for all things in common:

> It were better to have this communitie,
> Than to have this difference in degrees
> . . . make division equally,
> Of each mans good indifferently,
> And rightly may you follow Armes,
> To rid you from the civill harmes.
>   (ll. 84–85, 106–9)[33]

Here is the very Tudor nightmare of "the Multitude a Beast of many heads" (l. 188), spouting communistic doctrine of leveling all "difference in degrees." Ironically, the same Tudor authorities who passed laws restricting enclosures in an attempt to preserve common fields and wastes and reduce the numbers of displaced poor were at the same time frightened of the idea that *all* things should be in common. Few were willing even to entertain such radical solutions as one reformer proposed: "Unless private property is entirely done away with, there can be no fair or just distribution of goods, nor can mankind be happily governed."[34] Thomas More, to return to where we began, proposes an economic solution that follows quite logically from the enclosure paradigm he established. In *2 Henry VI*, Cade's solution—"all things shall be in common"—also follows from the grievances of the commons.

In one telling incident in *2 Henry VI* the petitioners in act 1 mistake Suffolk for the Lord Protector, and among the complaints Suffolk reads is one explicitly against him: "Against the Duke of Suffolk, for enclosing the commons of [Long] Melford." The petitioner defends himself from the angry duke by noting, "I am but a poor petitioner of our whole township" (1.3.20–24). At this point, at least in *The First Part of the Contention*, Suffolk "teares the papers" and says: "So now show your petitions to Duke *Humphrey.* / Villaines get you gone and come not neare the Court, / Dare these pesants write against me thus[?]"[35] Suffolk's act of enclosure is Shakespeare's invention, not present in any of the sources. In Hall, Suffolk is vaguely said to have "vexed, oppressed and molested the poore people," merely "for lucre of money," but enclosure is nowhere specifically mentioned.[36] It is fitting that Suffolk's agrarian exploitation is linked to the conditions that helped create the rebellious multitude that now calls for his head.

But not all enclosures are inherently evil, as we have seen. Shakespeare counterbalances Cade's desire to have all things in common with the antithetical agrarian position of Cade's nemesis, Alexander Iden of Kent, in whose enclosed garden Cade is slain. An experienced poacher, the "originall of vagabonds," Cade climbs over the "brick wall" into the garden, like any famished beggar looking for food. Iden is described as "the lord of the soil," who holds his "fee-simple" as an "inheritance my father left me" (4.10.6–25). Iden is designed as the virtuous contrast to the usual rural oppressors, the greedy cormorants who rapaciously enclose or raise rents; rather, Iden is a Horatian figure, an ideal of the landowner protecting his property: "I seek not to wax great by others' waning, / Or gather wealth I care not with what envy: / Sufficeth, that I have maintains my state, / And sends the poor well pleased from my gate" (4.10.20–23). His charity is such that he forbears "to combat a poor famish'd man," but when challenged slays the trespasser, only then discovering it is Cade, at which point all his charitable instincts vanish as he proceeds to mutilate and behead the corpse. Cade's headless body is dragged "into a dunghill," where it will presumably help one day to fertilize the gardens and enclosed fields of Kent. But in *The First Part of the Contention*, Iden accuses Cade of trespassing in somewhat different terms: "Thou hast broke my hedges, / And enterd into my ground without the leave of me the owner."[37] Recasting the historically contested term "hedges" as a "brick wall," and the "ground" to a private "garden," the Folio version ensures that Iden will be seen not as a potential encloser, a "greedy cormorant," but an emblematic version of the happy rural man. The Folio also adds several lines to Iden's initial speech about rural contentment, including his charity to the poor, as well as Cade's extremely explicit reference to the "fee-simple" and Iden's right to impound him as a trespassing "stray." Iden's Eden is thus more firmly established as legitimate in the Folio text, as one kind of enclosure is idealized and another condemned.

Cade is vanquished, at least on the London stage circa 1592, but his memory continued to live within the culture, as did his associations with masterless men and revolt from below. Tudor and Stuart governments regulated enclosure from a complex of often contradictory motives: the obligations of Christian charity, the need to increase agricultural productivity, and the need to ensure social and political stability in the body politic, among others. Parliamentary actions were often simply contradictory: acts against enclosures were passed and investigatory commissions formed to expose abuses, even while acts *for* enclosure were being passed for the benefit of individual landowners, frequently members of Parliament themselves—simply another form of "robbery," in Marx's view.[38]

Certainly one recurring argument in the Tudor-Stuart discourse on enclosure was that masses of beggars and masterless men in the countryside stood ready to join their cousins, the loose apprentices and vagrants in the cities, in armed rebellion. The descendants of Cade were allegedly immediately at hand in figures such as Bartholomew Steer of Oxfordshire. Cecil offered the conventional assessment in remarks to the Privy Council in 1598: "I have no fear of men of worth; when has England felt any harm by soldiers or gentlemen of worth? The State has ever found them truest. Some Jack Cade or Jack Straw and such rascals are those that have endangered the kingdom."[39] The comment was made, ironically, not in regard to a lower-class uprising, but in a discussion following the Earl of Essex's rebellious return from Ireland.

Whatever the facts about sedition from the top, the enduring myth in Tudor-Stuart political discourse was of sedition from below. Bacon described the masses of masterless men as "a seed of peril and tumult in a state," and in his essay on sedition offered a Brechtian warning: "The rebellions of the belly are the worst."[40] It is this fear that gave shape to much of the Tudor-Stuart discourse of enclosure, and helped produce in Jack Cade one rebellion of the belly, the poaching vagabond, "ready to famish! These five days have I hid me in these woods and durst not peep out, for all the country is laid for me; but now am I so hungry, that if I might have a lease of my life for a thousand years, I could stay no longer" (4.10.2–6). The conflicts in 2 *Henry VI* enact a characteristically Shakespearean ambivalence, reflecting both sides of the contemporary enclosure debates—inventing enclosure abuses and giving the rebels legitimate grievances, but at the same time undermining the rebels' ideological position through excess and ridicule. Still, though Cade's end is an ignominious one, he spoke on the London stage as one of the "hungry," "ready to famish," more likely to rob than to beg.[41]

NOTES

Research for this essay was assisted by a grant from the National Endowment for the Humanities.

1. Sir Thomas More, *Utopia*, ed. Robert M. Adams (New York: Norton, 1975), pp. 14–16. On the connections between enclosure and vagrancy, I have

found these sources particularly helpful: E. M. Leonard, *The Early History of English Poor Relief* (1900; reprint New York: Barnes & Noble, 1965); R. H. Tawney, *The Agrarian Problem in the Sixteenth Century* (London: Longmans, 1912); John Pound, *Poverty and Vagrancy in Tudor England* (London: Longman, 1971); Joan Thirsk, "Tudor Enclosures," in *The Tudors*, ed. Joel Hurstfield (New York: St. Martin's, 1973); Roger B. Manning, *Village Revolts: Social Protest and Popular Disturbances in England, 1509–1640* (Oxford: Oxford University Press, 1988); and Paul Slack, *Poverty and Policy in Tudor and Stuart England* (London: Longman, 1988).

2. See the convenient account in Manning, *Village Revolts*, pp. 237–41.

3. Karl Marx, *Capital: A Critique of Political Economy,* ed. Frederick Engels (New York: Modern Library, 1906), pp. 808–9.

4. Quoted in *Tudor Rebellions*, ed. Anthony Fletcher (London: Longmans, 1968), p. 142.

5. Manning, *Village Revolts*, p. 93.

6. See Thirsk, "Tudor Enclosures," pp. 108–9; some "agreements" were clearly made under duress, however.

7. Tawney, *Agrarian Problem*, p. 216.

8. John Webster, *The White Devil*, ed. John Russell Brown (Cambridge: Harvard University Press, 1960), 1.2.95–97. For a discussion of the social and sexual metaphorics of enclosure, see Peter Stallybrass, "Patriarchal Territories: The Body Enclosed," in *Rewriting the Renaissance: The Discourses of Sexual Difference in Early Modern Europe*, ed. Margaret W. Ferguson, Maureen Quilligan, and Nancy J. Vickers (Chicago: University of Chicago Press, 1986), pp. 123–42.

9. Thirsk, "Tudor Enclosures," p. 109.

10. On the phenomenon of vagabonds generally, see A. L. Beier, *Masterless Men: The Vagrancy Problem in England, 1560–1640* (London: Methuen, 1985), as well as Slack, *Poverty and Policy in Tudor and Stuart England.*

11. Joan Thirsk and J. P. Cooper, eds., *Seventeenth-Century Economic Documents* (Oxford: Clarendon Press, 1972), p. 150; hereafter cited in the text as *SCED.*

12. John Taylor, *The Praise, Antiquity, and Commodity, of Beggery, Beggers, and Begging* (London, 1621), C2ʳ.

13. Quoted in Frank Aydelotte, *Elizabethan Rogues and Vagabonds* (1913; reprint New York: Barnes & Noble, 1967), pp. 145–47.

14. Philip Massinger, *A New Way To Pay Old Debts*, in *Drama of the English Renaissance: The Stuart Period*, ed. Russell A. Fraser and Norman Rabkin (New York: Macmillan, 1976), 4.1.124–27, 2.1.27–39.

15. Donald Lupton, *London and the Country Carbonadoed and Quartred into Severall Characters* (London, 1632), p. 107.

16. Philip Massinger, *The Guardian* 2.4, in *Philip Massinger*, ed. Arthur Symons (London: Vizetelly & Co., 1889), 2:219.

17. Anon., *A Knack to Know a Knave*, in *Old English Plays*, ed. W. Carew Hazlitt (London, 1874), 6:518.

18. Quoted in L. C. Knights, *Drama and Society in the Age of Jonson* (New York: Norton, 1968), p. 99.

19. R. H. Tawney and Eileen Power, eds., *Tudor Economic Documents* (London: Longmans, 1924), 3:23–24; hereafter cited in the text as *TED.*

20. Both passages quoted in Christopher Hill, *The World Turned Upside Down* (New York: Viking, 1972), p. 41.

21. See Manning, *Village Revolts*, p. 163.

22. On the development of the sedition laws, see John Bellamy, *The Tudor Law of Treason* (London: Routledge, 1979), and Roger B. Manning, "The Ori-

gins of the Doctrine of Sedition," *Albion* 12 (1980), 99–121. As Manning notes, "The enclosure riot remained the pre-eminent form of social protest during the period from 1530 to 1640" (*Village Revolts*, p. 27).

23. Manning, *Village Revolts*, p. 187. For a more recent reappraisal of the "crisis" in London, see Ian Archer, *The Pursuit of Stability: Social Relations in Elizabethan London* (New York: Cambridge University Press, 1991), pp. 1–17.

24. Thomas Lodge, *Works* (1883; reprint New York: Russell & Russell, 1963), 4:67.

25. Quotations are taken from John Walter, "A 'Rising of the People'? The Oxfordshire Rising of 1596," *Past & Present* 107 (1985), 98, 108, 107–8.

26. *A Students Lamentation . . . for the rebellious tumults lately in the Citie hapning* (London, 1596), B2ᵛ. The passage continues: "All these at the beginning would be Reformers, a wrongs forsooth they went about to right: but when they had got head, what wrong did they not count right?"

27. In Thomas Heywood, *The Dramatic Works* (1874; reprint New York: Russell & Russell, 1964), 1.9.

28. *1 Henry IV* 5.1.79–82. Quotations from Shakespeare are from *The Riverside Shakespeare*, ed. G. Blakemore Evans (Boston: Houghton Mifflin, 1974); subsequent citations appear in the text.

29. Anon., *The Life and Death of Jack Straw, 1594* (Oxford: Oxford University Press, 1957), l. 247; subsequent citations appear in the text.

30. Geoffrey Bullough, *Narrative and Dramatic Sources of Shakespeare* (New York: Columbia University Press, 1975), 3:114.

31. Samuel Rowlands, *The Complete Works* (New York: Johnson Reprint, 1966), 2:44–45.

32. *Thomas Dekker*, ed. E. D. Pendry (Cambridge: Harvard University Press, 1968), p. 287.

33. Part of the preceding argument is developed more fully in my discussion of the political dimensions of Cade's language, "Language, Politics, and Poverty in Shakespearian Drama," *Shakespeare Survey* 44 (1992), 19–21.

34. More, *Utopia*, p. 31.

35. B2ᵛ, in *Shakespeare's Plays in Quarto*, ed. Michael J. B. Allen and Kenneth Muir (Berkeley: University of California Press, 1981), p. 49.

36. Bullough, *Narrative and Dramatic Sources*, 3:109.

37. G4ʳ, in *Shakespeare's Plays in Quarto*, p. 70; my colleague James Siemon first pointed out this detail to me.

38. Marx, *Capital*, p. 796.

39. *Calendar of State Papers Domestic, 1598–1601*, p. 352.

40. Francis Bacon, *Works*, ed. James Spedding, Robert Ellis, and Douglas Heath (London: Longmans, 1870), 6:409. Bacon notes two fundamental causes—"the matter of seditions is of two kinds; much poverty and much resentment" (p. 408)—and recommends, as prevention, that government suppress "or at the least [keep] a strait hand upon the devouring trades of usury, ingrossing, great pasturages, and the like," while at the same time working (he does not say how) toward "the improvement and husbanding of the soil" (p. 410).

41. Shakespeare himself, in 1614, was embroiled in an enclosure dispute surrounding his Welcombe property, which eventually led to hedge breaking by citizens of Stratford and Bishopton and a prolonged legal action settled by no less a figure than Chief Justice Coke, who, in 1616, ruled that William Combe "should never enclose nor lay down his common arable land." Quoted

in S. Schoenbaum, *William Shakespeare: A Compact Documentary Life* (Oxford: Oxford University Press, 1977), p. 285. But Shakespeare's way would be different from Cade's: shortly before the dispute began, Shakespeare had prudently entered into an agreement guaranteeing compensation to him or his heirs for any loss suffered "by reason of anie inclosure or decaye of tyllage there." E. K. Chambers, *William Shakespeare: A Study of Facts and Problems* (Oxford: Clarendon Press, 1951), 2:142. Shakespeare was equally careful in his will to leave these properties to his daughter Susanna.

3. Jack Cade in the Garden: Class Consciousness and Class Conflict in 2 *Henry VI*

THOMAS CARTELLI

I

In Shakespeare's 2 *Henry VI* the notorious career of Jack Cade concludes with the starving rebel's defeat at the hands of Alexander Iden, a self-styled "poor esquire of Kent" whom Cade formally terms "the lord of the soil" that provides the setting for their notably unequal combat. The end of Cade's career ironically becomes the occasion for a sudden turn in Iden's fortunes when Iden is "created knight for his good service," given a reward of a thousand marks, and effectively transformed into a courtier.[1] I say "ironically" because what may be termed the "garden scene" of 2 *Henry VI* is initially framed in the manner of a pastoral interlude as Iden enters and criticizes the lust for worldly advancement which has made Cade a desperate fugitive and encouraged many of Iden's social superiors to turn the "garden of England" into a site of fraternal bloodletting. The pastoral note is first sounded by Cade himself, whose representation of Iden's garden is, however, decidedly more utilitarian than conventional versions of pastoral:

> Fie on ambitions! fie on myself, that have a sword, and yet am ready to famish! These five days have I hid me in these woods and durst not peep out, for all the country is laid for me; but now am I so hungry, that if I might have a lease of my life for a thousand years, I could stay no longer. Wherefore, on a brick wall have I clim'b into this garden, to see if I can eat grass, or pick a sallet another while, which is not amiss to cool a man's stomach in this hot weather. (4.10.1–9)

Cade proceeds in a casually self-deprecating vein to play on the word "sallet" in a manner that suggests a crucial difference between his version of pastoral and Iden's. While he curses the ambitions that have brought him there, Iden's garden offers Cade merely the possibility of refreshment and a temporary respite from his flight from a "country" that is "laid for me," not an Arden-like retreat from the stresses of life.

Iden's construction of his garden state is notably more idyllic and mines the same conventions as Thomas Wyatt's anticourt pastoral, "Mine Own Join Poins."[2] Like the disaffected speaker in Wyatt's poem, Iden is "in Kent and Christendom" where "in lusty leas at liberty" he may walk. Unlike Wyatt's speaker, Iden enjoys a liberty that is unenforced, apart, that is, from the constraint of "this small inheritance my father left me," out of which Iden makes a virtue of necessity:

> Lord! who would live turmoiled in the court,
> And may enjoy such quiet walks as these?
> This small inheritance my father left me
> Contenteth me, and worth a monarchy.
> I seek not to wax great by others' waning,
> Or gather wealth I care not with what envy:
> Sufficeth, that I have maintains my state,
> And sends the poor well pleased from my gate.
>   (4.10.16–23)

As William Empson has taught us, pastoral effusions of this variety are seldom free of contextual qualification. In this instance we may observe that the self-congratulatory note Iden sounds harbors a discernible compensatory component, as if Iden were cheering himself up for his small inheritance by disparaging the profane pleasures the court offers those who can afford them and by overstating the worth of what the court would sneer at. Two additional qualifications are noteworthy. The first concerns Cade's altogether more material appraisal of Iden's "quiet walks" and "small inheritance." To Cade, Iden is less a poor esquire grazing on the pastoral margins of political life than the walking embodiment of established authority. Whereas Iden conceives of his walk in the garden as one in a series of daily demonstrations of an unturmoiled life neatly balanced between private pleasure and social obligation, Cade believes that "the lord of the soil" has walked forth expressly "to seize me for a stray, for entering his fee-simple without leave" (4.10.24–25).

Cade's legalistic and oppositional estimate of his imminent encounter with Iden demonstrates both his incapacity to appreciate Iden's version of pastoral and his complete exclusion from the privileged position that enables it. Unlike the poor who are sent "well pleased" from Iden's gate, Cade appears to be a complete stranger to the custom of feudal hospitality, of the mutual obligations that obtain, or are supposed to obtain, between prosperous giver and impoverished receiver. As befits the leader of a popular rebellion, Cade approaches his encounter with Iden from a thoroughly class-conscious and class-stratified position. For Cade, all possible relations between himself and Iden are construed in terms of the normative positioning of "stray" and "lord," hence in terms of mutual suspicion and hostility. From his perspective as a threatened stray, Iden's garden is *"enclosed private property*, not in any sense . . . a public or common domain."[3] And anyone in Cade's position would know that "a poacher could be . . . hanged for invading a park in search of what previously could be had for the taking in open countryside."[4] Cade's estimate of his position thus reveals the extent to which Iden's version of pastoral operates as a deeply privileged ideological construction.

Iden's effusion is further qualified by his own behavior during and after his encounter with Cade. Although Cade's aggressive challenge— "Ah, villain, thou wilt betray me, and get a thousand crowns of the King by carrying my head to him; but I'll make thee eat iron like an ostrich, and swallow my sword like a great pin, ere thou and I part" (4.10.26–29)—understandably discourages Iden from sending this particular poor man well pleased from his gate, the speed with which Iden confirms Cade's legalistic estimate of their relationship profoundly qualifies Iden's more placid conception of relations between rich and poor:

> Why, rude companion, whatsoe'er thou be,
> I know thee not; why then should I betray thee?
> Is't not enough to break into my garden,
> And like a thief to come to rob my grounds,
> Climbing my walls in spite of me the owner,
> But thou wilt brave me with these saucy terms?
>
> (4.10.30–35)

Iden's initial effort to allay Cade's anxieties suggests that Iden may be a more complex figure than Cade imagines, as does his subsequent reluctance to engage "a poor famish'd man" in combat. But as the passage moves—without further provocation from Cade—into a more magisterial restatement of Cade's own estimate of his transgression, Cade is summarily cast in the unvarying likeness of a "thief" who has "come to rob my grounds." Stephen Greenblatt notes, with respect to this encounter, that "status relations . . . are being transformed before our eyes into property relations, and the concern . . . for maintaining social and even cosmic boundaries is reconceived as a concern for maintaining freehold boundaries."[5] Although Greenblatt is certainly right to notice the crucial role that property plays in this transaction, Cade's braving of Iden with "saucy terms" seems to arouse Iden more than does his mere transgression of freehold boundaries. I would submit that it is primarily Cade's obstreperousness—his offensive refusal to maintain the habit of servility Iden expects both from "strays" who break into his fee-simple and from the poor who leave his gate well pleased—that motivates the violent turn in this encounter and consequently transforms Iden's pastoralized estimate of his garden state into a spirited defense of property rights.

Cade brings to Iden's garden a fully developed habit of resistance to even the most liberal ministrations of those who tower over him in the social order. His defiance rests partly on an overestimation of his notoriety, but largely on a conviction in his self-worth which has been fueled by his leadership of a rebellion that has already successfully leveled competing claims to distinction: "Brave thee! ay, by the best blood that ever was broach'd, and beard thee too. Look on me well: I have eat no meat these five days; yet, come thou and thy five men, and if I do not leave you all as dead as a door-nail, I pray God I may never eat grass more" (4.10.36–40). It is this that finally forces the issue between Cade and Iden, while Iden's response and the brief combat that follows ironically reveal the "true" nature of the relationship between social unequals:

> Nay, it shall ne'er be said, while England stands,
> That Alexander Iden, esquire of Kent,
> Took odds to combat a poor famish'd man.
> Oppose thy steadfast-gazing eyes to mine,
> See if thou canst outface me with thy looks:
> Set limb to limb, and thou art far the lesser;
> Thy hand is but a finger to my fist;
> Thy leg a stick compared with this truncheon;
> My foot shall fight with all the strength thou hast;
> And if mine arm be heaved in the air
> Thy grave is digg'd already in the earth.
> As for words, whose greatness answers words,
> Let this my sword report what speech forbears.
> (4.10.41–53)

Iden's speech fully appreciates and elaborates on the social disparity between the combatants by rendering it physical. Its comparative inventory of body parts casts Iden in the likeness of a giant and reduces Cade to the proportions of a dwarf. Although Iden's defeat of Cade may be accounted for—as Cade asserts—by the latter's current status as a starving fugitive, the text suggests that Cade is undone "naturally" in daring to contend with someone whose social superiority also makes

him his superior in strength and skill. Iden's conscientiously degrading
treatment of Cade's body—which Iden says he will drag "headlong by
the heels / Unto a dunghill," leaving Cade's "trunk for crows to feed
upon" after cutting off his head (4.10.75–83)—offers a last ironic gloss
on the futility of Cade's defiance and on the curse that Cade lays on
Iden's garden: "Wither, garden; and be henceforth a burying-place to
all that do dwell in this house, because the unconquer'd soul of Cade is
fled" (4.10.62–64).

This culminating act of enclosure also radically reorients Iden's attitude toward his own, previously celebrated, social position. Iden will
"cut off [Cade's] most ungracious head" and "bear [it] in triumph to the
King," thereby exchanging his garden state as a "poor esquire of Kent"
for the status of a knight, having clearly "waxed great" by another's
"waning," despite his earlier admonitory remarks. Cade's misadventure
in Iden's garden thus becomes the medium through which Iden exercises his own desire for social advancement, one that may be said to be
modeled on Cade's status as a very different kind of stray than Iden
initially imagines. As Iden leaves his garden behind for what he has
earlier appraised as the "turmoiled" life of a courtier, the notion of the
garden itself as an unturmoiled place apart, untouched by the social
strife that reigns elsewhere, also becomes radically qualified. In bringing to his encounter with Iden a deeply rooted, polarized, and polar-
izing consciousness of class, Cade elicits from Iden a response premised
on the same which effectively demystifies Iden's conception of a private space where rich and poor can meet on common ground. Cade's
violation of Iden's pastoral does not summarily transform Iden's garden into a site of social contestation; rather, it reveals the extent to
which its unbreached walls had previously functioned as a facade of the
imaginary, both for Iden himself and for the poor who came as sup-
plicants to its gates. In contesting the ideological hold that the garden
has heretofore maintained over all concerned parties, Cade effectively
unlocks its actual status as a space intersected by mutually exclusive and
competing class interests.

II

By assigning to a dramatic character a consciousness of something as
problematic as our modern notion of class, I run the risk of being discredited on both interpretive and historical grounds. But I believe that
a politically motivated class consciousness was capable of being both experienced and represented in early modern England, and that Jack
Cade constitutes the most realized example in Shakespeare's work of a

character who is able to transform his political subjection into something amounting to our modern sense of class-based resistance.[6] The
few historians daring or reckless enough to use the word *class* in their
representations of the period are usually careful to distance themselves
from the implication that its use indicates "either the existence of a
class society in the period or of class conflict."[7] Most seem content to
accept Peter Laslett's argument that in early modern England "there
were a large number of status groups but only one body of persons capable of concerted action over the whole area of society, only one class
in fact."[8] Where Laslett's argument falls flat is in its determination that
a social class must possess power commensurate with that of a ruling
party in society. Class conflict, for Laslett, requires the capacity or potential of an oppositional party to contest successfully the ruling party's
privileges or prerogatives: a formulation that—given the alleged lack
of a duly qualified opposition—appears always and ever to guarantee
the presence and predominance of a single class. R. S. Neale, by contrast, subscribes to E. P. Thompson's view "that class struggle precedes
class"; in Thompson's words, "Class defines itself as, in fact, it eventu-
ates."[9] Neale concludes that "the absence of a contemporary language
which would enable men to express such relationships [as class] should
not prevent historians from categorizing the past in ways unknown or
only vaguely understood by men in the past."[10]

In her own recent essay on *2 Henry VI*, Annabel Patterson demonstrates that "there *was* a cultural tradition of popular protest" in early
modern England, "a tradition in the sense of something handed down
from the past, cultural in the sense that what was transmitted were
symbolic forms and signifying practices, a history from below encoded
in names and occasions, a memorial vocabulary and even a formal
rhetoric."[11] In so doing, Patterson incisively redresses the traditional
neglect of the incipiently class-based ideologies of oppositional movements without, however, specifically nominating class as a discursive focus of her own.[12] Nonetheless, *2 Henry VI* is sufficiently abundant in
examples of a contemporary language expressive of class relationships
to satisfy the evidential demands of the majority of critics. Most of this
language is spoken by or through Jack Cade and his confederates, who
supply a variety of statements expressive of a deep and divisive consciousness of class. Although Shakespeare draws from these statements
no explicitly class-interested conclusions of his own, his characters
frequently do, as, for example, Jack Cade does in this exchange with
Lord Say:

Cade.   . . . Thou dost ride in a foot-cloth, dost thou not?
Say.   What of that?

Cade. Marry, thou ought'st not to let thy horse wear a cloak,
when honester men than thou go in their hose and doublets.
(4.7.44–49)

I choose this early moment in what soon becomes a notoriously violent encounter to demonstrate how commonplace signs of social distinction can be made to appear symptomatic of social inequity in *2 Henry VI*. In this instance a seemingly negligible privilege enjoyed by a representative of the ruling class is subjected to the sharp-tongued scrutiny of a representative of the class that both suffers and provides for it. By being placed in direct relation to the impoverishment of workingmen, the previously freestanding and therefore "innocent" social distinction is transformed into a corrupt social practice.

Although it could be argued that Cade's subsequent execution of a character who pleads "so well for his life" retrospectively cancels any incursion Cade may make against the ruling order's mystification of social injustice, such an objection would be hard to sustain in the context of a play that is largely devoted to dramatizing the predatory behavior of England's ruling establishment.[13] In 4.2., the first scene in which Cade's rebellion is represented, the ruling order is arraigned in a particularly resonant manner by two of Cade's confederates, one of whom proclaims, "Well, I say it was never merry world in England since gentlemen came up" (4.2.7–9). The wording of this statement notably anticipates a presentment made several years after this play's initial production by a participant in the 1596 Oxfordshire rising. According to Buchanan Sharp, "The miller Richard Bradshawe was reported to have declared 'that he hoped that before yt were long to see some of the ditches throwne downe, and that yt wold never be merye till some of the gentlemen were knocked downe,'" a sentiment, Sharp notes, "which recurred frequently in the examinations of the principal suspects."[14] Rather than claim that Bradshaw and his fellow suspects got their language from Shakespeare, one may more reliably assume that Shakespeare was appropriating an expression that would have been familiar to many well before the Oxfordshire rising and the initial performances of *2 Henry VI*.

By having his character rehearse a rallying cry that may well have been a contemporary commonplace, Shakespeare was bringing the successive histories of past risings and rebellions (beginning with accounts of the Peasants' Revolt of 1381, which he deploys throughout his dramatization of Jack Cade's rising) into direct contact with latterday representations of class conflict, thereby giving added currency to an apparently old complaint.[15] As Sharp observes: "Popular feeling in the Tudor-Stuart period reserved its most intense outbursts for . . . 'the rich.' As expressed in anonymous libels, seditious utterances reported from alehouses, and the few surviving examinations of rioters and insurrectionaries, the opinions of common folk reveal a deep hatred of the people possessed of the power, social standing, and landed wealth denied to them."[16] Shakespeare, of course, balances his representation of the poor's complaints against the rich by emphasizing the rashness and brutality of the rebels in his play. But in also choosing to emphasize the derisive manner in which characters such as Suffolk speak of "the rascal people"—for example, he calls his pirate captors "paltry, servile, abject drudges" (4.1.104)—and the indifference with which they hear and address the common people's seemingly modest petitions (see, e.g., 1.3.), Shakespeare demonstrates that the hatred of poor for rich is but "the mirror image of the contempt and fear with which their superiors regarded the poor."[17]

The predictability of the terms that rich and poor employ to speak of each other in 2 *Henry VI* has a contemporary Elizabethan analogue in the development of a "language of sorts," which, according to Keith Wrightson, "appears to have been used primarily to express a dichotomous perception of society." As Wrightson notes:

> Such language clearly reveals a world of social meanings untapped by the formal social classifications of the period—and arguably it was so widely used because it was of greater practical significance. Its utility lay above all in the fact that it was a terminology of social simplification, sweeping aside the fine-grained (and highly contested) distinctions of the hierarchy of degrees and regrouping the English into two broad camps which were clearly held to reflect the fundamental realities of the social and economic structure and the basic alignments of social relations. . . . It was a language of radical differentiation, cleaving society into the haves and have nots, the respected and the contemned. It was a language pregnant with conflict, aligning the "richer" over against the "poorer," the "better" over against the "meaner," "vulgar," "common," "ruder" or "inferior" sorts. It was also a language of radical dissociation, usually found in the mouths of those who identified themselves with the "better" sort and stigmatised those whom they excluded from that company with a barrage of pejorative adjectives.[18]

In 2 *Henry VI* the "better sort" variously refer to the commons as "the abject people" (Duke Humphrey, 2.4.11); "an angry hive of bees / That want their leader, [who] scatter up and down, / And care not who they sting" (Warwick, 3.2.124–26); and as "rude unpolish'd hinds" (Suffolk, 3.2.270). But what is perhaps more notable is the extent to which the rising commons themselves appropriate the stigmatizing function of the language of sorts to "align" themselves in prosecuting their rebellion.

Their initial, generalized animus against gentlemen is, for example, soon extended to include "all scholars, lawyers, [and] courtiers," other "false caterpillars" such as magistrates, those who "can write and read and / cast accompt" (4.2.81–82), and anyone who speaks Latin (4.7.55). Reacting against the "scorn" the nobility reserve for those who "go in leather aprons" and the lack of regard shown to "virtue in handicrafts-men," the rebels invert the criteria by which honor is measured by con-tending that "there's no better sign of a brave / mind than a hard hand (4.2.10–20). For his part, Jack Cade brings this tendency to its logical conclusion when he calls the Staffords "silken-coated slaves" (4.2.122), traces his artisanal nobility back to Adam, who "was a gardener" (4.2.128), and identifies "such as go in clouted shoon" as "thrifty hon-est men":

> And you that love the commons, follow me.
> Now show yourselves men; 'tis for liberty.
> We will not leave one lord, one gentleman:
> Spare none but such as go in clouted shoon,
> For they are thrifty honest men, and such
> As would, but that they dare not, take our parts.
>
> (4.2.175–80)

What is especially revealing about Cade's call to arms is that its direct challenge to the very people Cade presumes to represent—namely, "the commons"—expresses a tolerance for (and expectation of) their failure to respond to it. Cade attempts to claim here a representative political character for his rebellion by presuming to speak on behalf of those who "dare not" join in it but are joined *to* it both by their status as workers and by their unvoiced allegiance to its aims. Although Cade's confident assumption that he speaks on behalf of those who dare not speak for themselves may well be mistaken, it *be*speaks a con-sciousness of collective interests and shared goals that is, for all rights and purposes, a consciousness of class. And it also demarcates that piv-otal moment when "a class 'in itself' become[s] a class for 'itself.' "[19]

It is, of course, commonly held that Cade is represented as "a cruel, barbaric lout, whose slogan is 'kill and knock down,' and whose story as 'the archetype of disorder' is one long orgy of clownish arson and ho-micide fuelled by an infantile hatred of literacy and law." Shakespeare's decision to degrade the figure "whom [even the historian Edward] Hall respects as 'a youngman of godely stature and pregnaunt wit' . . . whose advisers were 'scholemasters' and 'teachers' " may well reflect his own negative appraisal of Cade.[20] But it does nothing to diminish the delegation to his character of an acute consciousness of class. Indeed, by separating *his* radically disorderly Cade from Hall's more respectable figure, Shakespeare may be said to have foregrounded class distinctions which a more accurate (or less prejudicial) estimate of the historical Cade would have occluded.[21]

The class distinctions Shakespeare foregrounds are almost exclusively those that distinguish the "better sort" from the "meaner sort," those who are socially and culturally privileged from those who privilege their own social and cultural dispossession. The "middling sort" play a much more negligible role in the physical conflict represented onstage, as the following example suggests. After announcing that "Jack Cade hath almost gotten London Bridge," a messenger to the king reports that "the citizens fly and forsake their houses," while "the rascal people, thirsting after prey, / Join with the traitor; and . . . jointly swear / To spoil the city and your royal court" (4.4.48–52). In addition to distinguishing the (victimized) citizens of London from the (victimizing) people, this passage implicitly draws a connection between the interests of "the city" and those of the "royal court." This connection is elaborated in the brief scene (4.5.) that ensues, in which a textually identified "citizen" (apparently speaking at the behest of the Lord Mayor) exchanges information with Lord Scales, who urges the Londoners to "fight for your king, your country, and your lives" (4.5.11). This they apparently do under the leadership of Matthew Goffe. But apart from the evidence provided by a stage direction that reads "Alarums. Matthew Goffe is slain, and all the rest" (4.7.), Shakespeare appears to have chosen not to stage at any length the bloody battle between citizens and rebels for London Bridge which Hall represents in graphically lurid detail:

> The multitude of the rebelles drave the citezens from the stoulpes at the bridge foote, to the drawe bridge, and began to set fyre in divers houses. Alas what sorow it was to beholde that miserable chaunce: for some desyrynge to eschew the fyre, lept on his enemies weapon, and so died: fearfull women with chyldren in their armes, amased and appalled, lept into the river: other doubtinge how to save them self betwene fyre, water, and swourd, were in their houses suffocat and smoldered.[22]

Shakespeare not only fails to include a single dramatic reference to Hall's account in the text of *2 Henry VI;* he also fails to provide the kind of detailed commentary on undramatized action that would have lent a great deal more judgmental fervor to his representation of the episode in question. Conjoined with Cade's subsequent (and wildly anachronistic) order for "some" to go "and pull down the Savoy" (4.7.1) and "others" to do likewise to the Inns of Court—both references to actions undertaken during the rising of 1381—Shakespeare's deviations from

Hall appear to repress the role played by citizens of "the middling sort" as opponents and victims of Jack Cade and as allies of the royal party. Rather than emerging as an "enemy of the people," whose conception of class warfare pits the commons against the citizens of London, Cade is consequently represented in a manner that more closely approximates his own self-estimate as protector or defender of "the people" against the depredations of the high and mighty.

The negligible role played by the citizen class or "middling sort" in Shakespeare's dramatization of Cade's rebellion does not, however, entirely mystify the position Shakespeare adopted in staging a conflict that primarily pits rich against poor. In largely choosing to remove citizens from the scene of Cade's rebellion and, for that matter, from the far more numerous scenes that portray the struggles between royalty and aristocracy which eventuate in civil war, Shakespeare may well be representing, as well as promoting, the point of view of the one component of English society that presumably remained both stable and reliable in the face of wholesale social disorder: namely, the literate, industrious, law-abiding citizen class. In identifying the point of view of *2 Henry VI* with the interests of what we today would term the "middle class," I am attempting to give some ideological basis to this play's author function while at the same time avoiding the facile equation of biography and ideology which makes Shakespeare a reactionary mouthpiece for the historically inevitable triumph of what Richard Wilson calls "the literate bourgeois."[23] Wilson detects nothing but "animus" in those episodes of the play that record "the people's garbled testimony or laboured puns" and that dramatize their "long orgy of clownish arson and homicide fuelled by an infantile hatred of literacy and law."[24] I detect, on the contrary, a politically astute reckoning with a long list of social grievances whose inarticulate and violent expression does not invalidate their demand for resolution. And I attribute the astuteness of that reckoning to a playwright whose manifest literacy and identification with citizen values may actually have made possible his sympathetic appraisal of the people's claims.

Garbled though they may be, the people's grievances are not, in any event, first expressed in the context of Cade's rebellion. They are, in fact, repeatedly addressed in the long series of events that lead up to it in the life of this particular play, beginning with the abortive presentation of the petition against the enclosure of Long Melford (1.3.) and with Simpcox's wife's testimony that she and her husband pursued their fraud "for pure need" (2.1.250). Even within the context of Cade's rebellion, powerful appraisals of social injustice are attached to ostensibly more intemperate diatribes against schooling and literacy, as is the case, for example, in Cade's rambling indictment of Lord Say:

It will be prov'd to thy face that thou hast men about thee that usually talk of a noun, and a verb, and such abominable words as no Christian ear can endure to hear. Thou hast appointed justices of peace, to call poor men before them about matters they were not able to answer. Moreover, thou hast put them in prison; and because they could not read, thou hast hang'd them; when, indeed, only for that cause they have been most worthy to live. (4.7.36–44)

Whereas Wilson employs such examples to demonstrate Shakespeare's revulsion toward those members of his audience and his society who, like his own father, lacked the capacity to write, we would do better to view such passages as symptomatic of Shakespeare's representation of literacy as a crucial bridge between powerlessness and empowerment. Cade and his cohorts repeatedly revile the practices of reading, writing, and printing, and the collateral institution of grammar schools and printing mills, less out of ignorance than out of an assured belief in the role they play in dividing society into haves and have-nots. They read into such practices and institutions their own marginal status as dispossessed subjects ("because they could not read") of all-possessing masters ("thou hast hang'd them").

Illiteracy was surely not a capital offense in Shakespeare's England, but it would be disingenuous to contend that Cade radically misrepresents the legal implications of a social structure in which illiteracy could, indeed, have mortal consequences. As late as 1663 George Swinnock noted that "some for want of reading their neck-verse have lost their lives."[25] And as David Cressy notes with respect to more fortunate participants in the customary reading of the neck-verse, "the opportunity remained in Tudor and Stuart England for the literate felon to claim 'benefit of clergy' and escape the full severity of the law."[26] Cressy also reminds us of the social consequences of membership in that class of subjects Jack Cade claims to represent—a grouping that closely resembles what Thomas Smith identified as that "fourth sort or class" that had "no voice nor authoritie in our common wealth," which comprised "day labourers, poore husbandmen, yea, marchantes or retailers which have no free land, copiholders, and all artificers, as Taylers, Shoomakers, Carpenters, Brickemakers, Bricklayers, Masons, & c."[27] The evidence assembled by Cressy suggests a close correlation between illiteracy and the lack of "voice or authoritie" of the majority of subjects in this class. In a ranking of trades by illiteracy, Cressy's samples indicate that approximately half the tailors, blacksmiths, joiners, wrights, and butchers in rural England in the period 1580–1700 were functionally illiterate. Between 60 and 75 percent of the carpenters, glovers, shoemakers, masons, and bricklayers fall into this category as well (pp. 132–33). In virtually all the samples assembled "labourers" and "husbandmen" vie with women of every class for the claim to complete illiteracy.

Cressy also supplies evidence that helps explain the connection between Jack Cade's animosity toward literacy and its enabling institutions and his specific singling out of "all scholars, lawyers, courtiers, [and] gentlemen" as enemies of the people. A division of early modern English society into discrete classes on the basis of literacy would, for example, directly link members of the clergy, the professions, and the gentry in ways that other measurements—say, on the basis of property, wealth, or political power—would not (pp. 119–21). According to Cressy: "The gentry, clergy and members of the professions were so similar in their literacy that they can be regarded as inhabiting a single cluster at the accomplished end of the literacy scale. Thirty percentage points or more usually separated them from the next most literate cluster, the yeoman and tradesman" (p. 124). Cressy's findings offer a possible rationale for what is often construed to be Jack Cade's irrational and indiscriminate attack on citizens who would initially appear to operate at some remove from the most obvious structures of power. If, as Cressy's evidence suggests, Cade and his followers are correct in perceiving a connection between those who appear to be only culturally privileged and those who are socially and economically privileged as well, then conventional estimates of Cade's demagoguery and his followers' barbarity may themselves be in need of correction. Indeed, Shakespeare may be attributing to Cade and his rebels what is at once a critically acute and an ideologically predictable piece of social analysis, grounded in a consciousness of class differences and opposing class interests similar to that which appears to have characterized the attitude of the Elizabethan poor toward the rich.

In commenting on the nature of the connections between the educationally and socially privileged, Cressy would appear to confirm this possibility: "The social standing of priests and professionals depended on their training and function as well as on their connections and wealth. They were essentially skilled literate specialists, agents and associates of the ruling class. By virtue of their profession alone they were accorded a kind of honorary gentle status and were grouped with the gentry in most contemporary social classifications" (p. 122). Instead of engaging in a complicated bout of self-hatred in representing Cade's attack on literacy and the literate, Shakespeare instead provides Cade with an argument consistent with convictions that not only may have been shared by contemporary working men, but continue to characterize the struggle for control of the "means of communication" in societies similarly divided between literate haves and illiterate have-nots.[28] In its effort to root out such "false caterpillars" as "scholars and lawyers," Cade's "ragged multitude" of illiterate "hinds and peasants" effectively identifies these "skilled literate specialists" as "agents and associates of the ruling class." Although the attendant scorn directed at literacy itself may constitute a displaced (and arguably self-defeating) symptom of political dispossession, the indictment of its beneficiaries could not be more apt.

Like other positions taken by Cade and his followers, the animus toward literacy is rooted in a collective valorization of prevailing differences, a nostalgia for a simpler time of undistinction, and a correspondingly defensive anxiety regarding change which has at least some basis in contemporary events. At the beginning of his encounter with Lord Say, for example, Cade identifies Say's educational philanthropy as one of the chief sins he has committed against the commonwealth: "Thou hast most traitourously corrupted the youth of the realm in erecting a grammar-school; and whereas, before our forefathers had no other books but the score and the tally, thou hast caus'd printing to be us'd" (4.7.30–34).

The terms of Cade's indictment initially seem to subordinate willful ignorance to a conscious cultivation of comic effect, as Cade appears to relish his exaggeration of the threat posed to civil society by Say. But if we choose to take Cade at his word, his indictment may instead express the same nostalgia for a "bookless" existence presided over by satisfied forefathers, which Nicholas Breton describes in his representation of the semiliterate countryman's pastimes: "We can learne to plough and harrow, sow and reape, plant and prune, thrash and fanne, winnow and grinde, brue and bake, and all without booke. These are our chiefe businesse in the Country, except we be Jury-men to hang a theefe, or speake truth in a mans right, which conscience and experience wil teach us with a little learning."[29] Cade's claim that the heritage of this simpler state of affairs is jeopardized by the unsettling changes wrought by grammar schools may also be more broadly placed in the context of the "educational revolution" that took place in the first half of the Elizabethan period and that reached its peak in 1580. According to Cressy, "The reign of Elizabeth saw a solid improvement in literacy among tradesmen and craftsmen in all parts of England," with tailors and weavers in particular making considerable gains (p. 153). This "revolution" witnessed the dissemination of schoolmasters throughout the countryside and may have been directly responsible for making Shakespeare's own generation more literate than that of either his ancestors or his descendants. Of course, such a revolution may also have worked to create divisions between generations, to arouse anxiety among those incapable of benefiting from it, or to exacerbate already prevailing tensions and differences between the latter and those who could employ their newly acquired literacy in the interests of social mobility.

Rather than speculate further in this vein, I would prefer to explore the connection between Cade's scorn for literacy and valorization of il-literacy with the positions he and his followers take toward property, power, and status relations. In the course of the play we get from them an inventory of claims, principles, and resolves that identifies the "fall" of the "merry world" that was England with the institution of a system of distinctions whose beneficiaries are gentlemen, magistrates, lawyers, and scholars, among others. England's redemption is premised on a series of utopian proposals that variously call for the termination of distinction ("All the realm shall be in common" [4.2.65]); the extermi-nation of those privileged by distinction ("The first thing we do, let's kill all the lawyers" [4.2.73]); and the absorption of those privileged by distinction into the great mass of the undistinguished ("Let the mag-istrates be laboring men" [4.2.16–17]). Having leveled distinction, Cade would apparel all "in one livery, that they may agree like broth-ers, and worship me their lord" (4.2.70–72). Cade's determination to reserve this pivotal distinction for himself is expressed with a good deal more consistency than are his other positions. Calling for the burning of "all the records of the realm," Cade claims that "my mouth shall be the parliament of England" (4.7.12–14). And in the same scene he as-serts, "The proudest peer in the realm shall not wear a head on his shoulders, unless he pay me tribute" (4.7.114–15).

It is commonplace for commentators on the play to emphasize the many contradictions in Cade's positions, the most notable one involv-ing Cade's demagogic claim to absolute power in a society in which all things are to be held "in common." But it is Cade's *impulse* to change radically the system by which goods and offices are distributed that might better occupy our attention. We learn from the examples the play gives us that what motivates Cade and his confederates most in-sistently is the wholesale destruction of a system of privileges which renders them visibly and permanently powerless. Gentlemen, magis-trates, lawyers, and scholars are portrayed as accomplices in a ruling-class conspiracy to cheat working men out of their "ancient rights." This conspiracy has been institutionalized in a rule of law, permanently housed in "the records of the realm," and handed down in incompre-hensible Latin tags by magistrates who will excuse only those who are as literate as they are. Enclosures, price-fixing, coining, the control of surpluses, and the delegation of easily distinguished vocational liveries, are all represented as activities that advance the interests of the ruling order at the expense of those who suffer them. Cade's communistic al-

ternative is an oppositional dream of simplification and uniformity—
of *undistinction*—of an equity born out of an intolerance with inequity,
though, given its genocidal and demagogic components, hardly identifiable with what we today would call social justice. The root of the
dream, in an apparent but fully explicable reversion to mystification, is
Adam in the Garden, the common father of common men, who, as in
the passage from Breton, can do "all without book."

III

As others have noted, one may trace the communistic dream in
2 Henry VI to a common ideological source which helped define a
succession of other popular uprisings and rebellions, succinctly summarized in John Ball's catchphrase, "When Adam delv'd and Eve span
/ Who was then the gentleman?"[30] Shakespeare's familiarity with
Grafton's and Holinshed's representations of John Ball and the Peasants' Revolt of 1381 has long been recognized and acknowledged. It is
especially obvious in his anachronistic decision to have Cade and his
followers destroy the Savoy and attack the Inns of Court, and in Cade's
response to Stafford's attempt to belittle him:

> *Staf.*   Villain! thy father was a plasterer;
>   And thou thyself a shearman, art thou not?
> *Cade.*   And Adam was a gardener.
> *Bro.*   What of that?
>   (4.2.126–28)

But the question asked by Stafford's brother, to which Cade gives a
characteristically arch and contradictory reply, is one that John Ball
answered more incisively in the sermons reproduced by Grafton
and Holinshed.

Richard Grafton offers a reconstruction of the commonplace address
Ball would give his parishioners after Sunday services:

> Ah good people, matters go not wel to passe in England in these dayes,
> nor shall not do untill every thing be common, and that there be no Vil-
> leynes nor gentlemen but that we be all as one, and that the Lordes be no
> greater then we be. What have we deserved, or why should we be thus
> kept in servitude and bondage? We be all come from one father and one
> mother, Adam and Eve. Wherefore can they saye or shewe that they are
> greater Lordes then we be? savyng in that which we get and labour for,
> that doe they spend.[31]

Tracing the human family back to its presumptive source in Adam and Eve, Ball effectively declares that the oppressive divisions of the contemporary social order constitute an unauthorized deviation from a divinely ordained equality. He further identifies the distinctions that currently obtain between lords and commons in terms that would be familiar to any latter-day cultural materialist. According to Ball, social dominance is now delegated to those who consume but do not produce, while those who produce but do not consume are "kept in servitude and bondage." Given this state of affairs, the return he envisions to an originary condition in which "there be no Villeynes nor gentlemen but that we be all as one" would appear to require either the dissolution of differences among men or the elimination of one of the contending social classes.

In his famous speech to the rebels at Blackheath, Ball offered his auditors a solution to this dilemma based, like Cade's, on an inverted valorization of workers. Ball addressed his audience as "good husbands" who must set about to transform the decaying garden of England in a thoroughly class-conscious manner, and not merely restore it to an Edenic state that has its human counterpart in an all-inclusive equality. According to Holinshed:

> He counselled them . . . that after the manner of a good husband that tilleth his ground, and riddeth out thereof such evill weeds as choke and destroie the good corne, they might destroie first the great lords of the realme, and after the judges and lawiers, questmoongers, and all other whom they undertooke to be against the commons, for so might they produce peace and suertie to themselves in time to come, if dispatching out of the waie the great men, there should be an equalitie in libertie, no difference in degrees of nobilitie, but a like dignitie and equall authoritie in all things brought in among them.[32]

Ball's emphasis on the destruction of judges and lawyers provides another basis for understanding Shakespeare's delegation to Cade of an emphasis on the same and on the destruction of the "records of the realm." It may be traced to the same rationale that motivated "the common uplandish people" during the Peasants' Revolt "to burne and destroie all records, evidences, court-rolles, and other minuments," the rationale being "that the remembrance of ancient matters being removoved out of mind, their landlords might not have whereby to chalenge anie right at their hands."[33] What Ball, Cade, and the "uplandish people" want, in the end, is less the return to a garden state that antedates the history of their disenfranchisement than the recovery of an "ancient freedom" that will supersede the memory of their servitude and dispossession. That Cade ultimately meets his end at the hands of a powerfully endowed "lord of the soil" while hunting up a salad in that man's garden graphically demonstrates the nostalgic basis of this shared dream of undistinction at the same time as it validates its construction of prevailing class differences.

N O T E S

1. 2 *Henry VI* 5.1.64–82. All quotations from 2 *Henry VI* are from the Arden edition, ed. Andrew S. Cairncross (London: Methuen, 1969); subsequent citations appear in the text.

2. In his own commentary on this scene, William Carroll calls Iden "an Horatian figure" and offers an illuminating comparison of the language delegated to him in the Folio version—from which my quotations are drawn—and in *The First Part of the Contention*. Although I agree with Carroll that the evidence for viewing the *Contention's* Iden as "a potential encloser" becomes flimsier in the Folio, I find other reasons to question his alleged standing as "an emblematic version of the happy rural man," as I suggest later in this chapter.

3. Stephen Greenblatt, "Murdering Peasants: Status, Genre, and the Representation of Rebellion," *Representations* 1 (1983), 24.

4. Simon Pugh, *Garden—Nature—Language* (Manchester: Manchester University Press, 1988), p. 11.

5. Greenblatt, "Murdering Peasants," p. 25.

6. As Michael Hattaway writes in "Rebellion, Class Consciousness, and Shakespeare's 2 *Henry VI*," *Cahiers Elisabethans* 33 (1988), 13–22: "What Cade proclaims constitutes a cause, . . . a cause that emerges from class oppression" (p. 13). Hattaway also claims that the nobility in the *Henry VI* plays "constitute a class—or if we prefer, an elite—defined by the conflict between individual aspirations of its members and everything that constitutes the culture or cultures of the plebeians" (p. 16).

7. Susan Amussen, "Gender, Family, and the Social Order, 1560–1725," in *Order and Disorder in Early Modern England,* ed. Anthony Fletcher and John Stevenson (Cambridge: Cambridge University Press, 1985), p. 206, n.33. Michael Hattaway offers this commentary on the similar conclusion reached by the editors of the volume in which Amussen's essay appears: "Working from an analysis of cultural models, patterns of behaviour and local community, Anthony Fletcher and John Stevenson conclude that 'a class society had not in our period yet arrived' [ibid., p. 4]. I cannot dispute their conclusion if I work from the same material and the same premises. But it seems that yet again literary critics have something to offer the cultural historians" ("Rebellion, Class Consciousness," p. 16). On this subject, see note 12.

8. Peter Laslett, *The World We Have Lost* (New York: Scribner's, 1965), p. 23. A possible exception is David Underdown, who notes that "a heightened polarization of society . . . makes this period [1540–1640] an important stage in the long process of class formation. England was still very far from being a class society, but the lines were beginning to sharpen, the horizontal ties linking the 'respectable' and dividing them from the poor to cut across the vertical

ones of local identity." David Underdown, *Revel, Riot, and Rebellion: Popular Politics and Culture in England, 1603–1660* (Oxford: Oxford University Press, 1985), p. 20.

9. R. S. Neale, *Class in English History: 1680–1850* (New York: Barnes & Noble, 1981), pp. 97–98.

10. Ibid., p. 99

11. Annabel Patterson, *Shakespeare and the Popular Voice* (Oxford: Basil Blackwell, 1989), p. 38.

12. In her editor's note to *Shakespeare Quarterly* 42, 2 (1991), Gail Kern Paster calls attention to the lack of reciprocity of social historians to the work of literary scholars, who have been greatly influenced by their findings and methodologies. Paster notes that not even avowedly revisionist historians "seem as prepared as most literary practitioners to investigate the ideological or material consequences of dramatic representation, either on lived practices or on the social formation of consciousness" (p. vi). Although I do not claim that "literary evidence, the evidence of imaginative texts," should "be allowed a referential function, a power to give material and concrete evidence about the past" (p.iii)—a possibility that Paster poses without actually endorsing—I *do* think historians should attend more closely to the representational claims of what is imagined in such eminently social texts as *2 Henry VI*.

13. As Michael Hattaway writes, "The *Henry VI* plays offer a searing indictment of aristocratic factionalism and the haughtiness of prelates" ("Rebellion, Class Consciousness," p. 16).

14. Buchanan Sharp, *In Contempt of All Authority: Artisans and Riot in the West of England, 1586–1640* (Berkeley: University of California Press, 1980), pp. 38–39. See also Keith Wrightson, *English Society: 1580–1680* (New Brunswick, N.J.: Rutgers University Press, 1982), p. 150.

15. In *Shakespeare and the Popular Voice*, Annabel Patterson notes that in appropriating "the chronicle accounts of the Peasants' Revolt to thicken his description of Jack Cade's rebellion," Shakespeare "was clearly participating in an Elizabethan cultural practice, that of collating the popular protests of the past, both with each other and with the issues of the day" (pp. 38–39).

16. Sharp, *In Contempt*, p. 36.

17. Ibid.

18. Keith Wrightson, "Estates, Degrees & Sorts in Tudor and Stuart England," *History Today* 37 (1987), 21.

19. Anthony Giddens, *The Class Structure of the Advanced Societies* (New York: Barnes & Noble, 1973), p. 30.

20. Richard Wilson, " 'A Mingled Yarn': Shakespeare and the Cloth Workers," *Literature & History* 12, 2 (1986), 167.

21. In her discussion of Kett's rebellion, Annabel Patterson remarks the "self-conscious acceptance, by the rebels themselves, of a 'peasant' ideology of the primitive," and concludes that "it is no accident that Shakespeare's Cade makes [the 'clouted shoon'] his distinguishing mark of class" (*Shakespeare and the Popular Voice*, p. 40).

22. Edward Hall, *The Union of the Two Noble and Illustre Famelies of Lancastre and Yorke* (London, 1548), f. 160ᵛ.

23. Wilson, "A Mingled Yarn," p. 168. As Wilson writes: "Son of a provincial glover whose only testimony is the mark he left beside his name in borough records, Shakespeare used his professional debut to signal scorn of popular culture and identification with an establishment in whose eyes authority would henceforth belong exclusively to writers" (ibid., p. 169).

24. Ibid., pp. 168, 167–68.

25. George Swinnock, *The Christian mans calling . . . the second part* (London, 1663), pp. 22–23. Quoted in David Cressy, *Literacy and the Social Order: Reading and Writing in Tudor and Stuart England* (Cambridge: Cambridge University Press, 1980), p. 3. According to Cressy, "In medieval England, when literacy was virtually a clerical monopoly and criminous clerks were judged more leniently than lay felons, the ability to read a set text of the Bible was regarded as a competent proof of clerkship. The criminal had only to ask for the book and read the standard verse, the 'neck-verse,' to escape the gallows" (p. 16).

26. Cressy, *Literacy*, pp. 16–17; subsequent citations appear in the text.

27. Sir Thomas Smith, *De Republica Anglorum* (London, 1583; rpt. Cambridge: Cambridge University Press, 1906), p. 46.

28. See Bill Ashcroft, Gareth Griffiths, and Helen Tiffin, *The Empire Writes Back: Theory and Practice in Post-Colonial Literatures* (London: Routledge, 1989), pp. 78–85.

29. Nicholas Breton, *The Court and Country* (1618), rpt. in *The Works of Nicholas Breton*, ed. Ursula Kentish-Wright (London: Cressett Press, 1929), 1:203.

30. See, e.g., Hattaway, "Rebellion, Class Consciousness, pp. 18–20, and Patterson, *Shakespeare and the Popular Voice*, pp. 38–40.

31. Richard Grafton, *A Chronicle at Large and meere History of the affayres of Englande and Kings of the same* (London, 1569), p. 330.

32. Raphael Holinshed, *Holinshed's Chronicles* (London, 1589, rpt. 1807), 2:749.

33. Ibid., p. 737. See also Hattaway's treatment of the same passage in "Rebellion, Class Consciousness," pp. 19–20.

4. Foreign Country: The Place of Women and Sexuality in Shakespeare's Historical World

Phyllis Rackin

I

I originally thought of calling this essay "Shakespeare and Sexuality: It Really *Was* Different"; but then I decided not to because, of course, we have no way of knowing how "it" really was. The questions with which we approach the past are the questions that trouble us here and now, the answers we find (even when couched in the words of old texts) the products of our own selection and arrangement. These difficulties are especially troublesome in the case of gender and sexuality—subjects that tend to be occluded in the historical records of the past and are heavily fraught with present concerns and controversies.[1] Moreover, since both women and sexuality were largely unwritten, there is always the temptation to universalize, to assume that because neither has a written history, neither has a history—that both were always and everywhere what they are now and here.[2]

This essay is an attempt to articulate some of the distinctions between the terms that shaped people's understanding of sexual difference in Shakespeare's time and those that obtain today. I have two interests at stake in this project. The first is scholarly: it seems to me that current discussions of the representations of gender and sexuality in Shakespeare's plays are often distorted because they are shaped by anachronistic conceptions of gender and sexual difference. The second is political: to historicize and thus demystify the assumptions that underlie current discussions of those issues—the beliefs that personal identity depends on sexual difference and that sexual difference is immutably grounded in the body.[3]

Governed by those assumptions, current scholarship on Renaissance gender ideology tends to focus on the body. Failing to discover a stable theory of sexual difference in Renaissance representations of the body, many scholars conclude that Renaissance gender ideology was incoherent and sexual difference indeterminate.[4] What I propose is that although Renaissance gender ideology, like our own, was conflicted and contradictory, it was not incoherent—that, instead, it was constructed on different principles and within different discourses. I believe the reason we cannot locate gender difference in Renaissance accounts of the body is that the body itself—male as well as female—was gendered feminine; and the reason we cannot find it in medical texts is that the distinctions that separated men from women, like those that separated aristocrats from commoners, were grounded not in the relatively marginal discourse of the new biological science but in the older and traditionally privileged discourses of theology and history.

I begin, however, by citing some Shakespearean passages that challenge modern conceptions of gender and sexuality and assumptions about the ways gender difference is grounded in the embodied experience of sexual desire. One crucial difference is that a man's desire for a woman, now coded as a mark of masculinity, is repeatedly associated in Shakespeare's plays with effeminacy. Romeo claims that his passion for Juliet has incapacitated him for the manly activity of fighting. "O sweet Juliet," he complains, "thy beauty hath made me effeminate, / And in my temper soft'ned valor's steel!"[5] In *Antony and Cleopatra*, Caesar charges that Antony's passion for Cleopatra has compromised his sexual identity. Antony, he says, "is not more manlike / Than Cleopatra; nor the queen of Ptolomy / More womanly than he" (1.4.5–8). Cleopatra herself describes a gaudy Egyptian revel which culminated, she recalls, when "I drunk him to his bed; / Then put my tires and mantles on him, whilst / I wore his sword" (2.5.21–23). The same assumption that passionate love for a woman would render a man effeminate, counterintuitive to modern consciousness, appears in Sidney's *Arcadia*, where Pyrocles dresses as an Amazon in order to be near the woman he desires, a transformation that Sidney emphasizes by using feminine pronouns to refer to the disguised lover. As Pyrocles' friend Musidorus remarks, "This effeminate love of a woman doth so womanize a man."[6]

By contrast, extreme virility, manifested in Spartan self-denial and military valor, is not only depicted as consistent with men's erotic desire for other men, it also seems to be expressed in it. In Shakespeare, as in Plutarch, Coriolanus is the supreme exemplar of the manly valor the Romans called *virtus;* but when Coriolanus greets his general on the battlefield, he exclaims: "O, let me clip ye / In arms as sound as when I woo'd, in heart / As merry as when our nuptial day was done / And tapers burnt to bedward!" His general responds with the loverlike epithet "Flower of warriors" (*Coriolanus* 1.6.29–32). An even more explicit expression of homoerotic desire between manly warriors occurs when Coriolanus joins forces with his old enemy, Aufidius. Embracing Coriolanus, Aufidius declares,

> Know thou first,
> I lov'd the maid I married; never man
> Sigh'd truer breath; but that I see thee here,
> Thou noble thing, more dances my rapt heart
> Than when I first my wedded mistress saw
> Bestride my threshold. . . .
>   Thou hast beat me out
> Twelve several times, and I have nightly since
> Dreamt of encounters 'twixt thyself and me;
> We have been down together in my sleep,
> Unbuckling helms, fisting each other's throat,
> And wak'd half dead with nothing.
>   (4.5.106–26)

Neither Coriolanus nor Aufidius is effeminated by this passion; neither is incapacitated for war, and neither is incapacitated for heterosexual love. Both speeches begin, in fact, with an acknowledgment of the speaker's passion for his wife. The homoerotic passion exceeds the heteroerotic one, but it does not displace it.[7]

Desire for another man, then, fails to compromise these characters' masculinity; instead, it reaffirms it. Desire for a woman, by contrast, incurs the risk of feminization. For women the situation was more complicated, since to become manlike was often construed, especially in theological discourse, as an elevation, a transcendence of both flesh and femininity,[8] while a man effeminated by passion for a woman suffered a double degradation: the enslavement of his higher reason by his base, bodily appetites, and the subjection of the superior sex to the inferior one. The asymmetry is probably most apparent in the case of cross-dressing, which, then as now, constituted a dressing up for women but a dressing down for men. Shakespeare's only cross-dressed hero is the Falstaff of *Merry Wives of Windsor,* for whom the disguise of a woman is quite literally a travesty, and also a guise in which he is beaten. A medium for Falstaff's degradation, cross-dressing is, by contrast, a source of empowerment for a number of Shakespearean comic heroines. What remains constant, however, is that in both cases the cross-dressing is associated with heteroerotic desire.

This association becomes explicit as double entendre in Shakespeare's *Merchant of Venice,* when Portia tells Nerissa her plan for the two of them to disguise themselves as lawyer and clerk. Nerissa asks, "What, shall we turn to men?" Portia's response—"Fie, what a question's that, / If thou wert near a lewd interpreter!"—articulates the connection between turning *to* men and turning *into* them (3.4. 78–80).[9] Portia takes on her masculine disguise *after* her marriage, and she does so in order to save her husband's friend. Like the other Shakespearean comic heroines who dress as men, she does so not to repudiate heteroerotic desire but to fulfill it. Rosalind uses her disguise as Ganymede to court Orlando; Viola, disguised as Cesario, serves the man she loves; and so does Imogen, the model of wifely fidelity, who disguises herself as the boy Fidele to follow and serve the husband who unjustly rejected her. Portia's disguise can be seen as an expression of assertiveness, Imogen's as a model of submission, but both are motivated by their love for men.

The connection between cross-dressing and heteroerotic desire is remarkably consistent: it applies to women as well as to men, and to bad women as well as to good ones. Joan in *1 Henry VI* is the first of Shakespeare's cross-dressed heroines, and probably the most masculine. She wears armor, she engages in onstage swordfights with male characters, and she leads the French army to victory. At the beginning of the play, she defeats the Dauphin in single combat, but the French courtiers punctuate the encounter with lewd comments, and even the words with which Joan accepts the Dauphin's challenge, "while I live, I'll ne'er fly from a man" (1.2.103), invite sexual interpretation—an interpretation confirmed at the end of the play when she claims to be pregnant with a bastard child, having engaged in illicit sex with the Dauphin and a number of his courtiers as well.

The same associations between heteroerotic passion and loss of gender identity appear in *2 Henry VI,* where the only erotic moment is the anguished leave-taking between Margaret and her adulterous lover, Suffolk, a scene charged with erotic power. "If I depart from thee," Suffolk declares, "I cannot live":

> And in thy sight to die, what were it else
> But like a pleasant slumber in thy lap?
> Here could I breathe my soul into the air,
> As mild and gentle as the cradle-babe
> Dying with mother's dug between its lips.
> (3.2.388–93)

Suffolk's passion for Margaret deprives him of his manhood, reducing him to the condition of a gentle, genderless infant; and Margaret, like Joan, is not only dangerously sexual but also dangerously masculine, depicted, in fact, as the epitome of all those masculine qualities "unbe-

seeming" her "sex." Like Joan, Margaret usurps the masculine prerogative of warfare; like Joan she appears, shockingly, onstage in
masculine battle dress. In *3 Henry VI* the Duke of York elaborates the
many ways in which Margaret is no true woman. "Women are soft,
mild, pitiful, and flexible," he complains, "Thou stern, obdurate,
flinty, rough, remorseless." Denouncing Margaret as an "Amazonian
trull," he links the masculinity of the female warrior with the sexual
promiscuity of the harlot (1.4.113–42).[10]

Shakespeare was not the only playwright to associate masculine behavior in women with heteroerotic promiscuity. In Jonson's *Epicoene*, a
group of mannish women live apart from their husbands and call
themselves "collegiates." Before any of them appears onstage, we learn
that they "cry down or up what they like or dislike . . . with most masculine or rather hermaphroditical authority."[11] Nonetheless, their masculinity is expressed not in passion for one another but in aggressive
courtship of the play's male hero.

In life as on the stage, masculine women were regarded as whores.[12]
In *The Description of England*, published in 1587, William Harrison complains about the female habit of wearing masculine clothing: "I have
met some of these trulls in London so disguised that it hath passed my
skill to discern whether they were men or women." The misogynist
pamphlet *Hic Mulier; or, The Man-Woman*, published in 1620, described
the woman in masculine dress as wearing a "loose, lascivious . . .
French doublet, being all unbuttoned to entice . . . and extreme short
waisted to give a most easy way to every luxurious action."[13] All of these
authors were male, but, as Gwynne Kennedy has pointed out, when
one of the few female writers of the period, Lady Mary Wroth, wished
to condemn female characters in her *Urania* for overaggressive courtship of men, she made the same associations, comparing the lustful
women to boys playing women's parts onstage.[14] Driven by lustful desire for men, these women lose their femininity.

The point of all these examples is to suggest that historical differences make it difficult for us to understand the representations of gender and sexuality in Shakespeare's plays and that we should not be too
quick to assume we understand their implications. Consider, for instance, the evasions of scholarly editors confronted by the variously directed erotic passion of the speaker in Shakespeare's sonnets, the
difficulties encountered when twentieth-century productions of
Shakespearean plays have attempted to use all-male casts, or the perplexities and debates of recent critics as they try to decide whether the
erotic desire evoked by Shakespeare's cross-dressed heroines should be
characterized as "homosexual" or "heterosexual" or both.[15]

The examples I've cited and the critical perplexities they provoke suggest important points of difference between current assumptions about gender and sexuality and those implicit in Shakespeare's texts. The problem with all these examples is not that they are inexplicable: numerous, and conflicting, explanations have been advanced. The problem is that the associations they imply are counterintuitive to modern consciousness. They demand and resist explanation because they imply an ideology of sex and gender that is radically different from our own. In the case of the boy heroines, for instance, although most educated people know that transvestism is by no means inconsistent with what we call "heterosexual" desire and activity, our knowledge of that fact is insufficient to resist the pressure of a gender ideology that constructs cross-dressing as a mark of what we call "homosexuality." Grounded on sexual desire, our assumptions about gender are based on models of sexual *orientation*. Contemporary gender ideology constructs a kind of metaphysics of desire that assumes, first, that it is the norm to desire *either* men or women (not both) and, second, that the gender of the object of sexual desire determines the desiring person's psychic and gender identity. According to our culture's prevailing norms, a person, either male or female, who desires women is defined as "masculine," and a person, either female or male, who desires men is defined as "feminine." A person who desires both men and women we call "bisexual." In the last case, the desiring subject is conceived as divided (*bi*sexual) in order to maintain the ideologically motivated gender categories as inviolate.[16]

At this point you're probably saying, "Not me, that's not what *I* think." And I'm saying that too. The kind of large, schematic oppositions I am suggesting ignore the variety, the complexity, and the contradictions of the current discourse on gender, not to mention that of a remote—and finally inaccessible—past.[17] Discourse is polyphonic, expressing the myriad distinctions of class, geography, and gender that determine the cultural locations and interests of various speakers. Moreover, the dominant features of a culture coexist with residual "elements of the past" as well as "emergent" elements that are in the process of "being created."[18] Even in Shakespeare's texts, anticipations of the biologically grounded ideology of compulsory heterosexuality which authorizes the nuclear family can be found in plays that focus on the life of the proto-bourgeoisie. In *The Taming of the Shrew*, for instance, Kate's final speech rationalizes the submission of wives to husbands not only on the traditional analogy between husband and king ("Such duty as the subject owes the prince, / Even such a woman oweth to her husband" [5.2.155–56]), but also on the physical differences between male and female bodies ("Why are our bodies soft, and weak, and smooth, / . . . But that our soft conditions and our hearts / Should well agree with our external parts?" [5.2.165–68]). Renaissance texts contain anticipations of modern constructions of gender and sexuality as well as vestiges of medieval ones, and vestiges of earlier formulations persist in our own discourse. Nonetheless, I think it is important to mark the places where Renaissance gender ideology differed from our own because the differences are what tend to be occluded in much of what we write about the constructions of gender and sexuality in Shakespeare's time.

One place where those differences are clearly visible is in the way we dress our children. In early modern England sumptuary laws imposed elaborate regulations on male attire to ensure that men's clothing would express their exact place in the social hierarchy, but from 1510 to 1574 women's clothing was exempted from regulation.[19] Moreover, throughout the period male and female children were dressed in the same attire—in skirts—until they reached the age of seven.[20] The physical difference that separated boys from girls was insignificant: what mattered was the difference in social rank that separated one man from another. In our own culture, by contrast, clothing is gendered from birth, but it is rarely a reliable indicator of status and rank. The president of the United States may appear on television dressed in blue jeans, and teenagers from working-class families wear full formal regalia to their high school proms. But we wrap our children in pink or blue blankets even in the hospital nursery, insisting on the innate, biological difference between male and female while eliding the distinctions of status and privilege that the egalitarian ideology of modern American democracy denies.

Less clearly visible—at least in current scholarly discourse—is the fact that in the Renaissance sexual passion had not yet achieved the privileged position it now holds, especially for men.[21] Excessive passion in either sex was condemned, but it was especially dangerous to men because it made them effeminate. Women were believed to be more lustful than men (in contrast to the still prevalent Victorian assumption that it is men who have those strong-animal-drives-which-cannot-be-denied). Female images of angels on commercial Christmas cards express popular notions that asexual purity is feminine. In sharp contrast, the sculptured images of the deadly sins that adorned medieval cathedrals depicted Lust as a woman.[22] Valuing sexual passion, the popular wisdom of contemporary culture associates it with the more valued gender, assuming that men feel it more often and more strongly. Despising lust as a mark of weakness and degradation, Renaissance thought gendered it feminine, attributed more of it to women, and regarded excessive lust in men as a mark of effeminacy. Reduced to its simplest terms, it's the difference between seeing heterosexual sex as the place where manhood is proved and affirmed in a conquest of the female and seeing it as the place where manhood is contaminated and lost in congress with her. The danger was that husband and wife would become, quite literally, one flesh, a fantasy that was expressed in fables and images of passionate lovers transformed into monstrous hermaphrodites.[23]

In modern terms that danger might be understood as a loss of identity, the fictions of individual identity being highly prized and identity being incomprehensible to us without gender. According to Rosi Braidotti, in fact, "The privilege granted to the discourse of sexuality and reproduction as the site of production of truth about the subject is the trademark of modernity."[24] It is not at all certain that either of those assumptions obtained at the time Shakespeare wrote. It seems more likely to me that such a union was seen as dangerous not simply or even primarily because it was a union but because it was a union of *flesh*. Spiritual union, even the union of male and female, was highly prized. The image of the hermaphrodite as a medical monstrosity or social misfit had its positive counterpart in the idealized image of the androgyne, represented in Neoplatonic, alchemical, and biblical tradition as a symbol of prelapsarian or mystical perfection.[25] If sensual lovers risked degenerating into the beast with two backs, spiritual lovers could transcend the limitations of fallen physical life in the perfection of androgynous union. One has only to think of the lovers in Donne's "Valediction: Forbidding Mourning" or Shakespeare's "Phoenix and Turtle": "Single nature's double name / Neither two nor one was called."

Modern valorization of the body has produced a nostalgic conception of the Renaissance as a period when, as Francis Barker has argued, "the body [had] a central and irreducible place"—"fully and unashamedly involved"—"in the social order."[26] But fear and loathing of the body was a living legacy in the Renaissance, rationalized in medieval Christian contempt for the flesh, grounded and verified in a present material reality of stinking bodies, desperately vulnerable to disfiguring disease and early death.[27] In medieval thought, the body itself, male as well as female, tended to fall on the wrong side of the binary opposition that divided masculine from feminine gender. Woman, said Saint Jerome, is "different from man as body is from soul."[28] These associations did not disappear with the Reformation.[29] To Martin Luther, "We are the woman because of the flesh, that is, we are carnal, and we are the man because of the spirit. . . . We are at the same time both dead and set free." This same distinction between masculine spirit and feminine flesh can be seen as late as the middle of the seventeenth century, when Gerrard Winstanley condemned sinners who had "been led by the powers of the curse in flesh, which is the *Feminine* part; not by the power of the righteous Spirit which is Christ, the *Masculine* power."[30]

The gendered opposition between masculine spirit and female flesh, although rationalized in Christian theology, was not confined to theological discourse. In fact, it played an important part even in medicine, the discourse of the body. Medical accounts of procreation, despite the influence of Galenic theory, frequently echoed the Aristotelian explanation that the male parent contributes form and soul to the fetus, while the mother provides only its physical matter. According to Aristotle: "The female always provides the material, the male that which fashions it, for this is the power we say they each possess, and *this is what it is for them to be male and female*. . . . While the body is from the female, it is the soul that is from the male."[31] The same distinction between male form, equated with soul, and female matter is repeated in *The Problemes of Aristotle,* a popular Elizabethan medical guide: "The seede of the man doth dispose and prepare the seed of the woman to receive the forme, perfection, or soule, the which being done, it is converted into humiditie, and is fumed and breathed out by the pores of the matrix, which is manifest, bicause onely the flowers [the menses] of the woman are the materiall cause of the young one."[32]

This congruence between medical and theological discourse suggests a conception of gender difference just as coherent as our own although significantly different from it. Modern gender ideology, like modern racism, constructs its binary oppositions on the basis of physical difference.[33] Grounded in a mystified body, it finds a prehistorical basis for masculine privilege in male physical strength, an ahistorical explanation for psychic difference in one small idealized part of the male body. Mystified as phallic power, its presence or absence becomes the defining characteristic of an always already gendered subjectivity.[34] In the Renaissance, by contrast, masculine superiority tended to be mystified in the spirit, feminine oppression justified by the subordinate status of the body.[35]

As is well known, the body served as a map not of gender difference but of social and political hierarchy. The system of analogies that rationalized the social hierarchy included the subordination of women to men, but its essential axis of difference was social and political status rather than embodied sex.[36] The relation of the head to the lower parts formed the basis for the ideological representation of the state as the body politic—the king as its head, the lower orders as its subordinate members. The same analogy also rationalized the subordination of women: like common people of both sexes, women were regarded as appetitive creatures, easily enslaved by bodily lusts and irrational passions. Incapable of rational self-government, they were associated with the lower parts of the body. Male authority resided in the higher regions. The king was the head of the state; the husband was the head of the household. Their dominance, however, was justified by fictions of superior rationality embodied in the head rather than by fictions of phallic power embodied in the penis.

Looking for Renaissance conceptions of gender difference, scholars turn to Renaissance anatomy books only to discover that biological science itself was still subordinate to the authority of classical texts. Renaissance anatomists, unlike the ancients, performed dissections and illustrated their texts with pictures of what they saw. But, as Thomas Laqueur has brilliantly demonstrated, what they saw was framed and limited by their study of ancient models. In Renaissance drawings, he shows, the anatomical parts were often literally framed by classical models: the internal organs of the human body displayed within cavities excavated in the torsos of classical statues.[37] Conceptually framed by Galen's models of genital structures, the observable differences between male and female anatomy were reduced to terms of simple inversion. Empirical observation had resulted in the medical rediscovery of the clitoris, but the vagina was still conceived as an inverted penis. Male and female sexual organs were perfectly homologous, the women's simply remaining inside the body because they were less "perfect" than those of men; in many cases, in fact, women could turn into men. In the best known of these, repeatedly cited in recent scholarship, a fifteen-year-old girl, chasing her swine in a field, and leaping a ditch in hot pursuit, suddenly felt her genitalia extruded outward, impelled by the heat of the chase. Henceforth, she was recognized as a man. The reason, as reported by the famous sixteenth-century surgeon Ambroise Paré, was that

> women have as much hidden within the body as men have exposed outside; leaving aside, only, that women don't have so much heat, nor the ability to push out what by the coldness of their temperament is held bound to the interior. Wherefore if with time, the humidity of childhood which prevented the warmth from doing its full duty being exhaled for the most part, the warmth is rendered more robust, vehement, and active, then it is not an unbelievable thing if the latter, chiefly aided by some violent movement, should be able to push out what was hidden within.[38]

In Paré's account, masculine behavior transforms the body to produce the physical signs of male sex, thus inverting the modern assumption that embodied sex is the solid ground that regulates gendered behavior. This does not mean, however, that gender differences were irrelevant or that early modern Europe was a feminist utopia where real women could assume masculine identity and privilege by the simple expedient of running quickly and leaping across ditches—only that Renaissance gender ideology worked on principles radically different from our own.

II

The first wave of twentieth-century feminist Shakespeare criticism focused on the comedies, especially the ones involving cross-dressed heroines, to theorize a theater in which female spectators could find liberating images of powerful, attractive women who violated gender restrictions and were rewarded for those violations with admiration, love, and marriage—a utopian moment when gender identity was as changeable as the theatrical costumes that transformed boy actors into female characters. The romantic comedies were doubly satisfying to modern feminists, for at the same time that they empowered their female characters, they also celebrated the love between men and women which culminates in marriage. Shakespeare's transvestite comedies satisfied the desires of feminist readers for personal liberation without disturbing the dominant gender ideology of our own time, for they also celebrated the heterosexual passion that provides the basis for the ideal nuclear family, held together by the love between husband and wife, the avenue for personal self-fulfillment and the foundation for the good order of society.

Shakespeare's history plays, however, tell a very different, much less optimistic story. In a survey of feminist Shakespeare criticism, Ann Thompson remarks that feminist critics have tended to neglect the English history plays.[39] Given the roles of women in those plays, this omission is not surprising. Female characters and heteroerotic passion, both central to the comedies, are marginalized or vilified in the histories. The hierarchy of dramatic genres was also a hierarchy of social status: the subjects of history were kings and the great noblemen who opposed them; women and commoners occupied only marginal places in historical narratives.

To move from comedy and history is to move up the generic hierarchy, into the exclusions of the dominant discourse, which was also the discourse of patriarchal dominance. If theology was the master discourse of the Middle Ages, and biology and psychology are those of our own, the discourse that authorized the social hierarchy in Shakespeare's time was that of history. Tudor historians produced fables of ancient descent to authenticate a new dynasty's claim to the English throne. Tudor subjects provided a thriving business for the heralds who constructed the genealogies by which they attempted to secure their places in an unstable social hierarchy. The patrilineal genealogy that organized the structure of Tudor history and Tudor society alike required the repression of women, and of heteroerotic passion as well, because the invisible, putative connection between fathers and sons that formed the basis of patriarchal authority was—as Shakespeare's cuckold jokes endlessly insist—always dubious, always vulnerable to subversion by an adulterous wife. In the case of a king, however, cuckoldry was no laughing matter: not only a source of personal anxiety, it was also a threat to royal succession and therefore the worst possible crime against the state.[40]

In the few cases in which heteroerotic passion appears in the histories, it is represented as a dangerous, destructive force, even when it leads to marriage. The comedies look forward to the emergent bourgeois ideal of the loving nuclear family, but the histories look backward to an older conception of marriage as a political and economic union between feudal families—a model that did in fact last longer at the higher levels of the social hierarchy and one that persists to this day among royalty. Shakespeare's Henry VI and Edward IV both reject prudent dynastic marriages in order to marry on the basis of personal passion; both marriages are represented as disastrous mistakes that weaken the men's authority as kings and destabilize the political order of their realms. By contrast, the desirable marriage between Richmond and Elizabeth, the foundation of the Tudor dynasty, is totally uncontaminated by any hint of romantic love—or even by any appearance on stage of the bride-to-be.

Even in their own time the history plays were understood as a specifically masculine, hegemonic genre. Both the gendered opposition between history and comedy and the ideological uses of the history play can be seen in sixteenth-century debates about the theater. Thomas Nashe, for instance, based his defense of theatrical performance on the masculinity of the English chronicle play. The "subject" of plays, he claimed, is "(for the most part) borrowed out of our English Chronicles, wherein our forefathers valiant acts . . . are revived . . . than which, what can be a sharper reproofe to these degenerate, effeminate dayes of ours." Conflating Englishness with masculinity and both with a lost heroic past, Nashe opposes the masculine domain of English history to the degenerate, effeminate world of present-day English experience in order to defend theatrical performance as an inspiration to civic virtue and heroic patriotism. He also invokes the masculine purity of English acting companies. "Our Players," he boasts, "are not as the players beyond Sea, a sort of squirting baudie Comedians, that have whores and common Curtizens to playe womens partes."[41]

It is important to remember, however, that Nashe's argument that the plays would inspire their audiences to patriotism and manly valor represents only one side of a hotly contested debate. Nashe appropriates the authority of English history on behalf of theatrical performance, but in the eyes of its opponents, the theater was associated with the same destabilizing and effeminating forces of social change that the English chronicles were designed to oppose. Antitheatrical invective focused obsessively on the sexually corrupting allurements of bawdy comedies, the immorality of boys in female costume, and the contaminating presence of women in the theater audiences. As Stephen Orgel reminds us: "The English stage was a male preserve, but the theater was not. The theater was a place of unusual freedom for women in the period; foreign visitors comment on the fact that English women go to theater unescorted and unmasked, and a large proportion of the audience consisted of women."[42]

The opposition between the authoritative masculine discourse of history and the disreputable feminized world of the playhouse is clearly marked in Shakespeare's history plays. Aliens in the masculine domain of English historiography, the women in those plays are often quite literally alien. Beginning with *1 Henry VI,* in which all the female characters are French, the women are typically inhabitants of foreign worlds, and foreign worlds are typically characterized as feminine. Moreover, both the women and their worlds are repeatedly characterized as comic and theatrical. The marginal status of women in Shakespeare's historical sources is reproduced in his history plays by a process of geographic and generic containment, which also marks the boundaries between the idealized masculine England of historical narrative and the feminized scene of present theatrical performance. In *Henry IV,* for instance, women are completely excluded from the English historical action, but they play dominant roles in two marginal places—the contemporary, lowlife world of Eastcheap and the foreign world of Wales. Both Eastcheap and Wales are separated from the central scenes of English historical representation, and both are associated with the illicit powers of female sexuality and theatrical performance. This geographic marking also replicates the situation in the theaters of Shakespeare's time; for although English women never appeared on stage, French and Italian companies, which included women, did occasionally perform in England.[43]

The Boar's Head Tavern in Eastcheap is a plebeian, comic, theatrical, anachronistically modern world that mirrors the disorderly push and shove of the playhouse itself (the Boar's Head, in fact, was the name of at least six real taverns in Shakespeare's London, one of them used for a theater).[44] Shakespeare represents his Boar's Head as a kind of theater as well. Frequented, like the playhouse, by a disorderly, socially heterogeneous crowd, it is also the scene of playacting. Falstaff pretends to be Hal, Hal pretends to be Falstaff, and both degrade the dignity of royalty by playing the part of the reigning king. The pleasures of the Boar's Head are illicit, and they are also dangerous. The disreputable crowd the tavern attracts is given to every sort of transgression, from drunkenness and brawling to thieving and prostitution. Here, as in the antitheatrical tracts, the dangers of the playing house are most prominently represented by women and sexuality. Like the prostitutes who looked for customers in the theater audiences, Doll Tearsheet infects her customers with venereal disease; and at the end of 2 Henry IV, when Doll and the Hostess are arrested, we learn that "there hath been a man or two lately killed about her" (5.4.5–7). Whether "her" means Doll or the Hostess, and whether "about" means "concerning" or "near," the women are clearly a source of danger. A. R. Humphreys, the editor of the Arden edition, glosses this line with a quotation from Dekker's Honest Whore: "O how many thus . . . have let out / Their soules in Brothell houses / . . . and dyed / Iust at their Harlots foot" (3.3.77–80).

It is significant that the proprietor of the Boar's Head is a Hostess, not a Host, and that she speaks in malapropisms, disrupting the King's English just as the fictional scenes in her tavern disrupt—as they interrupt, retard, and parody—the historical action. The Hostess's economic power, as Jean Howard has observed, recalls the economic power of the women who were paying customers in the playhouse. Her linguistic deformities bespeak her exclusion from the dominant official discourse. Just as the fictional scenes in Eastcheap have no basis in history and no place in the historical action, neither do the women they contain.

It is also significant that although the tavern is clearly marked as a feminized, theatrical space, the character who dominates that space is not the Hostess, or any other woman, but Falstaff. Physically a man and a womanizer, Falstaff is plainly gendered masculine in terms of the binary logic of modern thought. The analogical patterns of Shakespeare's discourse, by contrast, place Falstaff in a feminine structural position. His incompetence on the battlefield, his contempt for honor and military valor, his inconstancy, his lies, his gross corpulence—and his womanizing—all imply effeminacy within the system of analogies that separated aristocrat from plebeian, man from woman, and spirit from body. Contemplating what he thinks is Falstaff's corpse at the end of the battle of Shrewsbury, Hal asks, "What, old acquaintance! could not all this flesh keep in a little life?" (5.4.102–3). Falstaff himself, in a usage that would have been clearly intelligible to Shakespeare's audience, refers to his fat belly as a "womb" (2 *Henry IV* 4.3.22: "My womb, my womb, my womb undoes me"); and he compares himself to a "sow that hath overwhelm'd all her litter but one" (1.2.12). Moreover, *1 Henry IV* ends with the spectacle of Falstaff mutilating Hotspur's corpse (5.4.128). Wounding the dead hero's thigh, he reenacts the female threat to manhood and military honor symbolized in the opening scene by the report of the Welshwomen's mutilation of the corpses of English soldiers (1.1.43–46).[45]

The parallel between the two veiled references to castration suggests an analogical relationship between the world of Eastcheap and that of Wales, both associated with the loss of masculine honor. Analogy, however, is not identity. Although both settings are plainly marked as comic and theatrical and thus as opposed to history, the low comic scenes in the Boar's Head Tavern recall the disorderly scene of present theatrical performance, whereas the scene in Wales, with its emphasis on magic and romantic love and its exotic setting, recalls the Shakespearean genre of romantic comedy. The women in the tavern are too familiar to enter history, too much like the disorderly women in the theater audience. The woman in Wales, by contrast, is marked as an exotic creature from another world, like the French and Italian actresses who occasionally appeared on the English stage, or the heroine of a narrative romance or romantic comedy.

Or, perhaps, like Queen Elizabeth herself. In this connection the epilogue to *2 Henry IV* is revealing. Despite the absence of women in the preceding scene, the representation of the great historical moment when the wild Prince Hal of popular legend takes his historical place as Henry V, the epilogue contains two references to female presence. One recalls the world of Eastcheap as it acknowledges the presence of women—and of sexual transactions between men and women—in the theater audience: "All the Gentlewomen here have forgiven me; if the gentlemen will not, then the gentlemen do not agree with the gentlewomen, which was never seen in such an assembly." The other acknowledges the presence of a woman on the English throne: "And so I kneel down before you . . . to pray for the Queen."

The matter of Wales, like the presence of a woman on the English throne, haunts the borders of the historical world that Shakespeare constructed in his Lancastrian histories. Both evoked powerful, and related, anxieties for the genealogically obsessed patriarchal culture ruled by Queen Elizabeth—a female monarch who traced her patriarchal right to a Welsh grandfather who had turned to the dim mists of

Welsh antiquity to buttress his tenuous genealogical authority, incorporating the red dragon of Cadwallader in the royal arms and giving his eldest son the name Arthur. Located at England's geographic border, Wales represents a constant military threat, but it also represents the unspeakable realities of female power and authority which threatened the idealized England of masculine longing constructed by Shakespeare's historical myths.[46]

At the beginning of *1 Henry IV*, the Earl of Westmerland comes to the English court with bad news from a Welsh battlefield: Mortimer's army has been defeated in battle, Mortimer captured by Owen Glendower, a thousand of his soldiers killed. Westmerland also reports that after the battle, the Welshwomen committed some "beastly shameless transformation" upon the bodies of the dead English soldiers—an act, he says, "as may not be without much shame retold or spoken of" (1.1.44–46). Refusing to describe the act, Shakespeare follows Holinshed, who anxiously reports: "The shamefull villanie used by the Welshwomen towards the dead carcasses, was such, as honest eares would be ashamed to heare, and continent toongs to speake thereof." In Shakespeare's historical source, as in his play, Wales is identified as the scene of emasculation and female power—and also as the site of a repression in the English historical narrative.[47]

The shame that narrative represses is clearly intelligible to modern readers: the threat of castration, the founding event in Freudian myths of gender differentiation, but a symbol that proliferates in Shakespeare's play in ways that cannot be contained within the binary logic of modern gender ideology.[48] Veiled references to castration reappear not only in Falstaff's desecration of Hotspur's corpse but also in Kate's playful threat to break Hotspur's "little finger" (2.3.87)[49] and— for playgoers well acquainted with Holinshed—in the description of Douglas's capture after the battle of Shrewsbury. Shakespeare follows Holinshed in reporting that the Douglas was captured in flight after the battle because "falling from a hill, he was so bruis'd / That the pursuers took him" (5.5.21–22); but Holinshed specifies the nature of the bruise: "Falling from the crag of an hie mounteine, [he] brake one of his cullions, and was taken."[50] In neither case, however, does the wound appear to be a cause for shame; in fact, both Shakespeare and Holinshed immediately add that Douglas was, because of his great valor, at once set free. Because of his "valiantnesse" (Holinshed), or his "valors" and "high deeds" (Shakespeare), Douglas is honored as a noble man, a status unaffected by the genital wound.

Moreover, although Westmerland's veiled reference to female savages who intrude on the masculine space of the battlefield to deprive the English soldiers of their manhood and honor characterizes the

Welshwomen in terms that signal "masculine woman" to us, that characterization appears to be completely reversed in act 3, when Shakespeare moves beyond the boundary of English historical narration to stage a scene in Wales. Mortimer is happily married to Glendower's daughter, and the castrating savages of Westmerland's report are nowhere to be seen. The only Welshwoman we see is perfectly feminine—Glendower's weeping daughter, who is so devoted to her husband that she cannot bear the thought of his impending departure. The lady cannot speak English, but her father translates. She also expresses her love in tears, in kisses, and in singing "the song that pleases" Mortimer. Music, as Shakespeare's Orsino tells us, was considered the "food of love." Philip Stubbes, well known for his warnings against the dangerous consequences of theatergoing, also warned that music could corrupt "good minds, [making] them womanish and inclined to all kinds of whoredom and mischief." In fact the spectacle of a woman singing was widely regarded in Shakespeare's time as an incitement to lust.[51]

Suffused with luxurious sensuality, the scene in Glendower's castle replaces the horrified report of Welsh barbarism with the glamour of Glendower's poetry and his daughter's singing, the castrating savages of the battlefield with the seductive allure of the lady in the castle. What makes this replacement baffling to modern consciousness is that Glendower's daughter is *associated* with the castrating women of the battlefield. Unwilling to part with her amorous companion, she resolves that "she'll be a soldier too, she'll to the wars" (3.1.193). Moreover, Mortimer's passion for his wife does indeed seem to emasculate him. Although Shakespeare emphasizes Mortimer's lineal claim to the English throne, Mortimer himself prefers what he calls the "feeling disputation" of kisses with his wife to military battle in pursuit of that claim. "As slow as hot Lord Percy is on fire to go" (3.1.263–64) to join the battle that will decide the future of the English kingdom, Mortimer has lost his manhood to female enchantment.[52] Hotspur's male "heat," by contrast, makes him eager to leave his wife for battle.[53]

Shakespeare's Welsh interlude replaces the unspeakable horror of castration with the theatrical performance of seduction. A similar displacement seems to characterize Shakespeare's relation at this point to his historical source. The love scene has no historical precedent, but its structural position in act 3 of the play is similar to that of a passage inserted by Abraham Fleming in the 1587 edition of Holinshed's *Chronicles* (the edition Shakespeare used). Fleming interrupts the account of a later battle to insert a detailed account of the act Holinshed had refused to describe: "The dead bodies of the Englishmen being above a thousand lieng upon the ground imbrued in their owne bloud . . . did the women of Wales cut off their privities, and put one part thereof into the mouthes of everie dead man, in such sort that the cullions hoong downe to their chins; and not so contented, they did cut off their noses and thrust them into their tailes as they laie on the ground mangled and defaced." Fleming seems delighted with the grisly story, introducing it with numerous references to gory atrocities committed by women against men in classical times, but he also feels constrained to defend his decision to write the problematic material into the English historical record. He notes the precise location in Thomas Walsingham's Latin chronicle where he found it and explains: "Though it make the reader to read it, and the hearer to heare it, ashamed yet bicause it was a thing doone in open sight, and left testified in historie; I see little reason whie it should not be imparted in our mother toong to the knowledge of our owne countrimen, as well as unto strangers in a language unknowne."[54]

Fleming's belated account of the atrocities performed by the Welshwomen seems to lie behind Shakespeare's deferred Welsh scene, but Shakespeare transvalues the terms of Fleming's gruesome description. Fleming's account of bloody corpses lying on the ground, their organs of bottom and top horribly transposed, becomes the lady's seductive invitation to Mortimer to lie down upon the "wanton rushes," his head luxuriously resting in her lap, while she sings to charm his "blood with pleasing heaviness," a delicious languor like the state "twixt wake and sleep." The strange tongue from which Fleming translated his gruesome story becomes the sweet babble of the lady's Welsh, a sound that Mortimer calls "ravishing" and compares to a song "sung by a fair queen in a summer's bow'r," and that Shakespeare represents by repeated stage directions, *The lady speaks in Welsh* (3.1.195–210).

Like the historical record of the Welshwomen's barbarism, and like the French that Katherine speaks in *Henry V*, the language Glendower's daughter speaks requires translation. Departing from theatrical convention to write the women's lines in foreign tongues, Shakespeare excludes them from the linguistic community that includes all of the male characters—French and Welsh as well as English—along with his English-speaking audience.[55] The difference, however, is that whereas Katherine learns English in order to communicate with Henry, Mortimer promises to learn Welsh. Bewitched and enthralled in Wales, he will abandon the King's English, the discourse of patriarchal authority, in order to enter the alien discourse of a world that lies beyond the bounds of English historical narration.[56]

Shakespeare's representation of Mortimer in Wales interrupts the progress of the English historical plot to depict the dangerous allure of a world that is feminine and effeminizing, and also theatrical. It enacts

Renaissance beliefs that excessive sensuality would make a man effeminate, and it recalls the antitheatrical arguments that the theater encouraged idleness and lechery. It also reveals the difficulty of writing sexuality into history. Geographically and dramatically isolated, the Welsh scene of sexual seduction anticipates modern conceptions of love and war as alternative activities, linked in gendered antithesis—the romantic interludes that interrupt the military action in modern war movies, the poignant juxtaposition of idealized love and dirty war in novels such as Hemingway's *Farewell to Arms,* and the famous rallying cry of the 1960s, "Make love, not war."[57] But it is difficult to find modern counterparts for Shakespeare's conflation of heteroerotic desire with the loss of sexual identity. The closest modern analogue I can think of is boys in a schoolyard, afraid to play with the girls because having a girlfriend will make a boy a sissy. But the analogy should not be pushed too far. By the time those boys are eighteen, they'll boast about "scoring" to prove their manhood. It really *was* different: on Shakespeare's stage the Welsh lady herself was a boy. Unwritten, the incomprehensible language that masks the lady's meaning changes with every performance. All we have to read is her father's translation.

N O T E S

I am indebted to helpful responses to earlier versions of this paper presented at the CUNY Graduate Center, the Riverside-Berkeley Shakespeare Conference, the Glasgow conference "European Renaissance: National Traditions," the Center for Twentieth-Century Studies at the University of Wisconsin-Milwaukee, the seminar on the Diversity of Language and the Structures of Power at the University of Pennsylvania, and the University of Wisconsin at Madison. I especially wish to thank David Lorenzo Boyd, Gregory W. Bredbeck, Margreta de Grazia, Heather Dubrow, Mary Hazard, Jean Howard, Ann Rosalind Jones, Constance Jordan, Gwynne Kennedy, Mary Ellen Lamb, Donald Rackin, Carroll Smith-Rosenberg, and Peter Stallybrass. This essay was previously published under the title "Historical Difference/Sexual Difference," in *Privileging Gender in Early Modern England,* ed. Jean R. Brink, vol. 23 of *Sixteenth-Century Essays and Studies* (Kirksville, Mo.: Sixteenth-Century Journal Publishers, 1993).

1. See, for example, two studies of sexual difference in the Henry plays, both published after I had written this essay: Alan Sinfield's discussions of "masculinity and miscegenation" in *Henry V* in *Faultlines: Cultural Materialism and the Politics of Dissident Reading* (Berkeley: University of California Press, 1992), pp. 127–42, and Jonathan Goldberg's chapter, "Desiring Hal," in *Sodometries: Renaissance Texts, Modern Sexualities* (Stanford: Stanford University Press, 1992), pp. 145–75. Sinfield anticipates my argument at a number of points, emphasizing the ways in which early modern conceptions of male "effeminacy" differed from our own and were "not specifically linked to same-sex

physical passion" (p. 134). Goldberg, by contrast, insists on the linkage, denouncing criticism that fails to discover it as "heterosexist" (p. 2).

2. This tendency is exacerbated by the fact that current discussions of gender and sexuality are most often framed in psychoanalytic discourse, which itself tends to dehistoricize.

3. Such a history might well begin with the passage in Plato's *Symposium* in which Aristophanes tells a comic fable to explain the origins of sexual desire and sexual difference. Before the fall, he explains, the world was populated by spherical creatures, each of which had two sets of genital organs: some were male-male, some were female-female, still others had the organs of both sexes. Dividing each of these happily spherical creatures into two halves, Zeus created a fallen humanity, driven by desire for reunion with their severed halves. The originally female spheres thus became women who desired other women, the originally male became men who desired other men, and the originally androgynous became lovers driven by heterosexual desire: "Men who are a section of that double nature which was once called Androgynous," he continues, "are lovers of women; adulterers are generally of this breed, and also adulterous women who lust after men: the women who are a section of the woman do not care for men, but have female attachments; the female companions are of this sort. But they who are a section of the male, follow the male, and while they are young, being slices of the original man, they hang about men and embrace them, and they are themselves the best of boys and youths, because they have the most manly nature. Some indeed assert that they are shameless but this is not true; for they do not act thus from any want of shame, but because they are valiant and manly, and have a manly countenance, and they embrace that which is like them. And these when they grow up become our statesmen, and these only, which is a great proof of the truth of what I am saying." See *The Works of Plato*, ed. Irwin Edman, trans. Benjamin Jowett (New York: Modern Library, 1956), pp. 355–56. I am not proposing that Shakespeare derived his conceptions of gender and sexual desire from Aristophanes' fable, but it is worth remembering that the *Symposium* was an influential text in the Renaissance. See, for instance, James M. Saslow, "The Tenderest Lover: Saint Sebastian in Renaissance Painting," *Gai Saber* 1 (1977), 61, for its influence on Ficino's analysis of homoerotic love.

4. The fullest treatment of the subject is Thomas Laqueur's *Making Sex: Body and Gender from the Greeks to Freud* (Cambridge: Harvard University Press, 1990), which concludes that Renaissance sexual theory was based on a one-sex model. For a thoughtful essay influenced by Laqueur's work, see Stephen Greenblatt, "Fiction and Friction," in *Shakespearean Negotiations: The Circulation of Social Energy in Renaissance England* (Berkeley: University of California Press, 1988), pp. 66–93. For a richly documented argument that early modern culture lacked a single normative system by which gender difference could be categorized, see Ann Rosalind Jones and Peter Stallybrass, "Fetishizing Gender: Constructing the Hermaphrodite in Renaissance Europe," in *Body Guards: The Cultural Politics of Gender Ambiguity*, ed. Julia Epstein and Kristina Straub (New York: Routledge, 1991), pp. 80–111.

5. *Romeo and Juliet* 3.1.113–15. All quotations from Shakespeare are from *The Riverside Shakespeare*, ed. G. Blakemore Evans et al. (Boston: Houghton Mifflin, 1974); subsequent citations appear in the text.

6. Cf. the description in North's Plutarch of Theseus' excessive lust as "womannisheness," cited by Louis Adrian Montrose in " 'Shaping Fantasies':

Figurations of Gender and Power in Elizabethan Culture," in *Representing the English Renaissance*, ed. Stephen Greenblatt (Berkeley: University of California Press, 1988), p. 38. For similar examples taken from a wide variety of texts, see Susan C. Shapiro, " 'Yon Plumed Dandebrat': Male 'Effeminacy' in English Satire and Criticism," *Review of English Studies*, n.s., 39 (1988), 1–13. See also Winfried Schleiner, "Male Cross-Dressing and Transvestism in Renaissance Romances, *Sixteenth-Century Journal* 19 (1988), 605–19; and Mark Rose, "Sidney's Womanish Man," *Renaissance Essays and Studies*, n.s., 15 (1964), 353–63.

7. Note, too, that Coriolanus is represented as a father as well as a husband. As Randolph Trumbach points out, "Men could be found into the early 18th century who married women and had as well a career of seducing the local boys, without any risk to their status as dominant males." See his "Gender and the Homosexual Role in Modern Western Culture: The Eighteenth and Nineteenth Centuries Compared," in *Homosexuality, Which Homosexuality?*, ed. Dennis Altman et al. (London: GMP Publishers, 1989), p. 152.

8. See Margaret R. Miles, " 'Becoming Male': Women Martyrs and Ascetics," in *Carnal Knowing: Female Nakedness and Religious Meaning in the Christian West* (Boston: Beacon Press, 1989), esp. pp. 53–62; and Leah S. Marcus, "Shakespeare's Comic Heroines, Elizabeth I, and the Political Uses of Androgyny," in *Women in the Middle Ages and the Renaissance: Literary and Historical Perspectives*, ed. Mary Beth Rose (Syracuse: Syracuse University Press, 1986), pp. 135–54.

9. For a suggestive gloss on this exchange, see Jacques Ferrand, *A Treatise on Lovesickness* (1640), trans. and ed. Donald A. Beecher and Massimo Ciavolella (Syracuse: Syracuse University Press, 1990), p. 230, where Ferrand speculates that "it is quite plausible that the genitals of a girl, overheated by the fury of love, would be pushed outside the body, because those parts are the same as the male parts reversed."

10. The same linkage appears in Shakespeare's representation of Tamora in *Titus Andronicus* and also in Renaissance descriptions of Amazons. See Ania Loomba, *Gender, Race, Renaissance Drama* (New York: St. Martin's Press, 1989), p. 47, and Simon Shepherd, *Amazons and Warrior Women: Varieties of Feminism in Seventeenth-Century Drama* (New York: St Martin's Press, 1981).

11. Ben Jonson, *Epicoene or The Silent Woman*, Regents edition, ed. L. A. Beaurline (Lincoln: University of Nebraska Press, 1966), 1.1.74–76.

12. For numerous examples of this association during the period, see Susan C. Shapiro, "Amazons, Hermaphrodites, and Plain Monsters: The 'Masculine' Woman in English Satire and Social Criticism from 1580–1640," *Atlantis* 13 (1987), 65–76. Carroll Smith-Rosenberg informs me that European medical discourse continued this argument through the nineteenth century, lesbianism being believed to be especially commonplace among prostitutes, and that Lombroso, in particular, saw lesbianism and prostitution as twinned atavistic phenomena.

13. William Harrison, *The Description of England*, ed. Georges Edelen (Ithaca: Cornell University Press, 1968), p. 147; *Hic Mulier; or, The Man-Woman*, in *Half Humankind: Contexts and Texts of the Controversy about Women in England, 1540–1640*, ed. Katherine Usher Henderson and Barbara F. McManus (Urbana: University of Illinois Press, 1985), p. 267.

14. In a valuable unpublished paper titled "Boy Actors and Unfeminine Women," Kennedy quotes three comparisons between female characters and boy actors taken from Wroth's *Countesse of Mountgomeries Urania*. In two of the

examples the female character is lecherously courting a man; in the third she is behaving madly. I am grateful to Kennedy for giving me permission to cite this work.

15. On the sonnets, see David Buchbinder, "Some Engendered Meaning: Reading Shakespeare's Sonnets," *Works and Days* 14 (1989), 7–28; and Gregory W. Bredbeck, *Sodomy and Interpretation: From Marlowe to Milton* (Ithaca: Cornell University Press, 1991), pp. 167–85. On the boy heroines, see Lisa Jardine, *Still Harping on Daughters: Women and Drama in the Age of Shakespeare* (Totowa, N.J.: Barnes and Noble, 1983), pp. 9–36; Stephen Orgel, *Nobody's Perfect: Or Why Did the English Stage Take Boys for Women?*," *SAQ* 88 (1989), 7–30; and Phyllis Rackin, "Androgyny, Mimesis, and the Marriage of the Boy Heroine on the English Renaissance Stage," *PMLA* 102 (1987), 29–41.

16. For a brilliant analysis of these issues, which anticipates mine at a number of points, see Valerie Traub, "Desire and the Differences It Makes," in *The Matter of Difference: Materialist Feminist Criticism of Shakespeare*, ed. Valerie Wayne (Ithaca: Cornell University Press, 1991), pp. 81–114.

17. Because heat was regarded as superior to cold, men were regarded as naturally "hotter" than women, but women were also regarded as more lustful than men. Men were considered more spiritual, but the ladies celebrated in Renaissance sonnets were often depicted as inspirations to spiritual transcendence. On the one hand, silence was considered naturally proper to women; on the other, women were typically condemned for the supposed tendency of their sex to loquaciousness. Renaissance gender ideology, like our own, was fraught with conflict and contradiction.

18. Raymond Williams, *Marxism and Literature* (New York: Oxford University Press, 1977), pp. 121–27. I am also indebted here to Carroll Smith-Rosenberg's adaptation of Bakhtinian theory. See her *Disorderly Conduct: Visions of Gender in Victorian America* (New York: Knopf, 1985). On the contradictions between divergent views of homoeroticism during the early modern period, see Bredbeck, *Sodomy and Interpretation*, esp. pp. 149–60, on the hostile reception of Richard Barnfield's celebration of homoerotic love in *The Affectionate Shepheard* (1594) and Barnfield's disclaimer in his next book, *Cynthia*, of any personal stake in the poetic speaker's passion.

19. Wilfred Hooper, "The Tudor Sumptuary Laws," *English Historical Review* 30 (1915), 433–49. Hooper points out that despite previous regulation of women's dress, "the act of 1510 excluded all women, without distinction" (p. 433), and that this exclusion persisted in every subsequent enactment until 1574 (p. 444). See Ruth Kelso, *Doctrine for the Lady of the Renaissance* (Urbana: University of Illinois Press, 1956), pp. 33–36, on the relative lack of attention paid by Renaissance writers to social distinctions among women and the contingency of women's status on that of their husbands.

20. For provocative discussion of the implications of this practice, see Orgel, "Nobody's Perfect," pp. 14–16. Equally revealing is the use of "it" rather than a gendered pronoun to refer to children. Barbara Traister informs me that medical casebooks of the period referred to children of both sexes as "it" until they reached puberty.

21. Thomas Greene makes this point in "Anti-Hermeneutics: The Case of Shakespeare's Sonnet 129," in *Poetic Traditions of the English Renaissance*, ed. Maynard Mack and George deForest Lord (New Haven: Yale University Press, 1982), p. 148. The sonnet describes "lust in action" as "th' expense of spirit in a waste of shame"; but, as Greene points out, "the sexual act is . . . impover-

ishing only if one holds the medieval and Renaissance belief that it shortens a man's life . . . in place of the restorative, therapeutic release our post-Freudian society perceives." See Michel Foucault's argument in *The Use of Pleasure*, vol. 2 of *The History of Sexuality*, trans. Robert Hurley (New York: Vintage Books, 1990), pp. 82–86, that for the Greeks the "dividing line between a virile man and an effeminate man did not coincide with our opposition between hetero- and homosexuality" but instead distinguished a man who yielded to his appe- tites from one who exercised control over them. Rebecca W. Bushnell demon- strates the persistence of this idea in Renaissance representations of tyrants in *Tragedies of Tyrants: Political Thought and Theater in the English Renaissance* (Ith- aca: Cornell University Press, 1990).

22. Bonnie S. Anderson and Judith P. Zinsser, *A History of Their Own: Women in Europe from Prehistory to the Present*, vol. 1 (New York: Harper and Row, 1989), p. 255. See also p. 435, where the authors describe the continuing belief during the Renaissance that women were insatiably lustful.

23. This fear is vividly figured in the words of the seventeenth-century French preacher Paul Beurrier, who warned, "Our bodies resemble glasses that break when they touch one another." See Jean Delumeau, *Sin and Fear: The Emergence of a Western Guilt Culture, Thirteenth–Eighteenth Centuries*, trans. Eric Nicholson (New York: St. Martin's Press, 1990), p. 445. For a variety of exam- ples from medieval and Renaissance texts that use the Ovidian figure of the hermaphrodite as a symbol of heterosexual lust, see Carla Freccero, "The Other and the Same: The Image of the Hermaphrodite in Rabelais," in *Rewrit- ing the Renaissance: The Discourses of Sexual Difference in Early Modern Europe*, ed. Margaret W. Ferguson, Maureen Quilligan, and Nancy J. Vickers (Chicago: University of Chicago Press, 1986), pp. 149–51.

24. Rosi Braidotti, "Organs without Bodies," *differences* 1 (Winter 1989), 147.

25. The term *hermaphrodite* was also used in a positive sense. See, e.g., the comparison of heterosexual lovers locked in passionate embrace to the figure of the hermaphrodite in Spenser's *Faerie Queene* 3.12.45. See also Phyllis Rackin, "Androgyny," and "Shakespeare's Boy Cleopatra, the Decorum of Na- ture, and the Golden World of Poetry," *PMLA* 87 (1972), 201–12. For a variety of positive images of the hermaphrodite and androgyne, see Edgar Wind, *Pa- gan Mysteries in the Renaissance* (London: Faber and Faber, 1960), pp. 211–14. For extensive studies of the ambivalence of the figure of the hermaphrodite, see Nancy Hayles, "The Ambivalent Ideal: The Concept of Androgyny in En- glish Renaissance Literature" (Ph.D. diss., University of Rochester, 1976), and Jones and Stallybrass, "Fetishizing Gender."

26. Francis Barker, *The Tremulous Private Body: Essays on Subjection* (London: Methuen, 1984), p. 23.

27. See Delumeau, *Sin and Fear*, esp. chap. 16, "The Ascetic Model." For a well-known Shakespearean example, see Sonnet 146 ("Poor soul, the centre of my sinful earth"), which draws on the same tradition of ascetic dualism as the newly crowned Henry V's admonition to Falstaff, "Make less thy body (hence) and more thy grace, / . . . know the grave doth gape / For thee thrice wider than for other men" (2 *Henry IV* 5.5. 52–54).

28. Quoted in Anderson and Zinsser, *A History of Their Own*, p. 83.

29. See Rosalie Osmond, *Mutual Accusation: Seventeenth-Century Body and Soul Dialogues in Their Literary and Theological Context* (Toronto: University of Tor- onto Press, 1990); and Marilyn R. Farwell, "Eve, the Separation Scene, and the Renaissance Idea of Androgyny," *Milton Studies* 16 (1982), 3–20.

30. Gerrard Winstanley, *The New Law of Righteousnes*, in *The Works of Gerrard Winstanley*, ed. George H. Sabine (Ithaca: Cornell University Press, 1941), p. 157, and *Luther's Works*, ed. Jaroslav Pelikan (St. Louis: Concordia, 1955–86), 25:333, both quoted by Allison P. Coudert in "The Myth of the Improved Status of Protestant Women: The Case of the Witchcraze," in *The Politics of Gender in Early Modern Europe*, ed. Jean R. Brink, Allison P. Coudert, and Maryanne C. Horowitz, vol. 12 of *Sixteenth-Century Essays and Studies* (Kirksville, Mo.: Sixteenth-Century Journal Publishers, 1989), p. 81.

31. Aristotle, *Generation of Animals* 2.4.738b20–23; quoted in Laqueur, *Making Sex*, p. 30.

32. *The Problemes of Aristotle, with other Philosophers and Phisitions* (London: Arnold Hatfield, 1597), sigs E3–E4; quoted in Montrose, "Shaping Fantasies," p. 43. As Montrose explains, this text conflates Galenic and Aristotelian theories of procreation. For opposed views of the relative importance of Galenic and Aristotelian influence on early modern medical theory, see Laqueur, *Making Sex*, which emphasizes the Galenic influence, and "Destiny Is Anatomy," a review of Laqueur's book by Katharine Park and Robert A. Nye, *New Republic*, February 18, 1991, pp. 53–57.

33. Here again, anticipations of contemporary attitudes can be found in Renaissance texts. In *The Merchant of Venice*, for instance, although Venetian anti-Semitism is rationalized in terms of religion, Jessica's "Jewishness" does not disappear with her conversion, and Morocco's dark complexion is foregrounded as the mark of racial difference and inferiority. "Mislike me not for my complexion" is the burden of his opening speech (2.2.1–12). "Let all of his complexion choose me so" (2.7.78–79) is Portia's delighted response to his failure to choose the casket that would entitle him to claim her in marriage.

34. On the difficulty of separating "phallus" from "penis," see Jane Gallop, *The Daughter's Seduction: Feminism and Psychoanalysis* (Ithaca: Cornell University Press, 1982), pp. 95–100.

35. The body, in fact, was a site of radical instability. Classical myths of metamorphosis, popular in the Renaissance, make a similar point: the transformation of physical form by the pursuit, avoidance, or fulfillment of sexual desire. The transformation of ravished maidens reflects the sociological facts of a culture that defined women by their sexual status—as maidens, whores, wives, or widows—but the fact that male figures, including Jove himself, are often transformed in these stories implies that sexuality itself was held to compromise bodily identity.

36. Queen Elizabeth, for instance, habitually referred to herself as a "prince," even in statements in which she designated Mary, the deposed Queen of Scots, as a "princess." See Leah S. Marcus, *Puzzling Shakespeare: Local Reading and Its Discontents* (Berkeley: University of California Press, 1988), p. 56. See Alan Bray's argument in "Homosexuality and the Signs of Male Friendship in Elizabethan England," *History Workshop* 29 (1990), 3, that the offense of sodomy (designated by Edward Coke as a *crimen laesae majestatis*) was defined in political terms.

37. Laqueur, *Making Sex*, pp. 78, 79, 83.

38. Quoted by Thomas Laqueur in "Orgasm, Generation, and the Politics of Reproductive Biology," *Representations* 14 (Spring 1986), 13. For other cases in which masculine behavior produced the physical marks of male sex in people who had formerly been known as women, see Greenblatt, "Fiction and Friction," pp. 66, 73–86, 175–78; and Laqueur, *Making Sex*, pp. 126–28.

39. Ann Thompson, "'The Warrant of Womanhood': Shakespeare and Feminist Criticism," in *The Shakespeare Myth*, ed. Graham Holderness (Manchester: Manchester University Press, 1988), p. 85.

40. For a fuller development of this point, see chap. 4, "Patriarchal History and Female Subversion," in my book *Stages of History: Shakespeare's English Chronicles* (Ithaca: Cornell University Press, 1990).

41. Thomas Nashe, *Pierce Penilesse his Supplication to the Divell* (1592), rpt. in E. K. Chambers, *The Elizabethan Stage* (Oxford: Clarendon Press, 1951), 4:238–39.

42. Orgel, "Nobody's Perfect," p. 8. See also Ann Jennalie Cook, "'Bargaines of Incontinencie': Bawdy Behavior in the Playhouses," *Shakespeare Studies* 10 (1977), 271–90. On the role of gender in antitheatrical anxieties, see Jean Howard, "Crossdressing, the Theatre, and Gender Struggle in Early Modern England," *Shakespeare Quarterly* 39 (1988), 439–40; and Laura Levine, "Men in Women's Clothing: Anti-Theatricality and Effeminization from 1579 to 1642," *Criticism* 28 (Spring 1986), 131–37. On the presence of women in the commercial playhouses, see Andrew Gurr, *Playgoing in Shakespeare's London* (New York: Cambridge University Press, 1988), pp. 59–64 and appendixes 1 and 2; and Richard Levin, "Women in the Renaissance Theatre Audience," *Shakespeare Quarterly* 40 (1989), 165–74.

43. See Orgel, "Nobody's Perfect," p. 9 and p. 28, n.2. I am also indebted here to an unpublished paper by Frances K. Barasch, "The Lady's Not for Spurning: An Investigation of Italian Actresses and Their Roles in Commedia dell'Arte as Shakespeare's Inspiration." Barasch makes the intriguing suggestion that Shakespeare's witty, independent female characters may have been inspired in part by the performances of Italian actresses, who, because they worked from scenarios rather than from scripts, were in some measure the authors of their own theatrical selves.

44. See Samuel Burdett Hemingway, ed. *A New Variorum Edition of Henry the Fourth Part I* (Philadelphia: Lippincott, 1936), pp. 124–25; and Chambers, *The Elizabethan Stage*, 2:443–45.

45. On Falstaff's female characteristics, see Valerie Traub, "Prince Hal's Falstaff: Positioning Psychoanalysis and the Female Reproductive Body," *Shakespeare Quarterly* 40 (1989), 456–74.

46. Christopher Highley provides a rich topical context for the association of Wales with savagery and female power in "Wales, Ireland, and *1 Henry IV*," *Renaissance Drama*, n.s., 21 (1990), 91–114. It also has a precedent as ancient as Geoffrey of Monmouth's *Historia Regum Britanniae*, which records that the name Welsh derives "either from their leader Gualo, or from their Queen Galaes, or else from their being so barbarous." See *The History of the Kings of Britain*, trans, Lewis Thorpe (Harmondsworth: Penguin Books, 1966), p. 284. The country of the Others, a world of witchcraft and magic, of mysterious music, and also of unspeakable atrocity which horrifies the English imagination, Wales is defined in terms very much like those that define the woman. For an extended discussion of this point, see Rackin, *Stages of History*, chap. 4. A similar construction of Wales appears in *Cymbeline*, a play based on Holinshed and taking the name of its heroine from Innogen, the wife of the legendary Trojan founder of the British royal line. A land of miracles and music and also of mortal danger, the Wales of *Cymbeline* is also the place where the true heirs to the British throne (disguised with the historically resonant names Polydore and

Cadwal) are sequestered. For the mythic-historical associations of the Welsh material in *Cymbeline*, see Frances Yates, *Majesty and Magic in Shakespeare's Last Plays* (Boulder, Colo.: Shambhala, 1975), pp. 39–62; and Emrys Jones, "Stuart Cymbeline," *Essays in Criticism* 11 (1961), 84–99.

47. Raphael Holinshed, *Chronicles of England, Scotland, and Ireland* (1587; reprint London: J. Johnson et al., 1808), 3:20. The threefold association of female power, foreignness, and atrocity appears to be a persistent feature of early modern European discourse. Ralegh's *Discoverie of Guiana* (1596), quoted in Montrose, "Shaping Fantasies," p. 46, reports that Amazons "are said to be very cruel and bloodthirsty." Even more suggestive is a late sixteenth-century travel narrative quoted by Stephen Greenblatt in *Renaissance Self-Fashioning: From More to Shakespeare* (Chicago: University of Chicago Press, 1980), p. 181, which reports that "near the mountains of the moon there is a queen, an empress of all these Amazons, a witch and a cannibal who daily feeds on the flesh of boys. She ever remains unmarried, but she has intercourse with a great number of men by whom she begets offspring. The kingdom, however, remains hereditary to the daughters, not to the sons." What is especially interesting for my argument is that this account, like both Westmerland's and Fleming's accounts of the female atrocities in Wales, comes to its readers doubly mediated. It is recorded in the diary of Richard Madox, an English traveler in Sierra Leone, but Madox claims that he heard the story from a Portuguese trader. Still another account of female savagery, most closely resembling Fleming's, appeared in the *Columbian Magazine and Monthly Miscellany* 1 (Philadelphia, 1787), 549. This account is also represented as doubly mediated (told to the writer by an unnamed "gentleman" met "near Alexandria, in Virginia, in 1782"). In this report, a surveyor named Colonel Crawford, captured by Indians, "was delivered over to *the women*, and being fastened to a stake, in the centre of a circle, formed by the savages and their allies, the female furies, after the preamble of a war song, began by tearing out the nails of his toes and fingers, then proceeded, at considerable intervals, to cut off his nose and ears; after which they stuck his lacerated body full of pitch pines, large pieces of which they inserted (horrid to relate!) into his private parts; to all of which they set fire, and which continued burning, amidst the inconceivable tortures of the unhappy man, for a considerable time. After thus glutting their revenge, by arts of barbarity, the success of which was repeatedly applauded by the surrounding demons, they cut off his genitals, and rushing in upon him, finished his misery with their tomahawks, and hacked his body limb from limb." I am indebted to Carroll Smith-Rosenberg for the material from the *Columbian Magazine*.

48. As Stephen Greenblatt points out, images in Renaissance texts that seem "to invite, even to demand, a psychoanalytic approach" often turn out "to baffle or elude that approach." The "mingled invitation and denial," Greenblatt proposes, can be understood historically by considering that "psychoanalysis is at once the fulfillment and effacement of specifically Renaissance insights: psychoanalysis is, in more than one sense, the end of the Renaissance." Stephen Greenblatt, "Psychoanalysis and Renaissance Culture," in *Learning to Curse: Essays in Early Modern Culture* (New York: Routledge, 1990), p. 131.

49. See Coppélia Kahn's suggestive analysis in "Whores and Wives in Jacobean Drama," in *In Another Country: Feminist Perspectives on Renaissance Drama*, ed. Dorothea Kehler and Susan Baker (Metuchen, N.J.: Scarecrow Press, 1991), p. 255, of the incident in *The Changeling* in which De Flores gives

Beatrice-Joanna Alonzo's severed finger to prove his murder as "insinuat[ing] that the sexually active woman is a castrating woman."

50. Holinshed, *Chronicles*, 3:26.

51. Linda Austern, " 'Sing Againe Syren': Female Musicians and Sexual Enchantment in Elizabethan Life and Literature," *Renaissance Quarterly* 42 (1989), 397–419. Philip Stubbes, *Anatomie of Abuses* (1583), sig. D4, quoted ibid., p. 424. See also *2 Henry IV* 2.4.11–12, where it is the prostitute, Doll Tearsheet, who "would fain hear some music." Poetry was also considered effeminizing, as Mary Ellen Lamb demonstrates in a fine unpublished paper, "Apologizing for Pleasure in Sidney's *Apology for Poetry.*"

52. Matthew Wikander, *The Play of Truth and State: Historical Drama from Shakespeare to Brecht* (Baltimore: Johns Hopkins University Press, 1986), pp. 14–25.

53. Both Goldberg and Sinfield recognize Hotspur's misogyny as an expression of anxiety, but while Goldberg argues that the object of that anxiety is the "taint" that "lies in playing the woman's part with another man" ("Desiring Hal," p. 168), Sinfield associates it with the early modern assumption, grounded in Renaissance biological theory as well as gendered codes of behavior, that men could be rendered "effeminate" by "too much devotion to women" (*Faultlines*, p. 131). Cf. Hotspur's earlier declaration of independence from Kate: "When I am a' horseback I will swear I love thee infinitely" (2.3.102–3). The sexual symbolism is clearly intelligible in modern terms, but here, as in the case of Falstaff's "uncolting" in the preceding scene, the older commonplace analogy between rational control of the passions and a rider's control of his horse is at least as relevant.

54. Holinshed, *Chronicles*, 3:34.

55. With its insistent physicality and bawdry, the scene of Katherine's language lesson reiterates the foreign / female / illicit sexuality association that appears in the representation of Glendower's daughter. For a brilliant exposition of those associations in contemporary language texts, see Juliet Fleming, "*The French Garden:* An Introduction to Women's French," *ELH* 56 (1989), 19–51. For suggestive glosses on the women's exclusion from language and their association with body, see D. J. Gordon's observation in *The Renaissance Imagination*, ed. Stephen Orgel (Berkeley: University of California Press, 1975), p. 80, that in masques the visual aspect was called the body and the words the soul, and Hélène Cixous's argument in "Castration or Decapitation," trans. Annette Kuhn, in *Signs: Journal of Women in Culture and Society* 7 (1981), 41–55, that "the backlash, the return, on women of [masculine] castration anxiety is its displacement as decapitation" or the reduction to "complete silence." Women, Cixous argues, may "overflow with sound: but they don't actually *speak.* . . . They always inhabit the place of silence, or at most make it echo with their singing. . . . They remain outside knowledge" (pp. 43, 49).

56. Steven Mullaney points out—in *The Place of the Stage: License, Play, and Power in Renaissance England* (Chicago: University of Chicago Press, 1988), pp. 77, 162—that although Henry VIII had outlawed Welsh in 1535, the alien language ("nothing like, nor consonant to the natural Mother Tongue within this realm") consistently defied English efforts "to control or outlaw it." Resisting repeated "pressures of assimilation and suppression . . . Welsh remained a strange tongue, a discomfiting reminder that Wales continued to be a foreign and hostile colony, ruled and to an extent subjected but never quite controlled by Tudor power."

57. For an analysis of this coupling in a historically and culturally diverse series of examples, see Nancy Huston, "The Matrix of War: Mothers and Heroes," in *The Female Body in Western Culture: Contemporary Perspectives,* ed. Susan Rubin Suleiman (Cambridge: Harvard University Press, 1985), pp. 119–36.

5. Shakespeare and the English Witch-Hunts: Enclosing the Maternal Body

Deborah Willis

According to two documents among the state papers of 1590, an un-named London informer told the sheriff's office that a Mrs. Dewse had engaged the services of Robert Birche, by reputation a conjurer.[1] She sought through his magic art to revenge herself upon her enemies—the "theeves" and "villaynes" she believed were responsible for driving her husband, the Keeper of Newgate Prison, from office, "which would bee both her and her childrens undoinges." The first document names several men, among them "Mr. Younge," "Sir Rowland Heyward," and "Sye." Mrs. Dewse asked Birche to make wax images of these men and then "pricke them to the harte" to cause their death. Failing that, he was to use his art to make them die "in a damp"—that is, of typhus—as had happened in Oxford at the Black Assize of 1577, when a number of judges, jurymen, and lawyers had abruptly died of that disease. In that incident the "damp" was widely attributed to the sorcery of a bookseller, on trial for selling banned Catholic books.[2]

Birche, however, was reluctant to accommodate Mrs. Dewse. He was "lame," he said, and therefore unable to make the images. According to the second document, he even piously lectured her: "She were beste to take good heede how she dealte and whom she trusted in such mat-ters . . . . The best meanes was to pray to God that hee would turne her enemies hartes." But the angry wife was determined to make the im-ages herself, if only Birche would stand by and correct her mistakes. After several visits from Birche, Mrs. Dewse completed three pictures under his guidance. She made "one for Mr Younge & put a pynne into his harte, another for Sir Rowland Heyward & putt a pynne to his harte & another under his ribbes, & the third picture for Sye & put two pynnes into his eyes." Mrs. Dewse was apparently satisfied by the re-sults: "She thanked God that some of her pictures did work well."

Birche was paid a sum of money, sent a sugar loaf and lemons, and asked to come again "divers times."

As it happened, Mrs. Dewse had indeed placed her trust in the wrong man. Birche himself, after his very first visit, reported on their dealings to her enemy, Mr. Young—Justice Young, that is, as he is termed in the second document. Birche's subsequent visits could be considered something of a "sting" operation, as, under Young's direction, he cleverly but deviously gathered more information about Mrs. Dewse's intentions while leading her to commit the acts of sorcery on her own. The document closes with an account of the sheriff's search of her home, during which he found two pictures hidden in "a secret place" in her cupboard, "with pynnes sticked in them" just as the informant had said.

The second document is a statement taken from Birche himself after the sheriff's visit. Far from being discouraged, Mrs. Dewse now planned her revenge to extend up the social ladder to the Privy Council: she would add the sheriff, the Recorder, the Lord Chamberlain, and even the Lord Chancellor to her list of intended victims. This, apparently, was enough to prompt the sheriff to further action. She was apprehended that very day.

What happened to Mrs. Dewse? Was she charged and tried under the 1563 witchcraft statutes, which criminalized the use or practice of "anye Sorcery Enchantment Charme or Witchcrafte, to thintent . . . to hurte or destroye any person in his or her Body, Member or Goodes"?[3] If so—assuming none of her victims actually fell ill or died—she would have been subject to a one-year imprisonment, during which she would also be placed in a pillory on market day four times a year to "openly confesse" her error and offense. If her sorcery had been successful, of course, she would have been subject to the death penalty, joining the many hundreds of others—almost all women—executed for witchcraft in England between 1563 and 1736.

Her name is missing from the exhaustive lists compiled by historians of persons tried under the witchcraft statutes in this period, but other documents allow us to piece together more of Mrs. Dewse's story.[4] In the period preceding her involvement with sorcery, her husband, William Dewes, in his capacity as Keeper of Newgate, had been charged by one Humphrey Gunston of "sundry abuses and misdemeanours . . . concerninge her Majestie." Dewes, in response, had filed actions of slander against Gunston. But Gunston prevailed: the Keeper was about to be charged and bound over for trial for "treason, murder, or felony" around the time Mrs. Dewse contacted the conjurer Birche. Among Gunston's supporters were the three men targeted by Mrs. Dewse: Justice Young, a justice of the peace who frequently served as

examiner and torturer in numerous cases involving allegedly seditious
Catholics; Sir Roland Heyward, also a J.P. and twice mayor of London;
and Nicholas Sye, probably an underkeeper at Newgate Prison. These
men had petitioned the Lord Chamberlain and other officials on Gunston's behalf.

Mrs. Dewes herself mentions Gunston, naming him as one of
her husband's enemies, though the informant does not include him
among the targets of her image magic. It appears, then, that at the
time she was under investigation, her husband was on the verge of being forced out of office by the collaboration of two influential J.P.s and
a prison underkeeper, who were supporting Gunston's charges and
blocking Dewse's suits to the high officials who had formerly been his
patrons. That, at any rate, was what Mrs. Dewse believed: the "knaves"
Heyward and Young she complains, have "made the lord Chamber-
leyne that hee would not reade her husbandes peticions, and the Lord
Chauncelor who was ever her husbandes frend would do nothing for
her, & Mr Recorder whom she thought would not have bene her ene-
mie, he likewise did now (as shee heard) take his parte that should have
her husbandes office."

Was Gunston angling for Dewse's office, as Mrs. Dewse seemed to believe? Or were these men simply trying to remove from office a man
they considered corrupt? Perhaps Heyward and Young opposed Dewse
because they suspected him or his wife of Catholic sympathies—unde-
sirable especially in a keeper at Newgate, where many suspected Catholic conspirators were held. Mrs. Dewse reportedly told Birche that by
helping her to achieve her revenge he would "greatly please God, for
one of them was that thiefe Younge who lived by robbing papists." God
apparently would be pleased that they had punished an enemy of the
Catholic church, despite their ungodly methods. Moreover, her fallback
plan, to make these men die "as they did at the assises at Oxford," was
modeled on the sorcery of a seditious Catholic bookseller.

Or were the charges against the Keeper and Mrs. Dewse entirely
made up? Perhaps Young and Heyward wanted their own man in Dewse's office for personal advantage, not for religious reasons at all; perhaps Young and Heyward cynically concocted a tale of attempted
witchcraft in order to discredit Dewse further through his wife. As is
the case in most accusations of witchcraft, we have only the accusers'
statements to go on; the accused witch can no longer speak for herself.

What is clear enough in these documents is the way a charge of
witchcraft is embedded in a larger drama of intrigue, rivalry, and revenge, of power struggle over office and retaliation for its loss. Mrs.
Dewse's case, though it involves relatively minor players, resembles a
type of politically motivated witchcraft case which historians have con-

sidered especially characteristic of the medieval period, but which continued on into the Renaissance even after lower-class witches began to be persecuted as an end in itself—exactly the type of case that Shakespeare's imagination appears to have been engaged by at the time he was writing his early history plays. In such cases a charge of witchcraft is made against someone believed to have designs against the monarch or some highly placed official. It is frequently combined with accusations of treason or conspiracy against the state. The charge of witchcraft—and perhaps also its actual practice—may emerge, in fact, from factional struggle, part of one aristocratic group's attempt to displace its rivals and remove them from power. Shakespeare's first tetralogy focuses on a number of such politically embedded witchcraft cases: Joan of Arc, Eleanor, Duchess of Gloucester, Margery Jourdain, Margaret, Queen Elizabeth, and Jane Shore are all accused—and some convicted—of witchcraft in the course of these plays.

The case of Mrs. Dewse and the cultural practices that helped produce it provide an important context for Shakespeare's construction of witchcraft and political intrigue; but Shakespeare's plays in their turn, I believe, also provide a context for "reading" the historical phenomenon of witch-hunting. I would draw attention to the suggestiveness of Shakespeare for one issue in particular: the "woman question." Why were the victims of the hunt overwhelmingly female? Why, for example, is Mrs. Dewse the object of this particular investigation and not the male conjurer whom she engaged? Why Mrs. Dewse and not the husband who paid for and apparently endorsed, however fearfully, her involvement with sorcery?

Mrs. Dewse was caught in the cross fire of a power struggle between males over which she had little control. Assuming the charges against her to be at least partly true, she probably turned to sorcery as a last resort, when her husband's attempts to defend his position had faltered. In so doing, she stepped out of place as a woman, in a sense usurping her husband's role, appropriating for herself an agency usually restricted to males. But it is unlikely that the motives behind her arrest had much to do with the perception that her behavior had violated gender norms; rather, authorities were seeking to protect highly placed state officials from a magical threat to their lives. Yet what made that magical threat believable *as* a threat? What made authorities fear Mrs. Dewse and others like her, endowing them with a frightening power?

Witches were women, I believe, because women were mothers. To any reader of feminist theory, psychoanalysis, or Shakespeare criticism, it may seem obvious to say so.[5] Yet such a claim has seldom been tested in historians' analyses of the witch-hunts. Although historians have

been asking with increasing urgency why women formed the vast majority of those prosecuted under England's witchcraft statutes,[6] they
have not, by and large, focused on women's roles as mothers or caretakers of small children, or considered the psychological fallout of Renaissance mothering. The mother is absent from the most influential
studies of English and Scottish witchcraft, those by Alan Macfarlane,
Keith Thomas, and Christina Larner.[7] With some exceptions, the same
is true of studies of witchcraft in Europe and the American colonies.[8]

Mrs. Dewse was a mother, and she apparently turned to sorcery in
part because of that fact: her husband's loss of office threatened to be
the "undoing" of both her and her children. As mother and wife, she
was dependent on her husband for economic security and social position. Mrs. Dewse's interests intersected with his and her magical acts,
designed to help and avenge him, implicate her in his treasonous activities. Those acts eerily encode a nightmare version of her maternal
role; the doll-like wax images to be pierced by pins suggest children
over whom a controlling but monstrous mother holds the power of life
and death.

In Shakespeare's first tetralogy, witches, wives, and mothers are endowed with similar nightmare powers; by both magical and nonmagical
means they manipulate males and make them feel as if they have been
turned back into dependent children. Like Mrs. Dewse, these women
also use their powers to aid and abet "traitors" who threaten what other
characters see as legitimate political authority. But whereas Mrs. Dewse's maternal role is glimpsed only briefly in the documents connected
with her case, Shakespeare's plays foreground the links between the
witch and the mother, making a malevolent, persecutory power associated with the maternal body a central feature of their ability to
threaten order. In what follows I explore more fully the ways the first
tetralogy links the witch, the mother, and the rebel; after that, I return
to the witch-hunts and modern historians' intepretations of them. If
the maternal plays only a minor role in the case of Mrs. Dewse, when
we turn to the "mainstream" witchcraft cases taking place at the village
level, a distinct and, I hope to show, undeniable connection between
the witch and the mother will become clear.

                                 I

In *1 Henry VI* Joan—French rebel against English imperial claims,
base-born upstart who takes on the persona of the aristocratic military
hero—is represented as a witch whose supernatural power manifests
itself in exceptional physical strength and skill in combat. She would at

first seem an unlikely choice for an example of the linkage between witch and mother, given her highly masculinized role. Yet the sense of triumph the English males display when Joan is captured and set off to be executed derives not just from the fact that she is a national enemy and a vulgar upstart; it also stems from her clever manipulation of male ties to the mother. Initially associating herself with "God's mother" and a miraculous heavenly power to aid the Frenchmen, she is disclosed as demonically empowered and exploitive of both French and English males in her pursuit of purely personal "glory." On the battle-field she turns the Englishmen from fierce dogs into "whelps," by im-plication children. The language of "turning," "whirling," and shape changing is frequently used alongside the language of bewitchment to describe her effects on the English males: she "turns" Burgundy, the French duke initially loyal to the English, back into a loyal Frenchman by her appeal to his attachment to his native land, positioning him first as the mother himself: "Look on thy country . . . / As looks the mother on her lowly babe" as it dies in her arms.[9] After appealing to Bur-gundy's identification with the mother, Joan uses that identification to arouse guilt, as the country France becomes the mother—more spe-cifically, the mother's breast—which Burgundy has wounded with his sword: "Behold the wounds, the most unnatural wounds, / Which thou thyself hast given her woeful breast / . . . . One drop of blood drawn from thy country's bosom / Should grieve thee more than streams of foreign gore" (3.3.50–51, 54–55). The breast is also implicitly present later, when, as she begs her devils to continue their supernatural aid, she reminds them of her witch's teat, "where I was wont to feed you with my blood" (5.3.14). Later, Joan's father uses the breast to curse Joan after she denies her parentage: "I would the milk / Thy mother gave thee when thou suck'st her breast / Had been a little ratsbane for thy sake" (5.4.27–29). Here the breast is used in a retaliatory fashion, as if punishing Joan for her former appropriation of it—for, as it were, her fraudalent self-presentation as the nurturing breast, when all along she was a poisoning one. Her attempt to save herself from exe-cution by a last desperate appeal to pregnancy also brings the womb into play. As she is led away to be burned at the stake, it seems clear that in her the English are punishing not only a rebel and a class upstart but also a betraying mother, in this case a phallic mother, a mother who at first seemed to have it all—breast, womb, and phallus—now reduced to futile strategems that display only the relative powerlessness of the maternal body in the male public world.

Margaret—linked to Joan in numerous ways—is another version of the phallic mother. But whereas Joan's phallic power comes from su-pernatural sources, Margaret's comes from her "masculine spirit," her

potential to be a mother, and her commitment to the particular patrilineage with which she becomes associated. At the center of these plays
is a critique of the culture of aristocratic honor and the factional violence to which it gives rise, a violence Shakespeare also associates with
a problematics of "family": civil conflict is set in motion when fathers
can no longer control sons, wives, and younger brothers, and when
kings can no longer control individual patrilineages. As a "masculine"
mother in this world, Margaret comes to possess a witchlike power. She
is an object of desire in a world where fathers die prematurely; she is a
vehicle for "upstart"ambitions in a world where kings fail to rule. Later
her powers of attraction are revealed as humiliating or deadly to the
males who succumb to them—lover, husband, and son. Moreover, set
against the claims of the patrilineal family as a discrete unit are the
claims of a national "family." Viewed from this perspective, Margaret
paradoxically becomes linked to Medea, the witch-mother who kills her
own children, when her impassioned defense of her son's rights as
royal heir makes her the equally impassioned enemy of her husband's
rival's children—that is, when she authorizes the murder of "pretty
Rutland," the youngest son of her enemy York.

But it is the Duchess of York, mother of Richard III, who comes closest to the literal Medea. Her witchlike power mimics that of the real
witch Margery Jourdain (called Mother Jourdain, not incidentally),
glimpsed in 2 *Henry VI* as she raises spirits in order to prophesy the
future. Revenge and divine justice, witch's curse and godly prophecy,
merge as the words of the mother's final curse of her son seems to raise
the quasi-supernatural, ghost-filled dream that Richard has the night
before his final battle. Richard dies undermined from within as well as
without, "providentially" murdered not only by Henry of Richmond
but also by his unnerving, prophetic dream and, when he wakes, by an
inner voice that again echoes his mother's curse.

The first tetralogy thus inscribes the mother in the witch and the
witch in the mother. As the plays unfold, those terms also shift in value:
the Duchess of York's witchlike mothering makes her a hero more than
a villain in these final scenes. If at first the plays seem to substitute
mother-hunting for witch-hunting—inviting the audience to take pleasure in Richard's revenge on women while at the same time recognizing his misogyny—by the end of the tetralogy the witchy behavior of
mothers has taken on a more positive value. Whereas Margaret's
Medea-like complicity in the murder of her rival's son makes her a villain, the Duchess of York's willingness to "smother" her own son with
the words of her curse makes her the instrument of the play's restoration of order. In the interests of a national family, even participating in
the murder of one's own son can be a good thing. Richard's mother

becomes in a sense a 'white witch,' her behavior acquiring a positive value because it is deployed on behalf of this new, national family, thus making possible a partial disengagement from the fetishistic passion for "place," so closely associated with a primary narcissistic loyalty to patrilineage. Such loyalties, according to these plays, must be subordinated to other, quasi-familial ties to persons unrelated by blood or feudal contract if aristocratic civil wars are to cease. If the rhetoric of national family can all too easily be appropriated and used to mystify a state that serves only a small portion of that family—and so Shakespeare uses it for the House of Tudor and other elite interests—it is also true that this rhetoric makes possible a break from even more constricted forms of social organization and provides the play's more moving moments, in which new types of relatedness or social bonding can be glimpsed. Among such moments are those that involve the quasi-coven of mothers in *Richard III* 4.4., as Margaret teaches Queen Elizabeth and the Duchess of York, her old enemies, how to curse.

If Shakespeare at the end of this sequence opens up a space for the white witch who heals with her destructive violence, he also suggests that the national family must recognize a maternal inheritance as well as contain and redirect its destructive potential. In helping to destroy Richard, the three mothers aid the "milksop," mother-dependent Richmond; moreover, Queen Elizabeth helps Richmond consolidate his power by actively arranging his marriage to her daughter. These mothers still play a marginalized and subordinate role in this male-centered political world, but because they are outsiders they are also survivors, capable of action when the violence of masculinist honor has crippled that world. The plays do not subvert patriarchy, abandon their androcentric focus, or challenge the beliefs that informed the laws criminalizing witchcraft. But, as sons attempt to differentiate themselves from, as well as sustain a connection to, a problematic inheritance from the father, the plays do, I believe, open up a larger space within patriarchy for acknowledging an inheritance from the mother and for valorizing female solidarity and self-assertion, even when these take a violent form.

II

Shakespeare's first tetralogy foregrounds the way witch-hunting arises in response to a political crisis deeply intertwined with a breakdown in the family; as the consequences of that breakdown play themselves out, witch-hunting becomes mother-hunting, and the need for a reevaluation of both social practices becomes evident by the tetralogy's end. The destructive potential of the witch is closely tied to that of the murdering mother, and the punishment of both figures is instrumental in the construction of a new national identity—an identity that also depends, however, on recuperating aspects of their power. In Richard's narration of his childhood history, we glimpse the way an individual subject's desire is informed and fractured by his experience within a historically specific family unit, as women in caretaking roles employ a destructive patriarchal discourse about a (third) son's (deformed) body. If Richard's narrative at first encourages the audience to participate in the substitution of mother-hunting for witch-hunting, the tetralogy goes on to make visible the ironic sequence of misrecognitions involved in such hunts: Richard's attempt to repossess a magical omnipotence associated with the mother's body through the "Elysium" of the crown is exposed as fetishistic illusion; at the same time, his attempt to silence the punitive and rejecting mother's voice through acts of dominance falters as that voice is increasingly revealed to be, on the one hand, uncannily his own, and, on the other, patriarchal and divine.

For interpreters of the witch-hunts, these plays point in useful directions. They invite us to refocus our investigations by scrutinizing those social formations most directly involved in the construction of witch-hunting subjects, to attempt to chart the steps by which such subjects adopt and redeploy a language first uttered by the mother and encountered in the intersubjective context of specific families, a language that is then transferentially reworked later in life within larger networks of social relationships. Ideally such an attempt would also include an account of the way particular individual subjects are specially positioned to affect the state apparatus, which in its turn reaches out to affect the social institutions most directly involved in the production of individual subjects.

The witch-hunts were, of course, a highly complex, multidetermined affair, involving the poor and the very poor at the village level as well as a "prosecuting class" made up of gentry-level and aristocratic judges, justices of the peace, clerics, magistrates, and kings. Low, middle, and high, peasant and elite, male and female interests intersected in fear and loathing of the witch. Alan Macfarlane and Keith Thomas have offered the most powerful analysis of witchcraft at the village level, their explanatory paradigms concentrating on social structure, economic patterns, and popular belief. Christina Larner, exploring the Scottish witch-hunts, has integrated their approach with a closer examination of the role of the state apparatus and the ruling elites. As she remarks: "Peasants left to themselves will identify individuals as witches and will resort to a variety of anti-witchcraft measures in self-defence; they cannot pursue these measures to the punishment, banishment, or official execution of even one witch, let alone a multiplicity of witches, without the administrative machinery and encouragement of their rulers."[10]

Although these historians have little or nothing to say about the relation of witch to mother, they all take up the "woman question." For Keith Thomas, the fact that most of those accused of witchcraft were women is most plausibly explained "by economic and social considerations, for it was the women who were the most dependent members of the community, and thus the most vulnerable to accusation."[11] For Alan Macfarlane, it is not women's dependence but their social position and power that made them vulnerable; they were the "co-ordinating element" in village society, and "if witchcraft . . . reflected tensions between an ideal of neighborliness and the necessities of economic and social change, women were commonly thought of as witches because they were more resistant to such change."[12] Both Thomas and Macfarlane agree that the "idea that witch-prosecutions reflected a war between the sexes must be discounted," chiefly because village-level accusers and victims were at least as likely to be female as male, if not more so.[13]

Christina Larner, while stressing the political and religious factors involved in the hunts, has also argued that the witch-hunts were sex-related, though not sex-specific. For both elite groups and the peasantry, the women who became targets of the hunts had clearly violated norms regarding appropriate behavior of women; they were angry and demanding, not meek, mild, and compliant. She disagrees with the notion that a "war between the sexes" can be discounted as an element in the hunts merely because a majority of accusers were women themselves, as Thomas and Macfarlane suggest. Larner recognizes that patriarchal beliefs and practices often have the effect of dividing women against one another; because of their dependence on men, many women attempt to distinguish themselves from and even attack women who refuse to conform to patriarchal rules.[14]

Larner's argument is a more sophisticated version of one that has surfaced in less subtle form in many appropriations of the historical witch for feminist polemic.[15] The witch is a rebel against patriarchal oppression, a transgressor of gender roles, the innocent victim of a male-authored reign of terror that functions to keep all women in their place. If it is acknowledged at all in such texts that women were participants in as well as victims of the hunts, these women are represented as lackeys of patriarchy, conservative defenders of male-defined notions of women's roles, mere cogs in the phallocentric wheel. By contrast, the witch is the heroic proto-feminist who resists patriarchal technologies for producing the female subject and contests oppressive gender norms.

Patriarchal beliefs and practices do, of course, powerfully shape witchcraft accusations. But these polemical formulations, useful as they may be in some contexts, ascribe to the participants in the hunts a monologic unity of self that directs attention away from the tensions and discontinuities within early modern constructions of the subject. As I read the hunts, the woman accused of witchcraft is a profoundly liminal and ambivalent figure, especially in the early stages of a quarrel leading to a witchcraft trial. Although she is a transgressive figure in many ways, part of her power to arouse fear in her neighbors comes from her ability to appeal to communally recognized norms. The witch's discourse is simultaneously orthodox and transgressive; her curses call upon God, not the devil, even as she pursues her "unnatural" ends. Similarly, the woman who accuses her, though frequently protecting her claim to be recognized by the community as a good wife, mother, and neighbor, may also in some respects be renegotiating the definitions of those roles and practicing a resistance strategy of her own.

In what follows I attempt to build on the work of Macfarlane, Thomas, and Larner by pursuing a trajectory suggested by the Shakespearean text.

III

If, as Christina Larner makes clear, the impetus for the prosecution of witches ultimately came "from above," it was nevertheless primarily villagers who selected the specific individuals to be indicted for the crime and who thus played a decisive role in determining the witch's gender. And among these villagers, witch-hunting was especially women's work. Quarrels that led to accusation were significantly, though not exclusively, quarrels between older and younger women which focused on matters of feeding and child care. As a quarrel progressed, the younger woman came to see in the older one the attributes of a malevolent mother, who used her powers of suckling, feeding, and nurturing to enlist demonic aid in bringing sickness and death to the households of other mothers. For the younger woman, witch-hunting may have been a means of protecting herself from this malevolent maternal power by "enclosing" it in the witch.

The trial records analyzed by Macfarlane and Thomas reveal a profile of the witch that is remarkably similar in case after case. An older woman has a falling-out with a neighbor—in more than half the cases another woman.[16] The older woman is usually poorer, and often the falling-out has occurred after she has gone to her neighbor with a request for food or some domestic item, or for access to land. The request is denied. The woman goes away, cursing her neighbor openly, or murmuring in a sinister fashion under her breath. Later, some misfortune happens to the neighbor or her family. A child falls sick, a wife or husband dies, cattle or sheep die, a freak storm destroys the crops, the granary catches fire, the milk goes sour, the butter won't turn. The neighbor recalls the cursing of the old woman and suspects the misfortune is the product of her witchcraft.

What happens next? There are several possibilities. The neighbor might appeal to one of the local "cunning folk" to identify the witch and to procure some sort of magical protection against the witch's *maleficium*—her harmful magic. The neighbor might turn to the church or to prayer. She might also try to appease the witch in some way. But with the passage of the witchcraft statutes in 1563 she has a new option: she may appeal to the local justice of the peace, informing against the suspected witch and leading the J.P. to open an inquiry. Other informants are interviewed, and a grand jury then determines whether indictments should be handed down and a trial held. If so, the accused witch is on her way to imprisonment, execution, or possibly acquittal. The trial itself functions as a kind of countermagic, with judges and jury taking over some aspects of the role of the cunning folk, as the witch's exposure and forced confession also dissolve her magical powers.

What did it take to convict and sentence to death someone accused of witchcraft? It was not normally possible to catch the witch in the act of practicing her art; instead, the force of a gathering accumulation of circumstantial evidence determined her fate. Reports of the accused's curses, followed in a timely fashion by misfortunes, were key items in the circumstantial evidence leading to indictment. But so also were several other factors, such as observations of small animals around her home or in her vicinity (cats, weasels, ferrets, frogs, toads, "imps") and accounts of visions or dreams in which the accused appeared to the victim or the victim's relatives. By the time a woman was brought to trial, she had already developed a reputation for troublesome behavior and hostility toward her neighbors, and her suspected acts of *maleficium* had often taken place over many years. Indictment was most likely when a number of neighbors came forward to testify about the same woman—when, in other words, she was "notoriously defamed" by the "better sort" in her village community. For the death penalty to apply, her magic had to be believed to have resulted in someone's death. Once a trial was under way, the accused woman's body was examined for the devil's mark or "teat"; any unusual fleshy protuberance, especially one in a "private place," would be taken as further confirmation of the charge of witchcraft. Finally, a confession (extracted under duress, but seldom torture) would help ensure the witch's fate.

Some of the connections between the witch and the mother will already be obvious. The beliefs instrumental in conviction associate the malignant power of the witch with the maternal body. The teat which marks her as a witch, for example, is also the means by which she acquires her demonic power; it is in effect a third nipple by which she feeds her familiars, or "imps," the demonic spirits who inhabit the bodies of small animals and who help her carry out her magic. The witch, moreover, is an older woman, usually postmenopausal; beliefs about the witch may also register anxiety about the changes age brings to the female body.[17] It is as if her body encodes maternal rejection of the human child: her womb no longer fertile, her breast no longer capable of producing milk, she nevertheless can feed a counterfamily of demonic imps. Her witchcraft is frequently directed against the children of her neighbors, and almost always against domestic activities associated with feeding, nurturance, or generation. When animals rather than people are targets of the witch's magic, cattle and the milk they produce are especially likely to be affected.

Village-level witchcraft beliefs encode a fantasy of the witch as mother—a mother with two aspects. She is a nurturing mother who feeds and cares for a brood of demonic imps, but a malevolent anti-mother to her neighbors and their children. Over and over again in the trial records, the accused women are addressed as "Mother"—Mother Grevell, Mother Turner, Mother Dutten, Mother Devell, Mother Stile—following general village convention.[18] These women continue to be associated with the social role of mother even after they have aged and their own children are grown. But they are mothers who refuse to act like mothers. What is at stake here, however, is not their refusal to mother their own children; in a sense they are doing that by nurturing demonic imps. Rather, they refuse to play the quasi-maternal role expected of them by the larger community.

The witch's symmetrical opposite in the village community is the "gossip," a word derived from *godparent* and still related to that more specialized role. (Fairy tales in which the witch is set against the fairy godmother have an obvious relevance here.) The "gossip" is the female neighbor called in to assist at childbirth and during the "lying-in" period, who acts as midwife and helps to care for her neighbor's children, who participates in an informal village network in which women offer one another aid and advice about child care, sickness, and other areas of domestic management. These women are mothers in several senses: they "mother" one another, they mirror one another as mothers, and they act as substitute mothers for one another's children. The aid and advice they offer often involves magic; midwifery, for example, includes a range of magical techniques for helping ensure the safety of mother and child during the difficult time of childbirth. The witch is the female neighbor who brings a malevolent magic into the cultural spaces where mother and child are most at risk, introducing suspicion and fear into a community's informal network of female neighbors.[19] She uses the maternal body to betray the maternal body.

Given the fragmentary and problematic nature of the trial records, it is difficult to reconstruct the series of events that made a particular woman a target of suspicion. It is clear, however, not only that many quarrels involved women but also that the informal networks of shared mothering involved competition and conflict as well as mutual support. For example, there is the 1581 case of Cicelly Celles, an Essex woman. In one informant's statement she is seen "chiding and railing" at another woman who was engaged to replace Cicely as a wet nurse for a neighbor's child. "Thou shalt lose more by the having of it than thou shalt have for the keeping of it," Cicely reportedly threatened the woman; within a month the woman's own four-year-old daughter was dead. According to another statement, Cicely was involved in an incident with a young mother preparing to take her new baby to church. Several women, including Cicely, gathered around. After the other gossips had cooed over the baby and complimented it, Cicely uttered a dark prediction: the child would die soon and the mother would never bear another. And indeed, a short time later, the child died. (The incident recalls the christening scene in "Sleeping Beauty.") The mother, however, refused to accuse Cicely of witchcraft, instead praying God to forgive Cicely if she had "dealt in any such sort." But the husband of the woman who replaced Cicely as wet nurse was not so forbearing. He came forward to accuse Cicely in the death of his young daughter, and it was on account of the death of this child that Cicely was indicted—along with her husband—for witchcraft. Her husband was acquitted; Cicely was convicted and sentenced to death.[20]

Thomas and Macfarlane read the psychology of witchcraft accusation in the light of a conflict between "neighborliness" and "individualism." The accusers' actions, as they see it, are largely shaped by the guilt they experience after denying their neighbors' request for help—an "individualistic" transgression of traditional codes of communal sharing. Guilt manifests itself in some of the dreams and visions experienced by the accusers and their families and in the apparently psychosomatic illnesses that sometimes befall victims; it manifests itself

especially in the accusers' habitual interpretation of subsequent misfortunes as retaliation for the injury to the neighbor refused aid.[21]
Thomas and Macfarlane cast the accusing neighbor in the role of "individualist," as opposed to the witch, who is the defender of older
norms of "neighborliness"—that is, of the norms in place before the
Protestant Reformation and the sixteenth-century Poor Laws. But in
the quarrels involving Cicely Celles, for example, it is difficult to see
what norm of neighborliness her opponents would have felt they were
violating. Rather it is Cicely herself who seems to have been out of
line.[22] One can be unneighborly by demanding too much as well as by
giving too little. Accusers do sometimes retrospectively come to view
their actions as lacking in charity. But in many quarrels the situation is
far more ambiguous.

Such cases suggest a more complex dynamic at work than Thomas
and Macfarlane's formulation allows for: violating the codes of neighborliness is unlikely to be the only cause of guilt. Modern psychology
and psychoanalytic theory would in any case suggest that the responses
underlying victims' illnesses, visions, and interpretations of misfortune
have roots in childhood.[23] Neighborliness is embedded in the child's
early experiences in a family context, where quarrels over sources of
nourishment and boundaries of identity first take place. Here the child
learns about sharing, hierarchy, and the regulation of envy from mothers and other female caretakers, and competes for access to the mother's body (especially as symbolized by the breast) among rivals.
Whatever guilt is incurred by denying a neighbor's request or violating
codes of neighborliness is likely to come with a history, largely unconscious, in which the mother is both the first victim and first persecutor
of the child's earliest attempts to control its environment.

Moreover, Renaissance family structure, gender norms, and popular
magical beliefs worked together to make it more likely that the maternal rather than the paternal body would arouse in both men and
women fears of a specifically *magical* persecution. When the child first
encounters the prohibitions of her mother or other female caretakers,
she is still very young and thinks magically, conflating angry wishes
with destructive acts. Inevitably ambivalent about the mother who nur-
tures but also eludes control and thwarts the will, the child may fear
that her hostile fantasies will actually destroy the mother—and that the
mother may retaliate in kind. By the time the father takes over the role
of prohibitor and is understood to be the ultimate power within the
family and the larger social world, the child is cognitively better developed, more able to test reality; transgression against paternal authority
may arouse fear of physical punishment (especially castration), but his
disapproval and anger is less likely to be experienced as magically dan-

gerous. Renaissance belief, moreover, reinforced the association of magic with the maternal body, constructing that body as especially unpredictable and difficult to control: woman was the "disorderly" sex, the site of a bewildering and often contradictory array of special dangers and powers, associated variously with her womb and its appetites, her milk and menstrual blood.

In a significant number of quarrels leading to witchcraft indictments, accusers experience symptoms of physical pain or illness shortly after the quarrels take place—what would be called today psychosomatic or hysterical symptoms. The injury to the witch uncannily reiterates itself in an injury to the accuser.[24] Accusers who fall ill in more or less direct consequence of a quarrel can be either male or female, but in either case such incidents are relatively rare. More commonly, illness or misfortune befalls some other member of the household with whom the accuser is associated: a spouse or child. In these cases retaliatory fears inform the accuser's mode of explanation rather than produce a hysterical symptom. Sickness and death are interpreted as unjust punishments, and the accuser feels persecuted. The punishment is out of proportion to the "crime" committed against the neighbor—but not, perhaps, to the unconscious fantasy that goes with it.

The accuser feels guilt and fears retaliation, I believe, not so much for violating the code of neighborliness as for injuring a body unconsciously associated with the mother of childhood. The accuser confronts in her neighbor a woman of her mother's generation. While she consciously expresses anger and perceives the older woman's request as too demanding or excessive, unconsciously she may feel that her refusal of the request injures a body with which she still feels partly fused. The misfortunes regularly attributed to the witch's malevolent magic involve the loss of things a child associates with the mother's body and believes she controls: milk, milk products, food, domestic space, babies, husbands. Having injured the source of milk, the accuser's own milk is threatened by a mother far more powerful than herself.

The witch's curse was believed to be carried out by her demonic "imps"—her children, who do her will in exchange for sucking her blood and other acts of nurturance. Imps appear with great frequency in informants' statements. They often seem to have a Janus-like aspect. On the one hand, they are extensions of the witch's malevolence, carrying illness to her victims, causing accidents, sometimes displaying hunger or nipping them. On the other hand, they make the witch herself a target of a good deal of oral greed, sucking blood not only from the "witch's tit" but from other parts of the body, leaving marks and causing the witch pain, and sometimes demanding to be fed milk, beer, or bread as well. Like children, the imps can get out of the witch's control: Elizabeth Bennet, for example, sent her imp to kill the animals of her neighbor, William Byett, but the spirit exceeded his instructions and "plagued Byett's wife to death."[25] If the imps enact the witch's destructive will, they also in a sense enact the child's rebellious resistance to the mother.

Sometimes, but by no means routinely, the witch is believed to employ wax images or doll-like figures to carry out her magic—that is, to use sorcery, like Mrs. Dewse. These images were called not only "puppets" (poppets) but also "child's babies" and "maumets" (mammets, a term for the breast-fed infant). Alice Hunt denied "having any puppets, spirits, or maumettes." Alice Manfield had an imp called "Puppet alias Mamet."[26] Employing a familiar, the witch is a mother who makes a sacrifice in order to acquire a magic power through her demonic "child." Employing image magic, the witch makes her enemy into a child, to be controlled and sacrificed.

Imps are sometimes actual animals—pets perhaps—kept by a witch or sighted in her vicinity; sometimes they are apparitions or fantasies. It is in the testimony of children, some of them children of the accused, that the demonic imps seem especially vivid. In one sense the imp is the child's "evil twin"; the child in fantasy disassociates itself from the sadistic or devouring oral impulses that threaten the mother with injury. In another sense the demonic imp is the rival child the mother appears to favor. It is difficult, of course, to tell from the statements what the child has really experienced. Has the child witnessed the mother with pets, or with creatures the mother actually treats as her familiars? Is the child reporting a fantasy or dream? Is the child merely saying what the examiner wants to hear? Some of the statements do seem believable as children's fearful fantasies of mothers they have come to distrust, and suggest a troubled family environment. Such is the case with the statements taken from Cicely Celles's two sons.[27] According to them, she fed and sheltered a rival set of demonic siblings, who threatened the sons in various ways. Henry, aged nine, described a spirit who came "one night about midnight" and took his younger brother John by "the left leg, and also by the little toe." The spirit, he said, resembled his sister, "but that it was all black." John, according to the statement,

> cried out and said, "Father, Father, come help me, there is a black thing hath me by the leg, as big as my sister": whereat his father said to his mother, "why thou whore, cannot you keep your imps from my children": whereat she presently called it away from her son, saying, "come away, come away," at which speech it did depart . . . . The next day he [Henry] told his mother he was so afraid of the thing that had his brother

by the leg that he sweat for fear, and that he could scarce get his shirt from his back: his mother answering "thou liest, thou liest, whoreson."

Henry also reported seeing his mother feed the imps "out of a black dish, each other day with milk," and carry them out to a hiding place in the roots of a crab tree near the house. One, "a black one, a he," was called Hercules or Jack, the other "a white one, a she," was Mercury, and they had "eyes like goose eyes." On the night a neighbor's maid reported a sudden but temporary illness, Henry said he heard his mother tell his father that she had sent Hercules to the maid, the father answering, "Ye are a trim fool."

Henry's story was corroborated by his brother John, though there are some discrepancies in their accounts. Taken together, the documents suggest a sadly conflict-ridden family, in which husband abuses wife, wife abuses children, and the children themselves fear further abuse from a set of rival "siblings." The cycle of conflict was undoubtedly intensified by the family's poverty, and the family is suggestively fractured along sex lines: the father protects his sons—"*my* children"—from the mother's "imps," who remind the sons of their sister. Does the mother neglect her sons while favoring a daughter as well as the alleged imps? Are the sons envious as well as afraid of the rival siblings, whom their mother feeds and sets against them? It is of course hard to draw any firm conclusions from such fragmentary evidence, but it is possible that the sons' destructive impulses toward other siblings and toward the mother who seemingly favors them are returning to haunt them in the form of fearful apparitions. These sons literally experience their mother as a witch—a witch who feeds and nourishes her brood of demonic imps while neglecting and tormenting her human children.

The revelation of the witch's teat was usually among the last pieces of evidence to be entered against the accused woman.[28] It is as if the full fantasy—of witch as malevolent mother feeding a brood of rival children— could be confronted only in the relative safety of the courtroom. Only then, in the presence of male authorities deemed to serve a power greater than that of the witch, and after a relative consensus about her danger to the community had been reached, could the ultimate source of conflict—the mother's breast—be confronted and allowed to become a target of aggression. That the witch's teat is an *extra* one seems significant here; it can be destroyed while leaving the "good" mother's body intact. The grotesque body of the witch could be punished and executed, leaving the community the maternal body in its "natural" and purified form. And since the trial was also a demonstration of the legal, paternal, and divinely sanctioned power of authority over the witch, the maternal bodies that remained—those of

the female accusers—had in effect found access to an orthodox magic
of the father's body far more powerful than the witch's own.

                                IV

   The villagers who accused women of witchcraft were intent on purging their community of a specific threat to specific individuals. The
prosecuting class, however, tended to be more interested in curing the
whole country; for them the witch was an abstraction, her punishment
sending a message far and wide. Elite texts about witchcraft appropriate aspects of village discourse about the witch but also rewrite it. A
case in point is the pamphlet containing the case of Cicely Celles, produced by one W. W., and composed almost wholly of "informations"
taken by the justice of the peace, Brian Darcy, for a series of witchcraft
trials in St. Osyth, Essex, during 1582. The documents are preceded by
a dedicatory epistle that provides something of a frame story.[29] Dedicated to the head of the ennobled branch of the Darcy family, distant
relation of Brian Darcy, it purports to show "what a pestilent people
witches are, and how unworthy to live in a Christian Commonwealth."
Punishing the witch with rigor, the author claims, is the most likely
means to "appease the wrath of God, to obtain his blessing, to terrifie
secreete offenders by open transgressors punishments, to withdraw
honest natures from the corruption of evil company, to diminish the
great multitude of wicked people, to increase the small number of virtuous persons, and to reforme all the detestable abuses, which the perverse witt and will of man doth dayly devise." Hanging, in fact, is too
good for the witch; the penalty that suits the ordinary felon and mur-
derer is hardly severe enough for the witch, who defies "the Lorde God
to his face." To do anything less than burn the witch is to eclipse the
"honour of God . . . and the glorye due to his inviolable name." The
witch here is not the antimother feeding demonic imps but the servant
of Satan who joins his "hellish liverie" and swears allegiance to him as
to a rebellious feudal lord. The dedicatory epistle is designed to foreground Justice Darcy's heroic efforts to preserve order through his rig-
orous prosecution of Satan's rebellious crew.
   Yet the documents that make up the rest of the pamphlet tell the
story of the antimother: the case of Cicely Celles is only one of a number of others in which accusations of witchcraft arise from quarrels
over sources of nourishment, milk, feeding, and child care, that record
attacks on the community's children and sightings of demonic imps. Inside the enemy of God and the rebel against the state there still lurks
the antimother: it is as if, despite the confident demonstration of dom-

inance and patriarchalism expressed in the dedicatory note, the male author still finds himself vulnerable to a threat associated with this earlier figure of authority. The witch as antimother who is also a rebel and enemy of God brings us back, of course, to the central tropes of Shakespeare's first tetralogy.

This pamphlet suggests that, for governing elites as well as for peasant women and men, fantasies of maternal persecution continued to organize discourse about the witch and may have been an important factor motivating the hunts, if only one among others. To varying degrees and with varying emphases, elite discourse about the witch was also concerned with promoting a new religious orthodoxy and maintaining political order and social hierarchy; the witch is a heretic, a class upstart, a traitor, and an unruly woman as well as a malevolent mother. As Christina Larner has argued, the witch-hunts were linked to the problems experienced by the post-Reformation state as it attempted to legitimize itself in an age of religious controversy. But for the prosecuting classes such problems may have been further complicated by the sixteenth-century reconfiguration of the honor code and its consequences for male identities, a reconfiguration in which Shakespeare's first tetralogy fully participates. The honor code was undergoing a shift away from late-feudal military values and an emphasis on kinship, lineage, and local ties toward a state-centered emphasis on administrative office, learning, and the arts. This values shift, I believe, required from the male of the prosecuting class a new involvement in his psychological inheritance from the mother. He had to integrate into his masculine identity more traits that carried cultural and intrapsychic associations with her; he could not wholly disassociate himself from a primary identification with the mother, as could the late-feudal male.

The witch trials, then, may have functioned as more than a satisfying demonstration of legitimacy by a state in religious and political crisis; they may also have provided a consoling ritual for males of the prosecuting class coping with feminization. Like the younger peasant women who became accusers of the witch, the state-centered, gentry-level male felt pressure to identify with, as well as differentiate himself from, the mother; he too might fear magical retaliation from a maternal body with which he felt unconsciously fused. If Shakespeare's first tetralogy is an especially powerful evocation of the disturbing connections between the witch and the mother, such connections were also made by some of his contemporaries. I close with one last example, from *A Dialogue Concerning Witches and Witchcraft*, a pamphlet written in the form of a dialogue by the Essex clergyman George Gifford in 1593, around the time the plays making up the first tetralogy were initially being performed on the London stage. In this text Samuel, one of the speakers in the dialogue, is asked why he thinks he is bewitched. He responds: "Trust me I cannot tell, but I feare me I have, for there be two or three in our towne which I like not, but especially an old woman, I have been as careful to please her as ever I was to please mine own mother, and to give her ever anon one thing or another, and yet me thinkes she frownes at me now and then." Samuel quite explicitly—and anxiously—experiences the old woman as a mother impossible to please, suspecting her of witchcraft merely for frowning at him. Assuming that she had a counterpart in real life, here was one old woman on her way to the gallows for little more than a bad mood.

NOTES

1. *Calendar of State Papers Domestic—Elizabeth*, vol. 2 (1581–90) p. 644; the documents are reprinted in W. H. Hart, "Observations on Some Documents Relating to Magic in the Reign of Queen Elizabeth," *Archaeologia: or, Miscellaneous Tracts Relating to Antiquity* 40 (1866), 395–96.

2. A brief account and list of documents associated with this case can be found in George Lyman Kittredge, *Witchcraft in Old and New England* (Cambridge: Harvard University Press, 1929), pp. 89, 419–20, n. 90.

3. C. L'Estrange Ewen, *Witch Hunting and Witch Trials* (London: Kegan Paul, Trench, Trubner, 1929), p. 17. The first witchcraft statute was passed in 1542, at the end of Henry VIII's reign, then repealed in 1547 under Edward VI. According to Ewen, only one case (which resulted in a pardon) has survived from this period; see pp. 11 and 13–18 for the texts of both the 1542 and 1563 statutes.

4. John R. Dasent, ed., *Acts of the Privy Council*, n.s., 25 vols. (London: Eyre and Spottiswoode, 1897), 16:388; 17:47–48; 19:111–112. In the documents the name Dewse is spelled a variety of ways, among them Dews, Dyos, Dios, Devyes, and Devies.

5. Two essays on Shakespeare are worth special mention: Janet Adelman, "'Born of Woman': Fantasies of Maternal Power in *Macbeth*," in *Cannibals, Witches, and Divorce: Estranging the Renaissance*, ed. Marjorie Garber (Baltimore: Johns Hopkins University Press, 1987), pp. 90–121, reprinted with revisions in Janet Adelman, *Suffocating Mothers: Fantasies of Maternal Origin in Shakespeare's Plays, "Hamlet" to "The Tempest"* (New York: Routledge, 1992); and Karen Newman, "Discovering Witches: Sorciographics," in *Fashioning Femininity and English Renaissance Drama* (Chicago: University of Chicago Press, 1991), pp. 51–70. My argument is especially indebted to Adelman's essay.

6. Some essays that take up this question include Alan Anderson and Raymond Gordon, "Witchcraft and the Status of Women—the Case of England," *British Journal of Sociology* 29 (June 1978), 171–84; and Clarke Garrett, "Women and Witches: Patterns of Analysis," *Signs: Journal of Women in Culture and Society* 3 (Winter 1977), 461–70. Both essays provoked subsequent commentary; see J. K. Swales and Hugh V. McClachlan, "Witchcraft and the Status of Women: A Comment," *British Journal of Sociology* 30 (September 1979), 349–57; Alan Anderson and Raymond Gordon, "The Uniqueness of English Witch-

craft: A Matter of Numbers?" *British Journal of Sociology* 30 (September 1979), 359–61; letters by Judith H. Balfe, Claudia Honegger, and Nelly Moia commenting on Clarke Garrett's essay, together with a reply by the author, appear in *Signs* 4 (Autumn 1978), 201–2, and *Signs* 4 (Summer 1979), 792–804.

Two books also provide lengthy treatments of the role of gender in the hunts as well as appraisals of current research. See G. R. Quaife, *Godly Zeal and Furious Rage: The Witch in Early Modern Europe* (London: Croom Helm, 1987); and Brian P. Levack, *The Witch-Hunt in Early Modern Europe* (London: Longman, 1987).

7. Alan Macfarlane, *Witchcraft in Tudor and Stuart England: A Regional and Comparative Study* (New York: Harper and Row, 1970); Keith Thomas, *Religion and the Decline of Magic* (New York: Scribner's, 1971), pp. 437–583; Christina Larner, *Enemies of God* (London: Chatto & Windus, 1981).

8. An important exception is John Demos, *Entertaining Satan: Witchcraft and the Culture of Early New England* (Oxford: Oxford University Press, 1983), esp. pp. 172–210. Although Demos's psychoanalytic assumptions are somewhat different from mine, his argument is in many respects similar to the one I offer here; I am indebted to it. In *The Devil in the Shape of a Woman: Witchcraft in Colonial New England* (New York: Norton, 1987), Carol F. Karlsen discusses motherhood in a more restricted sense; her major focus is on women and patterns of inheritance. It is perhaps significant that both of these exceptions come from studies of colonial American witchcraft, which has close affinities with English witchcraft. At the same time, because more complete records survive for many American cases, it is possible to reconstruct the relationships and family histories of participants in greater detail than in English cases. It may also be true that the role of mother is not as relevant to witch-hunting in continental Europe. There, witch-hunting was a far more virulent affair, and the social practices and psychological dynamics were significantly different from those informing the English hunts; accordingly, the profile of the typical witch was also different. Among other things, continental witch stereotypes emphasized sexual deviance.

9. *1 Henry VI* 3.3.44, 47. All quotations from Shakespeare's plays are from *The Riverside Shakespeare*, ed. G. Blakemore Evans et al. (Boston: Houghton Mifflin, 1974); subsequent citations appear in the text.

10. Larner, *Enemies of God*, p. 2.

11. Thomas, *Religion*, p. 568.

12. Macfarlane, *Witchcraft*, p. 161.

13. Thomas, *Religion*, p. 568; Macfarlane, *Witchcraft*, p. 160. Both men and women, of course, have mothers.

14. Larner addresses these issues most directly in "Witchcraft Past and Present," in *Witchcraft and Religion: The Politics of Popular Belief* (Oxford: Basil Blackwell, 1984), pp. 84–88; see esp. p. 86.

15. Some examples include Mary Daly, *Gyn/Ecology: The Meta-Ethics of Radical Feminism* (Boston: Beacon Press, 1978); Andrea Dworkin, *Woman Hating* (New York: E. P. Dutton, 1974), pp. 118–50; Robin Morgan, "The Network of the Imaginary Mother," in *Lady of the Beasts: Poems* (New York: Random House, 1970). WITCH was the acronym of a women's liberation group in the late 1960s, and the witch has continued to be a powerful symbol invoked by a wide range of feminist groups. See also Silvia Bovenschen, "The Contemporary Witch, the Historical Witch, and the Witch Myth: The Witch, Subject of the Appropriation of Nature and Object of the Domination of Nature," in *New*

German Critique 15 (Fall 1978), 83–119. Bovenschen describes, among other things, uses of the witch in European demonstrations by feminists; she celebrates the "anarchic" energies of the mythic impulse behind such uses while at the same time ridiculing the "rearguard" interest of "ivory tower" scholars, with their delusions of autonomy and their foot-dragging emphasis on historical accuracy. Her discussion, engaging as it is in its "bad girl" iconoclasm, reproduces the notion of an autonomous ivory tower sealed off from politics and masks the new possibilities that careful attention to historical texts can open up for feminists. But Bovenschen's point about the rearguard nature of scholars' work on witchcraft is well taken. The feminist texts I have listed are all products of the 1970s; although scholarly witchcraft studies have a long history, it was not, for the most part, until the 1980s that historians gave sustained attention to the question of gender in the witch-hunts. Larner's essay, "Witchcraft Past and Present," first appeared in 1981.

16. Macfarlane finds that as many women as men informed against witches in the 291 Essex cases he studied; about 55 percent of those who believed they had been bewitched were female (*Witchcraft*, pp. 160–61). It is possible that this figure is misleadingly low; in many cases the husband as "head of household" may have came forward to make statements on behalf of his wife, the initial or central quarrel being between her and another woman. Careful reading of the "informations" taken against the St. Osyth witches seems to bear out this observation: males testifying against a witch often are husbands of women who have quarreled with the witch or have been bewitched by her. See W. W., *A true and just Recorde, of the Information, Examination and Confession of all the Witches, taken at S. Oses in the countie of Essex: whereof some were executed, and other some entreated according to the determination of lawe* (1582; reprint Delmar, N.Y.: Scholars' Facsimiles and Reprints, 1981). In addition, George Gifford's *Dialogue Concerning Witches and Witchcraftes* (1593; reprint London: Shakespeare Association Facsimiles, 1931), makes it clear that Samuel, an accuser of witches who is one of the dialogue's main characters, is acting at the behest of his wife. It may be that many male accusers became involved in witchcraft cases in ways loosely parallel to the situation of males accused. The very small percentage of men charged with witchcraft often were the husbands or relatives of women who had already been accused of witchcraft; they suffered from guilt by association. In a similar way a quarrel between two women may have expanded to involve the males to whom they were attached.

17. Some historians have associated the behavior imputed to witches with menopause; see Quaife, *Godly Zeal*, p. 94. Reginald Scot makes a similar argument when he suggests that the fantasies of old women who think they are witches may be the result of menopause: such fantasies, "upon the stopping of their monethlie melancholike flux or issue of blood . . . must needs increase." This "weaknesse both of bodie and braine" makes them "the aptest persons to meete with such melancholike imaginations. . . . Their imaginations remaine, even when their senses are gone." Reginald Scot, *The Discoverie of Witchcraft* (1584; rpt. Carbondale: Southern Illinois University Press, 1964), pp. 65–66.

18. For some examples, see C. L'Estrange Ewen, *Witchcraft and Demonianism* (London: Heath Cranton, 1933), pp. 154, 158, 159. This highly useful book gives abstracts of depositions and confessions from a large number of English witch trials.

19. Michael Macdonald's study of the seventeenth-century physician Richard Napier provides some suggestive evidence. Napier's patients included hun-

dreds who suspected they had been bewitched. Macdonald's exploration of these cases led him to criticize Macfarlane's emphasis on quarrels over alms. He writes: "The [witchcraft] allegations Napier's clients made were occasioned by a wider range of social and personal obligations than almsgiving. The most interesting of these concerned the custom of inviting village women to assist at a childbirth. The agony of labor without anesthetic was no less intense for being familiar. . . . Nothing could make childbirth safer and easier, so contemporaries attended to reducing the fear it provoked. . . . When birth was at hand, village women were invited to attend. The importance contemporaries attached to these displays of feminine solidarity is plain. The law prevented midwives from delivering babies without other women present; women whose travails had been marred by strife were said to have consequently gone mad. Mary Aussoppe became anxious and utterly depressed after a disgruntled neighbor cursed her during her labor. The woman burst into the house, fell to her knees, and "prayed unto God that . . . the plague of God light upon her, and all the plagues in hell light upon her." Five of Napier's clients thought that women whom they had not invited to their deliveries had bewitched them: "Participation in this feminine rite was an essential duty and privilege of village women, and omitted neighbors had reason to be angry." Michael Macdonald, *Mystical Bedlam: Madness, Anxiety, and Healing in Seventeenth-Century England* (Cambridge: Cambridge University Press, 1981), pp. 108–9.

20. For abstracts of the documents connected to this case, see Ewen, *Witchcraft*, pp. 155, 162–63. See also W. W., *A true and iust Recorde*, C8–D4ff.

21. Macfarlane, *Witchcraft*, pp. 196–98; Thomas, *Religion*, 553–69.

22. In other cases quarrels begin when the witch is caught stealing wood; when she wants to buy wheat at too low a price; when she refuses to help heal a child whose illness she is believed to have caused.

23. A thoroughgoing psychoanalytic account of the role of childhood experience in the construction of witch-hunting lies outside the scope of this essay. But among psychoanalytic approaches the work of Melanie Klein and those who have built on her theories seems especially promising. Klein's central preoccupations seem highly relevant to the witch-hunts: she focuses, among other things, on persecutory anxiety and retaliatory fears as they arise within the early mother-child relationship. For an overview of her work, see Hanna Segal, *Introduction to the Work of Melanie Klein* (London: Hogarth Press, 1973), and R. D. Hinshelwood, *A Dictionary of Kleinian Thought* (London: Free Association Books, 1991); for an appraisal of her work by a feminist psychoanalyst as well as a selection of significant writings, see *The Selected Melanie Klein*, ed. Juliet Mitchell (New York: Free Press, 1987); for one attempt to adapt Klein's thought for social theory, see C. Fred Alford, *Melanie Klein and Critical Social Theory* (New Haven: Yale University Press, 1989). Of course, Klein's theories cannot be applied to the witch-hunts without also taking into account the historically specific aspects of early modern subject formation and family life.

24. Margery Stanton, for example, indicted as a witch, was blamed for the illnesses that followed her quarrels with numerous neighbors. Thomas Prat, after some angry words, "raced her face with a needle. 'What,' quoth she, 'have you a flea there?" The next night he was "grievously tormented in his limbs" (the limbs, presumably, with which he scratched her). In another incident, she was denied milk by the wife of Robert Cornell and defecated outside the door of the house in departing, presumably as a gesture of contempt. The next day the wife was "taken sick with a great swelling." See Ewen, *Witchcraft*, pp. 151–52.

25. Ewen, *Witchcraft*, pp. 144, 145, 149, 157–58, 159, 160, 167.

26. Ibid., pp. 158, 159. Ewen discusses "puppets" in his introduction (p. 79).

27. Their statements, from which the quotations in this discussion are taken, may be found in W. W., *A true and just Recorde*, pp. D–D2.

28. According to Ewen, the belief in the witch's teat was a peculiarly English variation on the notion of the devil's mark, the sign of the witch's servitude to the devil, rather like the liveries worn by servants identifying them with their feudal masters. The belief in the witch's teat, moreover, did not become widespread in England until the mid-sixteenth century—in other words, around the time witch-hunting began in earnest. See Ewen, *Witchcraft*, pp. 63, 73–74.

29. W. W., *A true and just Recorde*, pp. A3–6.

6. Observations on English Bodies: Licensing Maternity in Shakespeare's Late Plays

Richard Wilson

I

Shakespeare's son-in-law John Hall was a busy man. Commuting between Acton and Stratford and maintaining a medical practice throughout the Midlands, he left notes on patients that are models of bedside briskness and efficiency, a rapid, diagnostic glance turned impassively on his own body. He suffered from hemorrhoids, aggravated by riding "daily to several places to Patients," but applied leeches to them and a paste of "Emollient Herbs." Emetics, purges, bleedings, suppositories: Hall's prescriptions were the last word in seventeenth-century humoral therapy. He caught "a burning Fever" that "killed almost all it did infect," but though "much maciated and weakened, so I could not move myself in Bed without help," cured it by massive infusions of rhubarb, quaffed until "the disease was cast out by Urine which flowed very much for four days." Vitamin C was evidently also the secret of Hall's great panacea, his Scorbutic Beer, concocted from watercress and herbs rich in ascorbic acid, which he sugared and spiced as a remedy for scurvy. Pride of place in his collection of "Cures Historical and Empirical experienced on Eminent Persons" was given to his treatment of the "pious, beautiful, chaste" Countess of Northampton at Ludlow in March 1622, when gallons of his beer cured her ladyship of fainting and "Scorbutic ulcerations, beyond the expectation of her Friends." A century before lime juice was rationed to sailors, Hall's Beer was "thought so strange," his editors admitted, "that it was cast as a reproach upon him by those most famous in the profession"; but he "had the happiness to lead the way to that practice generally used by the most knowing."[1] Thus, if his theories were a last gasp of magic, his practice was the first glimpse of medicine, and Dr. Hall entered the pantheon of the Great Instauration: a country physician who stumbled on the truth along the lonely road from superstition to science.

His own father had bequeathed Hall his "books of physicks" but had left "all his books on alchemy, astronomy and astrology" to a servant, since John would "have nothing to do with these things."[2] The graduate of Queen's College, Cambridge, was selective about his intellectual inheritance, and grew to be a zealous Puritan whose motto was "Health is from the Lord." But if health came, as he wrote in his own file, "without any Art or Counsel of Man," one still had to guard its mystery, and his casebook was intended, according to its preface, "not to be published til his decease, when men more willingly part with what they have." He had, in fact, ordered his papers to be burned, but his wife, Susanna, flouted his will and in 1644 sold his notebooks to raise cash, pretending she did not recognize his handwriting. By a deliberate misreading, therefore, his text was preserved, and posterity received the prescription he was certain would save his own life: "a Pigeon cut open alive, and applied to my feet, to draw down the Vapours." If the record is believed, this was a rare failure, since his cases typically conclude that the patient was "delivered from all Symptoms." To modern minds Hall's *Select Observations on English Bodies* are a confection of proverbial lore and threadbare jargon, as plausible as the pills its author compounded from spiders' webs, excrement, and the windpipes of cockerels. The seventeenth century, which thought fruit juice "strange," had no qualms about such medications; but what interests us is that Hall's text convinced his editors that his clinical gaze revealed the secrets of the body at the patient's bedside. Hall's *Observations* were published in 1657; Foucault traces the origins of the clinic to the founding of the first teaching hospital in 1658. Book and institution mark that critical reversal in the organization of knowledge whereby experience supplanted theory; *seeing,* in Foucault's account, punctured the time-worn codes of *saying;* and, in the boast of Hall's editors, "Observation" became "the Touchstone of what is not good and what is Current in Physik."

Neutral, intent, self-effacing, a modern practitioner glides through Hall's Renaissance surgery, and what impresses his editors is not the exoticism of his pharmacopoeia but the cold eye with which he observes each body. Thus, "Mrs. Wincol, afflicted with a falling out of the fundament, was cured as follows: Camomile and Sack [were] infused on hot coals. Then with linen cloths the Anus was fomented as hot as could be endured. After the Fundament was put up with one's finger, a Spunge dipt in the said Decoction was applied, on which she sate. Note: the Flowers of Camomile are much better." As Foucault comments, "In the clinician's catalogue, the purity of the gaze is bound up with a silence that enables him to listen. The prolix systems must be interrupted and the suggestions of the imagination reduced. The gaze will have access to the truth of things if it rests on them in silence. The clinical gaze has a paradoxical ability to *hear as soon as it perceives a spectacle.*"[3] This was the mentality of the Paracelsians, who rejected the authorities in favor of experience, and Hall was at one with them in treating Shakespeare's daughter Susanna with an enema of carnations when she was "miserably tormented with the cholic. This injected gave her two stools, yet the Pain continued, being but little mitigated." Confounded in his theory, the doctor "therefore appointed to inject a Pint of Sack made hot. This brought forth a great deal of Wind, and freed her from all Pain." Thus, "Mrs. Hall of Stratford, my Wife, was cured"; and the disinterest of the observation is the condition of its truth. This was what made Hall's notes so valuable, according to Dr. John Bird's "Testimony" to the first edition: their pretense of banishing all language anterior to observation; so unlike "the learned Practitioners whose Works fall short in performing the cures they promise [because] they deliver up as their own what they took from other Men upon Trust, through how many hands we know not; likewise giving us as approved, things that had no other ground than their Imaginations."[4]

The novelty of Hall's case notes was not lost on his contemporaries. In fact, the concept of a medical history was an epistemological watershed in Shakespearean England, and is usually dated to 1611 and the arrival in London of the French physician Theodore de Mayerne, whose published notes became the model for English practitioners. Francis Bacon was one of the first to recognize the role of such records in the scientific movement, bemoaning in *The Advancement of Learning* (1605) that "much iteration but small addition" characterized current medicine, a failing attributable to "the discontinuance of the ancient and serious diligence of Hippocrates, which used to set down a narrative of the special cases of his patients, and how they proceeded, and how they were judged by recovery."[5] Hall's notes, which begin in 1616, are an answer to Bacon's dream of a classical renaissance, since their will to truth derives wholly, as Dr. Bird discerned, from their assumption of a privileged immediacy with nature. But what was truth in 1616 must have seemed faded even by 1657, and these wide-eyed transcriptions can now be read as instances of the myth of original presence which impels the Cartesian drive for certainty. In Hall's casebook writing has become what Socrates imagines it to be in the *Phaedrus*, a mere supplement to the spontaneous language of the body, which speaks imploringly through its symptoms and excretions of a truth prior to the administration of the *pharmakon*. While the therapeutic text thus effaces itself, the body of the patient is textualized as a narrative full of meaning that leads toward the happy closure of a fairy tale, with the recovery of that prime of health which originates in God. In Hall's pharmacy the primal truth of life is restored by the purging of the contingent falsehood of disease, and the folkloric formula that the patient lived happily ever after elides "the absolute invisibility of the origin of the visible, the good/sun/father, the unattainment of presence or beingness," which, as Derrida reminds us, is the *aporia* of all such phallogocentric stories.[6]

In the theater of John Hall's infirmary bodies disclosed the secret of their symptoms to his peremptory eye. Thus, "Wife was troubled with Scurvy, Pain of the Loins, Melancholy, difficulty of Breathing, Laziness, the Mother, binding of the Belly, and torment there. February 9 1630." An enema brought no relief: "She could not lie in her Bed, insomuch as when any helped her she cried out miserably. For which I used this Ointment: Oil of Almonds, Dil and Roses. After annointing she was quiet all night, yet in the morning was troubled with Wind." Comprehensive treatment was required, consisting of pills of "Gillyflowers, Bugloss and Damask-Roses," a "long Suppository" of honey and cumin, and Hall's Beer fortified with wine boiled "for eight days stirring twice a day. Dose is three spoonfuls, which may be increased if there be need. And by these was she cured." To contemporary readers it was their show of disinterestedness that made these notes "equal to the best published."[7] Nobody else had been scrutinized, if Dr. Bird is to be believed, with the cool regard Hall fixed on patients, and no other case had been recorded in as much detail as that which he wrote for "Elizabeth Hall, my only Daughter," in her sixteenth year. She suffered neuralgia, which Hall treated in January 1624 with purges and "Opthalmick Water, dropping two or three drops into her eye." Then, on April 22, she "took cold" traveling from London "and fell into distemper on the contrary side of her Face, before it was on the left side, now on the right." Resourcefully, Hall supplemented purges and eyedrops by massaging spices into his daughter's neck and squeezing oil up her nose: "She ate Nutmegs often. And thus she was restored." No emergency flustered Dr. Hall, as he showed that May, when Elizabeth "was afflicted with an Erratick Fever: sometimes she was hot, sometimes cold, all in the space of half an hour, and thus she was vexed oft in a day." Her father purged her with his beer and rubbed her spine with liniment. "An hour after, all the Symptoms remitted. Thus was she delivered from Death and Deadly Disease, and was well for many years."[8]

John Hall was a master of all "the signs of death," which his editor explained were so "uncertain: because God Almighty often pardons whom we give over to death, and takes away whom we acquit."[9] From the Shakespearean period, this testimonial confirms, medical science was convening around the spectacle of the body stricken in disease or death, as the anatomy theater became the locus of a knowledge signified not by the invisibility of health but in the "white visibility of the dead." By a "strange misconstruction," Foucault remarks, "that which hides and envelops" knowledge for early modern medicine, "a curtain of night over truth, is, paradoxically, life. . . . However, this projection of illness onto the plane of visibility gives medical science an opaque base beyond which it can no longer go. That which is not within the gaze falls outside the domain of what can be known."[10] Thus, science came to be defined by that which could *not* be seen. Anatomists such as Nicolaas Tulp, depicted by Rembrandt expounding the lesson of the cadaver, refused to use the early microscopes, on the grounds that "when one looks into darkness everyone sees in their own way";[11] and if such a science could see only last things and signs of death, its blindness was complete in the one recess that defied its gaze, the place of birth. An intricate knowledge of the dead was counterpart to an obtuseness about birth on the part of a profession still gripped by the Galenic theory that a woman was an inverted man, with ovaries, uterus, and vagina for testicles, scrotum, and penis. It was this androcentric anatomy which accounts for the perpetuation of the lore that two veins ran from the womb to the breasts to turn blood into milk; that the sex of an infant was determined by the testicle from which seed came; that a mother's imagination imprinted the fetus with characteristics; that the embryo sucked menstrual blood; and that the child bit its way out of the womb in hunger.[12] When the good doctor went on his rounds, then, the birth place was literally his blind spot.

In former times, writes Foucault, doctors communicated with the mystery of life "by means of the great myth of immortality. Now these men who watched over patients' lives communicated with their death, in the rigour of the gaze."[13] When healing came to depend on the pathologist's capacity to "divest / And strip the creature naked, till he find / The callow principles within their nest,"[14] obstetrics could advance, the author of the *Observations in Midwifery*, Percival Willughby complained, only in countries such as Holland, where "they have privileges we cannot obtain. They open dead bodies without mutterings of their friends. Should one of us desire such a thing, an odium of inhumane cruelty would be upon us from the vulgar."[15] Willughby based his obstetrics on those of the "Father of British Midwifery," William Harvey, but for want of executed pregnant mothers, even the discoverer of the circulation of the blood was thwarted in his craving to cut open a woman's body to probe for life's origin. Though he possessed some fetal bones and a pickled embryo, Harvey spent his career, from his first anatomy lecture on April 16, 1616, dissecting animals and breaking eggs in a manic search to "determine what the cause of the egg is," eventually deducing that if it was not demonstrable that "the cock were the prime efficient" of the chick, semen must fertilize by "celestial influence," like the sun. Male science demanded a male prime mover, and protested that it was kept from sight of this "vital principle" by being deprived of inseminated corpses. Despite access to the female body through every orifice, science could not see inside to instantiate its presence. In fact, the hunt for spermatozoa was doomed without a miscroscope, but Harvey persisted in believing he would catch an "image of the omnipotent Creator" in egg yolks or the wombs of deer, where "I have still thought much more remained behind, hidden by the dusky night of nature, uninterrogated."[16] Thus the great adventure of science was posited as the release of an original male power from the abyss of female darkness.

Dreaming of its primacy, the patriarchal text asserts its truth against the benighted opacity of the female body. Conspicuously absent from the circle of neighbors and nurses gathered around the childbed, male science viewed birth as an archaic mystery locked within "a dark chamber," as Willughby wrote, "with glimmering candlelight behind the woman and five or six women assisting."[17] Although Thomas Raynald's midwives' manual *The Birth of Mankind* had been in print since 1545, physicians still objected that it was offensive that this woman's world could be read about by "every boy and knave as openly as the tales of Robin Hood";[18] and when Nicholas Culpepper published his *Directory of Midwives* in 1651, it was scorned by "Gentlemen and Scholars" as "truly *Culpaper:* paper fit to wipe one's breech with." Even Culpepper was disgusted that conception occurred "between the places ordained to Cast out Excrements, the very sinks of the body";[19] and the biblical taboo about the "defilement" of birth ensured that no English book on midwifery appeared in the century between these publications. So, when Harvey's contemporary John Hall attended the childbed, it was only in emergencies caused, by his account, by negligent midwives, since birth was not his business. When Mrs. Hopper, aged twenty-four, lapsed into a coma because "the Afterbirth was retained, whence a dire stink ascended to the Brain so there was great danger of death," Hall strapped a hot poultice "to the belly" and "delivered her in twenty four hours."[20] Or when Mrs. Lewes took cold after birth and "fell into an ague, with torment of the Belly," an enema of milk and a steaming poultice ensured that "she was helped suddenly."[21] Likewise, "Mrs. Finnes, being delivered of her third child," suffered a fever when her midwife fed her cold chicken, and "fell into an Hydroptick swelling. I was sent for, and perceived it to be a Scorbutic Dropsy. She implored for my help, being in a desperate condition." Hall pumped an enema of his Scorbutic Beer into her, while "she had a Restorative framed of Snails and Earthworms. And so she was returned to her former health."[22]

The Harveian surgical regime exercises jurisdiction over death but has no power over generation. To witness a birth, indeed, Willughby confessed he had "crept into the chamber on my hands and knees, and returned, so that I was not perceived by the lady."[23] Historically, therefore, the childbed would become the threshold of male science, where a tense struggle was to place between doctor and midwife for authority over delivery. What was at stake in this contest was control of fertility, but before women's bodies could be situated in the operating theater, their subjection to medical knowledge had to be secured in the light of the new secular mystery. Carried out of the dim candlelight of vulgar error and superstition, women would become visible in the sunlit positivity of normality and health, which was nothing other than the brightness of "great creating Nature."[24] As Willughby declared, it was better for birth to be left to "the invisible midwife Dame Nature," than forced by "the officiousness of conceited midwives, whom I would I could bring to observe Nature's ways, how she ripeneth all vegetables and produceth all creatures, with greater ease and speed than art can do, which is but Nature's servant."[25] In the seventeenth century a benign Nature was constructed, then, in specific institutional contexts, at the point described by Foucault, where case studies were first collected and the observations of disease abstracted into an ideal of health. This is the site of the birth of the clinic, "that borderline but paramount area" where medicine commences "to dictate the standards of physical and moral relations of the individual" in the interests of "the order of the nation and the fertility of its people."[26] And if Hall's casebook helped to organize the new clinical regime, its foundations were also being laid at this time in the texts of his father-in-law, where in another narrative of wives and daughters the female body was observed behind a mask of comparable impersonality and regulated according to the same idea of a husbanded and licensed Mother Nature.

II

Louis Montrose has reminded us how often Shakespearean drama frets over "the physical link between a particular man and child. . . . whether to validate paternity or call it in question." Aggravating this anxiety, he discerns, is that "what we call the facts of life have been established as *facts* only recently. That seminal and menstrual fluids are related to generation, that people have both a father and a mother, are hardly novel notions, but in Shakespeare's age they remained *merely* notions. Although maternity was apparent, paternity was a cultural construct for which ocular proof was unattainable." So if, as Lancelot Gobbo warns, "it is a wise father that knows his own child" in Shakespearean culture (*The Merchant of Venice* 2.2.76–77), patriarchy idealized phallic power as a mystical presence, with semen as a prime "efficient beginning of the child," its "form or soul," and the "corrupt, undigested blood" of the mother its mere "material cause."[27] Tellingly, Shakespeare found a paradigm for this mastery in the proprietorial rights and productive relations of his own industry. Theseus puts it crudely when he tells Hermia her father is a god "to whom you are but as a form in wax / By him imprinted" (*A Midsummer Night's Dream* 1.1.49–50); but the *semantic* metaphor, with its metaphysical craving for an originary truth, prior to the corruption of the *corpus*, recurs in the last plays as punningly. When Leontes assures Florizel, "Your mother was most true to wedlock, Prince, / For she did print your royal father off, / Conceiving you" (*The Winter's Tale*, 5.1.124–26), this is because royalties have been exacted on the text a father claims as "a copy out of mine" (1.2.122). Authorship is protected in these plays, despite the dread of cuckoldry that convulses a father when he scrutinizes his "offprints" to decide whether "we are. . . as alike as eggs" (1.2.129–36), by securing copyright as strictly in human as in textual reproduction. Signifying only absence of certainty, the Shakespearean phallus thus figures as transcendentally as Lacan's.

John Hall arrived in Stratford in 1600, it is thought from Montpellier, the center of humanist surgery.[28] His training may inform the secularization of healing that occurs in the Jacobean Shakespeare, where "the powerful grace that lies / In plants, herbs, stones, and their true qualities" (*Romeo and Juliet* 2.3.11–12), which had been a natural magic for religious or demonic figures such as Friar Laurence and Puck, is a resource of practitioners such as the doctors in *Macbeth*, *King Lear*, and *Cymbeline*. But although their administration of "baleful weeds and precious-juiced flowers" is therapeutic, the prognostic problem they face remains the one that thwarted the Friar when he prescribed the drug that cast Juliet into the underworld, which is how to calculate the *pharmakon* when "within the infant rind of this weak flower / Poison hath residence, and medicine power". If "the earth that's nature's mother is her tomb: / What is her burying grave, that is her womb" (*Romeo and Juliet* 2.3.4–20)? The cavern of the female body is never penetrated by the obstetrician, who must accept, with Lady Macbeth's doctor, that "more she needs the divine than the physician" (*Macbeth*

5.1.71), or that to "cleanse the stuff'd bosom of that perilous stuff /
Which weighs upon the heart," the patient must minister to herself
(5.3.45–46). It is this *aporia* in male thought that is figured in the tragi-
comic bed trick, and if one solution is essayed in *Measure for Measure*,
where the Duke's superintendence of Mariana's conception allegorizes
a despotic coercion, the other is offered in *All's Well That Ends Well*,
where Helena's management of her own pregnancy gives surety that
what can never be witnessed by men is legitimate. The French setting
and Helena's physician father, Gerard de Narbon, may defer to Hall's
experience, but the importance of this Shakespearean play, then, is
that it is the first in which medicine, previously the mumbo jumbo of
a Dr. Caius or Pinch, can claim a positivity to ensure that "all's well,"
and in the hands of the most suspect of healers, the wise woman or female empiric.

"I say we must not / So stain our judgement," the King of France tells
Helena, "to prostitute our past-cure malady / To empirics" (2.1.119–
21). His suspicion of folk healing was shared by the medical establish-
ments of London and Paris, whose view of popular remedies was being
shaped, as Natalie Zemon Davis has shown, by authorities such as Lau-
rent Joubert, chancellor of the Montepellier medical faculty, and in
1578 the first collector of "Vulgar Errors." For Joubert and his imita-
tors, such as Sir Thomas Browne or James Primerose, author of *The
Errors of the People in Physick* (1651), "popular culture was shot through
with ignorance, and the village goodwives and midwives—practiced
yet illiterate, working only with memorized recipes—were its perfect
expression."[29] What made the sage women of the Languedoc or West
Country so vexing to the professionals, however, was not their error but
their accuracy, for as the jurist opined in judgment of a suit brought by
the Paris faculty against a countrywoman in 1575, "How many savants
have been outdone by a simple peasant woman, who with a single herb
has found the remedy for an illness despaired of by physicians."[30] A
deep rift ran through organized medicine, therefore, when its claim to a
monopoly of knowledge was exposed by the "empirics and old women"
whom Bacon admitted were "more happy many times in their cures,"
and whose consultation Hobbes rated more highly than that of "the
learnedst but inexperienced physician."[31] Though the Royal College of
Physicians hounded them, Paracelsians were willing to learn from
herbalists and wise women, whose influential champions included
Archbishop Abbot and James I. And since the orthodox doctors were
unable, as Robert Burton complained, to "cure many diseases at all, as
epilepsy, stone, gout: a common ague stumbles them all," their will to
truth was vulnerable to such competition. As Keith Thomas reveals, in

an age of "helplessness in the face of disease," the fable of the healing
of the "fisher king," which Shakespeare announced with the title of
All's Well That Ends Well, could not have been more fundamental.[32]

"If the world knew of the ignorance of the physicians," declared
John Aubrey, "the people would throw stones at 'em as they walked in
the streets."[33] It is the irreverence toward the truth claims of medical
science which is the occasion of Shakespeare's comedy, where the "most
learned doctors. . . and / The congregated college have concluded /
That labouring art can never ransom nature / From her inaidable estate" (2.1.115–18). Here, then, the *senex* wears the pantaloon and
academic gown "of all the learned and authentic Fellows" of the chartered institutions, "both of Galen and Paracelsus" (2.3.11–12), and is
challenged by an equally topical lobby of hitherto unlicensed practitioners. The sorority of widow, daughter, and pregnant wife which petitions the Crown in the final scene of this play is one that regroups
throughout the late plays, opposing a discredited patriarchy and be-
guiling "the truer office" of authority's eyes, as the King says (5.3.299),
with the blinding conundrum of sexual reproduction. Until the partu-
rient mother is acknowledged by her husband, she riddles, " 'Tis but
the shadow of a wife you see" (5.3.301); but the puzzle around which
this tragicomedy revolves, tantalizing the father—"Dead though she be
she feels her young one kick . . . one that's dead is quick" (5.3.296–
97)—is a mystery defying masculine enlightenment. Helena suggestively calls her sovereignty over the quick and the dead "a triple eye" to
be stored "safer than mine own two" (2.1.107–7); and Lafeu concurs
that her sexuality is prior to either sight or writing:

> I have seen a medicine
> That's able to breathe life into a stone . . .
> whose simple touch
> Is powerful to araise King Pippen, nay,
> To give Charlemain a pen in's hand
> And write to her a love-line.
>   (2.1.71–77)

For a science based on the phenomenological desire to speak directly to
a world flooded in natural light, the ambivalence of phallogocentrism
is here exquisite; for how can men lay claim to an immediacy prior to
the act of writing when it is the female body of which they write, and
that is their own biological origin? "They say miracles are past; and we
have our philosophical persons to make modern and familiar, things
supernatural and causeless. Hence is it that we make trifles of terrors,
ensconcing ourselves into seeming knowledge when we should submit
ourselves to an unknown fear" (2.3.1–6).

The Shakespearean text knows what Nietzsche and Derrida will intuit, that "our philosophical persons" fear "truth is a woman who has reasons for not letting us see her reasons [since] her name is *Baubo* [the female genitals]."[34] Patriarchy is emasculated by the female enigma in these plays, as Lafeu reports of Helena: "I have spoke / With one that in her sex, her years, profession, / Wisdom and constancy, hath amaz'd me more / Than I dare blame my weakness" (2.1.81–84). It was male futility before the "miracles" of life and death that accounted for the association of midwifery with witchcraft, and what Shakespeare stages in the collusion of patient wives and wise matrons in these comedies is the nightmare that haunted the witch-finders—that of maternal control of generation. The jurist Jean Bodin recorded as fact in 1581 that witches worked as midwives, and superstitions concerning the disposal of the afterbirth and burial of stillborn fetuses reflected a suspicion that midwives were the mistresses of infanticide and abortion.[35] The "weird sisters" of *Macbeth*, who concoct their brew from "finger of birth-strangled babe / Ditch-delivered by a drab" (4.1.30–31), are figments of this collective fantasy that unsupervised women might pervert the powers of reproduction by seizing fetal organs for black masses. One scene recurs throughout the last plays, therefore, as an organizing tableau. The presentation of pregnant mother or newborn infant by midwife to father paradoxically confronts paternity at its most powerful moment with its deepest fear of impotence. Bertram's bafflement at Helena's pregnancy will be repeated with mounting suspicion in these dramas until the perplexity finally enrages: "Out! / A mankind witch! Hence with her, out o'door: / A most intelligencing bawd!" (*The Winter's Tale*, 2.3.67–69). Leontes' fury at Paulina, as he spurns the "bastard" daughter born to Hermione, taps the paranoia of Jacobean patriarchy, and he vomits its litany of misogynistic stereotypes in his conflation of witch, scold, and unruly woman. The midwife is "dame Partlet," who has "unroosted" her husband, a "crone . . . A callat of boundless tongue," and a "gross hag!" (2.3.74–76; 90–91; 107). "I'll ha' thee burnt" he warns (2.3.114); and the threat, with its echo of actual prosecutions for delivering "some changeling" in exchange for "fairy gold" (3.3.117–21),[36] underscores the social urgency of the theme of illegitimacy at the climax of the English witch craze.

It was the invisibility of the reproductive matrix that had excited the misogyny of *King Lear*, where the patriarch's urge to "anatomize" a woman's body to see what breeds" within (3.6.74), and repulsion from the "darkness" of the "sulphurous pit" (4.6.125–27), was provoked by the male suspicion that "The dark and vicious place" where a father begot a bastard must "cost him his eyes" (5.3.171–72). In tragedy's story of the night, the terror of blindness as a form of castration

evinces a psychotic unease with the indeterminacy of the female body.
Janet Adelman has described how this nightmare of feminine power is
embodied by the figures of Lady Macbeth and the witches, in a play
that resolves the inscrutable problem of the mother "through a ruth-
less excision of all female presence, its own satisfaction of the witches'
prophecy."[37] In *Macbeth*, the cesarean surgery that tears the victor from
the womb renders him invulnerable, as the apparition of the "bloody
child" portends (4.1.77), since it identifies him as "he, / That was not
born of woman" (5.7, 2–3). Because "Macduff was from his mother's
womb / Untimely ripp'd" (5.8.15–16), this male child is violently exempted from the riddling bodies and language of the "juggling fiends"
(5.8.18), as, cutting the umbilical knot, he frees the royal line from
emasculating equivocation. Shakespeare earlier exploited Sir Thomas
More's testimony that Richard III was hurried into the world "feet
first" by cesarean section (*Richard III* 1.1.20–21), and he would have
known that Henry VIII had commanded the same Neronian operation
on Jane Seymour, "having the womb cut before she was dead, so the
child ready to be born might be taken out." This was the fatal delivery
that led Edward VI to be styled "he that was never born," and the dynasty to adopt its icon of the self-creating Phoenix. The flaming bird
was an appropriate image for delivery of a man "not of woman born,"
since the name of the father was never more autonomous than in the
incision carved into a mother's flesh, which in premodern conditions
meant certain death from infection.[38] Cesarean section recurs in the
tragedies and histories, then, as a final solution to the female puzzle
and fulfilment of the Lex Caesare, the Roman inheritance law that decreed the womb to be a place where the infant was merely "imprisoned," and from which, and by whatever means, an heir was justly
"enfranchised" into "light" (*Titus Andronicus* 4.2.124–25).

   "The midwife and the nurse well made way," Aaron schemes when
inserting a changeling into the royal bed. "Then let the ladies tattle
what they please"; and the fate of the "long-tongu'd babbling gossip,"
stabbed like "a pig prepared to the spit" for "caterwauling" his secret,
may stand for the violent remedies offered in the tragedies to stabilize
masculine truth and inheritance (*Titus Andronicus* 4.2.57; 146–51).
What marks the last plays as modern artifacts, however, is a shift from
corporeal oppression to cultural repression, which is what makes them,
as Terry Eagleton notes, truly *ideological:* "These comedies make much
of the child-father relationship as a paradigm of possession. My children are mine by derivation from Nature, yet they are also my inalien-
able products, stamped with my life and labour. . . . Private property is
thus naturalized."[39] But the question this analysis begs is the one that
these plays seek to answer: if patriarchy is natural, what is the status of

Mother Nature? They do so by a strategy that is a counterpart of John Hall's pharmacopoeia, when they surrender power over women's bodies in exchange for possession of their language. From the mid-sixteenth century, midwives and empirics were, in fact, brought under tight surveillance throughout western Europe, and an English act of 1553 instituted licensing by bishops. Powerless to intrude into the women's chamber, the legislators wrestled to dictate its discourse; the midwife's oath therefore swore her to "use no profane words . . . nor any kind of sorcery, invocations, or prayers," and to conduct baptism only according to the sacrament that made Eve the cause of woe. If Marianism, with its fertility charms and holy girdles, was a target of these prohibitions, the aim was above all to ensure paternity, as the oath made clear, when it bound a midwife not to "permit or suffer that women being in labour shall name any other to be the father of a child, than only he who is the true and right father."[40] It was an interdiction that would remain on the statute book until 1786, and provide a discursive foundation for the licensing of maternity in Shakespearean drama.

III

Liberal criticism has long identified an accommodation with motherhood in the romances, but as Peter Erikson has pointed out, "Men do not, through a simple identification, adopt the values of nurturance they learn from women" by this maneuver; "rather, men appropriate these values and translate them into patriarchal institutions that place limits on women, albeit in a harmonious atmosphere."[41] So, though Leontes assures Paulina, "Thou canst not speak too much, I have deserv'd / All tongues to talk their bitt'rest" (The Winter's Tale 3.2.215–16), when women speak in these works they will be subordinated to male primacy as strictly as the matrons who swore to "use no mass, Latin service or prayers, than as appointed by the Church of England" in their deliveries. Confined to the "apt and accustomed words" of baptism, women's role in the ceremonies of childbirth will be restricted, as Paulina promises, to actions as "holy as / You hear my spell is lawful" (5.3.104–5). By these means the "gossips" whom she nominates for the birth of Leontes' daughter as the customary witnesses of labor (2.3.41) will be drafted into "a gossips' feast" of sponsors (The Comedy of Errors 5.1.405), their "babbling gossip" (Twelfth Night 1.5.277) reduced to christening the infant in the name of the Father. "My noble gossips," Henry VIII dubs them, at the end of the most neurotic of all these psychodramas of paternity, since the "old duchess" and "Lady Marquess," godmothers to Anne Boleyn's child, have stilled their rumor-mongering voices (*Henry VIII* 5.2.202; 5.4.12). In fact, the Puritans forbade midwives to baptize at all after 1577; and the semantic demotion of the term *godsibling* to *gossip* indicates how in the discursive system that produced these works women's language was congealing into tattle, while men's attained the truth of "observation." The plays register the process whereby male sense was sifted from female nonsense, as the sage woman declined from the status of a folk healer to that of Sarah Gamp, or the derided "Lady Margery, your midwife" (*The Winter's Tale* 2.3.159).

The Prologue to *Henry VIII* declares that the aim of this drama will be "no more to make you laugh" but to ensure that "Such as . . . hope they may believe, / May here find truth." If "All is True" in this text, this is so, then, because ribaldry has been curtailed, as the Puritans struggled to suppress the "time of freedom" when gossips gathered at a birth to "talk petty treason."[42] "A sad tale's best for winter," we learn; but the seriousness of the story of the man who "Dwelt by a church-yard," whose suspicion of cuckoldry haunts these plays, runs counter to the mocking "wisdom" of the ladies Mamillius calls "crickets" by the hearth (*The Winter's Tale* 2.7.25–31). In *Henry VIII*, "our chosen truth" (*Prologue*, l. 18) has therefore to be asserted over the "mirth" of Anne's midwife, whose role is to "deliver" the "old story" of a lady "that would not be queen. . . . For all the mud in Egypt," who yet succumbed, "for little England," to "venture an emballing" (2.3.46–47, 90–92, 101, 106). A scandal of sexual heresy has to be suppressed before her "royal infant" can be christened a prince of peace (5.4.9–16); and the ploy is one familiar ever since the Nurse instructed Juliet: the representation of women's language as a superstitious "mumbling . . .o'er a gossip's bowl" (*Romeo and Juliet* 3.5.174). This is a text that obliquely alludes to the indictment of Anne for adultery on the accusation of her midwife, Nan Cobham, when the Old Lady who delivers Elizabeth, palmed off by the king with a groom's payment, vows to "have more, or unsay" that the infant is as like him "as cherry is to cherry" (*Henry VIII* 5.1.168–75); but it stifles this seditious hearsay in favor of the martyrology that hailed the girl a Protestant Deborah. "Truth shall nurse her," her godfather Cranmer foretells, certain of a veracity that wrests the baby from female slander. Thus the male will to truth is predicated on an inquisitorial censorship of women's language, as Henry affirms, when he jests that the child will herself thank the archbishop, "When she has so much English" (5.4.14, 28).

Anne Boleyn was condemned on testimony that she had been delivered of a deformed fetus, which was taken as proof of her sexual relations with five men, alleged to have impregnated her by caresses and

French kisses.[43] In *The Winter's Tale,* where Hermione's ordeal recapitulates that of Elizabeth's mother, the same radical uncertainty about the facts of life prompts an identical demand about which acts are sufficient for consummation: "Is leaning cheek to cheek? is meeting noses? / Kissing with inside lip?" (1.2.285–86). Leontes' report on his wife's habit of "paddling palms, and pinching fingers" with Polixenes reads like a transcript of the Crown case in 1536, which was also reliant on the hypothesis that "to mingle friendship far, is mingling bloods" (1.2.109); but with Protestant claims dependent on Anne's exoneration, Shakespeare's brief was surely to discredit such suspicion. If the trials of successive Tudor queens are indeed "devis'd / And play'd to take spectators" in *Henry VIII* and *The Winter's Tale* (3.2.36–37), the romance, by disclaiming actuality, recounts what the history play obscures: patriarchy's inability to scrutinize the female body. Denying the Oracle, as Henry defied Rome, Leontes dooms a dynasty to extinction; yet the line descends through a princess lost in a northern land, to unite two kingdoms. For James I, who commanded a performance for the wedding of Princess Elizabeth in 1613, *The Winter's Tale* must have suggested that if absolutism can exercise no power over the female mystery, it must coopt it. And smarting at aspersions on Mary Stuart's relations with David Riccio, the royal house would follow the dramatic scenario by instituting, during its pregnancies, a cult of marital devotion. Shakespearean romance would have no more faithful sequel than the companionate marriage of Charles I and Henrietta Maria, in which sexuality would be purified with "All sanctimonious ceremonies," to make it a Neoplatonic idyll of "plain and holy innocence" (*The Tempest* 4.1.16; 3.1.82).

At the instant when the midwife cut the umbilical cord and held up the afterbirth, a Stuart royal baby was carried from its mother to be presented to the physicians and courtiers who thronged the threshold of the chamber. This ceremony contrasted grandly with the secretiveness of Tudor confinements, and symbolized the wary encirclement of maternity by absolutism. Yet if its intention was to oversee not only the facts of birth but their interpretation, the absolutist accouchement was not inviolable, as was demonstrated in 1688, when the entourage attending the birth of the Old Pretender failed, after the midwife vanished with her fee, to smother the rumor that he was a miller's son smuggled into the chamber in a warming pan.[44] Thus, Stuart history collapsed back into the folklore it had appropriated. For if the late plays, with their cast of changelings, estranged children, and wandering heirs, worked to legitimate the Scottish line, they also foretold how its sovereignty would be conditional on stories told by women. According to historians, the moral panic about the unruly woman as "a

common scold, raiser of idle reports and breeder of discord" in paternity disputes, reached fever pitch in the period of the romances,[45]
and the campaign to bridle gossip registers in the vigilance of the
Shakespearean fathers to guard themselves against sexual defamation.
What incenses Leontes is patriarchy's impotence to quell Paulina's assertions, which makes her husband a "lozel, worthy to be hanged, /
That wilt not stay her tongue" (*The Winter's Tale* 2.3.108–9). Yet the
male narrators of these texts must take up their dynastic story as it
emerges from the womblike "dark backward and abysm of time,"
where a husband takes it on trust that his wife "was a piece of virtue," because, as Prospero assures Miranda, "she said thou wast my
daughter" (*The Tempest* 1.2.50–57). The tale they "deliver" (5.1.113)
is as unverifiable as paternity, since, as the choric Gower concedes in
Pericles, it gestates in a matrix that is beyond the light of masculine observation:

> The cat, with eyne of burning coal
> Now crouches 'fore the mouse's hole;
> And crickets at the oven's mouth
> Sing the blither for their drouth.
> Hymen hath brought the bride to bed,
> Where by the loss of maidenhead
> A babe is moulded.
> (*Pericles*, 3.Chorus, 5–11)

Since "Lychorida, our nurse, is dead," Gower explains after the birth
of Marina, "the unborn event / I do commend to your content"
(4.Chorus, 42–46). A running metaphor analogizes these plays to the
doctor's supplement of the midwife. Playmaking and medicine both depend, we infer, on female delivery, and drama coopts lore which "were
it but told you, should be hooted at / Like an old tale" (5.3.116–17).
Earlier comedies had condescended to "the old and antic song" caroled
by "the spinsters and knitters in the sun" (*Twelfth Night* 2.4.3, 44); but
while Autolycus peddles broadsheets to girls who "love a ballad in
print . . . for then we are sure they are true" (*The Winter's Tale* 4.4.261–
62), drama cites its oral source from the same anxiety of representation
which Derrida finds in Rousseau's nostalgia for the song of the South
and the savage mind: "Like an old tale still, which will have matter to
rehearse, though credit be asleep and not an ear open" (5.2.62–63).
The Grand Narrative of modern knowledge legitimates itself, as Lyotard observes, by "smiling into its beard" at customary storytelling;[46]
yet the Jacobean antiquarian movement anticipated Rousseau's meta-

physics of presence by harkening to the dame who was ordinarily silenced with a ducking stool or bit. There were, in fact, affinities between the English cult of the "old wives' tale" and the French fad for fairy stories, which began, as Natalie Zemon Davis shows, in a similar context of centralizing absolutism. The publication of Charles Perrault's *Contes de ma mère l'loye* in in 1697 was dedicated to Louis XIV, when peasants' tales were retold in "Perrault's ironic voice" as human stories that naturalized the monarchy. Thus, Perrault, an architect of the Louvre, recruited "the old countrywomen of the Champagne" to serve the nation-state, complementing the researches of his brother Claude, the organizer of France's first public dissections.[47] The teenage girl anatomized in the earliest of these demonstrations, at Versailles in April 1667, may not have appreciated her grandeur, but for the brothers Perrault she yielded up her mystery in the interests of *la gloire*. If academicians could not fathom women, they would at least make them "speak" for the Sun King.[48]

The body politics of early modern storytelling are vividly displayed, Robert Darnton observes, in the frontispiece to the first edition of *Mother Goose*, which depicts "three well-dressed children listening raptly to an old crone in the servant's quarters." This image is a reminder that it was midwives and wet nurses who provided a physical link between elite and popular cultures, "for the audiences of Racine had imbibed folklore with their milk"[49] Old Mother Hubbard and Mother Goose (so-called from her cackle) were shadows of those real "goodwives" and "busybodies" whose lullabies for upper-class children seemed so suspect to seventeenth-century fathers, like the "Ladies" to whose "wisdom" the pregnant Hermione disposes Mamillius at a critical moment of her marriage: "Take the boy to you: he so troubles me, / 'Tis past enduring. . . . Pray you, sit by us, / And tell's a tale" (*The Winter's Tale* 2.1.1–23). As Leontes discovers, since husbands could not silence this *veillée*, they had to accept that the "stories grandmother told" were "words as medicinal as true, / Honest, as either, to purge him of that humour / That presses him from sleep" (2.3.37–39). So, laying "the old proverb" to his "charge, / So like you, 'tis the worse," Paulina "professes" to the king to be an "obedient counsellor" and "physician" in delivering his child (2.3.96–97, 54); but she warns that to "remove / The root of his opinion, which is rotten" (2.3.88–89), he must "awake [his] faith" in the efficacy of an "affliction" that "has a taste as sweet / As any cordial comfort" (5.3.76–77; 94–95). The faith healing the sage women prescribe in these plays, therefore, is truly a *pharmakon* that poisons to cure, being a purge of men's oldest fear. For the sugared pill they administer, with their aphrodisiacs of "Hot

lavender, mints, savory, marjoram" and "marigold" (4.4.104–5), contains the bitter cathartic that since it is a mother's body which has the
"ordering" of life, a father can only ever "print" his "copy" in the
"colours" she provides:

> Behold, my lords,
> Although the print be little, the whole matter
> And copy of the father: eye, nose, lip;
> The trick of's frown; his forehead; nay, the valley,
> The pretty dimples of his chin and cheek; his smiles;
> The very mould and frame of hand, nail, finger:
> And thou, good goddess Nature, which hast made
> So like to him that got it, if thou hast
> The ordering of his mind too, 'mongst all colours
> No yellow in't, lest she suspect, as he does,
> Her children not her husband's!
>
> (2.3.97–107)

Medical sociologists report that in Britain in the 1990s "one in ten
fathers is under a false impression that their children are their own,
while some studies put the figure at one in three."[50] What is remarkable, then, is that the fear of cuckoldry which features so obsessively in
medieval folktales should be so effaced in modern consciousness.
Shakespearean comedy suggests that if English husbands learned to
"take . . . no scorn to wear the horn" (*As You Like It* 4.2.14), this dates
from the licensing of maternity under such orderlies as Paulina. For
the "good goddess Nature" of the romances has become what Dame
Nature was for science: an archetypal "outsider inside," or Jacobean
equivalent of the *pharmakos*, the scapegoat/sorcerer whose remedies are
a necessary evil to prevent the greater ill. This sage matron enters the
Shakespearean polis as an indispensable Other who vouches for paternity; and it can be no coincidence that incorporation was the strategy
urged by obstetricians at the time. A material context for Paulina's actions may be found, for instance, in the petition for a midwives' charter
presented in 1616 to James I. Ostensibly drafted by London midwives,
this scheme for "the most skilful in the profession" to be "incorporated
into a Society" was promoted by Dr. Peter Chamberlen, head of a Hu-
guenot family which had invented the obstetric forceps. Though opposed by the Royal College, the Chamberlens lobbied for many years
against what they called "the uncontrolled female arbiters of life and
death," and, according to the midwives' spokeswomen, a Mrs. Hester
Shaw and a Mrs. Whipp, bribed a cohort of their "dear daughters" to
employ their "instruments by extraordinary violence." In 1634 sixty

midwives protested against "the molestation of Dr. Chamberlain and his project to have the licensing of them"; but science was with the doctor when he predicted dire "consequences for the health and strength of the whole nation if ignorant women, whom poverty or the game of Venus hath intruded into midwifery, should be insufficiently instructed." With projects for public anatomy lectures and baths, medical aid and poor relief, the Chamberlens were among those radical Protestants who wished to revolutionize the English municipality;[51] but the price exacted through the coopting of their "daughters" was paternal licensing of fertility itself.

IV

When Perdita disdains to force Nature by cultivating "carnations and streak'd gillyvors," she is lectured that "over that art / Which you say adds to Nature is an art / That Nature makes." In a reprise of her own story, Perdita is assured that Mother Nature legitimates those whom "some call . . . bastards" (4.4.82–92). Thus, Shakespeare's last plays make the same accommodation with the "gossip" of "an old tale" (5.2.62) as Hall's book does with folk healing, and it is piquant that their emblem for "great creating nature" should be his enematic flower. The doctor married Susanna on June 5, 1607, and *Pericles*, written during her pregnancy the following winter, immediately stages the conflict over the early modern childbed, when Thaisa dies delivering Marina, despite the efforts of her nurse, Lychorida, and her husband's prayers to "Lucina, Divinest patroness, and midwife gentle / To those that cry by night." If such charms and incantations for divine aid in labor contravened the midwife's oath, this one goes "unheard in the ears of death" (3.1.9–12). From the first Shakespearean scene of this text the discursive function of the romances is revealed, then, to be the Harveian project of separating childbirth from those wayward sisters already demonized in tragedy. So, after "a terrible childbed" with "no light, no fire," Thaisa's corpse is sunk "in the ooze" to appease the "superstition" of folk who are as "strong in custom" as they are weak in knowledge (3.1.50–57). Demographers estimate that in seventeenth-century England, in twenty-five out of every one thousand childbirths the mother died, and in time of plague and famine, the scenario of *Pericles*, mortality was much higher.[52] Yet out of this calamity the mother's body is salvaged when it is removed from the perils of the women's room and transferred to the safety of the clinic. Cerimon's surgery, where he calculates prescriptions and prognoses with cool exactitude, is imaged as the still center of a hysterical world, and in what reads like

a wedding gift to Hall, its ritual is valorized as a model of profession-
alism for the observation of the "disturbances" of the female body:

> I hold it ever,
> Virtue and cunning were endowments greater
> Than nobleness and riches: careless heirs
> May the latter two darken and expend,
> But immortality attends the former,
> Making man a god. 'Tis known I ever
> Have studied physic, through which secret art,
> By turning o'er authorities, I have,
> Together with my practice, made familiar
> To me and to my aid the blest infusions
> That dwell in vegetives, in metals, stones;
> And can speak of the disturbances that
> Nature works, and of her cures; which doth give me
> A more content in course of true delight
> Than to be thirsty after tottering honour,
> Or tie my treasure up in silken bags,
> To please the fool and death.
>
> (3.2.26–42)

The Shakespearean text foregrounds what Foucault would redis-
cover: the continuities between the old church and the new science.
Cerimon is reminded that by instituting his surgery on the site vacated
by a moribund religion, he has become a high priest of the modern cult
of welfare: "Your honour has through Ephesus pour'd forth / Your
charity, and hundreds call themselves / Your creatures, who by you
have been restor'd" (3.2.43–45). And this master's empiricism is confirmation that the war against disease is above all, as the Chamberlens
knew, a struggle against the nobility, won by "turning over authorities."
For, like the hospital regents painted by Rembrandt at this time, Cerimon sits at the apex of a system of chartered almshouses, bridewells,
madhouses, and schools that would make their president or professor,
as he brags, an institutional god. And the justification for the rise of
the medic to such status would have been the miracle of the surgery
or operating theater, performed as the doctor ministers to the body
of Thaisa, with all the genuflection formerly attending Mass. Christopher Hill has described the "spiritualisation of the household" accomplished by the Puritans; and Hall was foremost among those
"Physicians of the Soul," his editors declare, who perceived the close-
ness of the body and the soul and believed "that Sickness is commonly
a punishment for Sin."[53] So, as Cerimon operates on Thaisa to the
sound of "still and woeful music", this new Ephesian mystery literalizes
the Foucauldian thesis that to cure her of disorders of the "mother,"

the aim of medicine must be to penetrate not merely a woman's womb but her "o'erpress'd" soul:

> Make a fire within;
> Fetch hither all my boxes in my closet.
> Death may usurp on nature many hours,
> And yet the fire of life kindle again
> The o'erpress'd spirit . . .
>   The fire and cloths.
> The still and woeful music that we have,
> Cause it to sound, beseech you.
> The viol once more; how thou stirr'st thou block!
> The music there! I pray you, give her air.
> Gentlemen, this queen will live.
> Nature awakes a warm breath out of her.
> She hath not been entranc'd above five hours;
> See, how she 'gins to blow into life's flower again!
>   (3.2.82–97)

"When I leave his clinic", Freud would exclaim of Charcot's hypnotism of hysterics, "my mind is sated as after an evening at the theatre"; and the Chamberlens likewise promised to illuminate "Nature's most meandering labyrinths of Procreation."[54] Modern gynecology, Shakespearean catharsis predicts, will be a rite of exorcism. And with his histrionic cures, Hall was typical of the "godly sort" who approached the body at this time as a "temple" to be purified and cleansed. Thus, "Mrs Jackson," he records, "aged 24, being not well purged after birth, fell into a grievous Delirium; she was angry with those she formerly loved, yet her talk was very religious. By intervals there was a Frenzy. Yet there was a happy success by the following Prescriptions: To the Forehead was applied Water of Lettice. To the Head was applied a Hen new cut open. To the soles of the Feet, Radishes every third hour. There were also Scarifications to the Shoulders. And thus in seven days she was cured."[55] Like Cerimon, Hall evidently combined his clinical observations with the archaic belief in the uterine origin of hysteria: the "climbing sorrow" of the "mother" that "swells," in Lear's etiology, "upward toward [the] heart" whenever the womb wanders or overheats with humors (*King Lear* 2.4.56–57). Whether or not he knew Harvey, who he twice quotes, Shakespeare's son-in-law was at one with him in the conviction that "no one of experience can be ignorant what grievous symptoms arise when the uterus either rises or falls, is put out of place or is seized with spasm! Mental aberrations, delirium, melancholy, paroxysms of frenzy follow, as if the person were under the dominion of spells."[56] In Harvey's own lifetime his study of

parturition was as celebrated as his theory of circulation, so Hall's obstetrics could derive authority from the great man's treatment of postnatal "frenzy" by means of "musical sounds" to "dilate the uterine
orifice" and "release the foul vapours." And whatever operation Cerimon actually performs on Thaisa, with his "vi[a]l" and "fire and cloths"
to rouse her from her "trance," Harvey, who treated hysterics with in-
trauterine injections of "hot vitriol" or "cooling air," would surely have
certified his practice.[57]

Before he brings Thaisa to consciousness, Cerimon dedicates himself
to Apollo. Since the birth chamber had customs from which men were
excluded, its rites of confinement and delivery had to be institutionalized if they were to be authorized as a "lawful business" (*The Winter's
Tale* 5.3.96). In *Pericles* (which was registered just three months after
Susanna gave birth to Elizabeth), Thaisa therefore convalesces in "ves-
tal livery" as Diana's nun (3.4.9), her attendants reorganized into an order of "maiden priests" (5.1.240). The lying-in—during which a
mother remained housebound and sexually abstinent for thirty days
after delivery—is thereby appropriated as a Persephone-like poetic
myth: the postnatal resurrection of the so-called "lady in the straw," in
a purification ritual that fulfils the ordinance of Levitious, to decon-
taminate the mother "of the issue of her blood." So, "standing near the
altar . . . a number of virgins on each side" (5.2.), Thaisa removes her
"silver livery" to be reunited with her husband (5.3.7) in what seems to
be an imitation of the Anglican rite of churching, at which the mother,
surrounded by women, was led to church by her midwife and permitted to discard her veil to take communion, thus "bringing the world of
women back into contact with the literate world of men." With its "accustomed thank-offerings" for safe deliverance from the "snares of
death" and "pains of hell," churching was condemned by many as a
Jewish or papist superstition; but what is striking, according to social
historians, "is its high observance where it might be least expected: in
large, urban, Puritan parishes." Ninety percent of mothers were
churched after childbirth in early seventeenth-century Southwark.[58]
So, if Puritans objected to the mother's "coming forth covered with a
veil, as if ashamed of some folly,"[59] science and religion had little to
fear, it seems, from a *rite de passage* that reinstated the husband's claim
to his wife's body; as Leontes "will kiss her" when "the curtain" is
drawn from the face of Hermione (5.3.79).

With its blessing that "the sun shall not smite thee by day, nor the
moon by night," churching, Milton sneered, implied that the wife "had
been travailing not in her bed, but the deserts of Arabia."[60] Yet this is
the liturgy that the Shakespearean romances take seriously enough "to
lock up honesty and honour from / Th'access of gentle visitors," releas-

ing them, as Paulina says, with "such ado to make no stain a stain / As passes colouring" (*The Winter's Tale* 2.2.18–19). The final acts of these plays piously rehearse the service celebrated by Herrick in "Julia's Churching or Purification": "To th'Temple with the sober Midwife go, / Attended thus (in a most solemn wise) / By those who serve the Child-bed mysteries. / Burn first the Incense . . . and with reverend curtsies come. . . ."[61] This is dramaturgy that derives from the folklore that the woman who dies in childbirth, like Thaisa, or before she has "got strength of limit," like Hermione (3.2.106), can never rest in Christian burial or peace, and that defers to pagan superstition that "grass will never grow where they tread before they are churched."[62] For churching returns the childbearing women of these texts from an inscrutable darkness to the light promised in the service by a reading of Psalm 121: "I will lift up mine eyes unto the hills, from whence cometh my help." Thus, after enclosure "like one infectious" (5.2.98) in a "removed house," where she has been visited "twice or thrice a day" by her midwife (5.2.105), Hermione's sequestration from her family ends, as custom ordained, in liberation from night and immobility, when she is released from the woman's chamber: " 'Tis time, descend; be stone no more" (5.3.99). As Hermione is churched, Paulina allows that some "will think / (which I protest against) I am assisted / By wicked powers." This is a matter, as in Jacobean Stratford, of conscience: "Those that think it is unlawful business / I am about, let them depart" (5.3.89–97). But there was no reason for Puritans to "say 'tis superstition" when a mother was unveiled (5.3.43), since such cleansing of what preachers deemed "the stain" of sexual intercourse accorded exactly with their doctrine of the female body.[63] Hermione's isolation in her room, where she has been "kept / Lonely, apart" (5.3.17), is perfect confirmation of the thesis that rites of liminality work to reinforce the order they disrupt. Dame Margery the midwife tells Leontes not to "shun her," because his wife's body has been purged as thoroughly as those of the patients syringed by Dr. Hall: "O, she's warm! / If this be magic, let it be an art / Lawful as eating" (5.3.109–11).

By long seclusion in the woman's room, the female body is readmitted to society clarified of pollution. Although he sided with the vicar of Stratford against maypoles, there is no evidence that Hall opposed churching. The action of *The Winter's Tale* suggests why a doctor might find it expedient to cooperate with cunning women to invigilate a process he could never witness. For though Leontes rants that since maternity is "coactive" with "what's unreal. . . . And fellow'st nothing: then 'tis very credent [it may] conjoin with something . . . beyond commission" (1.2.141–44), he learns that there is no means for the "man [who] holds his wife by the arm" to verify his seed within the "sluices" of her

body: "Physic for't there's none" (1.2.192–200). His story seems, therefore, to warn the doctor to heal himself in the pandemic witch craze,
since "it is an heretic that makes the fire, / Not she which burns in't"
(1.2.114–15). Shakespeare had heralded the alliance of Dame Nature
and male science in the first play to record Hall's presence, yet there
Helena depended not on oral custom but her father's textual "notes":
"prescriptions / Of rare and prov'd effects, such as his reading / And
manifest experience had collected" (*All's Well That Ends Well* 1.3.216–
21). The wise woman of later comedies reverses this dependence, curing the "kingly patient" of his "distemperature," as Marina uses her
"utmost skill" on Pericles with a "sacred physic" that requires only "that
none but I and my companion maid / Be suffer'd to come near him"
(*Pericles* 5.1.27; 74–78). Complicit in their mystery, the father is restored to power when he accepts what these cloistered women have
"deliver'd weeping"—the biological conundrum of she "that beg'st him
that did thee beget"—and pledges that henceforth he will "never
interrupt" them (5.1.160–65;195) nor deny "the child-bed privilege ... which 'longs / To women of all fashion" (*The Winter's Tale*
3.2.103–4). For by dissociating from wayward women, like the witch Sy-
corax or the Queen in *Cymbeline*, these matrons and their "fellow
maids" (*Pericles* 5.1.49) are crucial in maneuvering the female body into
compliance. As they deliver their own sex at the altar of a masculine
religion, their role is to prepare a body such as Thaisa's or Hermione's:
immobile, aestheticized, and, above all, ready for inspection.

V

The theatricality of the operation Paulina stages helps explain why
the earliest entrance tickets were sold not for a playhouse but the anatomy theater at Padua, that "wooden O" where Harvey first looked
down from a darkened gallery to observe a spotlit corpse dissected. In
this new spectacular space the body would be reanimated, as Descartes
proposed in 1641, like a machine propelled by reflexes. This modern
body with pumping heart and automatic eyeblink is not the body
promised eternal life, but, in Descartes's image, a watch sprung for
motion.[64] And the medical gaze has no need of speech when it anato-
mizes such a mechanism because "silence ... the more shows off [its]
wonder." What it reads, of course, are the "wrinkled" signs of death;
but the question that it asks is Harvey's: "What was he that did make
it?" What master "deemed it breath'd? ... that those veins / Did verily
bear blood?" That "the very life seems warm upon her lip," and "the
fixture of her eye has motion in't"? "No longer shall you gaze on't,"

Paulina connives, "lest your fancy / May think anon it moves"; and the power that would have ripped open this womb, if necessary, to deliver a Macduff or Posthumus by cesarean section fancies it knows the mover. A "rare Italian master," the text calls him, punning art with nature (*The Winter's Tale* 5.2.21–96). But, as Harvey wrote, "I do not think we are greatly to dispute the name by which the first agent is to be called . . . . As the architect is more worthy than the pile he rears, as the king is more exalted than his minister, as the workman is better than his hands," so "the Supreme Creator is the father."[65] True to Harvey, it is the father who receives the child in these plays, as Cranmer carries the heir to the king at the end of *Henry VIII* and foretells a male inheritor who "shall star-like rise . . . and so stand fix'd" (5.4.44–45). No mother appears in *The Tempest*, since for Shakespeare, as for Harvey, male power is at last self-generating. But the beheading of Anne Boleyn and purging of Susanna Hall remind us how much the fiction of a masculine universe was the result of actual "observations" carried out on female English bodies.

The patriarchal myth of Pygmalion, who "could put breath into his work" to "beguile Nature of her custom" (*The Winter's Tale* 5.2.97–98), acquired new potency in an era when scientists such as Descartes hypothesized the origin of life in the fermentation of semen. Descartes's mechanistic physiology seemed, indeed, to contemporaries, to augur a final conquest by the "master" (5.2.96) of Nature's midwifery, as he pursued the dream of the Renaissance, to fabricate some "Diana as a man-machine". "Here is my library," he was reported to have said of his secret anatomy theater, "and this," gesturing to a dissected carcass, "the study to which I now attend." It was this preoccupation that must have accounted for "the strange tale circulated by his enemies" that he had usurped creation, and "made with much ingenuity an automaton in the form of a girl. Descartes was said to have taken this automaton on a vessel, packed in a box. The sailors had the curiosity, however, to open the box, and as the figure appeared to have life, they took it for the devil and threw it overboard."[66] With its analogues in Greek romance, this is a legend that provides a bearing on the Hoffmannesque riddle of the late plays, posed by Posthumus when he demands: "Is there no way for men to be but women / Must be half-workers?" (*Cymbeline* 2.4.153). In Shakespeare, however, an answer is given by the mothers and midwives themselves, who suffer the Caesarian law that, as Paulina assents, the "child was prisoner to the womb, and is / By law and process of great nature, thence / Free'd and enfranchis'd" (*The Winter's Tale* 2.2.59–61). Indeed, the dead mother in *Cymbeline* memorializes an entire medical revolution, when obstetric forceps displaced the healing art, as she laments how "Lucina lent me not her aid, / but took me in my throes, / That from me was Posthumus ript. . . . I died whilst in the womb he stay'd, / attending Nature's law" (5.4.37–45). Such cries witness how much the politics of early modern science, and of John Hall's family, underwrote the Harveian myths of "great creating nature" and the "right to life."

Attending a birth, the Chamberlens arrived with a giant trunk supposedly containing their miraculous "delivery machine," and after the mother had been blindfolded and the midwife locked out of the room, those "listening at the door could hear the ringing of bells and clapping of sticks." In this way the secret was kept for over a century that the trunk merely contained forceps, whose noise the music drowned.[67] Thus, to take control of birth, the new medicine required acts of faith as great as those of the old midwifery. But in July 1643, when Harvey was writing his book *On Generation,* his own faith faltered as he recalled how he had cut open a pregnant deer in Windsor Forest to show "the uterus to his majesty the king and satisfy him" as to the "prime efficient" of creation, only to discover in consternation "that there was nothing in the shape of semen to be found in the organ." And "whilst I speak of these matters," Harvey interjected, "forgive me, if I vent a sigh. This is the cause of my sorrow; whilst in attendance on his majesty during our late troubles, by command of Parliament rapacious hands stripped from my museum the fruits of years of toil. Whence it has come to pass that many observations have perished, with detriment, I venture to say, to the republic of letters."[68] At that moment, in the doctor's confusion, the fate of the "republic" of knowledge could not have been more tied to that of monarchy; but banished with the court to Oxford, the "father of English midwifery" recommenced his dissections undaunted, with "a Hen to hatch eggs in his chamber, which he daily opened to discern the way of Generation."[69] All might yet be well, the king restored, and the riddle of the chicken and the egg solved, if only Henrietta Maria could join her husband with reinforcements. But as Harvey cracked eggs and Charles fretted, the queen was enjoying unaccustomed power at the crossroads of different histories. She was at New Place in Stratford, the guest of Susanna Hall, a widow with chests full of her husband's casebooks and "play-writings" by her father,[70] which she was sorting for sale to the soldiers or for burning.

NOTES

1. John Hall, "To the Judicious Reader," in *Select Observations on English Bodies or Cures both Empirical and Historical performed upon Eminent Persons in Desperate Diseases* (London, 1657), p. 4. This text is published as an appendix to

Harriet Joseph, *Shakespeare's Son-in-Law: John Hall, Man and Physician* (Hamden, Conn.: Archon Books, 1964).

2. Quotes from Joseph, *Shakespeare's Son-in-Law,* p. 12; Hall *Observations,* 2nd Century, Observation 60, p. 149.

3. Hall, *Observations,* 1st Century, Observation 10, p. 10; Michel Foucault, *The Birth of the Clinic: An Archaeology of Medical Perception,* trans. Alan Sheridan (London: Tavistock, 1976), p. 107.

4. Hall, *Observations* 1st Century, Observation 19, p. 24: Hall, "To the Judicious Reader," pp. 10–11.

5. Francis Bacon, *The Advancement of Learning,* ed. W. Wright (Oxford: Clarendon Press, 1900), 2.10.2, p. 137.

6. Jacques Derrida, "Plato's Pharmacy," in *Dissemination,* trans. Barbara Johnson (Chicago: University of Chicago Press, 1981), p. 167.

7. Hall, *Observations,* 2nd Century, Observation 33, pp. 176–79.

8. Ibid., 1st Century, Observation 36, pp. 47–51.

9. Ibid., "Testimony," p. 8.

10. Foucault, *Birth of the Clinic,* p. 166.

11. Quoted ibid.

12. See Francis Joseph Cole, *Early Theories of Sexual Generation* (Oxford: Clarendon Press, 1930), and Noel Joseph Needham, *A History of Embryology* (Cambridge: Cambridge University Press, 1934).

13. Foucault, *Birth of the Clinic,* p. 166.

14. George Herbert, "Vanity," in *The Works of George Herbert,* ed. F. E. Hutchinson (Oxford: Clarendon Press, 1941), p. 85.

15. Percivall Willughby, *Observations in Midwifery* (Ms., 1863), ed. John L. Thornton (Wakefield, Eng.: S. R. Publishers, 1972), p. 254.

16. *The Works of William Harvey,* ed. Robert Willis (London, 1847; reprint New York: Johnson Reprint Company, 1965), pp. 364, 480–81.

17. Willughby, *Observations,* p. 65. For the "ceremony of childbirth" as a process of enclosure and confinement, see especially Antony Wilson, "Participant or Patient? Seventeenth-Century Childbirth from the Mother's Point of View," in *Patients and Practitioners: Lay Perceptions of Medicine in Pre-Industrial England,* ed. Roy Porter (Cambridge: Cambridge University Press, 1989), pp. 133–41. For male exclusion from the birth chamber, see also Adrienne Rich, *Of Woman Born: Motherhood as Experience and Institution* (New York: Norton, 1976), p. 134: "Misogyny attached itself to the birth-process so that males were forbidden to attend at births' because the church "saw woman—and especially her reproductive organs—as evil incarnate"; and Hilda Smith, "Gynecology and Ideology in Seventeenth-Century England," in *Liberating Woman's History: Theoretical and Critical Essays,* ed. Berenice Carroll (Urbana: University of Illinois Press, 1976), pp. 97–114.

18. Quoted in Jane B. Donegan, *Women and Men Midwives: Medicine, Morality, and Misogyny in Early America* (Westport, Conn.: Greenwood Press, 1978), p. 23.

19. Quoted in Margaret George, *Women in the First Capitalist Society: Experiences in Seventeenth-Century England* (Brighton: Harvester Press, 1988), p. 207; and in Lucina McGray Beier, *Sufferers and Healers: The Experience of Illness in Seventeenth-Century England* (London: Routledge & Kegan Paul, 1987), p. 44.

20. Hall, *Observations,* 2nd Century, Observation 56, pp. 221–22.

21. Ibid., 2nd Century, Observation 58, p. 223.

22. Ibid., 2nd Century, Observation 52, pp. 213–15.

23. Willughby, *Observations*, p. 233.

24. *The Winter's Tale* 4.4.88. All references to Shakespeare's plays are from the Arden edition, ed. Andrew S. Cairncross (London: Methuen, 1969); subsequent citations appear in the text.

25. Willughby, *Observations*, p. 233.

26. Foucault, *Birth of the Clinic*, pp. 34–35. For the place of midwifery and female healing in the medical marketplace, see especially Beier, *Sufferers and Healers*, pp. 15–19, 42–50, 211–17.

27. Louis Montrose, "*A Midsummer Night's Dream* and the Shaping Fantasies of Elizabethan Culture: Gender, Power, Form," in *Representing the English Renaissance*, ed. Stephen Greenblatt (Berkeley: University of California Press, 1988), pp. 42–43.

28. Hall, "To the Judicious Reader," p. 4. For Montpellier as a center of humanist surgery, see Vivian Nutton, "Humanist Surgery," in *The Medical Renaissance of the Sixteenth Century*, ed. Roger French, Ian Lowie, and Andrew Wear (Cambridge: Cambridge University Press, 1985), p. 81.

29. Natalie Zemon Davis, "Proverbial Wisdom and Popular Errors," in *Society and Culture in Early Modern France* (Stanford: Stanford University Press, 1975), p. 261.

30. Quoted ibid.

31. Quoted in Keith Thomas, *Religion and the Decline of Magic: Studies in Popular Beliefs in Sixteenth- and Seventeenth-Century England* (Harmondsworth: Penguin Books, 1978), pp. 16–17.

32. Robert Burton, *The Anatomy of Melancholy*, ed. Holbrook Jackson (London: J. M. Dent & Sons, 1932), 2:210; Thomas, *Religion and the Decline of Magic*, p. 17. The connection between *All's Well That Ends Well* and Harveian medicine is sketched in Charles J. Sisson, "Shakespeare's Helena and Dr. William Harvey," *Essays and Studies* (London, 1960), pp. 1–20.

33. Quoted in Thomas, *Religion and the Decline of Magic*, p. 17.

34. Friedrich Nietzsche, *The Gay Science*, trans. Walter Kaufmann (New York: Vintage Books, 1974), p. 38; quoted, with translation from the Greek, by Gayatri C. Spivak in the preface to *Of Grammatology* by Jacques Derrida (Baltimore: Johns Hopkins University Press, 1976), p. xxxvi.

35. Thomas Rogers Forbes, *The Midwife and the Witch* (New Haven: Yale University Press, 1966), pp. 117, 127–28. See also Jean Gibson, *Hanged for Witchcraft: Elizabeth Lowys and her Successors* (Canberra: Canberra University Press, 1988), pp. 96–106; and Jean Towler and Joan Bramall, *Midwives in History and Society* (London: Croom Helm, 1986), pp. 31–39.

36. Margaret Nelson, "Why Witches Were Women," in *Women: A Feminist Perspective*, ed. Jo Freeman (Palo Alto: Mayfield, 1975), p. 339. See also Towler and Bramall, *Midwives in History*, pp. 126–29.

37. Janet Adelman, "Fantasies of Maternal Power in *Macbeth*," in *Cannibals, Witches, and Divorce: Estranging the Renaissance*, ed. Marjorie Garber (Baltimore: Johns Hopkins University Press, 1987), p. 91.

38. For death from cesarean surgery, see Barbara Katz Rothman, *In Labor: Women and Power in the Birthplace* (New York: Norton, 1982), pp. 51–53. For the death of Jane Seymour, see Richard L. DeMolen, "The Birth of Edward VI and the Death of Queen Jane: The Arguments for and against Caesarian Section," *Renaissance Studies* 4 (1990), 359–91.

39. Terry Eagleton, *William Shakespeare* (Oxford: Basil Blackwell, 1986), pp. 92–93.

40. Towler and Bramall, *Midwives in History*, p. 56. Midwives were instructed to question the mother about paternity "when the pains of labour are greatest" so that her resistance would be overcome; see Margaret Wiesner, "Nuns, Wives, Mothers," in *Women in Reformation and Counter-Reformation Europe*, ed. Sherrin Marshall (Bloomington: Indiana University Press, 1989), pp. 24–25. For details of such interrogations, see also Martin Ingram, *Church Courts, Sex, and Marriage in England, 1570–1640* (Cambridge: Cambridge University Press, 1990), pp. 262–63.

41. Peter B. Erikson, "Patriarchal Structures in *The Winter's Tale*," *PMLA* 97 (1982), 827.

42. Quoted in Antony Wilson, "The Ceremony of Childbirth and Its Interpretation," in *Women as Mothers in Pre-Industrial England*, ed. Valerie Fildes (London: Routledge, 1989), p. 82.

43. See Retha Marvine Warnicke, *The Rise and Fall of Anne Boleyn* (Cambridge: Cambridge University Press, 1989), p. 203; Anne "was charged with inciting, in witchlike fashion, five men to have sexual relations with her by the use of touches and kisses that involved thrusting her tongue into their mouths and theirs in hers (called pigeon kisses). The kisses, touches, and caresses were minutely described."

44. For the Stuart rites of accouchement, see William F. Bynum, "Medicine at the English Court," in *Medicine at the Courts of Europe, 1500–1837*, ed Vivian Nutton (London: Routledge, 1990), p. 265. For the legend of the baby in the warming pan, see Henri and Barbara van der Zee, *1688: Revolution in the Family* (Harmondsworth: Penguin Books, 1988), pp. 73–77.

45. Quoted in David E. Underdown, "The Taming of the Scold," in *Order and Disorder in Early Modern England*, ed. Antony Fletcher and John Stevenson (Cambridge: Cambridge University Press, 1987), p. 119. See also Ingram, *Church Courts*, pp. 292–319.

46. Jean-François Lyotard, *The Postmodern Condition: A Report on Knowledge*, trans. Geoffrey Bennington and Brian Massumi (Manchester: Manchester University Press, 1986), pp. 18–41.

47. Davis, *Society and Culture*, pp. 252–53. For Perrault and Louis XIV, see also David Maland, *Culture and Society in Seventeenth-Century France* (London: Batsford, 1970), pp. 244–51, 274–75; and Louis Marin, *Portrait of the King*, trans. Martha M. Houle (London: Routledge, 1988), passim.

48. Seymour L. Chapin, "Science in the Reign of Louis XIV," in *The Reign of Louis XIV: Essays in Celebration of Andrew Lossky*, ed. Paul Sonnino (London: Humanities Press International, 1990), p. 185.

49. Robert Darnton, "Peasants Tell Tales," in *The Great Cat Massacre and Other Episodes in French Cultural History* (Harmondsworth: Penguin Books, 1985), p. 69.

50. Susan Macintyre and Anne Sooman, "Non-Paternity and Prenatal Screening," *The Lancet*, October 5, 1991, p. 869.

51. Jean Donnison, *Midwives and Medical Men: A History of Inter-Professional Rivalries and Women's Rights* (London: Heinemann, 1977), pp. 13–15; Towler and Bramall, *Midwives in History*, pp. 77–81; Peter Elmer, "Medicine, Religion, and the Puritan Revolution," in French, Lowie, and Wear, *The Medical Renaissance*, pp. 21–22. The official interpretation of the Chamberlen's petition as a

document in the history of feminism is offered in George Clark, *A History of the Royal College of Physicians of London* (Oxford: Clarendon, 1964), 1:236.

52. Shulamith Shahar, *Childhood in the Middle Ages* (London: Routledge, 1990), p. 35. See also Dorothy McLaren, "Fertility, Infant Mortality, and Breast Feeding in the Seventeenth Century," *Medical History* 22 (1978), 380–81.

53. Christopher Hill, *Society and Puritanism in Pre-Revolutionary England* (Harmondsworth: Penguin Books, 1986), chap. 13; Hall, "To the Judicious Reader," p. 7.

54. Ernest Jones, *The Life and Work of Sigmund Freud* (Harmondsworth: Penguin Books, 1964), pp. 173–74; Donegan, *Women and Men Midwives*, p. 29.

55. Hall, *Observations*, 2nd Century, Observation 54, pp. 216–18.

56. Ibid., 2nd Century, Observation 43, p. 131.

57. Kenneth David Keele, *William Harvey* (London: Nelson, 1965), pp. 82–83; Ilza Veith, *Hysteria: The History of a Disease* (Chicago: University of Chicago Press, 1965), pp. 130–31.

58. Wilson, *Participant or Patient*, pp. 38–39.

59. Quoted in Thomas, *Religion and the Decline of Magic*, p. 68.

60. Quoted ibid.

61. *The Poems of Robert Herrick*, ed. L. C. Martin (Oxford: Clarendon, 1965), p. 286.

62. Seventeenth-Century Welsh Superstition, cited in Thomas, *Religion and the Decline of Magic*, p. 43.

63. Quoted ibid., p. 68.

64. Elizabeth Sanderson Haldane, *Descartes: His Life and Times* (London: John Murray, 1905), pp. 376–77.

65. Harvey, *Works*, p. 367.

66. Quoted in Haldane, *Descartes*, p. 281. For Descartes's mechanistic theory of conception, see especially D. Fouke, "Mechanical and 'Organical' Models in Seventeenth-Century Explanations of Biological Reproduction," *Science in Context* 3 (Autumn 1989) 366–88.

67. James MacVicar, *Man-Midwife* (Leicester, Eng.: Leicester University Press, 1975), p. 6.

68. Harvey, *Works*, pp. 480–81.

69. John Aubrey, *Brief Lives*, ed. Oliver Lawson Dick (Harmondsworth: Penguin Books, 1949), p. 287; see also Louis Chauvois, *William Harvey: His Life and Times: His Discoveries: His Methods* (New York: Philosophical Library, 1957), pp. 142–45.

70. For Henrietta Maria as guest of Susanna Hall and the dispersal of Hall's library, see Stanley Schoenbaum, *William Shakespeare: A Documentary Life* (Oxford: Oxford University Press, 1975), p. 249; and *Shakespeare's Lives* (Oxford: Oxford University Press, 1970), pp. 125–26.

7. The Poetry of Conduct: Accommodation and Transgression in *The Faerie Queene*, Book 6

MICHAEL C. SCHOENFELDT

In countries where the populace is armed, people tend to be more polite.

— David Mamet

In a division that prefigures many of the signal differences between the idealizing tendencies of an older historicism and the materialist motives foregrounded by the new, Book 6 of *The Faerie Queene* oscillates between a definition of courtesy as an internal moral virtue and as a repertoire of shrewd social practices. Even the name of the exemplar of courtesy, Calidore, can be derived either from the Greek *kalla dora,* meaning "beautiful gift," or from the Latin *callidus,* meaning "cunning." Throughout Book 6 Spenser exerts immense effort in the attempt to reconcile grace and craft, the realm of ideal moral virtue and the region of practical politics. The strenuousness of the effort is disclosed in the violence with which he continually imbues the practices of courtesy. Courtesy, remarks David Norbrook, "needs to be supplemented by violence in the chaotic landscape of Book 6 in which brigands and wicked churls are constant menaces."[1] But in Book 6 Spenser is fascinated not only by the violence that supplements courtesy but also by the violence that suffuses it. "One of the most decisive transitions" in the civilizing process of western Europe, observes Norbert Elias, "is that of *warriors to courtiers.*"[2] In its portrait of the exemplar of courtesy as a warfaring knight, Book 6 of *The Faerie Queene* throws into relief the deep tensions inherent in this process, and exposes the vestiges of marital violence that linger in the purportedly genteel products of this transition. "Symbolic violence," writes Pierre Bourdieu, "is the gentle, hidden form which violence takes when overt violence is impossible."[3] As Spenser well knows, courtesy is among the gentlest but also the most potent of these forms. Throughout Book 6 he uses the language of courtesy to mystify but not to erase the violence that sustains the social hierarchy; in the process he exposes the brutal economy of exchange buried within courtesy's terminology of disinterested gift giving.

The fusion of gentility and violence which Spenser harnesses is built in to the linguistic structure and social ideology he inherits. "Arms," of course, are not just implements of death but also emblems of nobility. The medieval word *cortaysye,* according to W. O. Evans, "can refer not only to polite and correct procedure in chivalric matters but also to skill in fighting."[4] Indeed, Richard McCoy has argued that the chivalric ideology of Tudor England, because it at once "affirmed Tudor sovereignty" and "glorified aristocratic militarism and traditional notions of honor and autonomy, . . . combined deference and aggression, accommodating these dangerously incompatible, often contradictory impulses within its codes and customs."[5] In Book 6 of *The Faerie Queene,* Spenser goes to great lengths to accent these contradictions. His definition of courtesy encompasses not only Calidore's laying down his shield as a bier on which to carry the wounded Aladine but also Calidore's chopping off the head of a dead knight in order to help Priscilla save face with her parents. Relatedly, Spenser emphasizes the arresting power that flows from Calidore's courtesy: his "gracious speach, did steale mens hearts away" (6.1.2), while his every act is "like enchantment" (6.2.3).[6] Courtesy is never for Spenser simply a moral virtue; it frequently demands an exercise of martial power.[7]

In his compelling reading of Book 2, Stephen Greenblatt describes how *The Faerie Queene* is "driven by the will to deny its own perception of tragic conflict inherent in the fashioning of civility," a civility that "is won through the exercise of violence over what is deemed barbarous and evil."[8] In Book 6, though, violence is not only directed outward against that which one shuns but also turned by an outsider toward the circle of civility he desires to enter. Whether obliging inferiors or supplicating superiors, courtesy scales the hierarchical gradations it advertises. As a practice that allows one to cross social boundaries without threatening them, to enter a closed circle without puncturing it, courtesy is transgression under the guise of accommodation.

The son of a clothmaker, Spenser was acutely aware of the necessity of accommodating himself to the demands of the social hierarchy. He attended grammar school only by assuming the stigma of a "pore scholler." At Cambridge he was a "sizar," a student who received free room, board, and tuition in return for working in the kitchen and waiting on the tables of his wealthy and noble classmates. Throughout Spenser's career, success was inextricably linked to acts of service that allowed him access to a world otherwise closed to him. Like the natural mythology Spenser supplies for the germination of "comely courtesie," the exemplary virtue of Book 6—"though it on a lowly stalke doe bowre, / Yet brancheth forth in brave nobilitie, / And spreds it selfe through all civilitie" (Proem, l. 4)—Spenser's career delineates an ascent from lowly origins to noble aspirations.

Indeed, the originary moment of the narrative of *The Faerie Queene*, according to the letter to Raleigh appended to the 1590 edition, is an incident that reworks as romance motifs present in Spenser's own social experience. On the first day of the feast of Gloriana, the Faerie Queene,

> there presented him selfe a tall clownishe younge man, who falling before the Queen of Faries desired a boone (as the manner then was) which during that feast she might not refuse: which was that hee might have the atchievement of any adventure, which during that feaste should happen, that being graunted, he rested him on the floore, unfitte through his rusticity for a better place. Soone after entred a faire Ladye in mourning weedes, riding on a white Asse, with a dwarfe behind her leading a warlike steed, that bore the Armes of a knight, and his speare in the dwarfes hand. Shee falling before the Queene of Faeries, complayned that her father and mother an ancient King and Queene, had bene by an huge dragon many years shut up in a brasen Castle, who thence suffred them not to yssew: and therefore besought the Faery Queene to assygne her some one of her knights to take on him that exployt. Presently that clownish person upstarting, desired that adventure: whereat the Queene much wondering, and the Lady much gainesaying, yet he earnestly importuned his desire.

Finally his pleas are successful; he dons the "armour which [Una] brought," and "with dewe furnitures thereunto, he seemed the goodliest man in al that company, and was well liked of the Lady."[9] Although entering as a country lout, he leaves bearing the arms of a knight.

Beginning with an act of self-presentation at once brazen and deferential, and concluding with the triple fantasy of courtly employment, social elevation, and amorous favor, the story depicts not only the narrative genesis but also the social origins of *The Faerie Queene*.[10] By throwing himself at the feet of his queen and acknowledging that he is "unfitte through his rusticity for a better place" than her floor, the rustic discovers the literal and metaphorical launch pad for his physical and social "upstarting." The rustic clown—a social and literary figure with which Spenser identifies throughout his career—manages through the grace of the queen and his own ingratiating deference to break into a theoretically rigid hierarchy. By means of gestures which are at once transgressive and accommodating, he pays homage to the integrity of the closed circle he enters.

Book 6 of *The Faerie Queene* frequently formulates the social hierarchy Spenser likewise desires to enter as a series of closed circles. In the Proem to Book 6, for example, Spenser apologizes for interrupting a cycle which has Queen Elizabeth as its source and end:

> Then pardon me, most dreaded Soveraine,
> That from your selfe I doe this vertue bring,
> And to your selfe doe it returne againe:
> So from the Ocean all rivers spring,
> And tribute backe repay as to their King.
> Right so from you all goodly vertues well
> Into the rest, which round about you ring,
> Faire Lords and Ladies, which about you dwell,
> And doe adorne your Court, where courtesies excell.
>
> (ll. 1–9)

The poet is at once central and peripheral to the ecology he describes, delineating the closed circuit of courtesy that flows from and toward Elizabeth.[11] A similar set of concentric circles is traced in the vision on Mount Acidale, where Calidore sees "an hundred naked maidens lilly white, / All raunged in a ring, and dauncing in delight," surrounding "three other Ladies" who dance around "another Damzell, as a precious gemme, / Amidst a ring most richly well enchaced" (6.10.11–12). The former fluvial cycle represents the economy of the courtly world in which the poet wishes to play a productive role; the latter series of terpsichorean circles delineates a delicate but ephemeral vision available only to the poet. Yet ultimately for Spenser the ephemerality of the latter is surpassed only by the impenetrability of the former.

Book 6 makes powerful but contradictory claims about whether courtesy is bestowed at birth or attained by practice. The works of Renaissance courtesy literature from which Spenser draws—primarily Baldassare Castiglione's *Courtier*, Stefano Guazzo's *Civile Conversation*, and Giovanni della Casa's *Galateo*—frequently assert that true grace is innate, and cannot be acquired by effort.[12] Yet the very existence and immense popularity of these works belies the assertion.[13] Throughout Book 6 Spenser too insists that "some so goodly gratious are by kind, / That every action doth them much commend" (6.2.2), that

> a man by nothing is so well bewrayd,
> As by his manners, in which plaine is showne
> Of what degree and what race he is growne
> . . . gentle bloud will gentle manners breed.
>
> (6.3.1–2)

Yet Calidore's first adventure involves the teaching of courtesy to Briana and Crudor. Moreover, Calepine, another exemplar of courtesy, describes the child he gives to Sir Bruin as a "spotlesse spirit, in which ye may enchace / What ever formes ye list thereto apply, / Being now soft and fit them to embrace," and proposes that many "of the like, whose linage was unknowne, / More brave and noble knights have raysed beene . . . / Then those, which have bene dandled in the lap" (6.4.35–36). By likening the child to a soft and malleable substance, and linking noble action to those of unknown lineage, he indicates that education rather than blood is the crucial determinant of character. Most significant, both accounts are in circulation on Acidale: although Colin declares that "these three [Graces] on men all gracious gifts bestow, / Which decke the body or adorne the mynde," implying that courtesy is an unearned and unsought gift, he nevertheless proposes in the same stanza that they "teach us, how to each degree and kynde / We should our selves demeane, to low, to hie: / To friends, to foes, which skill men call Civility" (6.10.23). The distance between a gift and a lesson, between courtesy as the product of education and courtesy as the product of birth, is the space into which Spenser hopes to insert himself.[14] His partial endorsement of the mystification of courteous conduct as the exclusive province of nobility demonstrates his ambivalence toward his own project: he wants not to threaten the social hierarchy but to validate it while discovering a place for himself within it.[15]

This uneasiness about the source of true courtesy precipitates anxiety about the self-improvement that such mobility necessarily entails. In an often-quoted passage from the letter to Raleigh, Spenser alleges that "the generall end . . . of all the booke is to fashion a gentleman or noble person in vertuous and gentle discipline" (p. 15). The work, then, seems premised on just the kind of narrative self-fashioning that Greenblatt has persuasively shown to be central to the Renaissance.[16] In Book 6 Calidore endorses this notion of the malleability of personality and status, declaring that "in each mans self . . . It is, to fashion his owne lyfes estate" (6.9.31). Even in *A View of the Present State of Ireland*, a work dedicated to the policy of "reducing that savage nation to better government and civility," Spenser expresses a grudging admiration for the rebel Hugh McHugh, who, "being of himself of so base condition, hath through his own hardiness lifted himself up to that height that he now dare front princes."[17] Nevertheless, in Book 6 he censures Mirabella, who manages through her "wondrous giftes of natures grace" to rise above her "meane parentage and kindred base" (6.7.28). Moreover, when Calidore sees a woodman on foot kill a knight on horseback, his class prejudice causes him to censure the woodman as an ungrateful upstart: "Why hath thy hand too bold it selfe embrewed / In blood of knight, the which by thee is slaine, / By thee no knight; which armes impugneth plaine" (6.2.7). Only when the circumstances of Tristram's bold actions are made known, along with the crucial revelation that he is in fact the son of a Briton king, is the accusation of social transgression defused. The anxiety about such class war lingers, however. In its simultaneous celebration of those who rise above their birth and castigation of the upstart, the text of *The Faerie Queene* displays the uneasiness with which Spenser imagines his own capacity to make literature the vehicle of self-improvement.

A similar ambivalence imbues Spenser's attitude toward the court itself. In Book 3 the narrator expresses surprise that Belphoebe could have acquired such refined behavior "so farre from court and royall Citadell, / The great schoolmistresse of all curtesy" (3.6.1). But in Book 6 Spenser can only suggest that courtesy derives etymologically from the court:

> Of Court it seemes, men Courtesie doe call,
> For that it there most useth to abound;
> And well beseemeth that in Princes hall
> That vertue should be plentifully found,
> Which of all goodly manners is the ground.
>   (6.1.1).

It is obvious but deeply significant, however, that Book 6 contains no glimpses of these halls. As Michael O'Connell suggests, "The book intends more to qualify than to substantiate this etymology" linking courtesy and the court.[18] Throughout the book the absent court is identified with "fayned showes," and "colours faire," even as Spenser goes to great lengths to insulate Elizabeth's court from his devastating critique of courtly shallowness and hypocrisy.

Indeed, although there is no court in Book 6, the episode ostensibly furthest from the court—the pastoral interlude—provides an intensified version of courtly existence played out in pastoral guise. Just as Pastorella seems a shepherdess but is really the daughter of a queen, so is the entire world of the shepherds a projection of the court in miniature.[19] The moment when Calidore hides his armor under shepherds' weeds in order to rescue Pastorella from the brigands lays bare the covert political functioning of the entire episode. Calidore's courtship of Pastorella—a shepherdess who is really the daughter of a queen—requires great courtly dexterity. Like an expert courtier attending at all times to the pleasure of his monarch, Calidore speaks with a continual awareness of Pastorella as his ultimate audience, even

when addressing the shepherds: "Evermore his speach he did apply /
To th'heards, but meant them to the damzels fantazy" (6.9.12). Likewise, when Calidore expresses conventional pastoral sentiment by crit-
icizing the court and praising the shepherd's life, it is only "to occasion
meanes, to worke his mind, / And to insinuate his harts desire" (6.9.27).
Ironically, he praises the unambitious life of shepherds in order to advance his own erotic ambitions. Even his friendships among the shepherds are tainted by the duplicity and ambition that pastoral ostensibly
repudiates. Calidore

> did not despise [Coridon] quight,
> But usde him friendly for further intent,
> That by his fellowship, he colour might
> Both his estate, and love from skill of any wight.
> (6.10.37)

Such subterfuge exemplifies rather than opposes courtly practice.

Calidore's courtship of Pastorella, however, is initially unsuccessful.
Although Calidore "entertaine[s]" Pastorella "with all kind courtesies,
he could invent," she, who "had ever learn'd to love the lowly things /
Did litle whit regard his courteous guize." Pastorella views Calidore's
"knightly service" as an affectation, a "queint usage" (6.9.34–35). He
thus must accommodate his courtly behavior to her pastoral tastes,
altering

> the manner of his loftie looke;
> And doffing his bright armes, himselfe addrest
> In shepheards weed, and in his hand he tooke,
> In stead of steelehead speare, a shepheards hooke.
> (6.9.36)

Even as he takes off his knightly garb, however, Calidore manifests a
primary lesson of courtly conduct: adapting oneself to the inclinations
of those whom one desires to please. As Castiglione recommends, the
good courtier should "reverence the prince he serveth above all other
thinges, and in his wil, manners and fashions, to bee altogether plyable
to please him."[20] Calidore's surrender of his arms, and his adoption of
shepherds' weeds, measures his courtly pliability to Pastorella's fashions. As Louis Montrose has demonstrated, in Renaissance pastoral the
humble attire of a shepherd can function as an intensification of political ambition rather than a repudiation of it.[21]

Paradoxically, this pliability to Pastorella's tastes is the source of his
ultimate power over her. His courtship of Pastorella is successful pre-

cisely because of his willing submission to her: "So well he woo'd her, and so well he wrought her, / With humble service, and with daily sute, / That at the last unto his will he brought her" (6.10.38). By showing how Calidore gains authority over Pastorella through graceful gestures of self-abasement, Spenser exposes the aggressive undercurrents of courtly submission. As Stanley Stewart argues, "Calidore designs his 'courtesies,' not as a gift, but as a means to *acquire* the gift of Pastorella's love."[22] Like Spenser himself, Calidore deploys the currency of gifts as the medium of his own aspirations. Indeed, it is only after Calidore kills a threatening tiger and chops off its head as a present to Pastorella that she is fully won over: "From that day forth she gan him to affect, / And daily more her favour to augment" (6.10.37). The violence of arms at once supplements and suffuses the acts of courtship.

In his courtship of Pastorella, furthermore, Calidore practices the sublimation of competitive impulses so necessary for survival at court. "Sordid rivalry among authors," remarks Phoebe Sheavyn, "was the inevitable consequence of the struggle for favour" in the Elizabethan patronage system.[23] Where Coridon, who also loved Pastorella, "would loure, / And byte his lip" for jealousy of Calidore, Calidore by contrast continually applauds Coridon's clumsy efforts. He commends Coridon's pastoral gifts to Pastorella. When appointed to lead the ring of dances among the shepherds, moreover, he defers to Coridon, and "set[s] [Coridon] in his [own] place." Even when Pastorella places a garland on Calidore's head, he "did not soone displace, / And did it put on Coridons in stead" (6.9.39–42). Precisely by demonstrating through such gestures that he is above the competition, Calidore succeeds in the competition for favor. When the symbolic violence of their battle for place erupts in the actual violence of a wrestling match, Calidore nearly breaks Coridon's neck, then places the oaken crown bestowed by Pastorella upon the head he almost dislodged. Such behavior brilliantly but exasperatingly defuses the ill will that competition for favor can breed; ultimately "even they, the which his rivals were, / Could not maligne him, but commend him needs" (6.9.45). Frank Whigham has catalogued the "tropes of personal rivalry" available to the Renaissance courtier for the stifling of courtly rivals by calling them upstarts or accusing them of affectation.[24] Calidore exercises a subtler but far more effective strategy than those Whigham discovered in courtesy literature, silencing a rival by deferring to him, and denying that a rivalry exists. Calidore succeeds because he seems to scorn success. In doing so, he exercises the essence of courtly *sprezzatura*, which entails a kind of stylish feigning of modesty about one's own immensely artful performances. Aptly described by Whigham as "the master trope of the courtier, the dynamic mode of the fundamental stylistic category of grace," *sprezzatura* involves the expression of graceful contempt for one's highest efforts.[25] Calidore advances his amorous and political interests by means of an elegant combination of submission to pastoral convention, condescension to inferiors, and maintenance of an aristocratic distaste for the vulgar search for favor, in which he nevertheless participates.

Critics have been rather hard on Calidore for taking leave of his quest of the Blatant Beast.[26] But to reproach him for ignoring his mission while among the shepherds is to fail to see the close linkage between his pastoral activity and his heroic quest. In *The Civile Conversation,* Stefano Guazzo laments the existence of those "biters," out of "whose mouth proceede certaine short nips, which pearce our hearts more than sharpe arrows."[27] In the pastoral episode we watch Calidore deal brilliantly with the verbal violence epitomized in the wagging tongues of the Blatant Beast. When the narrator steps back at the beginning of Canto 12 to defend Calidore's pastoral retreat, he asserts that this long delay from Calidore's appointed mission—to catch the Blatant Beast—"hath not bene mis-sayd, / To shew the courtesie by him profest, / Even unto the lowest and the least" (6.12.2). As Richard Helgerson suggests, "The prime virtue of Courtesy seems better exemplified by Calidore's truant pastoral retirement than by his heroic pursuit of the Blatant Beast."[28] The pastoral respite, then, entails the practice of the modes of courtship it ostensibly disputes.

Similarly, its apotheosis—the vision of the Graces on Acidale—is deeply implicated in the political pressures it purportedly escapes. The landscape itself is endowed with social meaning. The wood bordering the hill, composed of "trees of honour," is "of matchlesse hight, that seem'd th'earth to disdaine"; at its foot is "a gentle flud" which debars the approach of both "wylde beastes" and "the ruder clowne" (6.10.6– 7). Geography generates a "natural" version of the social exclusivity which marks the court Spenser himself hopes to enter. Calidore feels himself drawn to this profoundly enclosed place but also fears trespassing upon it:

> He durst not enter into th'open greene,
> For dread of them unwares to be descryde,
> For breaking of their daunce, if he were seene;
> But in the covert of the wood did byde,
> Beholding all, yet of them unespyde.

Calidore becomes a voyeur on "an hundred naked maidens lilly white, / All raunged in a ring, and dauncing in delight," a vision so alluring that "even he him selfe his eyes envyde." The fear of intruding upon the scene chafes against the desire—at once social and erotic—which it stirs.[29]

At the center of the hundred maidens are the three Graces, themselves circling "Another Damzell." All are dancing to the piping of Colin Clout, the epitome of pastoral poetry, and a figure with whom Spenser had identified himself since his first book of poetry, *The Shepheardes Calender*. Somewhat unexpectedly, Spenser compares the "beauty of this goodly band" to a mistaken conflation of mythological accounts of battle and of marriage:

> Looke how the Crowne, which *Ariadne* wore
> Upon her yvory forehead that same day,
> That *Theseus* her unto his bridale bore,
> When the bold *Centaures* made that bloudy fray
> With the fierce *Lapithes*, which did them dismay.
>   (6.10.13)

As many critics have pointed out, Spenser here confuses the wedding of Theseus and Ariadne with that of Pirithous and Hippodamia, at which one of the centaurs in attendance drunkenly tries to rape the bride.[30] But equally notable is Spenser's placing the violence of the "bold Centaurs" and "fierce Lapithes" at the center of his emblem of harmony, courtesy, and grace. In doing so he reveals the "bloudy fray" at the core of even the most idealized vision of courtesy, the violence it (in both senses) *contains*.[31] Adumbrating both Calidore's subsequent interruption of this vision and the concurrent invasion of the pastoral world by the brigands, this image of vehement rapacity amid harmonious betrothal betrays the permeability of the highest social bonds, and the most refined social practices, to duress from within and without.

Calidore's invasion of Colin's private piping to the Graces is the culmination of a series of interruptions in Book 6. Calidore, for example, stumbles "rudely" upon Calepine and Serena making love (6.3.21). Priscilla and Aladine thought they had found "a covert glade / Within a wood, . . . free from all gealous spyes" (6.2.16), only to be surprised by an envious and discourteous knight. Arthur "troubles" the Hermit by unintentionally interrupting his devotions (6.5.36). Ideally, courtesy assuages the immense social anxiety that issues from the accidental invasion of private space. On Acidale, however, the approach of the exemplar of courtesy shatters rather than reestablishes social harmony, and causes Colin to break his pipe. Calidore apologizes profusely and often for "this luckelesse breach" (6.10.29) but even his ravishingly gracious words seem incapable of compensating for the loss of the vision of the Graces, a vision beyond the control of mortals, "For being gone, none can them bring in place, / But whom they of them selves list so to

grace" (6.10.20). Both the practices of courtesy and the powers of poetry are finally revealed to be inadequate to sustain the grace Spenser
desires. The consummate vision of courtesy cannot bear the invasive violence that its exemplar ideally should subdue.

By having the Graces dance to the tune of a shepherd poet and vanish when approached by a courteous knight, Spenser would appear to
privilege the accomplishments of poetry over the practices of courtesy.
As Daniel Javitch argues, "Spenser reveals the courtier's dependence
on the poet's 'gracious gifts' by presenting Calidore's encounter with
Colin Clout as a rite of initiation. The poet has become the high priest
of Courtesy. It is under his inspired guidance that the courtier as aco-
lyte may be initiated into its mysteries."[32] Yet the power Colin exercises
over his vision is extremely limited; he is unable either to prevent the
incursion of Calidore or to call back the Graces once they have fled. He
is more the victim of Calidore's interruption than he is tutor to Calidore's socialization. The emphasis in this canto is not on the romantic
withdrawal into an imaginative landscape that many readers have suggested but rather on the debilitating vulnerability of all imaginative
space.[33] The episode concludes not in an endorsement of the powers of
the creative imagination but rather in a demonstration of the fragility
of its products. Despite the noted inversion by which a rustic shepherd
has access to something unavailable to a courtly knight, and the equally
suggestive displacement of Queen Elizabeth by Colin's country lass at
the center of the poet's world, the scenario demonstrates what the last
lines of the book will bemoan: the subjugation of poetry to the social
and political forces Spenser wishes it could control.[34]

The manner in which these forces permeate literary conduct is chill-
ingly embodied in the conduct of the cannibals and the brigands. The
cannibals who capture Serena, for example, behave remarkably like
courtly poets in blazoning the qualities of their delectable captive:
"Some with their eyes the daintest morsels chose; / Some praise her
paps, some praise her lips and nose; / Some whet their knives, and
stript their elboes bare" (6.8.39). Nancy Vickers has proposed that the
dissection of the female body in conventional Petrarchan blazon functions as a ritual dismemberment of the female corpus it celebrates.[35]
The syntactic parallel between praising paps and whetting knives demonstrates the structural similarity between the symbolic violence of
courtly panegyric and the actual violence of cannibalism. Likewise, the
brigands who capture Pastorella engage in standard panegyric of female beauty, but only in order to increase the fee they will get for her
at the slave market: they "gan her forme and feature to expresse, / The
more t'augment her price, through praise of comlinesse" (6.11.11). Although supplying the absolute gauge of incivility, the violent cannibals

and the mercantile brigands also function as materialistic versions of
the literary behavior that ideally opposes them.

Unlike the brigands, however, who attempt to market their captives,
the cannibals reject all economic activity:

> ne did [they] give
> Them selves to any trade, as for to drive
> The painefull plough, or cattell for to breed,
> Or by adventrous merchandize to thrive;
> But on the labours of poore men to feed.
>
> (6.8.35)

The opposite of gracious beneficence, remarks Daniel Tuvill, is "the
barbarous ingratitude of inhuman cannibals."[36] Rather than feeding
others—the essential gesture of courtesy—Spenser's cannibals "eate
the flesh of men, whom they mote finde, / And straungers to devoure,
which on their border / Were brought by errour" (6.8.36). The cannibalism of the Salvage Nation is, as Cheney argues, "presented as a logical consequence of their refusal to participate in any productive
activity."[37] The very opportunity for courtesy, Spenser implies, depends on one's prior engagement in some form of productive activity.

Yet Spenser's deep antipathy to the rapacious nonproductive economy of the Salvage Nation does not make him sympathetic to the cause
of wage labor. Indeed, he reserves some of his bitterest invective for the
two knights Sir Turpine hires to help him get revenge on Arthur. Sir
Turpine promises the knights that if they will revenge the "great dis-
courtesie" Arthur has inflicted on him, "they should accomplish both a
knightly deed, / And for their paines obtaine of him a goodly meed"
(6.7.4). When Arthur kills one and defeats the other, Spenser un-
leashes cutting irony against their having acted "for promise of great
meed," declaring "now sure ye well have earn'd your *meed*" (6.7.12, 13;
my italics). Spenser is so hard on these unfortunate knights in part because their motives impinge so closely on his own. Despite (or perhaps
because of) Spenser's unmistakable hope that his own literary efforts
will be rewarded materially—one does not preface a work with seventeen dedicatory sonnets plus an overarching dedication to the queen
for absolutely uninterested motives—his censure of the hireling
knights involves what Pierre Bourdieu terms the "censorship of direct
expression of personal interest" necessary to the production of the
myth of voluntary and nonbinding service.[38] The knights, by contrast,
possess no devotion to the fiction of disinterested giving, and turn the
acts of chivalry into affairs of the marketplace. The surviving knight
laments "that ever I for meed did undertake / So hard a taske, as life

for hyre to sell" (6.7.15). Meliboe uses precisely this mercantile terminology to describe his courtly experience; the court for him is the
place "where I did sell my selfe for yearely hire" (6.9.24) As Calidore's
violence exposes the symbolic duress of courtesy, so does the hireling
labor of these knights lay bare the mystified economy of social exchange. Indeed, when Calidore promises Meliboe "golden guerdon"
for his hospitality, the veil transmuting vulgar hire into courteous reward begins to disappear (6.9.32). But by misrecognizing the "naked
self-interest" of his own productions, and by projecting his critique
of such activity onto the two hireling knights, Spenser maintains the
illusion that his creation is like that of the shepherds, who sing only
to one another and their sheep: "For other worldly wealth they cared
nought" (6.9.5).

Opposing both cannibalistic predation and mercenary motivation is
the economic process represented by Colin's interpretation of the
dancing posture of the Graces: "two of them still forward seem'd to
bee, / But one still towards shew'd her selfe afore; / That good should
from us goe, then come in greater store" (6.10.24). Deploying a pun on
then designating a sequential relation between giving and receiving and
than designating a comparative relation between giving and receiving,
these dense and heavily annotated lines are, as Thomas P. Roche argues, "genuinely ambiguous."[39] Tracing an alternating rather than a
direct current of commodities, the ambiguity allows Spenser to oscillate
between an account of our own good coming back to us redoubled and
a notion of our own efforts always being greater than the rewards they
attain. The former traces the hope of a poet in a patronage system; the
latter exposes the frustrations of one who feels himself inadequately
rewarded. Thomas Cain argues that on Acidale, Calidore "sees verbal
courtesy transfigured from social manipulation to a system of creative
giving and receiving."[40] Although Spenser does imagine here a cycle
of unlimited reciprocity that escapes the vulgar competition of the
potlatch and enriches all who participate in it, he does not force the
evacuation of manipulative energies from his description of verbal
courtesy. Rather, he creatively delineates the circulatory processes he
hopes his own gifts will enter, and proposes an economic model for the
dispersal of grace which should ensure their proper reward. "Distinctions and lasting associations," proposes Bourdieu, "are founded in the
circular circulation from which the legitimation of power arises as a
symbolic surplus value."[41] Spenser is divided between his allegiance to
a model of the monarch as the source of all value and his devotion to
the social importance of his own literary labors. As the Proem to Book
6 delineates a flow of gifts which belies our experience of the fluvial
metaphor—"So from the Ocean all rivers spring, / And tribute backe

repay as to their King" (6.Proem. 7.4–5)—so does Spenser on Acidale superimpose competing models for the circulation of courtly favor. By emphasizing within his literary production the circulatory processes he hopes it will enter, describing in detail the surplus of grace at its center, and depicting a model for the distribution of that surplus, Spenser imagines an economy of infinite increase for his own act of deeply interested presentation.

The 1596 *Faerie Queene* was published without the seventeen dedicatory sonnets and the letter to Raleigh which circumscribe the 1590 edition. This may have been accidental. It is unlikely that Spenser would forget, however, since the exclusion of a sonnet to Burleigh in the 1590 edition had led to a hastily arranged insertion of seven dedicatory sonnets. The dedication to Elizabeth, moreover, was expanded in 1596, with phrasing "that accentuates the grandeur of the queen and the humility of the poet."[42] The sonnets may have been left out because Spenser was discouraged about his courtly prospects; or perhaps they were left out because the narrative structure of Book 6 absorbs their supplicatory energies and performs their courtly tasks more effectively. Continually in these sonnets Spenser asks his superiors to behave in ways that are exemplified by the narrative of Book 6. For example, he asks the Earl of Oxford to "defend" his work "from foule Envies poisnous bit," seeking from his patron chivalric protection from a bite very much like that of the Blatant Beast. Likewise, he asks Thomas Sackville to protect his text against "vile Zoilus backbitings." In the dedicatory sonnet to Lord Grey of Wilton, whom he served as secretary in Ireland, Spenser implores Grey to "vouchsafe" to receive these "rude rymes, the which a rustick Muse did weave / In savadge soyle." He thus asks Grey to exercise that form of courtesy which Calidore practices toward the shepherds, and which Calepine and Serena display toward the Salvage Man—graciously accepting the fruits of inferiors, "howsoever base and mean" (see 6.5.15 and 6.9.7). Likewise, he requests the Earl of Ormond to "receive . . . a simple taste / Of the wilde fruit, which salvage soyl hath bred" (pp. 25–33). By strategically depicting and praising Calidore's demonstrations of courtesy "even unto the lowest and the least," Book 6 functions as a covert act of courtship, quietly exemplifying the kinds of generous behavior for which Spenser overtly pleads in the seventeen dedicatory sonnets. Like Calidore, whose "faire usage and conditions sound . . . in all mens liking gayned place, / And with the greatest purchast greatest grace," Spenser hopes his own fair usage will purchase for him both grace and place (6.1.2, 3).

But the final lines of Book 6, where Spenser tells his "rimes" to "seeke to please, that now is counted wisemens threasure," imply that such an economy remains an impossible fantasy in Elizabethan En-

gland, where the upstart poet's tenuous claims to authority remain separate from the power bestowed by one's place in the social hierarchy
(6.12.41). As a result, the poet must engage in the potentially corrupting act of pleasing superiors in order to survive. Divided between the
imposition of discipline as a principle of social reform and the need to
placate the powers that be, between paying accommodating tribute to
a closed circle of power and transgressively attempting to enter it,
Spenser in *The Faerie Queene* records the immense strain involved in his
position as both aspiring court poet and cultural critic.

The situation in Ireland as Spenser describes it in *A View of the Present
State of Ireland,* however, was quite different, and illumines from the
side his view of the failures of English culture. Although complaining
that the Irish bards "through desire of pleasing perhaps too much . . .
have clouded the truth" of Ireland's antique past, he proceeds to
project onto Irish society his own unfulfilled wishes for the role of poetry in English culture.[43] The "profession" of the bards, he relates, is
"to set forth the praises and dispraises of men, in the poems or rhymes,
the which are had in so high regard and estimation amongst them that
none dare displease them for fear to be run into reproach through
their offense and to made infamous in the mouths of all men; for their
verses are taken up with a general applause, and usually sung at all
feasts and meetings by certain other persons whose proper function
that is, which also receive for the same great rewards and reputation
besides" (pp. 72–73). Rather than having to please authority, as
Spenser laments his lines must do at the end of Book 6, Irish bards are
so powerful that "none dare displease *them.*" This barbarous country, so
unlike "civil" England, considers poetry a profession of "great rewards
and reputation." Since Irenius had begun this discussion under the ru-
bric of "their customs [I] dislike of," Eudoxus expresses great surprise
"that you blame this in them, which I would otherwise have thought to
have been worthy of good account . . . than to have been disliked" (p.
73). Irenius concedes that "such poets as in their writing do labour to
better the manners" of "young spirits" are "worthy to be had in [such]
great respect" (p. 73), implying that a poet such as Spenser, whose
project, as described in the letter to Raleigh, was to "fashion a gentleman or noble person in vertuous and gentle discipline" (p. 15), would
justly thrive in such a system. "But these Irish bards," Irenius continues, "are . . . so far from instructing young men in moral discipline,
that they themselves do more deserve to be sharply discipl[in]ed." "For
little reward or a share of a stolen cow," he complains, they will praise
even "the most licentious" and "rebellious" dispositions, affiliating the
bards with a menial status and mercantile motives that belie the exalted role he has just granted them (pp. 73–74). Nevertheless, com-

pared to the fragile and ephemeral vision of the power of poetry on Acidale—a vision whose spell is broken neither by some ferocious beast nor by a tribe of barbarians but rather by the accidental incursion of a courteous knight—Irish bards exercise an enviable degree of power and influence, however misapplied, over their culture. Although *A View* is dedicated to the policy of "reducing that savage nation to . . . civility," England, Spenser seems to whisper, could learn much about the use as well as the abuse of poetry from this society it wishes to suppress.

In an appropriately graceful phrase, C. S. Lewis terms courtesy "the poetry of conduct, an 'unbought grace of life' which makes its possessor immediately loveable to all who meet him."[44] In the social and political world of late sixteenth-century England, however, both poetry and conduct were shaped by the need to please those in whose interest it was to privilege courtesy as a discourse that transcended the material pressures of the social world. As a form of suasive verbal behavior, moreover, poetry functioned as courtesy in verse, a formalized negotiation between the aspirations of the self and the demands of the social hierarchy. Spenser had praised his friend Gabriel Harvey as one who

> Ne fawnest for the favour of the great:
> Ne fearest foolish reprehension
> Of faulty men, which daunger to thee threat.
> But freely doest, of what thee list, entreat,
> Like a great Lord of peereless liberty.[45]

Rather than becoming a lord of interior liberty delivered from the servility demanded by the social hierarchy, however, Spenser became a lord of colonial repression, taking possession of the estate of Kilcolman, Ireland, in 1590. Ireland—the site of Spenser's fantasy of bardic power—was appropriately the locus of his attainment of social status. The previous owner of the estate Spenser controlled, Sir John of Desmond, was a rebel whose rotting body dangled for years on the North Gate of Cork.[46] By siding with such violence in the name of civility, then, Spenser did succeed in fashioning himself into a sort of colonial gentleman, traversing in reverse the social and geographic distance covered by Calidore, a knight who traded his armor for shepherd's attire. Spenser's gentility, however, proved as fragile as the vision of the Graces on Acidale. In October 1598 the estate was burned to the ground during Tyrone's rebellion, by the very forces of incivility Spenser's fiction and his position as a plantation landlord had tried to harness. As in Book 6 of *The Faerie Queene*, the transgressive violence and economic coercion which courtesy disguises in order to sustain itself could no longer be contained within an accommodating fiction of civility.

N O T E S

1. David Norbrook, *Poetry and Politics in the English Renaissance* (London: Routledge and Kegan Paul, 1984), p. 144.

2. Norbert Elias, *Power and Civility,* vol. 2 of *The Civilizing Process,* trans. Edmund Jephcott (New York: Pantheon, 1982), p. 259.

3. Pierre Bourdieu, *Outline of a Theory of Practice,* trans. Richard Nice (Cambridge: Cambridge University Press, 1977), p. 196.

4. W. O. Evans, " 'Cortaysye' in Middle English," *Medieval Studies* 29 (1967), 147.

5. Richard C. McCoy, *The Rites of Knighthood: The Literature and Politics of Elizabethan Chivalry* (Berkeley: University of California Press, 1989), p. 3.

6. Edmund Spenser, *The Faerie Queene,* ed. Thomas P. Roche, Jr. (Harmondsworth: Penguin, 1987); all citations refer to this edition.

7. I take explicit issue here with the arguments of Dorothy Woodward Culp, "Courtesy and Moral Virtue," *Studies in English Literature* 11 (1971), 37–51.

8. Stephen Greenblatt, *Renaissance Self-Fashioning: From More to Shakespeare* (Chicago: University of Chicago Press, 1980), pp. 178, 186.

9. *Faerie Queene,* p. 17.

10. On the characteristically Spenserean quality of this act of self-presentation, see Richard Helgerson, *Self-Crowned Laureates: Spenser, Jonson, Milton, and the Literary System* (Berkeley: University of California Press, 1983), chap. 2, "The New Poet Presents Himself," pp. 55–100.

11. In "Exchanging Gifts: The Elizabethan Currency of Children and Romance," chap. 2 of *Cultural Aesthetics: Renaissance Literature and the Practice of Social Ornament* (Chicago: University of Chicago Press, 1991), pp. 29–66, Patricia Fumerton explores the social processes behind Spenser's portraits of the circulation of gifts, and argues that *The Faerie Queene* "is a circle of gift, an endlessly transformational round wherein all loss is gain, all giving taking, all dying living" (p. 58).

12. In a letter to Spenser, Gabriel Harvey lists the books most popular at Cambridge: "Machiavelli, Castilio, Petrarch, Boccacio, della Casa, Guazzo, and Aretino are greatly enjoyed"; quoted in Alexander C. Judson, *The Life of Edmund Spenser* (Baltimore: Johns Hopkins University Press, 1945), p. 38.

13. Moreover, as Frank Whigham argues, such literature aided the very mobility it intended to repress; see *Ambition and Privilege: The Social Tropes of Elizabethan Courtesy Theory* (Berkeley: University of California Press, 1984).

14. As Marvin Becker proposes, "Spenser contested the reigning public fictions while embracing them"; see *Civility and Society in Western Europe, 1300–1600* (Bloomington: Indiana University Press, 1988), p. 136.

15. Indeed, as Norbrook points out, part of Book 5 was reprinted as an anti-Leveller pamphlet in 1648 titled *The Faerie Leveller;* see *Poetry and Politics,* p. 151.

16. Spenser's dedicatory sonnet to the young earl of Cumberland suggests one way in which this fashioning might occur, promising the earl that he will find in the text "brave ensample of long passed daies, / In which trew honor yee may fashiond see," and that this example "to like desire of honor may ye raise" (*Faerie Queene,* p. 27).

17. Edmund Spenser, *A View of the Present State of Ireland,* ed. W. L. Renwick (Oxford: Clarendon Press, 1970), pp. 1, 117. Spenser's admiration for

McHugh must be tempered by his denigration of Hugh O'Neal, who was, he relates, "lifted up by Her Majesty out of the dust to that he hath now wrought himself unto." Spenser compares O'Neal to a "frozen snake, who being for compassion relieved by the husbandman, soon after he was warm began to hiss, and threaten danger even to him and his" (p. 114).

18. Michael O'Connell, *Mirror and Veil: The Historical Dimension of Spenser's Faerie Queene* (Chapel Hill: University of North Carolina Press, 1977), p. 165. The etymology Spenser questions is explored by Catherine Bates, " 'Of Court It Seemes': A Semantic Analysis of *Courtship* and *To Court*," *Journal of Medieval and Renaissance Studies* 20 (1990), 21–57, expanded in *The Rhetoric of Courtship in Elizabethan Language and Literature* (Cambridge: Cambridge University Press, 1992), chap. 2.

19. My argument in this and the following paragraph has been anticipated in part by Jacqueline T. Miller, "The Courtly Figure: Spenser's Anatomy of Allegory," *Studies in English Literature* 31 (1991), 51–68; Miller argues that Pastorella "is, despite her name, the object of a very courtly desire and aspiration" (p. 59).

20. Baldassare Castiglione, *The Book of the Courtier,* trans. Thomas Hoby (1561; reprint London: Dent, 1928), p. 106.

21. I am thinking particularly of Louis Adrian Montrose, "Gifts and Reasons: The Contexts of Peele's *Araygnement of Paris*," *English Literary History* 47 (1980), 433–61; "Of Gentlemen and Shepherds: The Politics of Elizabethan Pastoral Form," *English Literary History* 50 (1983), 415–59; and "The Elizabethan Subject and the Spenserian Text," in *Literary Theory / Renaissance Texts,* ed. Patricia Parker and David Quint (Baltimore: Johns Hopkins University Press, 1986), pp. 303–40.

22. Stanley Stewart, "Sir Calidore and 'Closure,' " *Studies in English Literature* 24 (1984), 79.

23. Phoebe Sheavyn, *The Literary Profession in the Elizabethan Age* (Manchester: Manchester University Press, 1909), p. 32.

24. Whigham, *Ambition and Privilege,* pp. 147–69.

25. Ibid., p. 93. *Sprezzatura* is derived from the verb *sprezzare,* which means "to disdain" or "to hold in contempt." Hoby translates it as "a certaine deigracing to cover arte withall," and argues that "of this doe I believe grace is much derived"; Castiglione, *Courtier,* p. 46.

26. See, for example, Harry Berger, "A Secret Discipline: *The Faerie Queene* VI," in *Form and Convention in the Poetry of Edmund Spenser,* ed. William Nelson (New York: Columbia University Press, 1961), pp. 35–75, and "The Prospect of Imagination: Spenser and the Limits of Poetry," *Studies in English Literature* 1 (1961), 93–120; and Richard Neuse, "Book 6 as Conclusion to *The Faerie Queene*," *English Literary History* 35 (1968), 329–53.

27. Stefano Guazzo, *The Civile Conversation,* trans. George Pettie (1581), ed. Edward Sullivan, 2 vols. (London: Constable, 1925), 1:72.

28. Helgerson, *Self-Crowned Laureates,* p. 90.

29. In *Gazing on Secret Sights: Spenser, Classical Imitation, and the Decorums of Vision* (Ithaca: Cornell University Press, 1990), Theresa M. Krier explicates the complex dynamics of such voyeurism throughout *The Faerie Queene.*

30. On the sources for this passage, see Edwin Greenlaw et al., eds., *The Works of Edmund Spenser: A Variorum Edition,* 6 vols. (Baltimore: Johns Hopkins University Press, 1938), 6:251.

31. Donald Cheney, by contrast, reads this as an emblem of the principle of *discordia concors;* see *Spenser's Image of Nature: Wild Man and Shepherd in The Faerie Queene* (New Haven: Yale University Press, 1966), p. 235.

32. Daniel Javitch, *Poetry and Courtliness in Renaissance England* (Princeton: Princeton University Press, 1978), p. 150.

33. I am thinking here of Arnold Williams, *Flower on a Lowly Stalk: The Sixth Book of "The Faerie Queene"* (East Lansing: Michigan State University Press, 1967); William V. Nestrick, "The Virtuous and Gentle Discipline of Gentlemen and Poets," *English Literary History* 35 (1968), 357–71; Berger, "The Prospect of Imagination" and "A Secret Discipline"; Humphrey Tonkin, *Spenser's Courteous Pastoral: Book VI of "The Faerie Queene"* (Oxford: Oxford University Press, 1972); David Miller, "Abandoning the Quest," *English Literary History* 46 (1979), 173–92; and John D. Bernard, *Ceremonies of Innocence: Pastoralism in the Poetry of Edmund Spenser* (Cambridge: Cambridge University Press, 1989).

34. In "Spenserean Autonomy and the Trial of New Historicism: Book Six of *The Faerie Queene*," *English Literary Renaissance* 22 (1992), 299–314, Robert E. Stillman develops a historical reading of the episode on Acidale by linking it to Spenser's colonial experience in Ireland.

35. Nancy Vickers, "Diana Described" Scattered Woman and Scattered Rhyme," in *Writing and Sexual Difference*, ed. Elizabeth Abel (Chicago: University of Chicago Press, 1982). In "The Comedy of Female Authority in *The Faerie Queene*," *English Literary Renaissance* 17 (1987), 164–65, Maureen Quilligan develops a similiar account of Spenserean blazon in Book 3.

36. Daniel Tuvill, "Of Gifts and Benefits," in *Essays Politic and Moral and Essays Moral and Theological* (1609), ed. John L. Lievsay (Charlottesville: University Press of Virginia, 1971), p. 106.

37. Cheney, *Spenser's Image of Nature*, p. 104.

38. Bourdieu, *Outline*, p. 194.

39. Roche, *The Faerie Queene*, p. 1228, links these two accounts to a tension between "the late classical view that good should from us go, then come in greater store" and the Christian view that "greater good should from us go *than* come in greater store."

40. Thomas H. Cain, *Praise in "The Faerie Queene"* (Lincoln: University of Nebraska Press 1978), p. 176.

41. Bourdieu, *Outline*, p. 195.

42. Judson, *Life*, p. 179.

43. Spenser, *A View*, p. 40; subsequent references to this work are cited in the text.

44. C. S. Lewis, *The Allegory of Love: A Study in Medieval Tradition* (New York: Oxford University Press, 1936), pp. 351–52.

45. "To the right worshipfull, my singular good friend, M. Gabriell Harvey, Doctor of the Lawes," cited from *The Shorter Poems of Edmund Spenser*, ed. William A. Oram et al. (New Haven: Yale University Press, 1989), p. 773.

46. Judson, *Life*, p. 129.

8. Submitting to History:
Marlowe's *Edward II*

JUDITH HABER

Marlowe's presentation of the brutal, iconographically "appropriate" murder of the king in *Edward II* has often posed a problem for critics. Traditionally, those who wished to avoid an orthodox interpretation of the play have appealed to some version of ambiguity, and this strategy survives in many current, historicized reconsiderations. In a discussion of closure and enclosure in Marlowe's plays, Marjorie Garber has provided a particularly cogent statement of this position, using Mortimer's "unpointed" Latin letter as support. The letter, designed to hide "the cause of Edward's death" (5.4.1–17),[1] is unpunctuated ("unpointed") and therefore ambiguous;[2] it can mean either "Fear not to kill the king, 'tis good he die," or "Kill not the king, 'tis good to fear the worst." Garber comments: "The letter reflects the essential ambiguity of the play. Is it good to kill the king, either politically or morally? . . . The letter sums up the conflict in the center of the play, for both of its statements are true."[3] Although I would agree that the letter is presented as centrally important, I believe that this formulation underestimates its force; the conflict between the two possible, positive interpretations of the letter—and of the play—is subsumed in, and ultimately negated by, a dialectic between socially constructed causal meaning and the threat of no meaning at all, a dialectic (in the play's terms) between "point" and pointlessness.

This paradoxical dialectic operates in some form in all of Marlowe's works, but nowhere so killingly as in *Edward II*. The idea of "pointlessness" emblematized by the letter pervades the play. In contrast to Marlowe's other plays, which repeatedly invoke Christian structures in the process of contesting them, *Edward II* contains few theological references (one of the few times God is mentioned Edward asks, "Who's there?" [1.2.199]). In the absence of a clear external point of reference,

structure and meaning become undecidable: the act of reinterpreta-
tion necessitated by the letter becomes the characteristic action of the
play. The audience is, of course, repeatedly forced to shift its sympathies, and is manipulated generally from a position opposing Edward
to one supporting him.[4] These shifts occur, however, not for the positive reasons that Garber and others have suggested, but as each successive position becomes insupportable—as Kent is compelled to shift,
in the space of a few minutes onstage, from the condemnation of an
"unnatural king" to the condemnation of an "unnatural revolt" (4.1.9;
4.5.18).

The audience's perplexing experience is encapsulated in a remarkable scene in which the barons are forced to reinterpret their own actions (1.4.187ff.). Having succeeded in banishing Gaveston, they are
persuaded to recall him, on the grounds that the significance (the consequence, the "point") of these acts is exactly the opposite of what it
originally appeared to be. During the course of this scene, almost everyone echoes the Archbishop of Canterbury's earlier resolution concerning the banishment—"Nothing shall alter us, we are resolved"
(1.4.74, cf. 214, 231, 233, 251)—and then discovers that "his mind is
changed" (1.4.236), until Lancaster finally erupts in despair:

> Can this be true 'twas good to banish him?
> And is this true to call him home again?
> Such reasons make white black and dark night day. . . .
> In no respect can contraries be true.
>
> (1.4.244–49)

He is, of course, right. The situation here (and throughout *Edward II*)
is not one in which contraries are equally "good" and "true" (the equiv-
alence made by Lancaster's elision) but one in which they are equally
false and "unnatural." The linguistic and structural contradictions that
pervade the play serve to unsettle the category of the natural and to
subvert significance itself. During their meeting the barons criticize
Mortimer for "play[ing] the sophister," and declare, "All that he speaks
is nothing" (1.4.255, 251). These comments come to define not a particular fault but the normal condition of speech in the play: unfixed,
arbitrary, reversible, and self-canceling—that is, pointless. It is this condition that paralyzes Isabella just before the meeting, when she wishes
she had been "stifled" by Edward's first marital embrace, since whether
she cries out unthinkingly against her husband's actions or attempts,
craftily, to "speak him fair," her efforts necessarily return on themselves and undermine her position (1.4.175–86). And it is this condition that is evoked by the characteristic linguistic tic of the play, the
antithetic exchange between adversaries.[5] To cite but a few examples:

Edward: Lay hands upon that traitor Mortimer.
Mortimer Senior: Lay hands upon that traitor Gaveston.

(1.4.20–21)

Queen: Villain 'tis thou that robbst me of my lord.
Gaveston: Madam, 'tis you that rob me of my lord.

(1.4.160–61)

Kent: Sister, Edward is my charge; redeem him.
Queen: Edward is my son, and I will keep him.

(5.2.114–15)

And of course, last but not least:

Warwick: St George for England
And the barons' right!
Edward: Saint George for England and King Edward's right!

(3.3.33–35)

Each of these exchanges (and there are many such in the play) is a contest over the definition and ownership of the signs of hierarchical structure—political, religious, familial, or rhetorical; they all serve to destabilize these structures, to reduce them to indefinition.

Throughout most of *Edward II* the only consistent reference point is death—which is viewed variously as an end, a consummation, and a center, and which is specifically termed a "period" (3.1.4–5; 4.6.61–62). But death is presented as an empty center, a hole in the middle of meaning, whose point is precisely its pointlessness, its capacity for erasing distinctions. Gaveston declares, when he is accorded the "honor" of an aristocratic beheading (rather than suffering the humiliation of being hanged): "Then I perceive, / That heading is one, and hanging is the other, / And death is all" (2.5.29–30).

The nominal center of the play is, of course, Edward; and Edward—who is "loose, " "pliant," and "flexible" (all similarly multivalent terms), impotent, theatrical, sexually ambiguous, and endlessly self-contradictory—is the embodiment of "pointlessness" in all its senses. The various connotations of the word coalesce in his homoerotic relationship with Gaveston, which is repeatedly presented as pointless play ("frolicking"), and is opposed (theoretically at least) to the productive—and reproductive—business of the kingdom. (Edward, a nineteenth-century editor of the chronicles tells us, was "the first king after the Conquest who was not a man of business.")[6] His attachment causes him to disregard his father's commandment, to neglect his queen—"the sister of the King of France," "sole sister of Valois" (1.4.187; 2.2.172)—

and it threatens to open a gap in the orderly process of dynastic succession. Edward tells the peers:

> Make several kingdoms of this monarchy
> And share it equally amongst you all,
> So I may have some nook or corner left
> To frolic with my dearest Gaveston.
>   (1.4.70–73)

The "nook or corner" that he claims as his own is imagined as a place apart, a site of insignificance: it is what is left over after the kingdom has been meaningfully divided, the socially and sexually unmarked locus of unproductive play.

This representation of Edward's relationship with Gaveston reflects conventional Renaissance definitions (if not conventional evaluations) of sodomy. As the work of Alan Bray and Jonathan Goldberg has demonstrated, "sodomite" was effectively a nonidentity in the Renaissance.[7] Not only did it not designate a particular sexual identity, not only did sodomitical actions become visible only when connected with other subversive activities, "sodomy" was formally defined as the principle of sexual indefinition (or nonidentity) itself: neither of God nor of the devil, outside the intelligible order of creation ("the universal and public manuscript" of nature),[8] it signified precisely "nothing"—nonmeaning, chaos, and indeterminacy. For this reason it was a particular focus for the fears of the antitheatrical writers, who were consumed by anxieties about destabilizing reality and unfixing gendered identity, anxieties that are perfectly captured in Philip Stubbes's famous warning against the transvestite theater: "These goodly pageants being done," Stubbes asserts, "every mate sorts to his mate, every one brings another homeward of their way verye freendly, and in their secret conclaves (covertly), the play the Sodomits, or worse."[9] The terms of Stubbes's fears seem strikingly continuous with those of Edward's fantasies. Like Edward's anal "nook or corner," Stubbes's "secret conclaves" are invoked as the socially un(re)marked sites of indeterminacy; and the sexual "play" that occurs there, Stubbes suggests, is inseparable from other subversions of ordered reality, linguistic, political, and religious: "Playes and Enterluds," he continues, teach us "to play the Hipocrit, to cogge, lye, and falsifie; . . . to jest, laugh, and fleer, to grin, to nodd, and mow; . . . to playe the vice, to swear, teare, and blaspheme both Heaven and Earth."[10]

The implications, attractions, and threats of this "pointless play" are most fully developed in Edward II in two lyric, descriptive speeches, neither of which, significantly, is spoken by Edward himself. The first is Gaveston's description of the king's sports, his delight in "music," "poetry," and "pleasing shows." This soliloquy begins as a dramatic response, as Gaveston acknowledges the parting words of the emblematic "three poor men" ("We will wait here about the court" [1.1.48]). He then explains his need for a different sort of "discoursing" (1.1.31) than they can provide:

> These are not men for me;
> I must have wanton poets, pleasant wits,
> Musicians, that with touching of a string
> May draw the pliant King which way I please;
> Music and poetry is his delight,
> Therefore I'll have Italian masques by night. . . .
>   (1.1.49–54)

His explanation clearly and logically subordinates the power of play to his manipulative purpose. As he proceeds, however, his speech far exceeds its explanatory point. Metamorphic in both content and form, it momentarily dissolves linear time and detaches itself from the action of the drama as it focuses on a series of transformations that repeatedly blur distinctions between play and reality, male and female, human and beast:

> Therefore I'll have Italian masques by night,
> Sweet speeches, comedies and pleasing shows;
> And in the day, when he shall walk abroad,
> Like sylvan nymphs my pages shall be clad,
> My men like satyrs grazing on the lawns
> Shall with their goat feet dance an antic hay;
> Sometime a lovely boy in Dian's shape,
> With hair that gilds the water as it glides,
> Crownets of pearl about his naked arms,
> And in his sportful hands an olive-tree
> To hide those parts which men delight to see,
> Shall bathe him in a spring, and there, hard by
> One like Actaeon peeping through the grove
> Shall by the angry goddess be transformed,
> And running in the likeness of an hart,
> By yelping hounds pulled down, and seem to die;
> Such things as these best please his majesty.
>   (1.1.54–70)

At the center of the speech is the myth of Actaeon's vision of Diana. This is, of course, a fable of sexual differentiation: the forbidden sight of female difference or "lack" causes fear of castration in the male. In a brilliant analysis of Petrarch's poetry, Nancy Vickers has demonstrated that it is also the founding myth of Renaissance lyric: the suspended moment between seeing and dismemberment is the space in which the lyric poet writes, asserting his mastery over the female by scattering her body in rhyme.[11] The vision in Gaveston's speech is similarly suspended: forward movement is halted for an indeterminate span ("sometime") while Diana is described. But here the Actaeon myth is turned back on itself; the "castrated"—and castrating—female is male after all:

> Sometime a lovely boy in Dian's shape,
> With hair that gilds the water as it glides,
> Crownets of pearl about his naked arms,
> And in his sportful hands an olive-tree
> To hide those parts which men delight to see,
> Shall bathe him in a spring.

The primary effect of this transformation, however, is not to stabilize sexual identity but to dissolve it. By ambiguating male and female "parts," the real and the artificial, the hidden and the seen (note particularly the fetishistic "olive-tree" held in appropriately "sportful" hands), these lines manage to suggest that sexual difference itself is merely an artificial construct.[12] And they threaten to uncover (to make seen) the possibility that the Actaeon myth is constructed to hide—the possibility that there is never really any "point" to see at all.

This threat is gradually contained as the passage returns, in succession, to verbal action ("shall bathe"), to Actaeon ("hard by"), to Gaveston's purpose ("Such things as these best please his majesty"), and to the action of the play: "My lord! Here comes the king and the nobles / From the parliament; I'll stand aside" (1.1.71–72). It resurfaces quite clearly, however, in Mortimer's condemnation of Edward and Gaveston. Mortimer's speech is prompted by his uncle's defense of male sexual relations, a defense that gives them a lineage and portrays them as properly patrilineal—and as utterly unlike anything we ever see in the play:

> The mightiest kings have had their minions,
> Great Alexander loved Hephaestion,
> The conquering Hercules for Hylas wept,
> And for Patroclus stern Achilles drooped;
> And not kings only, but the wisest men:
> The Roman Tully loved Octavius,
> Grave Socrates, wild Alcibiades.
>   (1.4.390–96)

Though Edward himself once applies the Hercules-Hylas comparison to his relationship to Gaveston (1.1.143), the clearly defined, hierarchical relation that it implies seems wholly inadequate to describe their bond. And the elder Mortimer implicitly acknowledges this disjunction in his next lines, when he characterizes Edward's attachments as "toys" from which "riper years will wean him" (1.4.400).

After listening to his uncle's defense, Mortimer dismisses Edward's "wanton humour" as beside the point. But its pointlessness returns in a series of other wanton transformations of the signs of stable hierarchy and order:

> Uncle, his wanton humour grieves not me,
> But this I scorn, that one so basely born
> Should by his sovereign's favor grow so pert
> And riot it with the treasure of the realm,
> While soldiers mutiny for want of pay;
> He wears a lord's revenue on his back,
> And Midas-like he jets it in the court,
> With base outlandish cullions at his heels,
> Whose proud fantastic liveries make such show,
> As if that Proteus, god of shapes, appeared;
> I have not seen a dapper jack so brisk.
> He wears a short Italian hooded cloak
> Larded with pearl, and in his Tuscan cap
> A jewel of more value than the crown.
>
> (1.4.401–14)

Here Mortimer moves freely among, and implicitly equates, a number of affronts to and inversions of traditional values: the "base" is raised above the noble, the foreigner above the native-born, the frivolous above the serious and practical, the superficial above the substantive. And, as he focuses on the excessive "show" that Gaveston's clothing makes, his speech begins to participate in the disruptions it describes. Like Gaveston's earlier speech, which it parallels, this descriptive passage exceeds its putative point, painting a strangely compelling picture of Gaveston's metamorphoses before it issues (oddly but appropriately) in a complaint that Edward and Gaveston are not taking the barons (or the signs of their station) seriously, that they are watching the peers as if they were characters in a show:

> While others walk below, the King and he
> From out a window laugh at such as we
> And flout our train and jest at our attire.
> Uncle, 'tis this that makes me impatient.
>
> (1.4.415–18)

This complaint more or less accurately describes Gaveston's position after his earlier lyric speech: he stands "aside" and comments scornfully on the actions of "the king and the nobles." And the charge is repeated in a later description of Edward on the battlefield:

> When wert thou in the field with banner spread?
> But once, and then thy soldiers marched like players,
> With garish robes, not armour, and thyself
> Bedaubed with gold, rode laughing at the rest,
> Nodding and shaking of thy spangled crest,
> Where women's favours hung like labels down.
>
> (2.2.182–87)

By "playing the sodomites" (playing, in effect, the players), Edward and Gaveston continually threaten to demystify the signs of hierarchy and order, to expose the serious, productive business of the realm as pointless, as necessarily an exercise in "playing the sophister."

The reading I have proposed so far would seem to support Edward's position—except, of course, for the fact that Edward is incompletely self-conscious about his own pointlessness (making him the perfect embodiment of the idea). While Mortimer and Gaveston attempt (with some regularity, if with predictable lack of success) to manipulate and control indeterminacy, Edward veers back and forth between painfully inadequate attempts to seize control and equally inadequate attempts to cede it. Simon Shepherd has called him "inconsistently masculine";[13] it is but putting the same idea the other way around to note that he is consistently inconsistent. His self-contradictions reach a height in the speech in which he debates whether or not he is willing to resign his crown: he repeats the word "but" so frequently here that it assumes the force of a contradiction even when it means otherwise (e.g., "But what are kings when regiment is gone / But perfect shadows in a sunshine day?" [5.1. 26–27; and see ll. 9, 11, 24, 36, 43, 56, 59, 69, 76, 82]). Edward is not deliberately inverting conventional structures; neither is he attempting (like Tamburlaine) to be paradoxically "on top" of impotence and indeterminacy. He simply doesn't know which way is up. Nevertheless—in fact, as a result—he gets the point in the end.

Edward's incapacity suggests that it is impossible effectively to escape socially constructed, determinate meaning. And this idea is emphasized throughout the play. It seems appropriate that the only articulate defense—really the only clear articulation—of homoerotic relations we hear is both strikingly patrilineal and wholly inadequate to the play. Attempts to escape orthodox logic and hierarchy here invariably return on themselves. There's even a joke to this effect early on: Baldock says, "I am none of these common pedants, I, / That cannot speak without *propterea quod* [that is, 'because']"; and Spencer replies, "But one of those that saith *quandoquidem* [that is, 'because']" (2.1.52–54). His jest echoes grimly through all the characters' various, contradictory attempts to find a "cause" for the confusion that surrounds them:

> Here comes she that's cause of all these jars.
> (Edward on Isabella [2.2.223])

> Corrupter of thy King, cause of these broils.
> (Mortimer on Gaveston [2.5.10])

> Misgoverned kings are cause of all this wrack.
> (Isabella on Edward [4.4.9])

Gaveston's and Mortimer's lyric flights (paltry when compared to Tamburlaine's) *are* finally contained, and they are unusual moments in the play. Evocations of pointlessness and nonmeaning are regularly presented in emblematic or aphoristic form;[14] while interrogating conventional moral structure, they insistently acknowledge their indebtedness to it. Attempts to enunciate death seem especially sententious and medieval. One thinks, for example, of the peers' standards for the tournament, all of which exceed their bearers' intentions, but all of which return to the same point—*undique mors est, aeque tandem*, "death is everywhere," "equal at last" (2.2.20, 28)—or of the "gloomy" Mower in the mead, who leaves requesting that the peers "remember [him]" (4.6.29, 115), or of the many heavy-handed references to the deadly "name of Mortimer" (e.g., 2.3.23, 4.6.38). The unpointed letter is, of course, itself such a carefully packaged piece of nonmeaning. And although Mortimer (and the play) make much of its indeterminancy, no one, in fact, has any great difficulty construing it. Gurney (who is not too bright) does complain, "I know not how to conster it," but Matrevis easily explains its meaning: it was, he notes, "left unpointed for the nonce," that is, on purpose, for a point (5.5.15–18). And Edward III treats it as completely transparent (5.6.44–48).

Neither do we have any difficulty construing the end. Not only does Edward get the point here, we all do; we are unable, finally, to avoid it. Critics have appealed to "the complex, sympathetic human feeling[s] evoked by the play,"[15] but the only character who effectively articulates and enacts those feelings—Edward III—supports by his very existence an orthodox interpretation of the play. In fact he does so precisely because he does articulate and enact those feelings: "Traitor," he says to Mortimer, "in me my loving father speaks / And plainly saith 'twas thou that murderedst him" (5.6.41–42). His assertions of pity for Edward slide inexorably into assertions of patriarchal and kingly rights—rights which are affirmed by the spectacle ("to witness to the world") of Mortimer's head upon the dead king's hearse:

> My father's murdered through thy treachery,
> And thou shalt die and on his mournful hearse
> Thy hateful and accursed head shall lie,
> To witness to the world, that by thy means
> His kingly body was too soon interred.
>   (5.6.28–32)

The decapitation of his enemy, of course, effectively "answers" both the manner and the fact of Edward's death, and it fulfills the (pointed) threats of decapitation made by the king's party throughout the play:

> Brother, revenge it, and let these their heads
> Preach upon poles for trespass of their tongues.
>   (1.1.116–17)

> Strike off their heads and let them preach on poles.
>   (3.2.20)

And the new king makes a similar point when he promises his mother that "if [she] be guilty" and "unnatural," she will not "find [him] slack or pitiful" (5.6.76, 81–82). His painfully firm resolution is particularly striking in a play in which almost everyone has been presented as "slack" or "drooping."[16]

It seems fitting (and I use that word advisedly) that the image of Edward's death is an image of submission. The play as a whole, I would suggest, records a submission to history—to history as "the dominant ideology," and (what is the same thing) to history as "the literal truth."[17] That submission is reflected in the relatively linear action of the play—for which Marlowe has been much praised, and which has often been seen as marking a positive development over his other works, which mount a more frontal assault on causality.[18] The play evidences a clear awareness of the ways in which, to invoke Laura Mulvey's reversible formulation, "sadism demands a story," and a story demands sadism.[19] And this story—which is history (and his story)—finds its origin and its end in the figure of Edward's death. That figure claims to be literally true, and the force of this claim is brought out (unintentionally) by a comment in one critical essay: "The first point to note is that the 'punishment-fitting-the-crime' aspect of Edward's death is not an invention of Marlowe's to add thematic unity to the play, but the literal truth as recorded in the chronicles"[20] (that is, the literal *English* truth, the only kind that really deserves the name of history). As this comment suggests, not only is the manner of Edward's murder literally true but, in its logical " 'punishment-fitting-the-crime' aspect," it is a figure *for* the literal truth, for the intelligible, the determinate, the (patri) linear, the causal—the historical.

That figure also, one could add, gestures toward its own figurality, toward the ways in which the determinate is created out of indeterminancy. As many readers have noted, it fulfills the promise of the Actaeon image in Gaveston's early speech. But it does so by resolving the hidden/seen, male/female parts of the vision of Diana into the indeterminate anus, which Drayton, in his version of this story, calls Edward's "secret part,"[21] and which, according to Holinshed (Marlowe's primary source), was chosen so that "no appearance of any wound or hurt outwardlie might be once perceived."[22] As its presence in chronicles, poems, and plays testifies, this indeterminate, imperceptible wound is, of course, seen by all; it stands (in Edward III's phrase) "to witness [the truth] to the world." No longer vaguely evoked as something extrinsic to meaningful order, it is situated at the center of meaning itself. "Nothing to see" becomes the sign of something to see, as the invisible, indeterminate act of sodomy, punished and pinned down, becomes the visible guarantee of the existence of a point.

The play as a whole implicitly acknowledges the process of scapegoating that is occurring. It certainly suggests that the series of humiliations Edward is made to suffer in a "dungeon . . . / Wherein the filth of all the castle falls" (5.5.55–56) answers not simply to his own character and condition but to the condition of a country overflowing with blood and gore, in which all enclosures are threatened and all boundaries seem in danger of being erased.[23] And it perhaps also implies, in its repeated focus on the word "gore," that the action of a point is inevitably implicated in the mire it opposes. Mortimer threatens:

> Upon my weapon's point here shouldst thou fall
> And welter in thy gore.
>
> (2.5.13–14)

Edward promises:

> If I be England's King, in lakes of gore
> Your headless trunks, your bodies will I trail,
> That you may drink your fill and quaff in blood.
>
> (3.2.135–37)

And Isabella laments:

> A heavy case
> When force to force is knit and sword and glaive
> In civil broils makes kin and countrymen
> Slaughter themselves in others, and their sides
> With their own weapons gored. But what's the help?
>
> (4.4.4–8)

Isabella's image of her countrymen "with their own weapons gored" completely erases the distinction between "my point" and "thy gore" that Mortimer had attempted to establish. But Isabella no sooner opens the possibility of indeterminacy than she tries to close it:

> Misgoverned kings are cause of all this wrack,
> And, Edward, thou art one among them all,
> Whose looseness hath betrayed thy land to spoil
> And made the channels overflow with blood.
> Of thine own people patron shouldst thou be,
> But thou . . .
>
> (4.4.9–14)

And her own "overflowing" mouth is itself shut by Mortimer's interruption: "Nay, madam, if you be a warrior / Ye must not grow so passionate in speeches" (4.4.15–16).

So, too, is *Edward II* finally closed down and shut up.[24] The play repeatedly gestures toward—but cannot effectively counter—its own inadequacy. It does not finally allow us (as Edward wishes) to return as well as go (1.4.143), nor (and this is Matrevis not Macbeth) to render "undone" what has been "done" (5.6.1–2). It leaves us, instead, with an image of submission—of not entirely willing (Edward remains indecisive until the end), not entirely conscious submission (when he's finally murdered, he's half asleep) to something that is seen as brutal and violating, that is clearly perceived as fictional, and that is nevertheless represented as unavoidable. Or more precisely—and this drives the point home—it leaves us with Edward III.

NOTES

An earlier version of this essay was presented to a session of the Marlowe Society of America, chaired by Constance B. Kuriyama, at the 1990 MLA. I thank Bonnie Burns, Richard Burt, Lee Edelman, Marshall Grossman, and Charles Trocano for their comments, suggestions, and advice.

1. All references to *Edward II* are taken from the New Mermaid edition, ed. W. Moelwyn Merchant (New York: Norton, 1987).

2. It is an example of the rhetorical form that Steven Mullaney, following George Puttenham, terms "amphibology," "the figure of the traitor"; see Steven Mullaney, "Lying Like Truth: Riddle, Representation and Treason in Renaissance England," *ELH* 47 (1980), 32–42. Patricia Parker also comments suggestively on amphibology (and on Renaissance puns on "point") in *Literary Fat Ladies: Rhetoric, Gender, Property* (London: Methuen, 1987), pp. 97–125. Throughout her book Parker makes illuminating connections between rhetorical forms and the construction of gender and sexuality.

3. Marjorie Garber, " 'Infinite Riches in a Little Room': Closure and Enclosure in Marlowe," in *Two Renaissance Mythmakers: Christopher Marlowe and Ben Jonson*, ed. Alvin Kernan (Baltimore: Johns Hopkins University Press, 1977), p. 16. For recent reformulations of this position see, e.g., Karen Cunningham, "Renaissance Execution and Marlovian Elocution: The Drama of Death," *PMLA* 105 (1990), 216, and Bruce R. Smith, *Homosexual Desire in Shakespeare's England: A Cultural Poetics* (Chicago: University of Chicago Press, 1991), p. 221.

4. David H. Thurn analyzes these shifts (and touches on some of the points I make in this essay) in his article "Sovereignty, Disorder, and Fetishism in Marlowe's *Edward II*," in *Renaissance Drama* 21 (1990), 115–42.

5. For extended analyses of this pattern (and of the other antitheses in the play) from significantly different perspectives, see Constance Brown Kuriyama, *Hammer and Anvil: Psychological Patterns in Christopher Marlowe's Plays* (New Brunswick, N.J.: Rutgers University Press, 1980), pp. 175–211, and Debra Belt, "Anti-Theatricalism and Rhetoric in Marlowe's *Edward II*," *English Literary Renaissance* 21 (1991), 134–60.

6. William Stubbs, *Chronicles of the Reigns of Edward I and Edward II* (1883), cited in *Edward II*, ed. H. B. Charlton and R. D. Waller (New York: Gordian Press, 1966), p. 37.

7. Alan Bray, *Homosexuality in Renaissance England* (London: Gay Men's Press, 1982); Jonathan Goldberg, "Sodomy and Society: The Case of Christopher Marlowe," *Southwest Review* 69 (1984), 371–78. In subsequent essays both critics have emphasized the extent to which sodomy is embedded in the order to which it is opposed: see Bray, "Homosexuality and the Signs of Male Friendship in Elizabethan England," *History Workshop* 29 (1990), 1–19, which includes a reading of *Edward II*, and Goldberg, "Colin to Hobbinol: Spenser's Familiar Letters," in *Displacing Homophobia: Gay Male Perspectives in Literature and Culture*, ed. Ronald R. Butters, John M. Clum, and Michael Moon (Durham: Duke University Press, 1989), pp. 107–26. The argument I present here is compatible with the underlying assumptions of these essays, although my account of *Edward II* is quite different from that advanced by Bray. For other recent perspectives, see Gregory W. Bredbeck, *Sodomy and Interpretation: Marlowe to Milton* (Ithaca: Cornell University Press, 1991), esp. chap. 2, Jonathan Dollimore, *Sexual Dissidence: Augustine to Wilde, Freud to Foucault* (Oxford: Clarendon Press, 1991), and Smith, *Homosexual Desire*, esp. chap 6. (Goldberg's important study, *Sodometries: Renaissance Texts, Modern Sexualities* [Stanford: Stanford University Press, 1992], published after the completion of this essay, contains versions of his article on Spenser and a reading of *Edward II*.)

8. Thomas Browne, cited in Bray, *Homosexuality in Renaissance England*, p. 23; see also Bredbeck, *Sodomy and Interpretation*, p. 91.

9. Philip Stubbes, *The Anatomie of Abuses* (1583), ed. Frederick J. Furnivall (London: N. Trubner, 1877–79), pp. 144–45 (sig. L8v). Laura Levine provides

an extremely perceptive and helpful analysis of the antitheatrical tracts in "Men in Women's Clothing: Anti-Theatricality and Effeminization from 1579 to 1642," *Criticism* 28 (1986), 121–43. She contends that sodomy is "a metaphor or a scapegoat or an attempt to give an account for the more disturbing idea at the center of these tracts, that under the costume there is really nothing there, or alternatively, that what is there is something foreign, something terrifying and essentially 'other'" (p. 135). I am indebted to Levine's formulation, although I am suggesting that the connection of sodomy with "the more disturbing idea at the center of these tracts" (and with the condition of being "a metaphor or a scapegoat") is less arbitrary than she allows. For interesting developments of Levine's ideas, see Stephen Orgel, "Nobody's Perfect: Or Why Did the English Stage Take Boys for Women?" in Butters et al., *Displacing Homophobia*, pp. 7–29; and Dollimore, *Sexual Dissidence*, pp. 239, 252.

10. Stubbes, *The Anatomie of Abuses*, p. 145 (sig. L8v).

11. Nancy J. Vickers, "Diana Described: Scattered Women and Scattered Rhyme," in *Writing and Sexual Difference*, ed. Elizabeth Abel (Chicago: University of Chicago Press, 1982), pp. 95–110. See also Vickers, "the Mistress in the Masterpiece," in *The Poetics of Gender*, ed. Nancy K. Miller (New York: Columbia University Press, 1986), pp. 19–41; and Parker, *Literary Fat Ladies*, pp. 62–66. For an analysis of the various uses to which the Actaeon myth was put in Renaissance literature, see Leonard Barkan, "Diana and Actaeon: The Myth as Synthesis," *English Literary Renaissance* 10 (1980), 317–59.

12. Cf. Thurn, "Sovereignty, Disorder, and Fetishism," pp. 120–21. See also Marjorie Garber's discussion of the fetish in *Vested Interests: Cross-Dressing and Cultural Anxiety* (New York: Routledge, 1992), pp. 118–27.

13. Simon Shepherd, *Marlowe and the Politics of Elizabethan Theatre* (Brighton, Sussex: Harvester Press, 1986), p. 204.

14. For a detailed discussion of Marlowe's emblematic method in the play, see David Bevington and James Shapiro, "'What Are Kings, When Regiment Is Gone?': The Decay of Ceremony in *Edward II*," in *"A Poet and a Filthy Play-Maker": New Essays on Christopher Marlowe*, ed. Kenneth Friedenreich, Roma Gill, and Constance B. Kuriyama (New York: AMS Press, 1988), pp. 263–78.

15. Stephen Greenblatt, "Marlowe and the Will to Absolute Play," in *Renaissance Self-Fashioning: From More to Shakespeare* (Chicago: University of Chicago Press, 1980), p. 203.

16. The primary exception is, of course, the murderous Lightborne, who is portrayed as unshakably "resolute" (5.4.22-23); cf. Spencer's advice to Baldock: "You must be proud, bold, pleasant, resolute, / And now and then stab as occasion serves" (2.1.42–43).

17. Phyllis Rackin points out in *Stages of History: Shakespeare's English Chronicles* (Ithaca: Cornell University Press, 1990) that, at the end of the sixteenth century, "history" was in the process of becoming "an autonomous discipline with its own purposes and methods, clearly distinct from myth and literature, and accountable to different formal requirements and different truth criteria. Rhyme gave way to reason, verse to prose. . . . Even the arrangement of incidents was strictly regulated" (p. 19). Rackin also notes that "the exclusive protocols of historical writing reproduced the divisions of the traditional social hierarchy" (p. 23).

18. As Sara Deats observes, the play's admirers have traditionally praised its dramatic structure, while its detractors have complained about its lack of poetic power; see Sara Munson Deats, "Myth and Metamorphosis in Marlowe's *Ed-*

ward II," Texas Studies in Literature and Language 22 (1980), 305, and "Marlowe's Fearful Symmetry in *Edward II*," in Friedenreich et al., *"A Poet and a Filthy Play-Maker,"* pp. 241–62.

19. Laura Mulvey, "Visual Pleasure and Narrative Cinema," *Screen* 16 (1975), 422; see also Teresa de Lauretis, "Desire in Narrative," in *Alice Doesn't: Feminism, Semiotics, Cinema* (Bloomington: Indiana University Press, 1982), pp. 103–57.

20. J. R. Mulryne and Stephen Fender, "Marlowe and the 'Comic Distance,'" in *Christopher Marlowe*, ed. Brian Morris (London: Ernest Benn, 1968), pp. 60–61.

21. Michael Drayton, *Mortimeriados*, l. 2053, in *The Works of Michael Drayton*, ed. J. William Hebel, Vol. 1 (Oxford: Basil Blackwell, 1931).

22. Raphael Holinshed, *Chronicles of England, Scotland, and Ireland* (London: J. Johnson et al., 1807), 2:587.

23. Cf. Julia Kristeva's formulation: "It is . . . not lack of cleanliness or health that causes abjection but what disturbs identity, system, order. What does not respect borders, positions, rules. The in-between, the ambiguous, the composite. The traitor, the liar, the criminal with a good conscience." Julia Kristeva, *Powers of Horror: An Essay on Abjection*, trans. Leon S. Roudiez (New York: Columbia University Press, 1982), p. 4. My attention was first drawn to the relevance of this passage by Lee Edelman's extraordinarily suggestive essay, "Tearooms and Sympathy, or, the Epistemology of the Water Closet," in *Nationalisms and Sexualities*, ed. Andrew Parker, Mary Russo, Doris Sommer, and Patricia Yaeger (New York: Routledge, 1992), p. 273.

24. It is useful here briefly to consider the somewhat different case of *Hero and Leander*. Marlowe is able to suspend the dialectic I have been discussing more completely in that poem than in any of his dramatic works largely because *Hero and Leander* is *not* a drama but a less pointed form of play, and (what is, fundamentally, the same thing) it lacks a conclusive end: it is theoretically "incomplete."

9. The 1599 Bishops' Ban, Elizabethan Pornography, and the Sexualization of the Jacobean Stage

Lynda E. Boose

To date, surprisingly little attention has been paid to a distinctly anomalous—and, I believe, portentous—political collision that occurred on June 1, 1599, between Elizabethan literary texts and the Elizabethan state. On that date John Whitgift, the Archbishop of Canterbury, and Richard Bancroft, Bishop of London, the official censors of the Elizabethan press, suddenly issued an order for the Stationers Company—the monopoly of licensed printers—to round up, burn, and ban from future printing a list of literary texts, named by title, and authored by nearly a dozen of London's major writers. The proscribed list includes works by John Marston, Joseph Hall, Christopher Marlowe, John Davies, Thomas Nashe, Gabriel Harvey, Edward Guilpin, Robert Tofte, Thomas Cutwode, and one "T.M.," identified as Thomas Middleton (see Figure 1).[1]

As we know from the edict issued three days later, the book burning took place and was followed by an official announcement dated June 4 (see Figure 2) that was posted in Stationers Hall, the site where the books had been burned. Apparently so thorough was the execution of the decree that "very few copies of any of these books survive and most of them disappeared entirely in the original editions."[2] Yet nowhere in the June 1 or the June 4 document is the reason for the ban or the nature of any violation ever stated. The second document, which duly records the names of those books that had been torched and those that, again for unstated reasons, had been reprieved (or "staied"), is of interest for several reasons, not only for the odd discrepancies it reveals between the two documents but also for what it inferentially tells us about the practices employed by the Elizabethan state in its censorship of printed material. Preceding its list of book dispositions, it asserts that the banning order is being published "to the Companye and especyally to the prynters, viz. . . ." It then goes on to list the names of fourteen men who turn out to be not the members of the Stationers Company to whom the order was issued but fourteen of the *un*privileged printers in London[3]—men who had no share in the patent, were obviously not members of the company, earned their living by printing under unauthorized conditions, and were therefore precisely the men from whose presses any future publication of these banned works might be expected to come. By posting such a list, the state was alerting the privileged printers to protect their own status and economic interests by whatever tactics necessary to contain their unlicensed rivals.

By thus deflecting the apparatus of regulating censorship into a socioeconomic machinery that was explicitly designed to control printers, not authors, the strategy effectively papered over the state's implication in the censorship of what authors could write—or, more precisely, of what authors could place into mass circulation by means of that potentially uncontrollable new medium of dissemination, the printing press. For censorship orders are really matters of selective dissemination. They are provoked not by the writing of a book nor even by the reading of a work in circulated manuscript, in which case the text in question reaches only an elite audience. What the state proscribes is the circulation of certain works among the proverbial masses. It is at that juncture that such works are imagined—and the metaphor here changes little from the sixteenth to the twentieth century—as acquiring a pervasive contagion that threatens the entire social body. To deter such threat of mass proliferation, the Elizabethan state depended on the self-interests of another elite: the privileged printers. And, indeed, the Stationers Company proved to be a most zealous detective, policeman, and prosecutor as well as advance censor of the Elizabethan printing trade, thereby becoming part of a system that, according to Frederick Siebert, "has long been considered a masterstoke of Elizabethan politics."[4]

By the 1590s, however, this strategically efficacious arm's-length model of control was showing signs of breakdown.[5] For while the nation's sense of political insecurity fulminated around the aging queen's approaching death and the escalating court intrigue being played out against the backdrop of unsettled succession, printing technology was simultaneously spreading beyond any immediate control. By this time it was producing its own street-corner demand for cheaply printed and practically untraceable polemical pamphlets, such as those of the nearly unsuppressible Martin Marprelate controversy of the 1580s. And it was in this kind of atmosphere of approaching crisis that the official censors apparently perceived some especially immanent threat to stability which persuaded them to issue the quite singular and apparently hastily drawn up decree on the night of June 1. By indicting London literati such as Marston, Hall, Middleton, Guilpin, Harvey, and Nashe, however, the censors were effectively throwing down their gage at the poetic authority of the city's increasingly influential literary community. And yet, even at this moment when censorship was forced to speak, to occupy the medium of print itself in order to secure its own authority, it managed to remain silent, mystifying its controlling say-so by effectively not saying anything about the nature of the imputed transgressions. Literary historians were thus left with only speculation to decode this strange decree.

To date, a single, rather dogmatic tradition has always dominated any discussion of the 1599 ban. According to this tradition, the ban was strictly an injunction against satire. As evidence, this line of thinking points to the statement of the June 1 decree that "noe Satyres or Epigrams be printed hereafter," and to the satiric category to which several of the major indicted works can be assigned—works such as Joseph Hall's *Virgidemiarum*, Marston's *Pigmalion with certain other Satyres*, and Marston's *Scourge of Villanye*, for instance. But behind this dominant tradition there has always lurked another view which holds that "satire" by itself is not an adequate category to cover all the works listed nor does it account for an equally prominent feature of the banned texts—the newly sexualized, salacious tone with which many of them seem to have been experimenting. That tone had first begun to seep into English literary texts, inspiring the condemnation of the moralists, about four or five years earlier.[6]

As far back as the 1940s, Arnold Davenport, the meticulous editor of Marston, Hall, and the Cambridge coterie's "Whipper Pamphlets," demurred from the tradition by asserting that the sexualization of the banned texts was an issue that could not be so easily dismissed. Furthermore, he was uneasy with restricting the issue behind the ban to satire—especially since the "Whipper Pamphlets," which are themselves satirical reactions to the ban, were published, apparently without problem, within a year of the decree.[7] But despite Davenport's reservations and an occasional murmur from scholars who have followed him, the academic discussion has nonetheless remained mired in the slough of satire, where it has generated a raft of adamantly overstated arguments in defense of its position. Of all such arguments, the most unwittingly revealing is the one put forth by Richard McCabe, whose claim actually demonstrates precisely the point it is trying to dismiss. By reasoning that Thomas Nashe's *Choice of Valentines* would surely have headed the list of specifically targeted works had the suppression of overt sexual discourse been a motive of the 1599 decree, McCabe concludes from its omission that the Bishops' Ban was directed wholly

[I. Binge.
  W. Ponsonby. } R. Newbery.   1 June 1599]   **316**

[41 *Reginæ Elizabethæ*]

Satyres tearmed HALLes *Satyres riz virgidemiarum or his tootheles or bitinge Satyres* /
[By JOSEPH HALL, afterwards Bishop of EXETER.   Licensed to **Robert Dexter** on 30th March 1598, see *p.* 109.]

PIGMALION with certaine other Satyres /
[By JOHN MARSTON.   Licensed to **Edmond Mattes** on the 27th May 1598, see *p.* 116 : and also *p.* 533.]

The scourge of villanye /
[Also by MARSTON.   Licensed to **James Robertes** on the 8th September 1598, see *p.* 125.]

The Shadowe of truthe in Epigrams and Satyres /
[*i. e. Skialetheia.*   Licensed to **Nicholas Ling** on the 15th September 1598, see *p.* 126.]

Snarlinge Satyres
[T. M. *Micro-cynicon. Sixe Snarlinge Satyres.*   Printed by **T. Creed** for **T. Bushell** in 1599.]

Caltha Poetarum /
[By THOMAS CUTWODE.   Licensed to **Nicholas Ling** on the 17th April 1599, see *p.* 143 : and also *p.* 581.]

DAVYES *Epigrams*, with MARLOWES *Elegyes*

The booke againste woemen   viz,   *of marriage and wyvinge* /

The xv ioyes of marriage
[For printing which disorderly, **Adam Islip** was fined ij^s vj^d on the 5th February 1599 : see II., 829.]

That noe *Satyres* or *Epigrams* be printed hereafter

That noe Englishe historyes be printed excepte they bee allowed by some of her maiesties privie Counsell /

That noe playes be printed excepte they bee allowed by suche as haue aucthorytie /

That all NASSHES bookes and Doctor HARVYes bookes be taken wheresoeuer they maye be found and that none of theire bookes bee euer printed hereafter /

That thoughe any booke of the nature of theise heretofore expressed shalbe broughte vnto yow vnder the hands of the Lord Archebisshop of CANTERBURYE or the Lord Bishop of LONDON yet the said booke shall not bee printed vntill the master or wardens haue acquainted the said Lord Archbishop, or the Lord Bishop with the same to knowe whether it be theire hand or no /

Jo[HN WHITGIFT] CANTUAR
RIC[HARD BANCROFT] LONDON

Suche bookes as can be found or are allready taken of the Argumentes aforesaid or any of the bookes aboue expressed lett them bee presentlye [*i. e. immediately*] broughte to the Bishop of LONDON to be burnte

Jo[HN] CANTUAR
RIC[HARD] LONDON

Sic examinatur /

III. 677

Figure 1. The decree of June 1, 1599

[316 b]   1—4 June 1599   R. Newbery. { I. Binge. W. Ponsonby.]

[41 *Reginæ Elizabethæ*]

Die veneris Primo Iunij / xlj° Regin[a]e /

The Commaundementes aforesaid were Delyuered att Croyden by my Lordes grace of CANTERBURY and the Bishop of LONDON vnder theire handes to master **Newbery** master[,] master **Binge** and master **Ponsonby** wardens, And the said master and wardens Did there subscribe two Coppies thereof, one remayninge with my Lords grace of CANTERBURY and the other with the Bishop of LONDON /

Die Lun[a]e iiij° Iunij [1599] Anno pr[a]edicto

The foresaid Commaundementes were published at Stacyoners hall to the Companye and especyally to the prynters. *viz*, **John wyndett Gabriell Simpson, Richard Braddocke, ffelixe kingston   william whyte, Raphe Blower, Thomas Judson   Peeter Shorte   Adam Islipe, Richard ffeild   Edmond Bollifante   Thomas Creed, Edward Aldee [and] valentyne Symes,**

[It is clear that these fourteen men comprised all the unprivileged printers at this date, and included all those from whose presses the works now condemned by episcopal authority might be expected. Compare this list with the list of printers in May 1583, at I. 242, and those on 9th May 1615, 8th October 1634, in 1635 and 1636, at *pp.* 699—704.]

Theis bookes presently therevppon were burnte in the hall /

viz /

>   PYGMALION

>   *The scourge of vilany*

>   *the shadowe of truthe*

>   *Snarlinge Satires*

>   DAVIES *Epigrames*

>   *Marriage and wyvinge*

>   15 *Joyes of marriage*

Theis [were] stai[e]d [*i. e. not burnt*]

>   *Caltha Poetarum*

>   HALLS *Satires*

WILLOBIES *Adviso* to be Called in /
[Licensed to **John Windet** on the 3rd September 1594, see II., 659; and also *p.* 466.]

III. 678

Figure 2. The decree of June 4, 1599

against satire.[8] Given the unconstrained ribaldry of *The Choice of Valentines; or, Nashe, his Dildo,* the argument seems persuasive enough—but persuasive only if one presumes that *Valentine* had indeed been published by 1599. *The Choice of Valentines* was clearly well known by the late 1590s and was frequently invoked by moralist writers such as Gabriel Harvey and Joseph Hall as evidence, variously, of the new salaciousness of literature or of Nashe's own personal immorality. The very frequency of its citation is most likely what led McCabe to the erroneous conclusion that the poem had been printed and, reasoning backward from there, to his inference that the Elizabethan censors were not averse to licensing such a work. But in fact it was to be three hundred years before this *Valentine* ever left the demesne of manuscript and became a publicly circulated text. When it was finally printed in 1899, even then it was issued with the reassuringly elitist imprimatur of being "for the private circulation of J. S. Farmer among circulators only."[9]

In trying to decode the silent semiotics of censorship, there is one earlier case that seems closely related to the implied issues and motives of 1599. This is the 1576 action that we can infer with fair certainty was taken against George Gascoigne, the promisingly witty young courtier-poet of 1573 who, by the time of his death in 1577, has been reduced to a court hack grinding out primly moralistic, didactic treatises with names such as "The Droomme of Doomes Day." As Richard McCoy describes Gascoigne's downfall, it seems quite clear that Gascoigne's 1573 masterpiece, *A Hundreth Sundrie Flowres,* was censored by the ecclesiastics because of its deployment of a newly frank sexual discourse of "wanton speech and lascivious phrase."[10] In 1575 Gascoigne tried to publish essentially the same text under the title of *The Posies of George Gascoigne* having made very few changes but hoping to sneak it past the censors by the addition of a prologue addressed to the bishops in which he claimed to offer them his "Poemata Castrata, gelded from all filthy phrases." Gascoigne probably sealed his fate with such thinly disguised aggression against those whom he recognized—and publicly identified—as his castrators.

Their response was, in effect, precisely as he had unhappily predicted: to cut off his authority and his authoriality, and to try even to efface his progeny. Had the censors been only slightly more effective, the comic masterpiece from *Hundreth Sundrie* that is probably the site of all the controversy, "The Adventures of Master F.J.," would never have survived—nor, most likely, would Gascoigne's name. Subsequent to the confiscation of the *Posies* in 1576, Gascoigne seems to have become a groveling court toady, forced to prostitute his talents in futile pursuit of the preferment that his violation of implicit court rules had already placed beyond him. In one of his last, insipidly moralistic works, *The Steel Glas,* his anger and self-contempt burst forth once more in the hostile creation of a poetic persona who has been emasculated—hence depotentiated into the feminine—only to be raped and then have her tongue cut out by the "Rayzor of Restraint." Although no originating censorship order survives to articulate the reasons for the ecclesiastical injunction of 1576, from the evidence Gascoigne himself bitterly etched for us it is clear that he understood the censorship to have been directed specifically against the overt sexuality of his work.

What seems crucial in the Gascoigne case is that he was one of the first Tudor poets to breach courtly decorum by publishing his own work, thus explicitly seeking a wider, less elite readership than manuscript circulation could afford. In doing so, he announced his intention to disseminate to a mass readership a book that contained as sexualized a narrative romp through the politics of courtly discourse as in anything yet written. McCoy argues that the work probably was, as Gascoigne claimed, innocent of any libelous motive. But because he had used an amoral, sexualized narrative set in contemporary time and inscribed within a loose allegory of courtiership as a form of complex courtesanship, the work apparently invited the kind of intrigue that condemned it to be read as libelous anyway. Gascoigne's intentions—whatever they may have been—would have been politically irrelevant to the censors. What the authorities would have cared about was how his book might possibly be read, especially since it was "about" courtiers and was intended to circulate among a mass readership.

What is dangerous about Gascoigne's comic narrative was the new site it uncovered. The sexual narrative provided a potentially hostile locus for satiric attack. Having written his "Master" story using sexuality as metaphor for the aggressions of discourse, when he then publicly tagged the bishops as castrators he only repeated the breach of decorum that no doubt had precipitated the first act of censorship. Under the pretense of speaking from the depotentiated location of castration and nonaggression, he had, of course, overtly deployed male sexuality as a hostile rhetorical strategy.

In 1599 the struggle between literary and state authority may have rested on grounds somewhat similar to these. But in 1599 the writers were not, like Gascoigne, would-be courtiers psychologically tied to introjecting the rules of the court. And the voice that speaks out in 1599—the voice the bishops are reacting against—is not couched in Gascoigne's elaborately decorous court rhetoric. This is a voice from the street—the same voice that a few years later would, from the stage, arouse the Venetian patriarch Brabantio with "timorous accent and

dire yell, / As when, by night and negligence, the fire / Is spied in pop-
ulous cities," the coarse voice of Iago, *Othello*'s "most profane and liberal counselor."[11] But Iago had learned that voice—and so had
Shakespeare's Thersites, and Webster's Bosola, and (Tourneur's) Vindice. And these malcontents and their brethren, who in a few short
years would so profoundly delineate the tone of what came to be
known as the "Jacobean" in drama, would all have learned that voice
from a writer who turned up not only in the middle of the 1599 ban
but at the center of almost every literary controversy of the era—John
Marston, whose career might serve as an abstract of the times.

As a new and aggressively sexualized form of distinctly English literature began emerging into definition in the 1590s, of all the writers
working within the paradoxes inherent in the demands of that form
the one who best understood them was not Thomas Nashe, whose
Choice of Valentines is too jocular and invests too much self-mocking humor in exposing the comedies of male impotence ever to reach the
dark depths and psychic defenses that underlie the pornographic. The
writer who best understood those depths was John Marston. And it was
Marston who understood the pornographic in the full range of its investments and negotiations with the reader. In *Metamorphosis of Pigmalion's Image*, one of his two works on the bishop's list, he deliberately
experiments with masturbatory strategies of inhibited desire designed
to stimulate the reader's arousal by creating a friction with it. As the
poem leads its (male) reader toward the given object of desire, the cen-
tripetal figure of the waiting female body, it alternately arouses him
with prurient questions much like those which Iago directs at Othello
and then prohibits him access by refusing to show what the reader has
been titillated to imagine, a denial technique that—like Iago's pursed
up thoughts, his "stops" and "close dilations" (*Oth.* 3.3.133, 136)—only
guarantees that the aroused reader will, like Othello, increasingly demand voyeuristic satisfaction: "Make me to see't" (3.3.380). At the end
of *Pigmalion* are appended some verses titled "The Authour in prayse
of his precedent Poem," where the poet radically switches his stance
and, in the voice of the moralist, scathingly attacks his readers as "lewd
Priapians" whose prurience has been "tickled vp" by the poem, which
the author now disclaims as a piece of "chaos indigest" which he just
"slubbered up" to "fish for fools." The poem and its annexed verses together constitute the paradox of this emerging genre's split mentality,
the seeming contradiction of Iago's dual stance which lies at the heart
of English pornography. By appropriating the voice of the moralist disgusted by what he graphically describes, the strategy neutralizes the
guilt of the sexualist and allows the two psychic figures to coexist in the
reader. Only because of such a split can the moralist revel in what he

simultaneously decries and the voluptuary be whipped for the pleasures that arouse him.

Perhaps because of the dual investments it must serve, English pornography came into the world with a voice all its own. What characterizes that voice is a language not of lascivious delight but of sexual scatology—of slime, poison, garbage, vomit, clyster pipes, dung, and animality—that emerges connected to images of sexuality in the vocabulary of Iago and his brethren. It is a language that flaunts a new coarseness in both its sound and its semantics. And, fittingly enough, this newly emergent English pornography adapts an important part of its native idiom from the moralists who had been writing against it. It was Marston who first contributed this language to English satire in his 1598 *Scourge of Villanie*, perhaps the most obscene piece of literature listed in the Bishops' Ban, yet one that purports to be an outraged attack on sexual writing spoken in the voice of the offended moralist. Throughout Marston's early satires an identifiable new fusion of sound and diction reshapes the possibilities for the stage and frames the extremities of the Jacobean discourse on the sins of sensuality.[12] In Marston's *Scourge* persona's new language of sexual bluntness the playwrights discovered a rich new muck pit for the drama to mine, and this voice seems to have provided what we might call the father tongue for figures such as Thersites, Vindice, Bosola, and other Jacobean malcontents who—along with Malevole/Altofronto and other of Marston's own dramatic scourgers of sexual vice—soon emerged on the English stage. But probably the *Scourge* speaker's closest descendant is Shakespeare's most famous villain. Like Iago, whom Othello describes as a man who "hates the slime / That sticks on filthy deeds" (5.2.154–55). Marston's speaker is a bluntly "honest" man who hates "the slime of filthy sensualitie" (xi l.207), which he endlessly describes in snarling ejaculations at

> *Aretines* filth, or of his wandring whore . . .
> of *Ruscus* nastie lothsome brothell rime,
> That stincks like Aiax froth, or muck-pit slime.
>   (xi ll. 144, 146–47)

> Out on this salt humour, letchers dropsie,
> Fie, it doth soyle my chaster poesie. . . . .
>   (xi ll.155–56)

In 1599, when the bishops ordered censorship and attempted to cut off the hostile, malcontented potential aggressions of the violently sexualized discourse they heard in these new hybrid literary constructions, the targeted authors reacted not, as Gascoigne had done, by becoming resentful castrati but by shifting venues. Now, as opposed to 1576, the writers had somewhere else to go, for 1599 almost pinpoints the shift in England from a poetry culture to a theater culture; it marks the beginning of the competition between a culture of print and one of performance. It also marks the theatrical shift to a style we generically associate with the core tragedies of Jacobean drama—a shift to the lurid, Italianate plots that were first contrived and put onstage by, once again, John Marston, who essentially transformed the narrative character of contemporary English drama with the very first play he wrote, *Antonio and Mellida,* probably composed in late 1599.[13]

But while English pornography developed in its own distinctive direction, the story of its origins and its relationship to the 1599 ban does have an outside agitator. What seems to have energized England's newly sexualized literature and in turn stimulated the peculiarly phallic aggressions of the Jacobean drama was the textual immigration of an Italian literary subversive—Pietro Aretino—whose arrival marks the entrance of vernacular pornography into England. *Pornography* means a written story of whores. And, indeed, this was the form in which pornography first arrived in England in 1584 under the title of Aretino's *Ragionimenti.* In his *Dialogues* the male fantasy of limitless sexual capacity is doubly displaced onto women's voices and a fantasy of women's limitless sexual insatiability. *The Dialogues* are spoken by an older and a younger woman debating the merits of becoming a nun, a wife, or a courtesan; the conversation is, of course, merely an excuse to describe and revel in the graphic "porntopia" fictionalized here as the older woman's experiences. The conclusion to the debate is that since all three choices are, quite literally, merely male "occupations," a woman ought best become a courtesan, in which "occupation" she at least gets paid for what the male author behind the female narrator invariably imagines as a repetition of endless pleasures.

Prior to 1584 Aretino had been known in England primarily as a political satirist and scourger of princes, a poet who had been compared even to Tasso and Petrarch by none other than Gabriel Harvey. Then word began to come from continental sources about Aretino's other productions, in particular his obscene sonnets. This soon-to-be infamous group of sonnets—which Aretino himself mockingly refers to as "I positzioni"—had originally been written to accompany a series of prints that Marcantonio Raimundi had made from Giulio Romano's erotic drawings, referred to in Italian treatises as "I modi," but coded in all English references as either "the postures" or "the pictures."[14] Not long after word of Aretino's association with "the postures" began to filter through to England, in 1584, *I ragionimenti* was published by John Wolfe, Gabriel Harvey's own publisher.[15]

The impact exerted by Aretino's *Dialogues* across Europe can perhaps be measured by the fact that the form which European pornography took for the next 150 years was that of Aretino's dialogue between two women—an emulation that has led modern biographers to call Pietro Aretino, appropriately enough, the father of modern pornography. And though we have no direct evidence that the pictures or Aretino's sonnets ever actually circulated in England, word about them most certainly did. Within ten years Aretino's name had come to be a layered metaphor occupying multiple grammatical positions (an "aretinized" discourse; an "aretine/aretin" idea; the "English Aretine"; the great "aretiner"; an "aretinizing" influence) and signifying both a certain type of salacious text and its aroused reader's response. Not surprisingly, the collocation also provoked a volley of self-legitimating political responses from various state and social institutions reacting against this newly available form of moral transgression.

No doubt because late Elizabethan culture recognized its own image in what it denounced as an invasion of literary filth from Italy, Aretino was not only well known by the 1590s—he was infamous. So much so that David McPherson has argued that the deluge of works in the 1590s depicting Italian diabolism owes its impetus more to England's contact with Aretino than with Machiavelli.[16] Within a decade of Aretino's arrival, writers such as Thomas Nashe and John Marston suddenly began experimenting with a type of literature that cannot be defined generically as either the Elizabethan bawdy or the Ovidian sensual. Marston's use of the epyllion form in *Metamorphosis of Pigmalions Image* marks a significant difference from that which Marlowe and Shakespeare had already established. This new type of literature, *Metamorphosis* included, bears the graphic stamp of Aretino.

Quite probably what had popularized Aretino as the exemplar of the obscene was the use that had been made of him in the scurrilous Harvey-Nashe pamphlet wars early in the decade, in which Harvey had attacked the immorality of Nashe's writing by calling its author "the English Aretine," an appellation Nashe apparently relished.[17] In *Machiavelli and the English Drama* (1897), Edward Meyer claimed to have found over five hundred references to Aretino in English texts printed before 1642 and even mentioned his belief that references to Aretino outnumbered those to Machiavelli.[18] Of all the contemporary responses, two by Ben Jonson and one by John Donne best demonstrate the range of uses. Jonson's two allusions illuminate the polarized responses of pleasure and outrage that characterize the English psy-

chic reaction to Aretino. In *The Alchemist,* Sir Epicure Mammon devises
a pleasure palace to excite his moribund sexual fantasies, and imagines
the palace as a room

> Filled with such pleasures as Tiberius took
> From Elephantis, and dull Aretine
> But coldly imitated.
>
> (2.2.43–45)

In *Volpone,* however, Corvino lashes out at

> . . . some young Frenchman, or hot Tuscan blood
> That had read Aretine, conned all his prints,
> Knew every quirk within lust's labyrinth,
> And were professed critic in lechery.
>
> (3.7.59–62)[19]

It is John Donne who situates Aretino politically. When Donne invokes
Aretino, he places the Aretino associated with the pornographic pictures in antithesis to the Aretino earlier praised as the scourge of
Princes. And from this intersection of the pornographic images and
the "pictures" of supposed virtue that a prince's court should model,
Donne reroutes the public lust to see "Aretine's pictures" into a complex site of political hostility directed against authority.

> Now; Aretines pictures have made few chast;
> No more can Princes courts, though there be few
> Better pictures of vice, teach me vertue.[20]

The Bishops' Ban marks an important line in literary representation
and speaks of the state's effort, in the final year of the sixteenth century, to plug the dike against a new kind of literature that the authorities saw inundating England.[21] The two forms of literature put in
focus by the ban are sexualized literature and the satiric invective, the
two newly emergent forms that had, by June 1, 1599, been so busily
cross-breeding as to become frequently indistinguishable from each
other. To constitute the two forms as binary and argue the intent of the
ban within that either-or context thus is not only unnecessary but
misses something vital. A new kind of subgenre—later identified as
England's only contribution to the genre of pornography—was, during
the late 1590s, being born. And as the Muse labored, it brought forth
a monstrously hybrid creature which combined the salaciously erotic
with the violent, misogynistic excoriations of the Juvenalian satiric

speaker, a literary genre which, thus parented, carried within it a newly destabilized discourse, an English pornography that brought together prurient lust and revulsionary loathing. With this admixture of scatology, misogyny, and revulsion, the pornographic pleasures of Aretino had at last become "Englished."

The ban did not therefore halt sexual representation so much as it politicized it by defining it as the contestatory site. By challenging the writer's autonomy, the ban effectively constituted sex and sexuality as the overt, primary, and reinvoked scene of primal struggle for the competitive assertion of authority. Like the confessional ecclesiastical authorities before them, the ecclesiastical censors of the Tudor state asserted their power over sexuality by situating it discursively.[22] But during the cyclonic heydey of the Jacobean stage, from 1600 to about the 1620s, the playwrights made a new claim on it: they claimed it representationally.

The theater that was created was a theater of the ego—a peculiarly narcissistic, sensationalized medium increasingly dependent on the ability of its self-dramatizing playwrights to dominate ever larger territories of sexual representation, the space over which they flaunted their dominion through their theatricalized and violent spectacles. The Jacobean theater is about power: sexuality becomes the vehicle for its expression. And the almost unavoidable cultural effect of framing the issue of authorial control as a male writer's battle for dominance and potency versus his acquiescence to gelded restraint is to produce—and by necessity reproduce—a medium, a metaphor, and, ultimately, a sensationalized message about male power welded to male violence. Translated from the well-known personal competitions among the brother playwrights into dramatic narratives to be played out on the stage, the contest is set up as an Oedipal struggle and a masculine battle for power. But within such an Oedipalized drama, the space for the female progressively becomes the site of a disturbingly new kind of male competition that resolves itself over, through, and in the annihilation of the female body through which the narrative has sexualized itself.

In 1599, when razors of restraint were effectively turned against the print medium, the writers had somewhere else to go. And Marston and Middleton set a pattern that, in a way, bespeaks the times: they ceased writing for print and turned their prodigious energies toward the medium where the most gratifying form of "publication" was instant, ephemeral, and constituted within performance. This move to the drama provided the Jacobean writers with a sanctuary that was itself strangely constituted by the spatial, the literary, and the cultural liminality of the theaters they wrote for. Inside that margin they could postpone any effective censorship of their texts by submerging themselves in the very instabilities of the medium they were producing,[23] a medium in which discourse is suspended inside dialogue, dialogue inside performance, and performance inside its own unlocatable ephemerality. Within their self-protected medium, where the real meaning of "publication" lay in stage production, these overreachers could literally get away with murder—with plots of fratricide, fantasies of matricide, violent assaults on the social body and body politic, and endless narrative refigurations of killing the king. When writers such as Marston and Middleton moved to the world of drama, the theater became almost simultaneously Italianized, sexualized, politicized, spectacularized, and, as Jonathan Dollimore defines it, also radicalized.[24] But from another perspective it also became even more profoundly homogenized, and, within such conscriptions, even more thoroughly misogynized.

N O T E S

A special thanks to Alexandra Halasz for contributing her knowledge of late sixteenth-century print and publication practices.

1. Edward Arber, ed., *A Transcript of the Registers of the Company of Stationers of London, 1554–1640*, 6 vols. (London, 1876), 3:677–78. "Snarlinge Satyres" by "T. M." is generally agreed to be Middleton's *Microcynicon*, also referred to as *Sixe Snarlinge Satyres*. See, for instance, Charles Ripley Gillett, *Burned Books: Neglected Chapters in British History and Literature*, 2 vols. (New York: Columbia University Press, 1932), 1:90, n.1.

2. Gillett, *Burned Books*, 1:90. Gillett then goes on to conjecture that, since most of the works can be known only from later editions, and comparison with the original edition is impossible, we cannot even know that these later editions had not undergone considerable revision, including the elision of objectionable passages. Arnold Davenport's introduction to *The Selected Poems of Joseph Hall, Bishop of Exeter and Norwich* (Liverpool: University Press of Liverpool, 1949) illustrates the scarcity of all the banned works by noting: "The STC records one copy of Davies's *Epigrammes*, four each of *Skialethia*, of *Pigmalion* and of *The Scourge of Villanie* (1598), and three of *The Scourge of Villanie* (1599)" (p. xxvii, n.1).

3. Arber, *Transcript*, p. 14.

4. Frederick Seaton Siebert, *Freedom of the Press in England, 1476–1776: The Rise and Decline of Government Controls* (Urbana: University of Illinois Press, 1952), is particularly shrewd in assessing how the political relationship between the government and the printers resulted in the printers' becoming their own censors; see pp. 4, 84.

5. See ibid., p. 63.

6. See David O. Frantz, " 'Leud Priapians' and Renaissance Pornography," *Studies in English Literature* 12 (1972), 157–72, 159. See also Frantz's *Festum Voluptatis: A Study of Renaissance Erotica* (Columbus: Ohio State University Press, 1989).

7. Arnold Davenport, ed., *The Whipper Pamphlets* (1601), Liverpool reprints, nos. 5, 6 (Liverpool: University Press of Liverpool. 1951). In *Censorship and In-*

terpretation: The Conditions of Writing and Reading in Early Modern England (Madison: University of Wisconsin Press, 1984), Annabel Patterson notes only that the ban "included, along with its prohibition of satire, the direction that 'noe English historyes be printed excepte they bee allowed by some of her maiesties privie Counsell" (p. 47). More recently, however, Bruce R. Smith, in *Homosexual Desire in Shakespeare's England* (Chicago: University of Chicago Press, 1991), takes a position closer to mine. Citing Foucault and noting the way that "satire puts the satirist in peril of getting caught up in the very vices he castigates . . . for the reader, what starts out as a homily can easily turn into a piece of pornography," Smith comments that "the Archbishop of Canterbury and the Bishop of London did not need Foucault to tell them that when they ordered the Stationers Company to round up all copies of Marston's *The Scourge of Villanie*, and . . . seven other satirical books" (p. 164).

8. Richard A. McCabe, "Elizabethan Satire and the Bishops' Ban of 1599," *Yearbook of English Studies* 11 (1981), 189.

9. It is Nashe's editor, R. B. McKerrow, who provides the publication information. The first edition was apparently set from two known surviving manuscripts of Nashe's poem, one of them from the Bodleian Library. See *The Works of Thomas Nashe*, ed. Ronald B. McKerrow (1910); rpt., ed. F. P. Wilson (London: Basil Blackwell, 1958), 5:141, n.1.

10. See Richard C. McCoy's essay, "Gascoigne's 'Poemata Castrata': The Wages of Courtly Success," *Criticism* 27 (1985), 29–55; the quotation is from p. 42.

11. *Othello* 1.1.77–79; 2.1.163–64. All quotations are from the Bantam edition, ed. David Bevington (New York: Bantam, 1988), and are subsequently cited in the text.

12. John Marston, *The Scourge of Villanie*, in *The Poems of John Marston, 1575?–1634*, ed. Arnold Davenport, Liverpool English Texts and Studies (Liverpool: Liverpool University Press, 1961). Davenport likewise sees Marston as instrumental in the creation of this new language of the Jacobean stage. See his introduction to *Poems*.

13. Marston's contribution of the Italianate plot is cited in Norman Sanders's introduction to the New Cambridge edition of *Othello* (Cambridge: Cambridge University Press, 1984), p. 18.

14. See David O. Foxon, *Libertine Literature in England, 1660–1745* (London: New Hyde Park, 1965), pp. 11–12. The most accessible version in English of the text and history of "I Modi" is *I modi: The Sixteen Pleasures: An Erotic Album of the Italian Renaissance: Giulio Romano, Marcantonio Raimondi, Pietro Aretino, and Count Jean Frederic-Maximilien de Waldeck*, ed. and trans. Lynne Lawler (Evanston: Northwestern University Press, 1988).

15. Besides John Marston, John Wolfe is the other "white rabbit" to follow. See Siebert, *Freedom of the Press*, p. 75.

16. David McPherson, "Aretino and the Harvey-Nashe Quarrel," *PMLA* 84 (1969), 1551–58.

17. From one of Gabriel Harvey's attacks on Thomas Nashe. See "Pierce's Supererogation," in *The Works of Gabriel Harvey*, ed. A. B. Grosart (London, 1884), 2:91–96. McPherson, "Aretino and the Harvey-Nashe Quarrel," traces Aretino's prominence in the quarrel and also details Harvey's shifting attitudes toward the Italian poet.

18. Edward Meyer, *Machiavelli and the Elizabethan Drama* (Weimar: Emil Felber, 1897), p. 4.

19. Ben Jonson, *Three Comedies: Volpone, The Alchemist, Bartholomew Fair*, ed. Michael Jamieson (Baltimore: Penguin Books, 1966).

20. John Donne, Satyre 4, ll. 70–72, in *The Satires, Epigrams, and Verse Letters*, ed. W. Milgate (Oxford: Clarendon Press, 1967).

21. See Frantz, "Leud Priapians," p. 159.

22. See especially Michel Foucault, *The History of Sexuality*, vol. 1, *An Introduction* trans. Robert Hurley (New York: Pantheon Books, 1978), p. 77.

23. Although the Master of the Revels was indeed a mechanism set up to provide this surveillance over dramatic scripts, the sheer conditions of burgeoning play production, the variety of sites at which plays were nightly being performed, and the impossibility of policing every performance severely limited the scope of what the Revels Office could even hope to control. Most of the censorship interventions that are discernible in late Elizabethan and Jacobean drama occur at one of two sites: dramatic characters who too closely resembled the politically influential (the Oldcastle-Falstaff transposition, for example, or the caricature of the Spanish ambassador which set off the furor over Middleton's *Game of Chess*) and the use of blasphemous oaths onstage. Especially in comparison to sexual reference, both these sites would be relatively easy for a censor at least to locate within a script. For a highly informative discussion of the Master of the Revels Office, see Richard Dutton, *Mastering the Revels: The Regulation and Censorship of English Drama* (Hampshire: Macmillan, 1991).

24. Jonathan Dollimore, *Radical Tragedy: Religion, Ideology, and Power in the Drama of Shakespeare and His Contemporaries* (Chicago: University of Chicago Press, 1984).

PART II

BOUNDARY DISPUTES:

CONSEQUENCES OF

CONSOLIDATION

10. This Is Not a Pipe:
Water Supply, Incontinent Sources,
and the Leaky Body Politic

Jonathan Gil Harris

My sister my spouse *is as* a garden inclosed, as a spring shut vp, *and* a fountaine sealed vp.
> —Song of Songs 4.12 (Geneva Bible)

In this verse of the Song of Songs, Solomon performs a double appropriation. At the moment when he borrows the traditional topos of the well of life to represent his bride, her body is transformed into *his* paradise regained, a sacramental but privatized *fons et origo* of erotic bliss. There is a further and perhaps unexpected dimension of the Song of Songs' appropriation of the "source" topos. The tropes of containment with which Solomon insistently figures the subjected body of his bride—an enclosed garden, a shut-up spring, a sealed-up fountain— cannot help but invoke by their negating force an alternative image of a nonenclosed, unsealed, and leaky spring, one resistant to his dominion. In the process, the Song of Songs implicitly suggests that the matrimonial Edenic waters are, in fact, preceded by another type of source: Solomon's "well of life" is predicated on the enclosure—the patriarchal appropriation and transformation—of a potentially unruly and incontinent spring.

The Song of Songs may seem to have very little to do with questions of origin and water supply in early modern England. But the suggestive tropes of containment which distinguish the Geneva Bible translation provide a useful starting point for understanding the notions of source that accompanied and were shaped by the enclosures, physical and symbolic, of the period. Several studies have provided invaluable insights into the literary versions of the source topos in the Renaissance.[1] Insofar as these have focused primarily on the typology of the waters of life, however, they have largely ignored a competing convention of source representation, one that may be discerned amidst the contradictory morass of Tudor and Stuart attitudes toward the origins of the body politic's water supply. As in the Song of Songs, the articulation of a life-giving source was frequently made possible only by the prior appropriation, enclosure, and/or disavowal of an altogether different kind of source—one apprehended, by contrast, as a contaminating and sometimes deadly incontinence.

I. Edward Forset's Leaky Garden

In November 1612, six years after the publication of his tract on the body politic, the London writer and lawyer Edward Forset became publicly embroiled in yet another political debate. But whereas his *Comparative Discourse of the Bodies Naturall and Politique* had endeavored to convince its readers of the righteousness of Stuart hegemony and judicial policy, Forset now found himself, if only briefly, at odds with the authorities. At stake this time was nothing as lofty as the "marking and matching of the works of the finger of God, eyther in the larger volume of the vniuersall, or in the abridgement thereof, the body of man."[2] The source (quite literally) of the dispute was a spring on the grounds of Forset's manor estate, located a few miles outside London. Dismayed by the damage that overflow from the spring was causing to his property, he had decided to enclose it within a brick wall. This in turn had enraged London's city officers, who, faced with desperate water shortages that year, demanded access to the spring. Forset, for whatever reasons he may have had, stubbornly refused. The argument dragged on for some months; in June of the next year the city authorities were still trying to make good their claim to the spring's waters.[3] On a technicality, however, Forset had the law on his side. Although an act of 1544 gave the mayor and commonalty of London authority to "enter into the grounds and possessions of the King, as well as every other person and persons, bodies politic and corporate, where they shall find or know any such springs to be . . . and there to dig pits, trenches, and ditches, to erect heads, lay pipes, and make vaults . . . for the conveyance of the said water and springs to the citie," they were nonetheless prohibited access to any property "inclosed with stone, brick or mud walls."[4]

Forset's method of containing the spring's flow illustrates the extent to which enclosure was employed to assert the primacy of boundaries—not simply the physical boundary dividing a rogue spring from a well-manicured garden, but also the proprietorial boundaries which, within the mercantilist society of Tudor and Stuart England, were commensurate with the growth of a bourgeoisie increasingly protected by law against the claims of the "commonweal." As the 1544 law governing water supply testifies, the civic *corpus politicus* was now capable of finding itself at odds with private "body politics," property owners who, like Forset, were ostensibly part of, but were also guaranteed a relative autonomy from, the larger social body. This is a development that lies outside the scope of this essay,[5] but it is worth noting the very different ways in which the two body politics, private and public, regarded water. Forset's irritation with the spring's leaky encroachment upon his property may recall (in a less extreme fashion) the attitude of John Davies, who, in his long poem about the body, remarked that just as "*hate* hauocks in each hole in al *vprores*," so "*water* hauocks *life* through all the *pores*."[6] By contrast, London's city officers lent voice to the claims of a civic body politic given to figuring its springs and piped waters as its very "life-blood." Samuel Rolle's *Burning of London* (1666) pursues the analogy in considerable detail:

> As nature, by veins, and arteries some great and some small, placed up and down all parts of the body, ministereth blood and nourishment to every part thereof, so was that wholesome water which was necessary for the good of London as blood is for the good and health of the body, conveyed by pipes wooden or metalline, as by veins, to every part of this famous City. If water were, as we may call it, the blood of London, then were its several conduits as it were the liver and spleen of that City; (which are reckoned the fountains of blood in human bodies,) for that the great trunks and veins conveying blood about the body, are seated therein as great roots fixed in the earth, shooting out their branches in divers and sundry ways.[7]

It would be a fundamental mistake, however, to assume that where private body politics depended on enclosure to assert their boundaries against the threat (or nuisance value) of water, the civic organism was characterized by an abundant, uncontained leakiness. The public body did, after all, enclose water in vaults, pipes, castellated conduits; water had to be contained and controlled for London's citizens to enjoy its not insignificant benefits. But a distinction between Rolle's and Forset's body politics and their attitudes toward water does need to be drawn. In Thomas Heywood's *If You Know Not Me, You Know No Bodie*, the young Queen Elizabeth begs her court to recognize "some difference . . . / Twixt Christall Fountayne, and foule muddy Springs."[8] Similarly, Rolle's "fountains" and Forset's "spring" demand a distinction between two very different types of source: one that "ministereth . . . nourishment to every part"; another that "hauocks" the body through

"every pore." As we shall see, these two notions were very much mediated by patriarchal constructions of gender and parenthood. The
first, beneficent source was often regarded as the animating and masculine principle of social order; the second, "havocking" source as grotesquely feminine and requiring surveillance and enclosure of the type
undertaken by Forset. But, as we shall also see, the masculine source of
the public body always had the potential to revert to its dangerous feminine antitype. As a consequence, attitudes toward civic water supply
were often ambivalent and contradictory. Various strategies of enclosure were mobilized to mitigate the dangerous, feminine attributes of
water supply—enclosures ranging from straightforward physical containment to the encircling trajectory of the royal gaze—all of which
were only partially successful.

Before critically reappraising notions of source from the vantage
point of gender, I shall attempt to sketch a poetics of the incontinent
body politic in early modern England.[9] Such a poetics is primarily designed to illuminate the complex cluster of somatic figures with which
the polis, its sources, and its boundaries were thought during the age of
enclosure, and to explain how water supply resisted total containment
within these figurations. But the characteristic leakiness of the incontinent body politic may also suggestively image the fluid interplay between Tudor and Stuart constructions of geography, gender, and
engendering which are the concern of this essay. Above all, this interplay shows that a lot can be learned from something as apparently
mundane as the metaphysics of Elizabethan and Jacobean plumbing.

II. Source Study: Where Does Water Come From?

Rolle's analogy between London's water supply and the body posits a
straightforward physical correspondence between the two. In certain
Jacobean texts this correspondence was developed to account for or
justify existing social hierarchies and modes of production. *The Dead
Tearme* by Thomas Dekker (1608), for example, offers an anatomy of
London in which the city's heart is represented by its clergy: "a goodly
Fountain, large, cleare, strongly, and curiously built, out of which come
a thousand pipes (some greater than the rest) thorough whome a
sweete water flowes, that giues life."[10] By contrast, Barnabe Barnes's
Foure Bookes of Offices (1606) compares the position of the treasurer in
the body politic to the "conduits of the liuer," from which are dispersed
riches for "the generall sustenation and nurriture" of the commonwealth.[11] The somatic models that Barnes and Dekker employ are recognizably pre-Harveian. Blood here does not circulate; instead it has

an origin and an end, an animating source (the heart or the liver), and a dependent recipient (the remainder of the body) to which it "trickles down."[12] In anthropomorphizing London's water supply, Rolle likewise pinpoints an origin within the body of the city: just as the liver and the spleen are "fountains of blood," the mainsprings of the city water supply are its "several conduits."

For most people living in London in the late sixteenth and early seventeenth centuries, conduits—public fountains—were indeed the "source" of their water. Although the first large conduits were constructed in the thirteenth century, they enjoyed their heyday during the reign of Elizabeth. In the first edition of his *Survey of London* (1598), John Stow makes reference to sixteen conduits in the city.[13] These were often impressive structures. Compared to the relative simplicity of the Great Conduit in Cheapside, rebuilt in 1479 as a battlemented stone building enclosing a large lead cistern, the conduit at Fleetbridge was ostentatiously ornate. Stow notes that its cistern was crowned by "a fair tower of stone, garnished with images of *S. Christopher* on the top, and Angels round about lower down, with sweet sounding bels before them, whereupon by an Engine placed in the Tower, they, diuers houres of the day and night, chymed such an Hymme as was appointed."[14] The grandiose design of the Fleetbridge conduit would appear to accord it the symbolic significance which the liver and heart enjoy in Rolle's, Dekker's, and Barnes's organic metaphors as London's "wells of life." But following Rolle and Barnes in characterizing conduits as sources of water *within* the civic body commits one to a significant confusion or elision: although some of London's conduits were erected on the sites of medieval wells, for the most part they received their water from pipes leading to springs—like Forset's—situated *outside* the city walls. Stow tells us that the Great Conduit contained "sweet water, conueyed by pipes of Lead vnder ground from Paddington." Similarly, the Cripplesgate conduit was serviced by pipes leading from Highbury, and others received water from springs at Hoxton and Islington.[15]

This confusion surrounding the city's sources of water was paralleled by the semantic ambivalence of the word "conduit" itself. It did not simply mean "source," although this was very much its dominant sense. In his portrait of the Castle of Alma in *The Faerie Queene*, Spenser presents an extended allegory of the body which employs a somewhat different sense of the word:

> But all the liquor, whiche was fowle and wast,
> Nor good nor seruiceable for ought,
> They in another great round vessell plast,

> Till by a conduit pipe it thence were brought:
> And all the rest, that noyous was, and nought,
> By secret wayes, that none may it espy,
> Was close convaid, and to the back-gate brought,
> That cleped was *Port Esquiline,* whereby
> It was avoided quite, and throwne out privily.[16]

Spenser's use of "conduit" in this stanza suggests not a source within the body but a pipe which, invested with the "secret wayes" of an orifice, leads through its outer limits. The conduit pipe did not simply convey waste from the body; it could also provide the body with material from the outside. A conduit (pipe) could therefore supply a conduit (source). The emphasis Spenser puts on the conduit pipe's "secret wayes" places it in sharp contrast to the spectacular visibility of the conduit buildings I have mentioned. Such a contrast, I would argue, facilitated the disavowal of the external source to which the conduit pipe led. When ostentatiously invested with the value of the internal source, therefore, the conduit was most assuredly not a pipe.

The extraordinary visibility of the conduit building often involved a second kind of displacement of source from outside to inside the city. Lamb's Conduit was an immensely extravagant, and from all accounts expensive, construction. It was decorated with four columns and a pediment surmounted by a pyramid, on which had been placed a statue of a lamb—a rebus on the name of the conduit's benefactor, William Lamb. In the process, not only did he become recognized as the human "source" of water in the city; additionally, his much-publicized donation of 120 pails to poor women so that they could obtain water from the conduit established him as London's "font of charity."[17] Human "font" thus contrived to occlude geographic origin.

What was at stake in repudiating the external sources of London's water supply? The answer is located in part, I think, in an ideology of determinate or bounded space which writers such as Dekker reproduced, and which materially instantiated itself in the many enclosures of land and water in early modern England. When indebted to an external source, a city's water supply involves a blurring of geosymbolic boundaries: elements of the "outside" are incorporated in the "inside." Thus figured, the city's body is in at least one respect reminiscent of Dante's depiction of Hell, which, as Robert M. Durling has shown, draws upon the traditional notion of the body of Satan as the blasphemous antitype of the body of Christ. Durling remarks that it "is surely significant that the rivers of Hell do not, like the river of blood in a human body, originate within the Body of Satan itself, but from outside."[18] This Satanic body image therefore possesses the distinctive qualities of what Mikhail Bakhtin, in his well-known study of Rabelais, calls the "grotesque" body image of popular festival and carnivalesque literature. In representations of the grotesque body, Bakhtin asserts, "the stress is laid on those parts of the body that are open to the outside world, that is, the parts through which the body itself goes out to meet the world."[19] If a city with an external source for its water supply approximated the Satanic or grotesque body, the representation of a city as a body with internal sources can be seen to have invoked the discursive norms of what Bakhtin calls the "classical," or official, body. This other body provides, by contrast, a "finished, completed" image; whereas the grotesque body disrespects both its own and other bodies' boundaries, the classical body's contours "acquire an essential meaning as the border of a closed individuality that does not merge with other bodies and with the world."[20]

Bakhtin, it is important to note, insists on the mediating role played by the two body images in organizing the structure and boundaries of different social formations in early modern Europe.[21] Just as the overflowing abundance of the grotesque body characterized the teeming, sensual throng of carnival and marketplace, the clearly delineated borders of the classical body frequently informed the ideological inscriptions of high or "official" culture. If the grotesque body possessed for Bakhtin an unproblematic utopian subversiveness, it acquired a very different accent for those Tudor and Stuart ideological institutions which legitimized their authority by appealing to the values of the exclusionary classical body. The grotesque body was *incontinent,* both in the modern somatic sense and in the earlier, broader meaning of "unrestrained."[22] Transcoded into the domain of organic political metaphor, these qualities were easily remodeled as the contaminating excrescences and incursions of a malevolent organism in opposition to which the civic body politic had to assert its recognizably classical boundaries, demanding from all its members an unconditional vigilance which would securely unite (and enclose) them against a common threat. In his *Picture of a Perfit Common Wealth* (1600), for example, Thomas Floyd told his readers that they needed "no more than the liuely example of Argos, which had his head inuironed with a hundred watching eies."[23]

Yet Floyd's figuration of the vigilant body politic and its "hundred watching eies" potentially increased rather than diminished the danger of a contaminating, grotesque incursion. "The outward senses," observed John Davies of both natural and political bodies in *Microcosmos,* "are the Doores where through Sin enters."[24] Writing of the symbolic formations of primitive and modern societies, Mary Douglas notes that "sometimes bodily orifices seem to represent points of entry or exit to social units."[25] In seeking to bar entry to its interior, the exclusionary classical body politic attempted to renounce its orifices. Not for it the grotesque contours of Panurge's Paris, enclosed by a wall made of women's "thing-o-my-bobs."[26] Instead, it hankered for the unpunctured walls of the fortress: "You are all knit together in one common wealth, as it were members in a naturall bodie," William Averell informed the readers of his *Meruailous Combat of Contrareties* (1588); "beware . . . that your enemies may have no gap whereby to enter."[27]

But a city whose pipes extended beyond its walls *did* have such vulnerable gaps, albeit "secret" ones such as that produced by the conduit pipe in Spenser's Castle of Alma. Christopher Marlowe illustrated the potential threat presented by an external source in *Tamburlaine the Great I* with Bajazeth's plan for winning the siege of Constantinople: "Cut off the water, that by leaden pipes / Runs to the city from the mountain."[28] In addition to such military threats, the awareness that London obtained it water through pipes leading beyond the city walls was also capable of producing a fear of contamination from the outside. Suspicions that London's water supply was being tampered with at its source were focused in an act that strictly prohibited people "to meddle with the spring at the foot of the hill of the said heath, called Hamsted Heath . . . or procure to be done, any thing, acts, or act, to the impairing, hurt, or diminishing, of the water of the same spring at any time hereafter."[29] As I shall argue, however, these fears are themselves symptomatic of a more fundamental nexus of phobias which clustered around the very notion of source.

III. Monstrous Parents

William Averell's exhortation that citizens ensure there is no gap in the body politic for the enemy to enter found a judicial parallel in the 1531 Statute of Sewers, which expressed concern about "the outrageous Flowings, Surges, and Course" of water, springs, and sewers in and near London. Authority was given to commissioners "to tax, assess, charge, distrain and punish" persons liable for the upkeep of sewers, vaults, and walls.[30] In the face of potential leakiness, therefore, London's citizens were expected to emulate the vigilant Dutch hero of Haarlem, who, noticing water seeping through a hole in the dike, saved his city from catastrophe by stopping the gap with his finger. Citizens who failed to display such vigilance were to be punished. Negligence in this matter represented a delinquency as intolerable as the leakiness itself: both required containment. The imperative to control water was therefore already inseparable from a process of social control. This connection was established in other ways. The twin tasks of containing "incontinent" water and "incontinent" citizens were constantly identified with each other: John Stow notes that the conduit at Cornehill was originally built in 1282 as a prison to contain "night walkers and suspicious persons," as well as those "suspected of incontinencie." He tells us also that water reservoirs were built at Newgate and Ludgate prisons.[31] Enclosure was thus a critical component in the articulation of classical boundaries between inside and outside, dry and wet, citizen and delinquent.

The link between incontinent water and antisocial delinquency was readily accessible to many writers in Tudor and Stuart England; it seems to have occupied a major place in the phobic imaginary of the period. Dekker provides a notable example in *The Dead Tearme*. In the course of anatomizing her body, London warns her neighbour Westminster of "all these Cankers of a State, that lye gnawing to eate thee vppe; All those sensuall streames, that flowe about thy body, and labour to drowne it in impieties, flowe in thy Veynes, but as little Riuolets, but in mine they exceed all boundes, and swell vppe to an Ocean. And that the very least of them vndermineth and shaketh my strongest buildings" (sig. E1v). Dekker here depicts the "waters" of London's body very differently from Samuel Rolle in *The Burning of London*. Whereas the latter views the city conduits as the sources of a "wholesome water . . . necessary for the good of London as blood is for the good and health of the body," Dekker uses water as a pathological figure for the threat presented to the body politic's health by the excessive incontinence of both its members and its enemies. Water no longer guarantees the maintenance of degree within the *corpus politicus:* it threatens instead to muddy the distinctions of the social order. Invoking a catastrophic scenario in which even gender difference has become grotesquely blurred, London proceeds to describe the nature of its "sensuall streames" which "exceede all boundes": "As for that Monster with many heades, that Beast (both Male and Female) I mean Letchery, it is within my Fredome more made of, then Island Dogges are amongest Cittizens Wiues: and when it gets out of my freedome, it is then like the place where it desires to lurke in, for then it lyes out of the circuite of all ciuill Liberty" (sigs E1v–E2). This hermaphroditic monster is the epitome of grotesque incontinence: it is to be found both outside and inside London, disrespecting the enclosing classical boundary of the civic body politic, described here as "the circuit of all civil liberty." Once outside this "circuit," Letchery is "like the place it desires to lurke in," uncontained by geography or civic jurisdiction. Dekker's similitude amounts to a literal *mapping* of delinquency, in which morality is topographized and topography moralized: the source of the city's sickness is located outside its body, in the ambivalent marginal space of the City Liberties.[32] Moreover, this mapping leaves the reader in no doubt as to the gender of the sinful source outside the "circuit of all civil liberty." In a move that serves to translate Letchery's multi-headed hermaphroditism into a specifically feminine threat to the social order, Dekker identifies its "outrageous waters" with prostitution. Both are characterized by a failure to keep within limits; in the past, fulminates Dekker, "orders were established to keepe this Sin within certaine boundes, but now it breaks beyond all limits" (sig. E2).[33] A delinquent, leaky femininity becomes symbolic shorthand, therefore, for the grotesque transgression or infiltration of London's city limits.

In contrast to this malevolent origin *outside* the city, Dekker elsewhere discusses what would at first appear to be an altogether more positive feminine point of origin *within* London's body. At the beginning of the pamphlet Westminster praises her neighbor: "A blessed Mother thou art, for no lesse than one hundred and threescore Emperours, Kinges, and Queens, hast thou borne in thy Wombe"(sig. A3). Yet if the womb here figures the "blessed" source of the body politic's royal (and patriarchal) authority, its reproductive power later assumes an altogether more ambivalent and threatening dimension that recalls the portrait of Letchery. Advising Westminster on how to eradicate sin from her body, London invokes her own experience as a mother and begs her to "presently beginne to rip open the adulterous Wombe of those sinnes that are euery day begotten vnder thy roofes" (sig. E1). The womb has degenerated here into an incontinent source, both corrupt and corrupting; its powers of generation are presented as no longer constitutive of but opposed to the body politic's health. Grotesque, contaminating, and ultimately as alien to the "circuit of all civil liberty" as Letchery and her "sensuall streames,"[34] the womb confronts here a fate that is disconcertingly grisly yet rife with significance—a disemboweling-cum-hysterectomy which allows Dekker to repudiate any maternal origin in and for the body politic.

The figural slipperiness of the womb in *The Dead Tearme* points to the profound disjunctions that characterize Renaissance representations of motherhood and childbirth.[35] Two distinct trends can be discerned. The first fetishizes the mother as the means of patrilineal (re)production: she provides her husband with male children to whom he passes the patrimony. This view serves to style the father as source, inasmuch as the child's discrete identity originates in, but is distinct from, the father's. Dekker's initial praise of London's "blessed . . . Wombe" from which countless monarchs have been born comes close to this construction of maternity: London is to be praised insofar as she has made possible the perpetuation of patrilineal monarchy. But if the mother is here celebrated as the mediator of a patriarchally interpellated identity which conforms to the exclusionary strictures of the classical body image, her reproductive body was itself readily associated with a grotesque doubleness which blurred the boundary between her child's and her own identity. As Dekker's later portrait of "the adulterous Wombe" of sin demonstrates, motherhood could thus be used to figure a polluting source indistinct from its effluvia.

This second view of motherhood is in accord with the biblical law that condemns the pregnant woman and new mother as polluted or impure: according to Leviticus 12:2–8, a woman shall be unclean for fourteen days after the birth of a girl, and for seven days after the birth of a boy.[36] Biblical law, however, cannot account on its own for the extreme vehemence and disgust that inform many Renaissance representations of childbirth and the womb. In the opening canto of the first book of *The Faerie Queene*, Spenser provides a particularly virulent instance which has certain affinities with Dekker's demonization of the womb in *The Dead Tearme*. Red Cross Knight has barely left the Faerie court (that is, he is in the marginal zone between "civility" and "barbarity") when he stumbles upon Errour, a "lothsom, filthie, foule" monster (1.1.14.9), half serpent, half woman. Attacking him by spewing out a vile-smelling "floud of poyson horrible and black" (1.1.20.2), Errour then proceeds to pour "forth out of her hellishe sinke / Her fruitfull cursed spawne of serpents small, / Deformed monsters, fowle and black as inke" (1.1.22.5–7).

Spenser's terminology here is significant. Errour's "sinke"—a common Elizabethan term for sewer—establishes her as a polluted and polluting source, a monstrous mother whose "cursed spawne" is a subspecies of vomit. Moreover, the conflation of stomach and womb represented by Errour's "sinke" intensifies the ambivalences of her brand of maternity: her excremental offspring's point of origin in her body is also their nemesis, a disjunction graphically reinforced by her practice of feeding on them. To explain Errour's grotesque coupling of reproductivity and infanticide, Spenser employs an extended analogy which reiterates the link between monstrous parenthood and incontinent water:

> As when old father *Nilus* gins to swell
>   With timely pride about the *Aegyptian* vale
>   His fattie waues do fertile slime outwell,
>   And ouerflow each plaine and lowly dale:
>   But when his later spring gins to avale,
>   Huge heapes of mudd he leaues, wherein there breed
>   Ten thousand kindes of creatures, partly male

And partly female of his fruitfull seed;
Such ugly monstrous shapes elsewhere may no man reed.

(1.1.21)

Spenser may call the river "father Nilus,"[37] but it is, after all, Errour's form of motherhood that he is describing. Like Errour and her "fruit-full cursed spawne," the parent-river is indistinct from his children, who are produced from his "fertile slime"; like Errour, who eats her "thousand young ones" (1.1.15.5), the Nile is an infanticidal parent, promising to devour his brood the next time his "fattie waues" burst their banks.

Spenser is drawing here on a stock representation of the Nile which provides the negative term in a related sequence of oppositions between clean and polluting, restrained and incontinent, paternal and maternal sources. William Averell, for example, concludes his tale of the body politic's mutinous members by thanking God for delivering England from the poisonous errors of the Mother Church of Rome: "Thou hast taken awaie our stinking waters of *Nilus,* and given us the christal stremes of the clean water of life."[38] A similar opposition obtains in Dekker's *Dead Tearme.* We have seen how the "stinking waters" of Letchery and the sinful womb constitute grotesque female or maternal sources derived from "outside the circuit of all civil liberty"; in so doing they contrast the unequivocally healthy and masculine "christal stremes" of the clergy, who, we recall, nourish the body and the soul of the *corpus politicus* through their thousand pipes. This rhetorical pattern—feminine source demonized, masculine source valorized—recurs throughout Dekker's text. It is perhaps most apparent with Westminster's near-comic paean to the pen: "What a rare inuention therefore was pen and incke, out of whom (as streames from a Fountaine), flow all these wonders? How much beholden are men to his witte, that out of a poore Goose-gull was the first deuiser of so strange an instrument as a Pen, which carries in it such power, such conquest, and such authority, that euen the greatest subiects in kingdomes are glad sometimes to be beholden to it, and as often to tremble when it is but held vp against them" (sig. C3). Unlike Letchery or the womb, the phallic "fountain" pen guarantees—somewhat coercively—the hierarchal differences of social order, according to which subjectivity is the result of subjection. In the process, the pen—like the clergy—is characterized as an indispensable member of the healthy body politic. With its deployment of organic analogy, therefore, *The Dead Tearme* not only performs a significant demonization and/or repudiation of any external feminine or maternal source; it also firmly locates and masculinizes the origin of social value and degree *within* the civic organism.

This process provides an illuminating parallel to the disavowal of an external source which informed the designs of London's conduits. But even if writers such as Samuel Rolle can be seen to have repudiated the grotesque and feminine dimensions of water supply by styling conduits as sources within London's body, these buildings, although classically enclosing water within their walls, had the potential to be viewed as themselves grotesque: in order to function, they still had to discharge water, to leak. Addressing London, Thomas Nashe begged it to contain its sinful proclivities and not "ouerflow like ful conduits."[39] Many representations of conduit buildings identified them with the body's orifices rather than the liver or heart. This was certainly the case with the so-called Pissing Conduit situated at the end of Cheapside. Indeed, the *OED* notes that "conduit" had by 1560 become available as a synonym for the pissing orifice itself.

Much insightful work has been done, notably by Peter Stallybrass and Gail Kern Paster, on the important role played by the grotesque and classical body paradigms in Renaissance constructions of gender.[40] Leakiness was proverbially associated with women, as Gonzalo's notorious remark in *The Tempest* suggests: "The ship were no stronger than a nutshell, and as leaky as an unstanched wench" (1.1.47–48).[41] The leakiness of the conduit was frequently employed to figure the congenitally grotesque female body. Juliet's father reacts to the spectacle of her tears with the remark: "How now, a conduit girl?" (*Romeo and Juliet* 3.5.129). More frequently the conduit was associated with women's alleged verbal incontinence: "She is like a conduit-pipe," Ben Jonson's Master Morose complains of Epicoene, "that will gush out with more force when she opens again."[42] The association was strengthened further by the fact that women rather than men were accustomed to obtaining water from London's conduits, as William Lamb's much-vaunted donation of pails to lower-class women indicates. With an image that naturalized the metaphorical link between the supposed incontinence of female mouths and the leakiness of conduits, a large woodcut accompanying a pamphlet titled *Tittle-Tattle; Or the Several Branches of Gossiping* (1603) depicts a scene, "At the Conditte," in which a group exclusively comprising women is gathered gossiping in whispers.[43] Moreover, the conduit as a specifically incontinent feminine site seems to have been positively appropriated by the near-legendary female transvestite and "roaring girl" Moll Cutpurse; rumor had it that she willed twenty pounds so that the city conduits would run with wine.[44]

If the sources of London's water supply readily presented themselves as incontinently feminine even when displaced into the enclosed interiority of the classical body politic, how did patriarchal authority undertake to reassert the masculinity of those sources? We have already seen how, in the case of Lamb's Conduit, the emblematic details of the structure attempted to displace public perception of the source of London's health from a geographic to a human, patriarchal point of origin. This process occurred in a much more complex manner in the coronation pageant of King James, during which the city's conduits and fountains participated in what can be recognized as a narcissistic articulation of royal power.

IV. Narcissus: Royal Reflections on Water

When King James arrived in London to claim the throne on March 15, 1603, he was greeted with a spectacular pageant. Marie Axton has noted how the poets and the dramatists who contributed to the pageant translated the legal theory supporting the new king into powerful theatrical emblems: "Their pageant iconography declared that it was not the land, or the estates of Parliament, but the King who represented the power of government and the perpetuity of the realm."[45] Jonathan Goldberg has gone ever further, claiming that the absolutist notions of regal power informing James's coronation pageant (and, indeed, his entire reign) are incompatible with conceptions of representative government: "As he arrived, like the sun giving life, like the groom entering the bride, like a king in court, the city sprang alive."[46] In other words, James did not owe his existence to the people; on the contrary, they owed theirs to him. Goldberg's sun metaphor is not an arbitrary one. Jacobean and Caroline writers frequently employed it to dramatize the configuration of power according to which the king was not the representative but the animating origin of the body politic. In his *Comparative Discourse of the Bodies Naturall and Politique,* Edward Forset asserted that "the resplendence and power of sovereignty in the royall person of a Sovereign," like that of the sun, is demonstrated "both in so great a majestie, as dazleth the eyes of all beholders, and in so admirable effects, as to transform savagenesse into civility, repugnance into concords, vices into virtues, procuring love, yet implying fear."[47] The bedazzling sun-monarch is thus understood to be the source of social and moral order, in a manner reminiscent of the fountain of the clergy in Dekker's *Dead Tearme.* The figures of sun and fountain uphold alike the Neoplatonic vision of the cosmos embedded in Jacobean and Caroline conceptions of royal power: a unitary, life-giving source—also imaged as a father—creates and sustains a qualitative hierarchy of spheres, whose values are determined by their relative proximity to the origin.[48] All of creation—that is, "everything under the sun"—constitutes the totality of signifiers representing the transcendental signified of the origin. The monarch fits into this schema in a somewhat ambiguous way. As Goldberg points out: "James was God's lieutenant, he stood in his place; re-placed him, represented him and doubled his power."[49] The king is thus both signifier and signified, both a representation of the font of being and the font itself.

Those who devised James's coronation pageant fully exploited the Neoplatonic dimensions of the figure of the fountain to legitimize his authority. In Thomas Dekker's *Magnificent Entertainment*, which recounts the various spectacles presented "vpon the day of his Maiesties Triumphant Passage (from the Tower) through his Honourable Citie (and Chamber) of *London*," particular attention is paid to a fountain near Soper Lane built especially for the pageant: "An artificiall Lauer or Fount was erected, called the *Founte of Araite (Vertue)*, Sundry Pipes (like veines) branching from the body of it: the water receuing libertie but from one place, and that very slowly."[50] King James, seated on a horse, beheld two allegorical figures, Detractio and Oblivio, asleep at the foot of the fountain. One held a cup around whose brim writhed snakes, "intimating that whosoeuer his lippes toucht, was poysoned;" the other held "a blacke Cuppe couerd, in token of an enuious desire to drowne the worth and memorie of Noble persons" (sig. E4). Detractio and Oblivio's "malitious intent" was stymied, however, by the abrupt revelation of the royal presence: "A strange and heauenly musick sudainly striking through their eares, which causing a wildnes and quick motion in their lookes, drew them to light vpon the glorious presence of the King, they were suddainly thereby daunted and sunke downe; The Fount in the same moment of *Tyme*, flowing fresh and abundantly through seuerall pipes, with Milke, Wine, and Balme" (sig. F1). A further allegorical figure, Circumspection, stepped forward to "deliuer to his Maiestie the interpretation of this dumb Mysterie":

> A *Phoenix* liu'd and died in the Sunnes brest,
> Her losse, made sight, in teares to drowne her eyes,
> The eare grew deafe, Taste like a sick-man lyes,
> Finding no rellish, euery other Sence,
> Forgat his office, worth and excellence,
> Whereby this Fount of Vertue gan to freeze,
> Threatned to be drinke by two enemies,
> Snakie *Detraction*, and *Obliuion*,
> But at thy glorious presence, both are gone,
> Thou being that sacred *Phoenix*, that doest rise,
> From th'ashes of the first: Beames from thine eyes
> So vertually shining that they bring,
> To *Englands* new *Arabia*, a new Spring.
>
> (sigs. F1v–F2)

Circumspection's gloss on the spectacle interpellates the king's identity in ambiguous relation to the Neoplatonic source. Initially, he is merely the most recent incarnation of the mystical body of royalty,[51] imaged as the phoenix which lives and dies "in the Sunnes brest." Ten lines later, however, he is more than Elizabeth reborn; he is the sun itself, and the "Beames" from his bedazzling eyes are understood to be the animating principle which bestows life upon "*Englands* new *Arabia*," not to mention the Fountain of Araite. James's ennobling effect on the corrupt fountain, a deft display of Neoplatonic plumbing, can be understood as the emblematic enactment of the sun-monarch's transformative power acclaimed by Forset: this episode in the pageant indeed saw James "transform savagenesse into civility, repugnance into concords, vices into virtues."

But this process involved further significant dimensions. James's transformation of the fountain was at once an act of appropriation and of self-fashioning. It was an appropriative gesture insofar as it marked the transfer of the English body politic to his rightful possession (and if this exchange recalls Solomon's appropriation of the bridal fountain in the Songs of Songs, the parallel is all the more trenchant, given James's well-documented perceptions of himself as a second Solomon and of his coronation as a marriage to the nation).[52] But, just as important, this appropriative gesture was also an act of self-fashioning. By transforming the fountain into a life-giving source, James recast himself allegorically within the spectacle. The Fountain of Virtue was the standard emblematic counterpart of the sovereign and his court: "a prince's court," observes Antonio in *The Duchess of Malfi*,

> Is like a common fountain, whence should flow
> Pure silver drops in general; but if't chance
> Some curs'd example poison't near the head,
> Death and diseases through the whole land spread.[53]

The figure of the fountain was commonly employed to characterize King James himself. In *The Advancement of Learning*, Francis Bacon describes James's speeches as "prince-like, flowing as from a fountain, and yet streaming and branching itself into nature's order, full of facility and felicity, imitating none, and inimitable by any."[54] The section of the coronation pageant that took place at Soper Lane therefore involved a fountain-king producing and recognizing his self-image in a fountain representation. But it is important to note that this was more than simply a specular encounter. James's self-fashioning as *fons et origo* of the nation was commensurate with his emblematic triumph over an alternative, poisonous source; more significantly, perhaps, his self-fashioning consisted also in the appropriation and transformation of that source into its healthy, life-giving opposite.

The encounter between royal source and water source was foregrounded at another point in the coronation pageant. James's tour of London involved his stopping at the city conduits, to which had been affixed "Moral Sentences." These were somewhat trite epigrams designed, presumably, to reflect the mind of their royal spectator. The conduit at Cornhill, for example, contained this profound insight: "When a Kinge's head but akes, / Subiects should mourne / For vnder their crownes / A thousand cares are worne."[55] In contrast to his complex interplay with the corrupt Fountain of Araite, the relationship between the king and the conduits seems much more straightforward: there were no spectacular, dramatic transformations of "savagenesse into civility," or "vices into virtues." Nevertheless, one may still view James's encounters with the conduits as performing a series of subtle appropriative transformations not dissimilar to that witnessed by his subjects in the episode at Soper Lane. First, the conduits' participation in the pageant as reflections of the royal source involved their temporary appropriation from a cultural system within which they were, as we saw earlier, coded as specifically lower-class feminine sites. For the duration of James's tour of London, in other words, the conduits ceased to be the incontinent accomplices of Moll Cutpurse, and were instead press-ganged into legitimizing the king and his authority.

Second, James's encounter with his royal reflection may be seen to have briefly repudiated the threat that conduits—or rather, the sources from which conduits derived their water—presented to the boundaries of the classical body politic. When the royal source—the sun of the nation, the font of virtue—saw himself reflected both allegorically and physically in the conduits, the "source" he contemplated momentarily occluded knowledge of a more disturbing, and potentially contaminating, point of origin outside the city walls. His self-recognition prompted him and his spectating subjects to invest the very notion of the conduit with the Neoplatonic associations characterizing his own self-image as a life-giving source *within* the body politic. In its repudiation of an external source as well as its containment of the city conduits' associations with feminine leakiness, the encircling trajectory of James's self-contemplating gaze may be regarded as having performed a double enclosure: it asserted the masculine impermeability of both the classical body politic and its internal sources. Nevertheless, this masculinization or "classicization" of the conduits has a problematic aspect, one that arises from the contradictory contemporary attitudes toward the very specularity that informed the pageant's articulation of royal authority.

Early in *The Magnificent Entertainment*, Dekker identifies the coronation pageant with masques (sig. C1). Not only did the iconography of
the pageant anticipate Inigo Jones and Ben Jonson's court masques, in
which the Neoplatonic motif of the sun as source was adapted to the
articulation of royal power; but more specifically, the encounter between fountain-king and fountain-representation, and the resulting
specularity of royal spectator and spectacle, also recalls one of the most
significant features of the Jacobean and Caroline court masque.
Stephen Orgel has directed critical attention to Ben Jonson's observation that masques are "the mirrors of man's life." In particular, Orgel
notes, they were presented as reflections of the royal mind: "What the
noble spectator watched he ultimately became."[56]

As many commentators have noted, Renaissance attitudes toward
mirrors were complex and contradictory. On the one hand, they signified self-knowledge; on the other, they invoked the folly of Narcissus,
bedazzled by his own reflection.[57] For a number of Elizabethan authors, Narcissus' crime was less self-love than the heinous overvalua-
tion of a mere image.[58] According to this reading, Echo, the
incorporeal nymph whose desire is spurned by Narcissus, assumes a
critical importance: in contrast to the falseness of Narcissus' reflection,
she is the "real" thing, a legitimate object of desire. For example,
Henry Reynolds tells the readers of his *Mythomystes* to "*adore Ecco*. This
Winde is . . . the Symbole of the Breath of God."[59] Reynolds's reading
produces Echo as the allegorical representative of the Neoplatonic
source; by contrast, I would argue that Narcissus' rejection of Echo in
favor of his own reflection parallels very closely patriarchal authority's
production of *itself* as the Neoplatonic origin through the appropriative transformation and/or repudiation of an incontinent female
source.

There is a further feature of the narcissistic encounter between
fountain-king and fountain-spectacle which contradicts most Tudor
and Stuart readings of Ovid's myth. Francis Bacon's interpretation of
Narcissus' crime asserts that excessive attention to one's reflection is inherently antisocial: "For it is the propertie of men infected with this
humour not to come much abroad, or to be conuersant in ciuill
affaires."[60] By contrast, James's coronation pageant encouraged its
spectators to regard his narcissistic self-contemplation as the very
source of social order and "ciuill affaires." In his outstanding study of
social and semiotic disorders in the Renaissance, Barry Taylor has convincingly argued that Jonson's play *Cynthia's Revels, Or the Fountain of
Self-Love* arrives at a similar understanding of Narcissus' self-
absorption: it "is not merely an abdication or standing aside from
meaning and socialisation, but rather a dynamic principle which ani-
mates and indeed originates society itself."[61] The play encourages this

interpretation, argues Taylor, because it somewhat unwillingly presents the Neoplatonic source as a surface image apprehended by narcissistic contemplation. Taylor's argument is worth rehearsing briefly here because it points to a cultural dynamic that is also embedded in James's appropriative transformations of London's fountains and conduits.

Cynthia's Revels sets out to satirize courtly life and, in particular, the narcissistic self-deceptions of courtiers who pay inordinate attention to the trappings of speech and dress. In contrast to such deceptive vanities, Queen Cynthia (the allegorical representation of Queen Elizabeth) stands as the reference point and guarantor of a supposed discourse of truth, one that appears to be embodied in the masque which her courtiers stage for her in the play's last act. But what does this "truth" amount to? Like the masques of the Jacobean and Caroline courts, the courtiers' entertainment endeavors to articulate in cryptic form the mysterious truth of the royal audience. To read the masque "correctly," however, Cynthia must suspend knowledge of her courtiers' vanity and privilege, in narcissistic fashion, the illusory truth of their appearances within the entertainment. The royal "truth" thus becomes the surface reflection which disavows—or is *superimposed* upon—the court's "fountain of self-love." As Taylor points out, Cynthia thus participates in what she claims to transcend: the fixation on "image" over "truth." Just as significant, perhaps, is the way in which she anticipates James by attempting to contain a potentially dangerous "fountain" by projecting onto it her own image, elevated to the status of the "true" source.

In foregrounding the narcissistic component of the masque, then, *Cynthia's Revels* critically interrogates the Neoplatonic notion of the source. Despite all its efforts, the play cannot break free from a universe of image and appearance; the "true" source it craves remains permanently inaccessible or deferred. Given the uncertainties that afflict the play's representations of origin, then, how does *Cynthia's Revels* depict Echo, Reynolds's "Symbole of the Breath of God"? Early in the play Echo has her powers of speech temporarily returned to her. She takes advantage of this reprieve in order to repeat the Neoplatonic dictum that Narcissus' death was caused by his failure to recognize truth:

> Had Echo been but private with thy thoughts,
> She would have dropped away herself in tears
> Till she had all turned water, that in her
> As in a truer glass, thou mightst have gazed,
> And see thy beauties by more kind reflection.[62]

The possibility of a reengagement with the "truth" of Echo, briefly intimated, turns out to be a false hope. She claims to offer Narcissus a "truer glass" than the spring that prompted this destructive self-love;

but this only ends up presenting him, once again, with the spectacle of his reflection. In a manner identical to both James's coronation pageant and Cynthia's masque, "truth" thus becomes indistinguishable from a narcissistic image which repudiates the source on which it is superimposed. Moreover, this source is momentarily identified with an incontinent feminine body image: Echo "would have dropped away herself in tears / Till she had all turned water." The unitary Neoplatonic origin which Echo is thought to personify, therefore, readily reverts to its leaky, unstanched opposite.

This counternarrative to the Neoplatonic interpretation of Echo betrays an uneasiness concerning the status of her identity, an identity that in its potential leakiness disregards the decorum of classical difference. Poststructuralist readings of the Narcissus myth have likewise subjected to critical scrutiny the issue of Echo's identity. In a study of the interplay between voice and writing in Renaissance texts, Jonathan Goldberg argues that Echo, as the image of voice, represents both identity and its loss.[63] John Brenkman, working with a similar paradox of presence/absence of the self, demonstrates how the narrative's desire for presence bestows identity on the otherwise selfless Echo: "The story of Echo emerges within the larger narrative as the drama of the self's identity and integrity restored. What could have been the mere play of significations left unattached to a speaker, a character, a consciousness, becomes the other side of an actual dialogue between autonomous speakers, between two equally realized characters."[64] Echo's assumption of identity thus mitigates a threat presented to selfhood by empty repetition; as a desiring subject, she lends her imitative utterances a presence or intentionality they would otherwise lack.

Goldberg and Brenkman are certainly right to recognize in Echo's utterances a problematic of identity. I would argue, however, that the threat Echo potentially presents—less visibly in *Cynthia's Revels*, perhaps, but more clearly in other Renaissance versions of the myth—consists less in the *mise en abîme* of deferred identity than in the danger of a catastrophic identification, or amalgamation, with an incontinent feminine source who blurs the boundaries of a classically conceived identity. For many of Jonson's contemporaries, the problem posed by Echo to Narcissus is not the *jouissance* of unattached signification, but the possibility that in both her amorous pursuit of him and her mimetic doubling of his utterances, she threatens to attach herself to and even merge with him.[65] A modern reader may be tempted to recognize in this phobic scenario of female invasion and erosion of discrete identity the dyadic structure of Julia Kristeva's conception of abjection.[66] More pertinent, however, is the extent to which Narcissus' fear of an identity-threatening engulfment by Echo resonates with the Tudor and

Stuart fear of an external, feminized source infiltrating the *corpus politicus*. Thus the desire for presence that transforms Echo into a "real" character is, perhaps, a desire for a specific *type* of presence: the enclosed presence of a self-sufficient, nonleaky, classical identity, such as informs Henry Reynolds's conception of Echo as the Neoplatonic source. Reynolds made this classical Echo replace her leaky doppelgänger in a fashion that not only recalls but is structurally identical to the enclosure or masculine "classicization" of London's conduits during James's coronation pageant. As an incontinent female source, however, Echo was relegated to the phobic imaginary of patriarchy, from which she nonetheless powerfully resurfaced in a number of guises: Dekker's Letchery, Spenser's Errour, and the external source of London's water supply.

N O T E S

I am immensely indebted to Alan Sinfield, Heather Findlay, Misha Kavka, Gail Paster, and Stephen Turner, who all made invaluable suggestions about this essay in its draft form.

1. See David Quint's important study, *Origin and Originality in Renaissance Literature: Versions of the Source* (New Haven: Yale University Press, 1983). Quint focuses primarily on the topos of the "global river source" in Renaissance literature and its derivation from Plato's *Phaedo* and Virgil's *Fourth Georgic*. See also Donald R. Dickson, *The Fountain of Living Waters: The Typology of the Waters of Life in Herbert, Vaughan, and Traherne* (Columbia: University of Missouri Press, 1987).

2. Edward Forset, *A Comparative Discourse of the Bodies Naturall and Politique* (London, 1606), sig. iiiv.

3. W. H. Overall and H. C. Overall, eds., *Analytical Index to the Series of Records Known as the Remembrancia* (London: E. J. Francis, 1878), p. 376.

4. The act is cited in William Matthews, *Hydraulia: An Historical and Descriptive Account of the Water Works of London, and the Contrivances for Supplying Other Great Cities, In Different Ages and Countries* (London: Simpkin, Marshall, 1835), p. 12.

5. For a fascinating discussion of relative autonomy in early modern England, see Richard Halpern, *The Poetics of Primitive Accumulation: English Renaissance Culture and the Genealogy of Capital* (Ithaca: Cornell University Press, 1991), esp. pp. 6–15.

6. John Davies, *Microcosmos: The Discovery of the Little World, with the Government Thereof* (London, 1603), sig. Y1.

7. Cited in Matthews, *Hydraulia*, pp. 21–22.

8. Thomas Heywood, *If You Know Not Me, You Know No Bodie* (London, 1606), sigs. C2–C2v.

9. The "poetics" of the incontinent body politic which I sketch here is very much influenced by the work of Peter Stallybrass and Allon White; see, for example, "The City: The Sewer, the Gaze, and the Contaminating Touch," in *The Politics and Poetics of Transgression* (Ithaca: Cornell University Press, 1986), pp. 125–48.

10. Thomas Dekker, *The Dead Tearme; Or, Westminsters Complaint for Long Vacations and Short Tearmes* (London, 1608), sig. F3; all further references are cited in the text.

11. Barnabe Barnes, *Foure Bookes of Offices: Enabling Privat Persons for the Speciall Service of all Good Princes and Policies* (London, 1608), sig. B1v.

12. William Harvey announced his discovery of the circulation of blood in *De Motu Cordis* (1628). There was considerable controversy among physicians and scholars over which organ was the body's "well of life." Aristotelians or Peripatetics (to whom Harvey was much indebted) favored the heart, but a considerable body of physicians working in the Galenic tradition preferred the liver. See Walter Pagel, *Religion and Neoplatonism in Renaissance Medicine*, ed. Marianne Winder (London: Variorum Reprints, 1985), pp. 42–45.

13. John Stow, *A Survey of London*, ed. Charles Lethbridge (Oxford: Clarendon Press, 1908), 1:17–19, 109–10, 114, 173, 211, 266, 283–84, 292–93, 330; 2:18, 34, 40–41, 79, 83, 173, 177, 179, 302.

14. Ibid., 2:41. The conduit in Bristol was equally ostentatious, castellated, and topped with a statue to commemorate the defeat of the Spanish Armada. See F. W. Robins, *The Story of Water Supply* (Oxford: Oxford University Press, 1946), p. 136.

15. Stow, *A Survey of London*, 1:264, 283, 293.

16. Edmund Spenser, *The Faerie Queene*, ed. Thomas P. Roche and C. Patrick O'Donnell, Jr. (Harmondsworth: Penguin Books, 1978), 2.9.32; all further references are cited in the text.

17. Ben Weinreb and Christopher Hibbert, eds., *The London Encyclopedia* (London: Macmillan, 1983), p. 928.

18. Robert M. Durling, "Deceit and Digestion in the Belly of Hell," in *Allegory and Representation*, ed. Stephen Greenblatt (Baltimore: Johns Hopkins University Press, 1981), p. 66.

19. Mikhail Bakhtin, *Rabelais and His World*, trans. Helene Iswolsky (Bloomington: Indiana University Press, 1984), p. 26.

20. Ibid., p. 320.

21. Here, as elsewhere, I am heavily influenced by the work of Peter Stallybrass and Allon White. For a discussion of the transcoding of the "grotesque" and "classical" body images into other symbolic domains, see *The Politics and Poetics of Transgression*, p. 21.

22. According to the *O.E.D.*, "incontinent" signified chiefly "wanting in self-restraint," particularly with regard to sexual passion; the modern sense, "unable to retain natural evacuations," dates from the early nineteenth century.

23. Thomas Floyd, *The Picture of a Perfit Common Wealth Describing as Well the Offices of Princes and Inferiour Magistrates Over Their Subjects, as also the Duties of Subjects Towards Their Governors* (London, 1600), sigs. F12v–G1.

24. Davies, *Microcosmos*, sig. P3.

25. Mary Douglas, *Purity and Danger* (London: Ark Paperbacks, 1984), p. 4.

26. François Rabelais, *Gargantua and Pantagruel*, trans. J. M. Cohen (Harmondsworth: Penguin Books, 1955), p. 219.

27. William Averell, *A Meruailous Combat of Contraretes, Malignantlie Striving in the Members of Mans Bodie, Allegoricallie Representing Unto Us the Enuied State of Our Flourishing Common Wealth* (London, 1588), sig. E1v.

28. Christopher Marlowe, *Tamburlaine The Great I*, 3.1.59–60, in *The Complete Plays*, ed. J. B. Steane (Harmondsworth: Penguin Books, 1969). Marlowe seems to have been among Elizabethan writers the most fascinated with the

possibility of illicit access to the body politic by way of its pipes and concealed orifices. After Barabas has staged his own death and his body has been thrown over Malta's walls, he covertly returns through its sewage outlet; see *The Jew of Malta* 5.1.88–90, in Marlowe, *Complete Plays*.

29. Cited in Matthews, *Hydraulia*, p. 13.

30. Cited in Ida Darlington, *The London Commissioners of Sewers and Their Records* (Sussex: Phillimore, 1970), p. 1.

31. Stow, *A Survey of London*, 1:188, 17.

32. For a critical study of the City Liberties and their ambivalences, see Steven Mullaney, *The Place of the Stage: License, Play, and Power in Renaissance England* (Chicago: University of Chicago Press, 1988).

33. Dekker's diatribe demonstrates how prostitution, like water, was often tolerated provided it remained confined within its "certaine boundes." Prostitution was even occasionally regarded as a necessary component of the body politic. Thomas Aquinas averred that "prostitution in the towns, is like the cesspool in the palace; take away the cesspool and the palace will become an unclean and evil-smelling place." Cited in Gamini Salgado, *The Elizabethan Underworld* (Gloucester, Eng.: Alan Sutton, 1984), p. 51. For fuller discussions of prostitution in Elizabethan and Jacobean England, see Anne M. Haselkorn, *Prostitution in Elizabethan and Jacobean Comedy* (Troy, N.Y.: Whitston, 1983); Wallace Shugg, "Prostitution in Shakespeare's London," *Shakespeare Studies* 10 (1977), 291–313; and Jonathan Dollimore, "Transgression and Surveillance in *Measure For Measure*," in *Political Shakespeare: New Essays in Cultural Materialism*, ed. Jonathan Dollimore and Alan Sinfield (Ithaca: Cornell University Press, 1985), pp. 72–87.

34. It is worth recalling here the notorious belief concerning the uterus that persisted among physicians well into the Renaissance: Plato had believed it to be "an animal in its own right, endowed with powers of movement and a sense of smell." See Ian Maclean, *The Renaissance Notion of Woman: A Study in the Fortunes of Scholasticism and Medical Science in European Intellectual Life* (Cambridge: Cambridge University Press, 1983), p. 41.

35. See, for example, Julia Kristeva, "Motherhood According to Giovanni Bellini," in *Desire and Language: A Semiotic Approach to Literature and Art,* ed. Leon S. Roudiez (New York: Columbia University Press, 1980), pp. 237–71. For an important discussion of the ambivalences of female reproductivity and the womb in Renaissance England, see Marion Wynne-Davies, " 'The Swallowing Womb': Consumed and Consuming Women in *Titus Andronicus*," in *The Matter of Difference: Materialist Feminist Criticism of Shakespeare*, ed. Valerie Wayne (Ithaca: Cornell University Press, 1991), pp. 129–51. Janet Adelman's *Suffocating Mothers: Fantasies of Maternal Origin in Shakespeare's Plays, 'Hamlet' to 'The Tempest'* (London: Routledge, 1992) offers a fascinating and exhaustive survey of Shakespeare's presentation of original sin as the sin of (maternal) origin, with many conclusions that are similar to my own. My ideas here and at other stages of my argument owe much to Julia Kristeva's *Powers of Horror: An Essay on Abjection,* trans. Leon S. Roudiez (New York: Columbia University Press, 1982).

36. These biblical utterances continued to resonate powerfully in European society more than two thousand years later. To protect the community, corpses of women who had died in childbirth were often buried in a secluded corner of the cemetery, or outside the cemetery wall entirely, next to murderers and suicides—outside, in other words, the "circuit of civil liberty." See Edward Shorter, *A History of Woman's Bodies* (Harmondsworth: Pelican Books, 1984), p. 291.

37. The gender of the Nile in classical and Renaissance literature has a complicated and fascinating history. The river was traditionally regarded as masculine; Ovid refers to it in Book 2 of the *Metamorphoses* as male, and his description in Book 1 appears to accord it a masculine procreative power in relation to the feminine "earth": after the Nile flooded, says Ovid, "the mud and soggy marshes swelled under the heat, and fertile seeds, nourished in the life-giving earth as in a mother's womb, grew and in the fullness of time acquired a definite shape." *The Metamorphoses of Ovid*, trans. Mary Innes (Harmondsworth: Penguin Books, 1955), p. 40. Ovid's account is ambiguous, however; it arguably presents the sun, rather than the Nile, as the masculine "inseminating" agent: "Other animals of different kinds were produced by the earth, of its own accord, when the long-lingering moisture was warmed through by the rays of the sun. . . . All things are born from these two elements. Although fire and water are always opposites, none the less moist heat is the source of everything, and this discordant harmony is suited to creation" (p. 40). This conception potentially serves to feminize the waters of the Nile, an interpretation that underlies Antony's swearing by "the fire / That quickens Nylus slime." (*Antony and Cleopatra* 1.3.68–69, in *The Riverside Shakespeare*, ed. G. Blakemore Evans et al. (Boston: Houghton Mifflin, 1974). Of course, Shakespeare implicitly feminizes the Nile by making it the dominant metonymy throughout the play of Cleopatra's own "fertile bounty": as Janet Adelman notes in *Suffocating Mothers*, "Egypt becomes the locus of the common mother's promiscuous generativity, indifferently producing figs and asps from its slime" (p. 175). The confusion surrounding the gender of the Nile is most glaringly apparent in Book 1 of *The Faerie Queene*. Spenser anticipates Shakespeare in appropriating the Nile and its "slime" as the prototype of a grotesque feminine fertility, yet remains faithful to his classical "sources" by paradoxically styling the river as "Father Nilus."

38. Averell, *A Meruailous Combat of Contrareties*, sigs. F2–F2v. Cf. Dekker's complaint to London in *The Seuen Deadly Sinnes of London* (London, 1606): "Who can denye now, but that Sinne (like the seuen-headed Nylus) hath ouerflowed thy banks and . . . made thee fertile in all kindes of Vices?" (sig. G2v). The parallel with Letchery in *The Dead Tearme*—another incontinent multiheaded source who overflows London's boundaries—is striking.

39. Thomas Nashe, *Christs Teares Over Jerusalem*, in *The Works of Thomas Nashe*, ed. R. B. McKerrow (London: A. H. Bullen, 1904–10), 2:158.

40. See Peter Stallybrass's essay "Patriarchal Territories: The Body Enclosed," in *Rewriting the Renaissance: The Discourses of Sexual Difference in Early Modern Europe*, ed. Margaret W. Ferguson, Maureen Quilligan, and Nancy J. Vickers (Chicago: University of Chicago Press, 1986), pp. 123–42. Stallybrass's essay breaks important ground in its examination of the reconstructions of body and gender that accompanied the enclosures of the sixteenth century. See also Gail Kern Paster's illuminating articles, "Leaky Vessels: The Incontinent Women of Jacobean City Comedy," *Renaissance Drama*, N.S., 18 (1987), 71–86, and " 'In the Spirit of Men There Is No Blood': Blood as Trope of Gender in *Julius Caesar*," *Shakespeare Quarterly* 40 (1989), 274–88.

41. Quotations from Shakespeare are from *The Riverside Shakespeare;* all further references are cited in the text.

42. Ben Jonson, *Epicoene* 4.2.142–44, in *Drama of the English Renaissance*, vol. 2, *The Stuart Period*, ed. Russell A. Fraser and Norman Rabkin (New York: Macmillan, 1976).

43. The picture is depicted in George Frederick Stephens, *Catalogue of Political and Personal Satires Preserved in the Department of Prints and Drawings in the British Museum*, vol. 1, *1320–1689* (London: British Museum Publications, 1978), p. 32.

44. See Norman Rabkin's introduction to Thomas Dekker and Thomas Middleton, *The Roaring Girl*, in Fraser and Rabkin, *Drama of the English Renaissance*, 2:333.

45. Marie Axton, *The Queen's Two Bodies: Drama and the Elizabethan Succession* (London: Royal Historical Society, 1977), p. 131. A useful discussion of the forms of power deployed in James's coronation pageant and their relevance for understanding Shakespeare's plays can be found in Leonard Tennenhouse, *Power on Display: The Politics of Shakespeare's Genres* (New York: Methuen, 1986), pp. 134–46. Jonathan Goldberg compares the forms of power employed by Queen Elizabeth and King James in their respective coronation pageants in *James I and the Politics of Literature: Jonson, Shakespeare, Donne, and Their Contemporaries* (Baltimore: Johns Hopkins University Press, 1983), pp. 28–54.

46. Goldberg, *James I and the Politics of Literature*, p. 31.

47. Forset, *A Comparative Discourse of the Bodies Naturall and Politique*, p. 34.

48. For a useful discussion of the sun-king's gaze, see Christopher Pye, "The Sovereign, the Theater, and the Kingdome of Darknesse: Hobbes and the Spectacle of Power," in *Representing the English Renaissance*, ed. Stephen Greenblatt (Berkeley: University of California Press, 1988), pp. 279–301.

49. Goldberg, *James I and the Politics of Literature*, pp. 153–54.

50. Thomas Dekker, *The Magnificent Entertainment* (London, 1604), sig. E3; all further references are cited in the text.

51. The important legal-ecclesiastical distinction between the king's political and natural bodies is examined in Ernst H. Kantorowicz, *The King's Two Bodies: A Study of Medieval Political Theology* (Princeton: Princeton University Press, 1955). Marie Axton supplements Kantorowicz's conclusions in *The Queen's Two Bodies* (see n.45).

52. See Goldberg, *James I and the Politics of Literature*, pp. 46–47.

53. John Webster, *The Duchess of Malfi* 1.1.11–15, in Fraser and Rabkin, *Drama of the English Renaissance*, vol. 2.

54. Francis Bacon, *The Advancement of Learning*, ed. G. W. Kitchin (London: Dent, 1973), p. 2.

55. Cited in Matthews, *Hydraulia*, p. 23.

56. Stephen Orgel, *The Illusion of Power: Political Theatre in the English Renaissance* (Berkeley: University of California Press, 1975), pp. 43, 39.

57. See, for example, ibid., p. 59, and Benjamin Goldberg, *The Mirror and Man* (Charlottesville: University Press of Virginia, 1985), chap. 8.

58. Louise Vinge summarizes the various readings of the Narcissus myth in her invaluable study, *The Narcissus Theme in Western European Literature up to the Early Nineteenth Century*, trans. Robert Dewsnap et al. (Lund: Skanska Centraltryckeriet, 1967).

59. Henry Reynolds, *Mythomystes* (London, 1630), sig. P3v.

60. Francis Bacon, *The Wisedome of the Ancients* (London, 1619), sig. A6v.

61. Barry Taylor, *Vagrant Writing: Social and Semiotic Disorders in the English Renaissance* (Toronto: University of Toronto Press, 1991), p. 181.

62. Ben Jonson, *Cynthia Revels* 1.2.31–37, in *The Complete Plays of Ben Jonson*, vol. 2, ed. G. A. Wilkes (Oxford: Clarendon Press, 1981). I diverge from Taylor's exemplary reading only with respect to his conclusion that the origin in

Cynthia's Revels remains ever deferred and inaccessible; this deferral, I would argue, is less the consequence of a self-deconstructing metaphysical system than a phobic response to a more dangerous, feminine, and potentially all-too-present "origin" (Echo) who is repudiated, or, to use the Kristevan terminology, abjected, in order to restore the classical differences informing the Neoplatonic schema of patriarchal order.

63. See Jonathan Goldberg, *Voice Terminal Echo: Postmodernism and English Renaissance Texts* (London: Methuen, 1986), esp. p. 12.

64. John Brenkman, "Narcissus in the Text," *Georgia Review* 30 (1976), 293–327; see p. 301.

65. Aspects of the malevolent feminine source haunt the representation of Echo in other Renaissance retellings of the myth. In James Shirley's poem "Narcissus, Or the Self-Lover," Echo first attacks, then takes the place of, an evil female spirit whom she believes to inhabit Narcissus spring. Shirley presents Echo's display of desire for Narcissus as a monstrous invasion of male identity, not to mention a usurpation of an exclusively male prerogative. See *The Dramatic Works and Poems of James Shirley*, ed. Alexander Dyce (London: John Murray, 1833), p. 488. In the anonymous student play *Narcissus* (1602), Echo chases Narcissus into a forest, where he "knowes the way in nor out"; his utterances start to merge with Echo's, thereby lending weight to his fear of an identity-threatening engulfment. See *Narcissus: A Twelfe Night Merriment Played by Youths of the Parish at the College of S. John the Baptist in Oxford*, ed. Margaret Lee (London: David Nutt, 1893), ll. 594–612.

66. See Kristeva, *Powers of Horror*.

11. The Enclosure of Virginity: The Poetics of Sexual Abstinence in the English Revolution

John Rogers

I

When in 1637 Milton published *A Maske Presented at Ludlow Castle,* he inserted lines that can be found neither in the poet's own early manuscript of the masque nor in the manuscript copied shortly after the original performance in 1634. Milton's primary insertion, an addition to an already substantial speech made by the masque's heroine, the Lady, alters significantly the ethical tenor of the text. The moral virtue to which the masque was pointing had originally been the temperance grounding the Puritan ideal of the disciplined marriage. But the Lady's new interposition redirects the masque's energies away from the temperate marriage. Hers, we learn now, is the distinctly unmatrimonial virtue of absolute virginity. It is my purpose in this essay to explore a brief chapter in the cultural history of the English Revolution, the elevation of the sustained life of virginity to a moral ideal, and, beyond, to a political principle. If we can think of this phenomenon of a revitalized virginity to have a temporal origin in the revised version of *Comus,* then its later manifestations in the years of the English Revolution can be said to proceed along similar literary lines: the affirmation of virginity as a viable source of power nearly always bears the status of a jarring interpolation, the unwanted intrusion of an ethic logically incompatible with the cultural expressions that surround it.

Many historians and critics of early modern literature and culture have labored to unveil the truths of patriarchal oppression behind the ideological facade of a cultural value such as virginity.[1] But these attempts, nearly all of them grounded on the analytic model of false consciousness, have risked, I think, overlooking the wide spectrum of social and cultural functions which an ideal as complex as virginity could serve. The task of this essay is to explore some of the theological and political symbologies that converge in the representation of virginity in the period between 1640 and 1660, a project that will require an attempt to uncover some of the sedimented layers of the history of virginity. I will examine the intercalated traces of an interest in a virginity that was not so easily appropriable by the dominant social powers that cultural historians continue to invoke as the wardens of the errant desires of women. And I will look at the faith—evident in a number of discursive modes, and with varying degrees of explictness—in the connection between sexual purity and human power, a power that for some could potentially alter forever the religious and political face of the English nation.

Let us first return to the disjunctive moment in Milton's masque. In an attempt to seduce the Lady, the magician Comus has marshaled a series of ingenious arguments for Nature's requirement of the full sexual participation of all her creatures. In opposition to his call for the obligation imposed by Nature's generous fecundity, the Lady delivers a plea, in all versions of the masque, for the temperate and just use of Nature's gifts. Nature has, she says, blessed us with a finite sum of consumable resources, and it is the duty of "every just man" to take "but a moderate and beseeming share" of this natural wealth (ll. 768–73).[2] Given the scene's figural link between the consumption of natural wealth and sexual consummation, the Lady's call for a tempered distribution and consumption of natural goods clearly points to a figuration of an attitude toward sex. She gives voice in this speech to the belief in the moderate marital sex advocated by Augustine in *De bono coniugali* and propounded in Milton's own time in a succession of Protestant theological tracts and secular conduct books. The Lady, whose journey through the forest will end when she is presented to her mother and father (ll. 965–75), and whose own eventual marriage is subtly prefigured in a vision of Cupid and Psyche (ll. 1003–11), articulates a figurative version of what was becoming in seventeenth-century England the normative affirmation of temperate conjugal sexual behavior, the doctrine of "married chastity."

It is this appeal to the ideal of married chastity in the name of moderation that constitutes the Lady's final words in the two extant earlier versions of the masque. But in the revised version of 1637, Milton reopens the thematically enclosed domain of the Lady's concluding argument, and permits his heroine another attempt at rebuttal:

> Shall I go on?
> Or have I said enough? To him that dares
> Arm his profane tongue with contemptuous words

Against the Sun-clad power of Chastity
Fain would I something say, yet to what end?
Thou hast nor Ear nor Soul to apprehend
The sublime notion and high mystery
That must be utter'd to unfold the sage
And serious doctrine of Virginity. . . .
Thou art not fit to hear thyself convinc't;
Yet should I try, the uncontrolled worth
Of this pure cause would kindle my rapt spirits
To such a flame of sacred vehemence,
That dumb things would be mov'd to sympathize,
And the brute Earth would lend her nerves, and shake,
Till all they magic structures rear'd so high,
Were shatter'd into heaps o'er thy false head.

(ll. 779–99)

It is clear, as critics have noted for some time, that Milton's Lady does not proceed, in this expanded version of the debate, to marshal further arguments for man's moderate fulfillment of natural, conjugal duty. She wrests the subject of her speech away from the virtue of moderation central to the doctrine of married chastity and bends it to the unyielding, absolutist virtue of sexual abstinence central to a very different kind of doctrine. In a few short lines the Lady has changed the subject of her diatribe from the "holy dictate of spare Temperance" to the "Sun-clad power of Chastity," and, in case we have not fully appreciated the distinction between the two models of sexual behavior she has introduced, she heightens the import of their difference with her final, most inflexible, appeal to "the sage / And serious doctrine of Virginity."[3]

It comes as no surprise that the Lady, or, for that matter, Milton himself, betrays some concern about resuming a previously concluded peroration: "Shall I go on? / Or have I said enough?" The expression of uncertainty here, a brief confession that what we are about to hear may very well exceed the implicit ideological limits of the Lady's position in the debate, signals quite pointedly the thematic excess of her new argument. Claiming for her capacity as virginal orator the potency at once of an Orpheus, a Prospero, and a Samson, she threatens her seducer with an apocalyptic power that far surpasses the strength required to destroy a petty magus such as Comus. The earth-shattering force putatively embodied in the doctrine of virginity would seem to give the Lady control even over the very authority she is journeying to honor. The Lady's father, newly entrusted by Neptune to govern Wales, has been divinely appointed "with tempered awe to guide / An old, and haughty nation proud in arms" (ll. 32–33). But the "awe," far from tempered, or temperate, with which the virgin is said to "[dash] brute violence" (ll. 447–52), seems in every respect, when compared to her father's, the "superior power." The "uncontrolled worth" of the pure cause of virginity should be capable of shattering not only the magic structures of her father's new dominion but the institutional structure of marriage, which is nothing other than the father's law. With a proclamation of virginal strength that logically overrides any need for the sanctioned transition to marriage, the Lady short-circuits the masque's generically and culturally defined movement toward marriage and married chastity. Her final words force the rhetoric of virginity to burst through its conventional enclosure within the confines of normative conjugal ideology.

In the end, the Lady has probably said more than enough in her testimony to the apocalyptic powers of the virgin. The strength of her virginity, as well as her capacity even to articulate that strength remains, throughout the course of the masque, untested and uncertain. It is true that the moral idealism informing the Lady's purely conditional threat exudes a force sufficiently powerful to make Comus shudder in recognition that "she fables not" (l. 800); nothing in the masque specifically calls into question the veracity of the Lady's claim for the power (which she refuses to unleash) of the doctrine of virginity. But the full force of this doctrine is nonetheless restrained, if not by necessity, then by the exigencies of Milton's romance narrative. The burst of apocalyptic energy does not alter, but only briefly interrupts, the predictable course of the masque's narrative, providing only a momentary vision of an alternative view of human power. The Lady's ability to wreak an apocalyptic justice is enclosed carefully within the realm of unrealized potential.

Not only does the Lady withhold a full account of her sage and serious doctrine, but Milton, too, refrains for the rest of his career from extolling the power and virtue of virginity. With the exception of some curious entries in his commonplace book in the early 1640s, the Lady's promise of a fully realized peroration on virginal power is not one that Milton, at least after 1639, ever attempts to fulfill.[4] As the political and religious conflicts with which he would so entangle himself were coming clearly into focus, Milton turned his thoughts to marriage and so abandoned his commitment to the special apocalyptic powers embodied in virginity. His exuberant faith in an apocalyptically driven English Revolution came to hinge not on the physical integrity of the Puritan saints but on a more loosely defined moral condition he referred to as "discipline."[5] But while Milton at midcentury remained as unwilling as the Lady to unfold a revolutionary doctrine of virginity, others in the period were not so reticent. The image of the power of virginity, which had been for Milton in 1637 not much more than a matter of moral idealism, began in the 1640s and 1650s to acquire a more distinctly political set of associations.

II

Before we can begin to examine the forms and functions of the century's later expressions of virginal power, it is necessary to confront the failure of cultural historians to acknowledge a new, or revitalized, Protestant affirmation of sustained sexual abstinence. Since the publication of William and Malleville Haller's ground-breaking article, "The Puritan Art of Love," it has become a commonplace to chart the shifts in seventeenth-century domestic ideology as a steady march toward a recognizably bourgeois idealization of married love. For all of their differences concerning the quality and the nature of marital relations in the century, nearly all social, religious, and literary historians have assented to the Hallers' thesis of the overwhelming new cultural sanction granted the institution of marriage, the practice that could now be named in the *Book of Common Prayer* that of "holy matrimony."[6] "The medieval Catholic ideal of chastity," writes Lawrence Stone, "as a legal obligation for priests, monks and nuns and as an ideal for all members of the community to aspire to, was replaced by the ideal of conjugal affection."[7] For Anglicans no less than Puritans, we are told, marriage and conjugal affection became increasingly idealized and encouraged, while the sustained life of celibacy was devalued and dismissed as sinful popery. Even the Neoplatonic chastity cult at the Caroline court placed its emphasis on chastity in its temperate, matrimonial guise, seeing the perfection of all chaste energies in the apex of married love.[8] Maidenly virginity maintained its status as a moral ideal, but it was strictly a temporary state, the condition of bodily integrity that best qualified an individual, usually female, for her proper entry into legitimate marriage.

There is, of course, an overwhelming amount of evidence to substantiate this now canonical understanding of seventeenth-century matrimonial discourse. I do not wish to question the undeniable ascent of conjugal sexuality as an ethical and religious norm in this period. This was a time, in fact, in which a slackening of regular sexual intercourse could be considered a sign not of a married couple's purity but of their possession by Satan, who "under colour of a better pureness . . . seekes to breed a wearinesse and disdeine of the ordinance" to be fruitful and multiply.[9] But although I am not doubting the generally escalated esteem in which conjugality was held, I do propose that one of the discursive phenomena that cultural historians have overlooked is the presence of a brief but striking Protestant opposition to the moral entrenchment of the ideal of married love. In exploring some of the counterevidence to the almost unquestioned thesis of the century's unequivocal demotion of virginity, it is the purpose of this essay, as it was indeed for the revised version of *Comus,* to resist the total enclosure of virginity within the larger temporal frame of marriage and married chastity.[10]

The literary praise of virginity, so popular in Elizabethan panegyric, and especially in the work of Lyly, Chapman, Raleigh, and Spenser, is not, of course, unique to the years of England's revolutionary struggles.[11] But there is in the mid-seventeenth century a marked redirection of that earlier interest in the power of virginity, a power that in the post-Elizabethan period need no longer be isolated in the authority, and the body, of a single historical personage. This later period sees the emergence, evident in a number of generic fields, of a general praise of a universally accessible bodily purity and a corresponding critique of sexual consummation. In the world of lyric poetry, a traditional poetic topos such as the antifruition theme informing Shakespeare's "Expense of Spirit" and "Love's Alchemy" by Donne is deployed and adapted with an almost obsessive regularity by the century's later poets.[12] And a historically specific revival also charges the field of mid-century natural philosophy: the renewed English interest in the 1650s in the esoteric, hermetic philosophers of the sixteenth century, Cornelius Agrippa and Paracelsus in particular, can in large part be attributed to the degree of mystical, almost alchemically based powers they bestowed on virginity.[13] The Dutch natural philosopher Jean Baptiste van Helmont, in fact, introduced to England in 1648 an entire system of materialist theology that held as a central component the mystical powers of the virginal body.[14]

While these admittedly peripheral, radical voices attempted to carve a privileged space for the virginal ideal in an intellectual culture increasingly given to the praise of wedded love and wedded sexuality, there is a striking, and largely unacknowledged, affirmation of virginity in the more sanctioned sphere of mainstream moral theology. It may in fact be the cultural preeminence of this field that lends a special potency to its insinuation of the value of virginity into the culture's hegemonic praise of married love. Historians of early modern English social life have noted with some embarrassment the exceptional status of the broadly popular Richard Baxter (1615–91), the Puritan minister who most adamantly refused to subject virginity to the patriarchal law of married chastity. Even among proponents of virginity Baxter is surely extraordinary, not only for his almost exclusive focus on male, clerical virginity, but for his painfully literal reading of Jesus' praise for those men "which have made themselves eunuchs for the kingdom of heaven's sake" (Matthew 19:12).[15] A less strident, and perhaps more characteristic, example of a mainstream interest in virginity can be found in one of the century's other most prolific and popular theologians, the Anglican Jeremy Taylor. Among the most frequently cited of the seventeenth-century proponents of the holiness of matrimony, Taylor is probably best known to modern readers for his orthodox claim that "marital love is a thing pure as light, sacred as a temple, lasting as the world."[16] But like many of the period's so-called champions of the new doctrine of holy matrimony and married chastity, Taylor reveals on closer scrutiny a rhetorical stance toward virginity quite at odds with his ethically normative claims for marriage.

Like Milton's Lady in her final speech to Comus, Jeremy Taylor begins a discussion of the two forms of chastity in his popular *Holy Living* (1650) with a capacious, and predictable, sense of the sanctity of the chaste and continent marriage. But also like Milton's Lady, Taylor begins to soar, at the very mention of virginal chastity, in a powerful and surprisingly countercultural lyrical flight:

> *Chastity* is either *abstinence* or *continence*. *Abstinence* is that of Virgins or Widows: *Continence* of married persons. *Chaste marriages* are honourable and pleasing to God: *Widowhood* is pitiable in its solitarinesse and losse, but amiable and comely when it is adorned with gravity and purity, and not sullied with remembrances of the passed license, nor with present desires of returning to a second bed. But *Virginity* is the life of Angels, the enamel of the soul, the huge advantage of religion, the great opportunity for the retirements of devotion: and being empty of cares, it is full of prayers: being unmingled with the World, it is apt to converse with God: and by not feeling the warmth of a too forward and indulgent nature, flames out with holy fires, till it be burning like the Cherubim and the most extasied order of holy and unpolluted Spirits.[17]

Upon issuing a claim for the virtue of chastity in its matrimonial, Protestant guise, Taylor explodes in beautifully rhapsodic prose to reveal a profound and unmistakable preference for chastity *tout court*. Like George Herbert's famous amplification in "Prayer," Taylor's definition of virginity expands into a litany of appositives that names the virtue in question as the only hope for intercourse between this world and the next. Certainly the strength of the paragraph's initial assertion, that "*chaste marriages* are honourable and pleasing to God," is consumed in the final assertion of the burning glory of virginal power. Milton's Lady had warned Comus that should she even try to unfold the doctrine of virginity, "the uncontrolled worth / Of this pure cause would kindle my rapt spirits / To . . . a flame of sacred vehemence." Although the Lady had not, to her mind, fully unfolded that doctrine, her anticipatory rhetoric seemed evidence enough of her kindled, rapt spirits. We are witness, in this closely related outburst in Taylor's *Holy Living,* to another example of the unwitting truth of the Lady's admonition. Within a text working ostensibly to affirm, among other things, the "holy living" possible within the state of marriage, Taylor deploys a rhetoric of apocalyptic virginity which itself "flames out with holy fires." In Taylor, as in Milton, the rhetorical affect of ecstasy that charges the unfolding of the doctrine of virginity functions, at least in the short term, to confirm the claim for the ecstatic and uncontainable position of the powerful virgin.

It is incumbent on us now, I think, to account for this literary and cultural phenomenon. How are we to explain the inconsistent and incompatible affirmations of the life of sustained virginity in a text seemingly devoted to the affirmation of the state of marriage? To what do we attribute the unarticulated conflict between virginity and married chastity that a text such as Taylor's makes so palpable? Possible answers to these questions abound, of course. A sociological approach to this historiographic problem might emerge from a study of wartime demographics: the new separation of eligible bachelors from their communities during the civil wars of the 1640s may have necessitated a compensatory idealization of celibacy, one that flew in the face of the otherwise prevailing prestige of marriage. Literary evidence for such a claim could even be culled from the parodic pamphlet of 1643, *The Virgins complaint for the losse of their sweet-hearts by these present wars: and their owne long solitude and keeping their virginities against their wills / presented in the names and behalfes of all the damsels. . . .*[18] But despite the real possibility that the exigencies of the civil wars may have temporarily altered the opportunity for physical relations between the sexes, it is not a statistical study of sexual activity that I wish to pursue here. The phenomenon of the new estimation of virginity does, I think, pick up speed from the radical energies fueling the English Revolution. But the new valuative inversion to which virginity is subjected finds its foundation less in social action than in the cultural, and specifically literary, realm of revolutionary sentiment. It is as a discursive event, with discursive consequences, that I hope to understand the curiously subversive effect posed by a rhetoric of celibacy within an otherwise conventional expression of normative social values.

In assessing the cultural origins of virginity's new prestige in this period, one might appeal to the possibility of a rear-guard Puritan response to the dominant elevation of physical conjugal pleasure. Or one might trace a residual interest in virginity, as Levin Schücking has, to

Protestant England's nostalgic refusal to forgo completely its pre-Reformation heritage.[19] But this historically late embrace of the ideal of sustained virginity seems less a case of Catholic atavism or Puritan prudery than a deliberate appropriation of Catholic, and Puritan, values for an entirely new, radical end. The new celibacy, I propose, may be seen to take two distinct forms, both of which are identifiable in the proleptic text of the revised *Comus*. We have examples in Milton's masque of what one might profitably label the "liberal" and the "radical" formulations of virginal power: the more common, liberal expression of virginity imagines the virgin's practical liberation from the social constraints that attend the institution of marriage, while the radical assertion of virginal power posits the virgin's magical capacity to effect change in the world by virtue of nothing more than a static condition of moral and physical purity. The liberal model of virginity, evident in the Lady's brief rhetorical release from the hierarchical constraints of marriage and paternal authority, can be seen to have an early proponent in the Paul of 1 Corinthians. In one of his many incitements to virginity, Paul explains that "she that is married careth for the things of the world, how she may please her husband," whereas the "unmarried woman careth for the things of the Lord" (1 Corinthians 7:34). Clearly, for Paul, virginity liberates one from lesser, earthly structures of authority, liberating even the unmarried woman from the struggle to please her husband which is the burden of her married sisters. For all his notorious misogyny, Paul holds in surprising esteem the woman who refuses to participate in the social and familial world of marriage and procreation. One of the cultural phenomena we can trace in our period is a recovery of what had been for Paul, and the early Christian writers of the late classical period, the central paradox of virginity.[20] Maidenly virginity, the very state that qualifies a woman for her subjection to the patriarchal law of marriage, is the same condition, if maintained, that best permits her to evade its hold.

A striking example of this liberal figuration of virginity can be found in a poem, written in 1648 but not published, by a very young Katherine Philips:

> A marry^{d} state affords but little ease:
> The best of husbands are so hard to please.
> This in wifes Carefull faces you may spell,
> Tho they desemble their misfortunes well.
> A virgin state is crown'd with much content,
> Its allways happy as it's inocent.
> No Blustering husbands to create your fears,
> No pangs of child birth to extol your tears,

No children's crys for to offend your ears,
Few worldly crosses to distract your prayers.
Thus are you freed from all the cares that do
Attend on matrymony and a husband too.[21]

Although Philips follows Paul in her claim that the "virgin state" offers
"few worldly crosses to distract your prayers," the dominant concern
here lies with the secular implications of the Pauline preference for virginity. The virginal life is simply freer from those mundane constraints,
at once social, physical, and psychological, that "attend on matrymony
and a husband too."[22] As practical as Philips's vision of virginal liberation may seem, we should not imagine that this virginal ideal had necessarily begun rooting itself in contemporary social practice: Philips
wrote this lyric shortly before her own marriage in 1648. It may in fact
be the invariable sway of marital obligation that is responsible for gen-
erating such figurations of the virginal ideal. The social reality of marital pressure gives force to the figure of sustained virginity as an
imagined release from what Jane Barker, one of Philips's seventeenth-
century poetic heirs, calls in her poem "A Virgin Life" "the power / Of
mans, allmost omnipotent amour" (p. 360).

The liberal image of virginity finds perhaps its most fascinating consequence in its capacity to represent the newly formulated ideal of liberal individualism. In response to the bourgeois culture's dominant
attempt to establish the ideal of marriage as the foundation for the private realm in which the individual flourishes, the antimarital figure of
virginity provided the image for privacy par excellence. Sexual abstinence, within the Catholic and the earlier Stoic traditions, had always
been figured as self-possession and self-control. But there is a literal
and highly physiological sense in which the female virgin provided a
symbolic model for the specifically seventeenth-century image of the
autonomous liberal self: she contained a physical guarantee of her privacy in the very existence of her hymen, the membrane defined by
"learned Physitians," according to Ambroise Paré, as "the enclosure of
the virginity."[23] It was her literal self-enclosure, her protection, however tenuous, from forces outside herself, that could render the female
virgin not only a pious participant in the private realm but a figurative
embodiment of the private realm itself. It was in respect to this isolate
self-sufficiency that the traditional image of the virgin, self-contained
and self-enclosed, found a fortuitous corollary in the rhetoric forged in
the Putney Debates and the Leveller controversies of a liberal political
philosophy. The language of virginal self-enclosure, a discourse that
seems at first blush to be firmly cloistered away from the struggles of
partisan politics, can be seen to drift almost imperceptibly into a dis-

cursive association with the emergent liberal rhetoric of individual self-ownership. Nonconventual virgins are to be considered, according to Leonardus Lessius, in his *Treasure of Vowed Chastity,* as "such as are at their owne disposing, and retaine their proper substance," a claim that bespeaks their legal independence no less than the originary purity of their bodily integrity.[24] How fitting, then, that the liberal figuration of virginity reemerges at the moment of the liberal call, formulated first in the 1640s, for individual human rights. "Every Individuall in nature," wrote Richard Overton in 1646, "is given an individuall property by nature, not to be invaded or usurped by any: for every one as he is himselfe, so he hath a selfe propriety, else could he not be himselfe."[25] The sage and serious doctrine of virginity, at least in its pragmatic and liberal guise, assumes the shape of a specific, and tangibly physical, corollary to the theory of possessive individualism.

As we have seen, the liberal model of virginal freedom, employed as an analogy for, or even a possible means to attain, the newly articulated ideal of liberal selfhood, was in no way a partisan practice. As the examples I have cited indicate, a heightening of the interest in sustained virginity in the middle years of the seventeenth century was open to Catholics and Protestants, republicans and Royalists alike. There was, however, another aspect of the virginity cult that found its home much more comfortably, though not exclusively, in the more radical spheres of revolutionary Puritan thought. The maintenance of virginity was not only a convenient symbolic assertion of the isolate, liberal self; it could also be imagined, far more radically, as an actual historical precipitant for a spiritual, even political, revolution. The new affirmation of the value of celibacy came to participate, much as it seemed to in the 1637 version of *Comus,* in the millenarian optimism charging the revolutionary aspirations of midcentury radicals.

Like the liberal figuration of virginity, this radical figuration of virginal power can also be seen to have a scriptural sanction in 1 Corinthians, a text that established a distinction between the two types of virginal force which continued to hold throughout the seventeenth century. Although virginity in its liberatory capacity was a condition meaningful primarily for women, it acquired its radical, millenarian force through the sexual abstinence not so much of women as of men: "The time is short: it remaineth, that . . . they that have wives be as though they had none . . . for the fashion of this world passeth away" (1 Corinthians 7:29). The hope that male sexual abstinence might actually trigger the eschatological union of heaven and earth seemed all the more reasonable in light of the passage in Revelation, so beloved by Milton, in which Saint John explains exactly which of the earth's inhabitants he saw in his vision of the multitude who "sung as it were a

new song before the throne" of the Lamb.[26] "No man could learn that
song," Saint John reports, "but the hundred and forty and four thousand, which were redeemed from the earth. These are they which were
not defiled with women; for they are virgins" (Revelation 14:1–5). The
force of John's heavenly vision lay in virginity's capacity to redeem the
celibate minority from the earth, a strategy for salvation that no doubt
accounts for the fact, noted by Schücking, that "well into the seventeenth century we still encounter the pious proverb that 'marriage fills
the earth but virginity fills the heavens.' "[27] But John's revelation
seemed to promise more than the individual salvation of the virgin; it
was easily extended to suggest virginity's power to redeem, and to reform, man's fallen world.

An explicitly political use of this revelation of a virginal future marks
the redemptive theology of the radical Digger, Gerrard Winstanley.
With a characteristic conflation of the body of the individual believer
and the body politic of the English nation, Winstanley, in his 1649 treatise *Fire in the Bush*, imagines the long-awaited millennial transformation as Christ's embrace of the virgin: "This chaste Virgine-state, that
hath no outward Lover, and that is not defiled, but cleansed from de-
formity, is this Virgine chaste state, in whom the Sonne of righteousnesse will arise, and take the man into union with himselfe."[28]
Certainly the most extreme proponent of a John-inspired virginal
apocalypticism was Roger Crab, the former soldier for the Parliamentarian army who went on, in the 1650s, to write a number of radically
inflected anti-Cromwellian religious pamphlets. For Crab, the twin
practices of celibacy and vegetarianism (both solutions to the endemic
English problem of "lusting after the flesh") are our primary means of
courting divine favor and initiating the long-awaited millennium. To
engage, in this late hour of human history, in a sexual practice of any
kind is first for Crab to invite God's justifiable punishment of the entire
nation: "The judgment of God may be seen to a *Sodomite* generation,
living now upon *English* ground."[29] The indulgence in sexual activity
will result as well in a more personal, and naturalistic, form of individual damnation: "For hee that dyeth with fleshly desires, fleshly inclinations, and fleshly satisfactions; this being a composure of the spirits
of darknesse in this body, must rise again in the same nature, and must
be taken into the centre of *Mars*, the god of flesh, blood, and fire, so
that every man shall receive the things which are done in his body, according to that he hath done, whether it be good or evill, *2 Cor.5.10.*"[30]
As if alluding to the Platonic account of unchastity's effect on the body
and soul related by the Elder Brother in Milton's masque (ll. 463–75),
Crab envisions a personal afterlife as a final physiological accounting,
man's ultimate reconciliation with "the things which are done in his

body." It is the practice of absolute sexual abstinence that can keep the human body from its terrifying journey "into the centre of *Mars*"; and sexual abstinence which can direct the human body, and, indeed, the virgin state of the entire body politic, to a higher, more spiritualist assumption into heaven.

Hardly a passive resignation from the world of affairs and the higher cause of political struggle, the practice of sexual abstinence could easily be imagined a likely cause for the long-awaited reign of the saints. Gregory of Nyssa, with whose *De virginitate* not only Milton but nearly all seventeenth-century proponents of virginity were familiar, had asserted that "those who refrain from procreation through virginity . . . bring about a cancellation of death" and the other effects of the Fall.[31] And the third-century celibate Methodius had noted that "nothing is superior to chastity in its power to restore mankind to Paradise."[32] The doctrine that virginity might help reestablish the lost paradise here on earth was not, of course, without its logical stumbling blocks: the likelihood that a sustained universal virginity would spell the end of the human race dogged some of England's most eloquent proponents of virginity. Thomas Browne, though no revolutionary, laments in *Religio Medici* man's inability "to perpetuate the world without this triviall and vulgar way of coition."[33] But the Church Fathers, upon whom all Protestant advocates of virginity relied, had happily addressed that problem, concluding that virginity's resistance to reproduction only contributed to its efficacy as a trigger of apocalypse. Tertullian had written that celibacy "conspires with the end of human time," and Susan DuVerger in 1652 invokes Augustine for support against the objection that a universal virginity would only bring the failure of all human aspirations:

> Continue your course [of celibacy], run perseuerantly that you may comprehend, and forciblely draw all that you can with you into the same course, as well by the good example of your life, as by your pious exhortations: and permitt not your selues to be diuerted from that earnest endeauour, (whereby you excite many to follow your footestepps) by the clamours of vane fooles, who say, how should mankind subsiste, if all were continent? as though, forsooth, this world were retarded for any other end then that the number of the elect might be accomplished, which being once accomplished, certes the world will presently haue an end.[34]

What, indeed, could more efficiently install the thousand-year reign of Christ than the "retarding" of population growth through the practice of sexual abstinence? A universal virginity would alone permit the number of the elect finally to be "accomplished," or completed, for, as DuVerger explains, it is only once we stop perpetuating the world "that the world [can] presently haue an end."

III

In this final section I turn to "The Picture of Little T.C. in a Prospect of Flowers," a short lyric by Andrew Marvell, who perhaps more than any other figure engages in all their complexity the shifting components and perspectives of the revolutionary period's virginal idealism. It usually comes as no surprise to readers of *Upon Appleton House* that the author of "To His Coy Mistress" should represent, in the early convent scene of the country-house poem, the sordid hypocrisy of the Catholic idealization of virginity (ll. 81–280).[35] Writing from a firmly Protestant perspective in the early 1650s, Marvell looks back to pre-Reformation England and calls on his strength as satirist to portray the ecclesiastical commitment to virginity as outmoded, and, ultimately, in light of his hint at the nuns' erotic intimacy, sinful. The poem's conventual virgins are seen to have attempted to prevent the destined birth of Marvell's employer and to thwart, by extension, the hope for dynastic continuity embodied in the anticipated marriage of Marvell's pupil, Mary Fairfax. All of this anti-Catholicism notwithstanding, Marvell, I submit, is no enemy of virginity itself. The elaborate caricature of conventual abstinence works in that poem to dispel from our ken the early Catholic practice of sexual self-denial, a practice that protected the purity of the body through a systematic deployment of external constraints, the most prominent of which was claustration, or the enclosure of virginal nuns. Marvell's country house poem distances itself from this older form of enclosure to establish an emergent Protestant abstinence that focuses on the contemplative purity and revolutionary power of virginal self-enclosure.[36] The ethically normative praise for Mary Fairfax's future marriage in *Upon Appleton House* is compromised, near the end of the work, by an affirmation of the magical power of her organically self-cultivated virginity (ll. 745–68). And it is this final, and radically Protestant, figuration of virginity—one that I will examine as it reappears in "Little T.C."—that responds, I propose, to the complex revolutionary engagement of virginity in the 1640s and 1650s.

In the brief and elusive "Picture of Little T.C.," as in *Upon Appleton House,* the cultural tension between the sanctioned model of married chastity and the new revolutionary stance of perpetual virginity manifests itself in poetic form as an unsettling thematic ambiguity. The poem begins by situating a young female virgin as a potential agent of an unknown revolution: "Who can foretel for what high cause / This

Darling of the Gods was born!" (ll. 9–10). The speaker anticipates with considerable anxiety the girl's ultimate participation, through the rituals of courtship, in the publicly sanctioned transition to married chastity, an alien realm envisioned as the erotic battlefield of Petrarchan love. He fears T.C.'s removal to a public world where her coy and guarded lovemaking could assault mankind with the violence of military attack: her "conquering Eyes" will some day be poised "with their glancing wheels" to "drive / In Triumph over Hearts" (ll. 18–21). As if in danger that he himself might fall victim to this cruel politics of eros, the narrator opts to shelter himself in virginal retirement: "Let me be laid, / Where I may see thy Glories from some Shade" (ll. 23–24).

Although it seems inevitable that T.C. will, at some point in the future, engage the public world of erotic combat, doubtless as a prelude to the ultimate goals of marriage and procreation, the speaker nonetheless idealizes that span of time in which the girl remains in a state of erotic innocence. Like the poet-tutor of *Upon Appleton House*, who posits a topographical transformation contingent on the maintenance of Maria's virginity (ll. 745–68), the speaker of "Little T.C." assumes the language of historical change—so charged in the early years of the English republic—as he exhorts the innocent girl to "reform" the verdure of her garden in the "mean time" of her virginal state:

> Mean time, whilst every verdant thing
> It self does at they Beauty charm,
> Reform the errours of the Spring;
> Make that the Tulips may have share
> Of sweetness, seeing they are fair;
> And Roses of their thorns disarm:
>> But most procure
> That Violets may a longer Age endure.
>> (ll. 25–32)

With the simple and unexpected verb "reform," Marvell presses the conventional elements of pastoral to serve in a most unconventional representation of the revolutionary spirit of his age. In asking T.C. to employ her virginal beauty to "reform" the floral world around her, the poet courts the question, so loaded in 1650, of the nature of the agency behind the array of political, religious, and social "reformations" that had already been effected, and were still being sought.

In enumerating the "errours of the Spring" in need of reformation, Marvell situates the now ideologically inflected natural world of this poem after the Fall, once death and imperfection, affecting the tulips and roses and violets, have already insinuated themselves into the garden. But even within the fallen world, as Gregory of Nyssa had written, the maintenance of bodily purity can return the virgin to a pristine, unfallen state. And so Marvell endues T.C. with that original Edenic power entrusted to the unfallen Eve: she "there with her fair Aspect tames / The Wilder flow'rs, and gives them names" (ll. 4–5). Representations of virginal power in Milton and in Taylor had focused on virginity's ability to transcend this world and begin communing with the celestial sphere. But the reformational energies of Little T.C. are to be directed toward the worldly improvements possible in that millennium before the end of earthly time. Her special status as unfallen virgin in a fallen world confers upon T.C. the radical capacity or "high cause" to "reform," perhaps even redeem, the postlapsarian world.[37]

In failing to understand the magical power that virginity could be seen to possess in this period, critics have struggled in vain to determine precisely what actions T.C. is being urged to take to effect such a remarkable reformation of the landscape.[38] But Marvell suggests quite clearly that T.C. need not *act* in any traditional, interventionist sense in order to effect these natural reforms. The competing spheres of courtly love, or even marriage, might require of her a certain militaristic activity, but the nymph of Marvell's lyric need do no more than lie "in the green Grass" (l. 3) to effect nature's gradual return to its unfallen state. The mere presence in the garden of her virginal body can elicit a natural force sufficient to redeem the "errours of the Spring." While "every verdant thing" charms itself at T.C.'s beauty, so will she respond to the fairness of nature's elements, "disarming" the roses as she preserves the benign and pacific tranquility of the self-enclosed, self-regarding realm of pastoral virginity. Like the passive exercise of abstinence employed by Roger Crab to counter Cromwell's reactionary use of military strength, T.C.'s virginity disarms the world of its physical means of force and exercises its power by virtue of the uncontrolled worth of its purity. This virginal reformation, while theoretically contained within the temporal limits of T.C.'s sexual innocence, works even to extend its own continued viability: in procuring the possibility that "violets may a longer Age endure," Little T.C. elongates indefinitely the meantime of virginity, as the short-lived violet, a traditional emblem of virginity, is returned to its Edenic condition of longevity and growth.[39]

However optimistic the lyric's figuration of a natural historical burgeoning, nothing in Marvell's poem prepares us for the shock of the final stanza:

> But O young beauty of the Woods,
> Whom Nature courts with fruits and flow'rs,
> Gather the Flow'rs, but spare the Buds;

Lest *Flora* angry at thy crime,
To kill her Infants in their prime,
Do quickly make th'Example Yours;
  And, ere we see,
Nip in the blossome all our hopes and Thee.
        (ll. 33–40)

It has been a frustration to Marvell's critics that this poem has not provided a more accessible referent for the speaker's powerful injunction to "gather the Flow'rs, but spare the Buds." In the context of the poem's investment in T.C.'s erotic innocence, however, this admonition surely concerns the young girl's future sexual behavior. To gather flowers, critics have implied, is to experience the sex sanctioned in marriage; to gather buds, as in Herrick's famous *carpe florem* "To the Virgins," is to seize a sexual experience to which one is not yet entitled.[40] The logic of Marvell's floral figuration, in other words, can be seen to close this lyric with an affirmation of the value of marriage. Little T.C. may be able as a maiden to employ her virginity in reforming the beauty of the garden, but she must now anticipate the perfection of her maidenhood in marriage, remembering, for the sake of that marriage, to keep her maidenhood from an untimely premarital loss.

Such, at least, is one of the ways to impose an ideological coherence onto this mysterious poem, a reading that privileges the final stanza's hint at the normative value of marriage at the expense of the claims of the preceding eight lines. But we are in a position now to ask whether we can accept without question this reading of the final stanza's incitement to marriage once we have envisioned the possibility of a reformation attainable solely through virginity. As in the other texts I have examined, the assertion of virginal power exercises a logically corrosive effect on the orthodox sanction of married sexuality. The wide-ranging implications of the virgin's ability to deliver the garden from its fallen condition both demand and make possible a reading of the poem that resists the enclosure of the penultimate stanza within the normative frame of marriage. With an eye to the significance of the promised virginal reformation, one may supply another meaning for the poem's deliberately elusive injunction to "gather the Flow'rs, but spare the Buds." Marvell's speaker can also be seen to urge the girl to avoid altogether the world of sexual consummation, to preserve the "bud" of her virginity even, in the words of Saint Paul, "if she pass the flower of her age" (1 Corinthians 7:36). As in the final movement of Marvell's *Upon Appleton House* (ll. 737–44), the gathering of the "bud" in "Little T.C." can signify the defloration even of the bride, the relinquishing of the bodily integrity that forms the basis of the virgin's magical relation with the natural world. The last stanza, then, can with an equal interpretive integrity be read to threaten T.C. with the possibility that any indulgence in the garden of desire—an indulgence that would include even a culturally sanctioned act of marriage—will result in her swift and certain sacrifice at the hand of the angry goddess. Far from fulfilling the "high cause" foretold at her birth, marriage can only thwart "all our hopes" in a millennial reformation contingent on virginity. Marvell's poem can from this perspective be seen to end with a tentative but sympathetic embrace of that hope in the redemptive power of virginity in which so many of his contemporaries were invested. The difficulties of this lyric arise, of course, from its seemingly definitive counsel to "spare the Buds," an injunction that acquires its poetic force by insisting on both premarital and, more radically, perpetual virginity. In the conflicting ends that the poem imagines for the future life of T.C. we see the faint but unmistakable traces of the midcentury struggle for the proper form of chastity, a contest between the competing alternatives of chaste marriage and sustained virginity.

It is fitting that this essay concludes with a consideration of a text positioned so firmly in the literary world of the *hortus conclusus*. In the seventeenth-century search for an authoritative sexual discourse, it is the image, and the literary practice, of enclosure that characterizes the competing attempts to establish both virginity and marriage as the superior ethical power. Little T.C., like perhaps all those whose virginity is imagined to be something more than passive resignation, is at once enclosed, placed by convention in a garden structured by traditional values, and self-enclosed, deploying a revolutionary force of virginal purity that promises to reform forever the nature and the rules of the *hortus*. The degree to which this revolutionary promise could realistically be fulfilled is a question that all proponents of virginity can be seen to worry. It would be folly, of course, to suggest that the mid-seventeenth-century assertion of virginal power ever seriously threatened the prevailing conjugal ideal: the unfolding of the radical doctrine of virginity could not shatter the magic structure of marriage. The cultural poetics of sexual abstinence involved instead the more insidious attempt to forward the pure cause of sustained virginity from within the enclosing walls of the sanctioned representation of holy matrimony. Although the radical claims for abstinence were never sufficient to destroy the ideological foundation of marriage, we can nonetheless detect the literary traces of a response to this heavily circumscribed revolutionary agenda: like the brute earth that Milton's Lady threatened to shake with the sacred vehemence of her virginal rhetoric, midcentury England lent its nerves and was moved to sympathize.

NOTES

I thank Cornelia Pearsall, Richard Burt, Kevin Dunn, and Barry Weller for their comments and suggestions on this essay, as well as the participants at a Huntington Library colloquium at which I presented an early version of this thesis.

1. Discussions of the esteem attached to sexual abstinence in the early modern period have focused exclusively on premarital virginity and its origin in the problem of property exchange and inheritance, or of church authority. Classic expressions of this line of analysis can be found in Keith Thomas, "The Double Standard," *Journal of the History of Ideas* 20 (1959), 195–216; and Jack Goody, *The Development of the Family and Marriage in Europe* (Cambridge: Cambridge University Press, 1983), pp. 212–21.

2. All quotations from Milton's poetry, and all line citations, are from *John Milton: Complete Poetry and Major Prose*, ed. Merritt Hughes (Indianapolis: Odyssey, 1957). All prose quotations are from *The Complete Prose Works of John Milton*, 7 vols. (New Haven: Yale University Press, 1962), hereafter cited as *CPW*. The two extant manuscript copies of *Comus* are reprinted in John Milton, *A Maske: The Earlier Versions*, ed. S. E. Sprott (Toronto: University of Toronto Press, 1973).

3. Arthur Barker, in noting the incompatibility of the two halves of the Lady's speech, explains that "what remains when these lines are omitted is a perfectly consistent debate in which Comus derides abstinence as the absurd alternative to his sensuality and the Lady neatly counters with her description of temperance." Arthur Barker, *Milton and the Puritan Dilemma, 1641–1660* (Toronto: University of Toronto Press, 1942), p. 339n. The most compelling analyses of the masque's thematic conflict can be found in William Kerrigan, *The Sacred Complex: On the Psychogenesis of Paradise Lost* (Cambridge: Harvard University Press, 1983), pp. 22–72; and Christopher Kendrick, "Milton and Sexuality: A Symptomatic Reading of *Comus*," in *Re-Membering Milton: Essays on the Texts and Traditions*, ed. Mary Nyquist and Margaret W. Ferguson (New York: Methuen, 1987), pp. 43–73.

4. The commonplace entries can be found in *CPW* 1:369–70, 1:371. Milton's youthful interest in celibacy is evidenced in the 1629 *Elegia Sexta*, the 1633 "Letter to a Friend" and *De Sphaerum Concentu*, and the ecstatic conclusion to the *Epitaphium Damonis* of 1639. Milton reviews this early obsession with celibacy, announcing at the same time his more recent commitment to married chastity, in the autobiographical sketch in the *Apology for Smectymnuus* of 1642 (*CPW* 1:891–93). The most complete account of Milton's interest in this subject is in E. M. W. Tillyard, *Milton*, rev. ed. (London: Chatto and Windus, 1966), pp. 318–26.

5. See "Of Reformation" (1641), in *CPW* 1:616, and "The Reason of Church Government" (1642), in *CPW* 1:751.

6. William Haller and Malleville Haller, "The Puritan Art of Love," *Huntington Library Quarterly* 5 (1942), 235–72. Jack Goody, in *The Development of the Family and Marriage in Europe*, pp. 78–79, discusses the Augustinian and Lutheran preference for marriage over virginity. See also Levin L. Schücking, *The Puritan Family: A Social Study from the Literary Sources*, trans. Brian Battershaw (New York: Schocken Books, 1970), pp. 18–55; Stephen Ozment, *The Age of Reform, 1250–1550: An Intellectual and Religious History of Late Medieval and*

Reformation Europe (New Haven: Yale University Press, 1980), pp. 381–96; and Mary Beth Rose, *The Expense of Spirit: Love and Sexuality in English Renaissance Drama* (Ithaca: Cornell University Press, 1988), pp. 14–29.

7. Lawrence Stone, in *Family, Sex, and Marriage in England, 1500–1800* (New York: Harper and Row, 1977), p. 135.

8. See Maryann McGuire, *Milton's Puritan Masque* (Athens: University of Georgia Press, 1983), pp. 130–66.

9. Daniel Rogers, *Matrimoniall Honour* (London, 1642), p. 176.

10. Heather Dubrow, one of the few critics to examine the complexity of the discourses of marriage and celibacy, writes perceptively of the residual attachment to the Catholic ideal of celibacy not only in Luther and Calvin but in seventeenth-century English conduct books as well in *A Happier Eden: The Politics of Marriage in the Stuart Epithalamium* (Ithaca: Cornell University Press, 1990), pp. 16–21.

11. For an analysis of the sixteenth-century's interest in the Virgin Queen, see Philippa Berry, *Of Chastity and Power: Elizabethan Literature and the Unmarried Queen* (London: Routledge, 1989).

12. Poetic praises of sexual abstinence, excluding those by Milton and Marvell, include Henry King's "That Fruition Destroyes Love," Suckling's "Against Fruition 1" and "Against Fruition 2," Denham's "Friendship and Single Life against Love and Marriage," Waller's "From a Child," Rochester's "Platonic Lady," Bold's "Chloris, Forbear a While," and Sedley's "To Chloris."

13. See Henry Cornelius Agrippa, *Three Books of Occult Philosophy*, trans. J[ohn] F[rench] (London: R.W. for Gregory Moule, 1651), esp. pp. 512–18 and 522–26; and Paracelsus [Theophrastus von Hohenheim], *Philosophy Reformed & Improved in Four Profound Tractates . . . Discovering the Wonderful Mysteries of the Creation, by Paracelsus: Being His Philosophy to the Athenians*, trans. H. Pinnell (London: M.S. for Lodowick Lloyd, 1657). The antisexual prejudices of Agrippa and Paracelsus, as well as the Paracelsian experiments with virginal procreation, are described in James G. Turner, *One Flesh: Paradisal Marriage and Sexual Relations in the Age of Milton* (Oxford: Clarendon Press, 1987), pp. 150–62. Allen Debus has characterized the 1650s as a decade in which "more Paracelsian and mystical chemical works were translated than in the entire century before 1650" in *The Chemical Dream of the Renaissance* (Cambridge: Heffer, 1968), p. 26.

14. Jean Baptiste van Helmont, *Ortus Medicanae* (1648); see the English translation, *Oriatrike or, Physick Refined* (London, 1662), pp. 652–87.

15. In his *Christian Directory* (London, 1673), Baxter refuses to rule out castration as a viable means to maintain male virginity: "Some think the help of a Surgeon may be lawful, to keep a *Vow* [of virginity], in case it be not an apparent hazard of life. For Christ seemeth to allow of it, in mentioning it without reproof, *Matth. 19.12.* if that text be to be understood of castration" (p. 479). The "exceptional position of Baxter" is noted by Schücking, *The Puritan Family*, pp. 21–25.

16. See Schücking, *The Puritan Family*, pp. 24–25; Stone, *Family, Sex, and Marriage*, p. 137; and Christopher Durston, *The Family in the English Revolution* (Oxford: Basil Blackwell, 1989), p. 32. The quotation can be found in Schücking, *The Puritan Family*, p. 48, and Stone, *Family, Sex, and Marriage*, p. 137.

17. Jeremy Taylor, *Holy Living*, ed. P. G. Stanwood (Oxford: Clarendon, 1989), p. 74.

18. *The Virgins complaint . . .* (London: Printed for Henry Wilson, 1642).

19. See Schücking, *The Puritan Family,* pp. 22–23.

20. For a reading of the social subversiveness of sexual abstinence in the late classical period, see Elaine Pagels, *Adam, Eve, and the Serpent* (New York: Random House, 1988), pp. 78–97; and Peter Brown, *The Body and Society: Men, Women, and Sexual Renunciation in Early Christianity* (New York: Columbia University Press, 1988), pp. 80–81. Constance Jordan has argued that for many "feminists," or prowoman intellectuals, in the Renaissance, virginity was revived as a socially liberatory force: "Chastity was important chiefly insofar as it could lead to a woman's escape from patriarchal proprietorship. A daughter who wished to remain a virgin—and thus to lead a celibate life—was legally under her father's control unless she entered a nunnery, but feminists generally portrayed her as possessing a kind of liberty that was, typically, devoted to intellectual and devotional pursuits." Constance Jordan, *Renaissance Feminism: Literary Texts and Political Models* (Ithaca: Cornell University Press, 1990), p. 30.

21. *The Collected Works of Katherine Philips, The Matchless Orinda,* ed. Patrick Thomas (Essex: Stump Cross Book, 1990), 1:254. See also Philips's poem "The Virgin," p. 207. Poems in praise of virginity written by women later in the century include Jane Barker, "A Virgin Life," from *Poetical Recreations: Consisting of Original Poems, Songs, Odes, &c. with several new Translations* (London: Benjamin Crayle, 1688); and "Innocence: Or the Inestimable Gemm. Written by a Young Lady," from *Miscellanea Sacra* (London, 1696). All of these poems are reprinted in *Kissing the Rod: An Anthology of Seventeenth-Century Women's Verse,* ed. Germaine Greer et al. (New York: Farrar Straus Giroux), 1988; subsequent citations appear in the text.

22. For a similarly pragmatic defense of virginity, see the Catholic text written a few years before Philips's poem, *The English Nunne, Being a Treatise Wherein the Author Endeavoreth to Draw Young and Unmarried Catholic Gentlewomen to imbrace a votary and religious life* (London, 1642). From the radical Puritan perspective, a powerful, if not exactly lucid, critique of marital injustice is provided by the millenarian celibate Roger Crab, who rants against the clerics who "engage the man to endow his Wife with all his Worldly Goods, and to Worship her with his body; yet as soon as they come home to their Habitation, if the Woman disposes of any of his Goods, they have another Law to fetch it again, and the Womans Power stands in no force without the man; but the Man may dispose of it by Law without the Woman: but her Pimp, her Priest prayes devoutly, *That this young couple may go together, and bring forth children in the order of God.*" *Dagons-Downfall* (1657), reprinted in Roger Crab, *The English Hermite and Dagons-Downfall,* ed. Andrew Hopton (London: Aporia, 1990), p. 30.

23. Ambroise Paré, *The Workes of that Famous Chirurgian Ambrose Parey,* trans. Thomas Johnson (London: Thomas Cotes, 1634), p. 937.

24. Leonardus Lessius, *The treasure of vowed chastity in secular persons. Also the Widdowes glasse,* trans. I. W[ilson] (1621: reprint London: Scolar, 1974), p. 46.

25. [Richard Overton], *An Arrow Against All Tyrants* (London, 1646). For an insightful analysis of the late classical attention to sexual austerity and the ethos of individualism it generated, see Michel Foucault, *The Care of the Self,* vol. 3 of *The History of Sexuality,* trans. Robert Hurley (New York: Vintage Books, 1986), pp. 39–68. Sexual austerity for Foucault "takes the form . . . of an intensification of the relation to oneself by which one constituted oneself as the subject of one's acts" (p. 41).

26. Milton reports his affection for the passage in Revelation, as well as his belief that unchastity in a man is "more deflouring and dishonourable" than unchastity in a woman, in *CPW* 1:892.

27. Schücking, *The Puritan Family*, pp. 22–23.

28. Gerrard Winstanley, *Fire in the Bush* (1649), in *The Collected Works of Gerrard Winstanley*, ed. George H. Sabine (Ithaca: Cornell University Press, 1941), p. 480.

29. Roger Crab, *The English Hermite* (1655), in *The English Hermite and Dagons-Downfall*, p. 1.

30. Ibid., p. 18.

31. Gregory of Nyssa, *On Virginity*, in *Ascetical Works*, trans. Virginia Callahan (Washington, D.C.: Catholic University of America Press, 1967), p. 48. Milton cites Gregory in his commonplace book (*CPW* 1:397).

32. Methodius, *Symposium: A Treatise on Chastity*, ed. Herbert Musurillo (London: Longmans, 1958), p. 75.

33. Thomas Browne, *The Major Works*, ed. C. A. Patrides (Harmondsworth: Penguin Books, 1977), p. 148.

34. Tertullian is quoted in R. Howard Bloch, "Chaucer's Maiden's Head: 'The Physician's Tale' and the Poetics of Virginity," *Representations* 28 (1989), 120. Susan DuVerger, a Catholic, demonstrates the degree to which England's virginal and millenarian enthusiasm was not confined to radical Puritans in *Dv Vergers Hvmble Reflections vpon Some Passages of the right Honorable the Lady Marchionesse of Nevvcastles Olio* (London, 1652), pp. 80–81.

35. Marvell's poems are cited by line number from *The Poems and Letters of Andrew Marvell*, ed. H. M. Margoliouth, vol. 1, rev. Pierre Legouis (Oxford: Clarendon, 1971).

36. See Marvell's praise of the virginal and Protestant Queen Cristina of Sweden, in "A Letter to Doctor Ingelo" (1653). A *"regia virgo"* (l. 16) like England's Eliza (l. 23), Cristina is granted elaborate praise as *"perpetuae virginitatis honos"* (the ornament of perpetual virginity).

37. Different perspectives on the apocalyptic implications of this stanza can be found in Joseph Summers, "Some Apocalyptic Strains in Marvell's Poetry," in *Tercentenary Essays in Honour of Andrew Marvell*, ed. Kenneth Friedenreich (Hamden: Archon, 1977), p. 188; and Margarita Stocker, *Apocalyptic Marvell: The Second Coming in Seventeenth-Century Poetry* (Sussex: Harvester, 1986), pp. 134–35.

38. Joseph Summers, for example, has ventured to guess that T.C. is manually dethorning roses and lending fragrance to the tulips with "a judicious bouquet arrangement," in "Marvell's 'Nature,'" *English Literary History* 20 (1953), 132.

39. Bruce King discusses the emblematic significance of T.C.'s flowers in "Marvell's Tulip," *Notes and Queries* 214 (1969), 100.

40. See Joseph Summers's reading of this lyric in "Marvell's 'Nature,'" or, more recently, the interpretation by Christine Rees, in *The Judgment of Marvell* (London: Pinter, 1989), pp. 142–43.

12. The Garden Enclosed / The Woman Enclosed: Marvell and the Cavalier Poets

CRISTINA MALCOLMSON

In a note on "The Mower against Gardens," Frank Kermode claims that in the poem Marvell rebukes the seduction poetry of the Cavaliers, like "The Rapture" by Thomas Carew, which celebrates a libertine garden of sexual freedom. According to Kermode's reading, Marvell speaks through the Mower: "The naturalist sensuality is not innocent, but corrupt, as Nature itself is corrupted by human pride and lust. The fields, inhabited only by the heroically simple Mower, alone 'dispense A wild and fragrant Innocence.'" Bruce King, by contrast, identifies the Mower with the Levellers, and argues that Marvell criticizes the Mower, and therefore the Levellers, "as ideologically and theologically unsophisticated." As King puts it, "Any Renaissance reader would recognize the enclosed garden of the poem as a place of meditation and contemplation of God, and therefore part of the process of restoration." Both of these critics use political or literary allusion to develop a version of Marvell's point of view, and it is characteristic of Marvell criticism that these views are diametrically opposed. The issue at stake here is the status of the garden as well as the enclosure that surrounds it: Is it the work of aristocratic self-interest, developing and carving up nature according to an artificial and corrupt set of values? Or does the structuring of the garden represent benevolent cultural forces, meant to overcome the failings of nature and society?[1]

In this essay I argue that in "The Mower against Gardens" Marvell alludes to both the Cavalier poets and the Levellers in order to dramatize the extent to which "nature" was used during this period to authorize as legitimate whatever was in the disputant's interest. His own strategy is to superimpose the wall of the garden onto the wall of the field and so to justify as "art" the process of improvement represented by agricultural enclosure. The poem criticizes the Mower, and the Lev-

ellers and Diggers, for their claim to a special understanding of
"natural law" and its ability to reveal as artifice the institutions of
seventeenth-century society, including the monarchy, the church, and
the class system, with its traditional disposition of property. Property is
in fact a central issue in all of Marvell's poems about gardens: who will
own it, who will cultivate it, and whether such ownership and cultivation can be justified. Enclosure as historical issue and literary metaphor lies at the heart of Marvell's interest in gardens because it
encapsulates in small the possibility of violence to the community and
yet the potential profit to be gained from acknowledging human civi-
lization as a matter of craft rather than part of some "natural" order.
But Marvell's use of the imagery of enclosure cannot be understood
apart from its relation to gender: in the Cavalier poems, from which
"The Mower against Gardens" takes its shape, enclosure is used as a
metaphor for marriage. In their poems on the libertine garden, the
Cavaliers conceitedly and pornographically describe women in terms of
the land and its fruits; in "The Mower against Gardens," Marvell reverses this process and describes the land and its fruits in terms of
women. The bodies of women become analogous to and emblematic of
the property whose ownership and government were in dispute in England during this period. The imagery of the enclosed garden of England and the enclosed garden of the chaste but generative wife blend
in new ways as the literature of the Civil War contests over the nature
of a proper "husbandman" for the country. As we shall see, this metaphoric link between property and women frequently structures arguments against the Levellers and Diggers, and bolsters their critics'
defense against the radical claims made by these sects. I mean to show
that whereas Marvell takes the Levellers and Diggers far more seriously than many of their critics, he nevertheless finally employs their
enemies' methods: the garden of England must be controlled by an upper class which can benevolently yet efficiently marshal the powers of
Mother Earth.[2]

The earnestness of Marvell's Mower gives him the moral edge over
his Cavalier predecessors, but Marvell nonetheless exposes the Mower's
lack of ideological and theological sophistication through the very
courtly wit the Mower impugns. When the Mower decries enclosure as
the corrupting work of the human imagination, he takes his cue and
his terms from the Cavalier poems to which Marvell responds: both
Mower and Cavalier argue that "Inclosures mans Inventions be." In
1640 Carew had written in "The Rapture" that honor or chastity is

> not as we once thought,
> The seeds of Gods, but a weake modell wrought

> By greedy men, that seeke to enclose the common,
> And within private armes empale free women.

The conceit that women are like land and the sexual act like plowing
and sowing the seed is no doubt traditional, but Carew adapts it to the
early seventeenth century by evoking the campaign against profit-
seeking landlords which resulted in public riots and legislation against
enclosure. Such riots were frequent in the early 1630s, and Carew may
have wryly reinvented the work of his pious contemporary George
Herbert, who by 1633 had used the conceit to support marriage rather
than to question it: "If God had laid all common, certainly / Man would
have been th' incloser: but since now / God hath impal'd us, on the con-
trarie / Man breaks the fence, and every ground will plough." Both
conceits work through a contrast between divine order and human disorder: since his gods have laid all common, Carew associates marriage
with the possessiveness of aristocratic capitalists; since property is divinely decreed, according to Herbert, he focuses on the unruliness of
the rioters. Both poets seem acutely aware of the arguments in favor of
and against enclosure as they turn the issue into a piece of wit.[3]

More is at stake than just wit, of course: for the writers of licentious
verse, the female body seems to evoke a dream of possession, and an
expression of unlimited desire which is both sexual and social or finan-
cial in nature.[4] Thus Donne's famous lines on his mistress going to bed
in Elegy 19:

> O my America, my new found land,
> My kingdom, safeliest when with one man manned,
> My mine of precious stone, my empery,
> How blessed am I in this discovering thee![5]

The eroticism of this desire for possession is strong but continually mediated by the clever use of language, as if the "treasure" or "fruits"
sought here are not in the female body at all but in the "flowers" of
literary generation.[6] Notice how this wit often takes on contemporary
political or social issues, particularly questions about government: "O
my America . . . / . . . safeliest when with one man manned." The link
between sexual and political relations seems wholly customary; the
point is to express it in a surprising, inventive way, as if mastery were to
be proved here more fully in the word than in bed.

In "Upon Love fondly refus'd for Conscience sake," which directly
influenced Marvell's poem, Thomas Randolph follows Carew in using
enclosure as an emblem for marriage, and more generally for any custom humanly derived:

> Nature, Creations law, is judg'd by sense,
>   Not by the Tyrant conscience . . .
> It was not love, but love transformed to vice,
>   Ravish'd by envious Avarice,
> Made women first impropriate; all were free;
>   Inclosures mans Inventions be.
> I'th'golden age no action could be found
>   For trespasse on my neighbours ground;
> 'Twas just with any Fayre to mix our blood;
>   The best is most diffusive good.
>   (ll. 1–2, 11–18)

The word "invention" alerts us to the double-edge motives of these seduction poems; they argue that sexuality and the female body should
be free from all restrictions imposed by human custom, yet the poems
are themselves catalogues of the ingenious inventions of the poet-
seducer, who rings the changes on the analogy between women and
land to achieve his erotic effect. Randolph's poem in fact shifts significantly from its advocacy of "Nature, creation's law" to an acknowledgment of the art of the gardener in a section that bears directly on
Marvell's poem:

> If the fresh Trunk have sap enough to give
>   That each insertive branch may live;
> The Gardner grafts not only Apples there,
>   But addes the Warden and the Peare;
> The Peach, and Apricock together grow,
>   The Cherry, and the Damson too.
> Till he hath made by skilfull husbandry
>   An intire Orchard of one Tree.
> So, least our Paradise perfection want,
>   We may as well inoculate as plant.
>   (ll. 41–50)

The erotic, pornographic joke works like the description of the female
body as eroticized landscape: the male "branch" inserted into the female "trunk" (l. 41) becomes another image for the sexual act. The
grafting imagery complicates the meaning, however, since it suggests
that generation by one kind of fruit tree or one partner is not enough:
if monogamy can be fruitful, then promiscuity yields even greater variety and enjoyment. Each woman should therefore bear the seed of as
many men as possible. These poems are not simple allegories of sexuality in terms of nature; each image of fruit, flower, valley, or mound
becomes a temptation and a challenge to the reader to unveil the poet's

ingenious euphemism for parts of the female body.[7] The acknowledgment in Randolph's poem of the "skilfull husbandry" of the gardener disrupts the speaker's contrast between nature and artifice, and highlights the immensely energetic and contrived "art" of poetic seduction. Randolph's poem contains its own critique, which is the starting point for Marvell's poem. Both evoke the more serious undertone of this poetry: like "The Flea" by Donne and "The Rapture" by Carew, the licentiousness of the poem allows the poet and the reader to speculate about what aspects of society are "mans Inventions," whether metaphor, marriage, Carew's "Goblin Honour," or enclosure.

Marvell's Mower would consider these ingenious poetic inventions just as perverted as the horticultural rarities he derides: "Tis all enforc'd."[8] As Kermode points out, one effect of the poem is to expose the vision of libertine sexuality as not natural but rather the work of a crafty seducer. Yet Marvell "turns" the Cavalier imagery of woman as land into the Moweresque imagery of land as woman, and presents us with a Mower-poet as inventive as his decadent predecessors. The cultivation of nature is condemned as a seduction: "Luxurious Man, to bring his Vice in use, / Did after him the World seduce" (ll. 1–2). Hybrid flowers display the gardener's corruption of "plain and pure" female beauty: "With strange perfumes he did the Roses taint, / And Flow'rs themselves were taught to paint" (ll. 11–12). Grafting is defined as a form of adultery (l. 25), since the gardener deals "between the Bark and Tree" (l.21), a phrase often used to refer to someone who interferes with the relations between husband and wife, but this poem adds a suggestion of voyeurism: "Forbidden mixtures there to see" (l. 22). The gardener becomes a Turkish sultan and the enclosure of the garden a palace imprisoning his harem: "His green *Seraglio* has its Eunuchs too; / Lest any Tyrant him out-doe" (ll. 27–28). The impulse of "luxurious man" to enclose "willing nature" and make it serve his interests is put in terms of the seduction and enslavement of women and the perversion of female sexuality.

In *A Letter to the Lord Fairfax and his councell of war*, written in 1649, Gerrard Winstanley compares enclosing property owners to the Diggers in their treatment of the land: "And we shall honor our Mother the earth, by labouring her in righteousnesse, and leaving her free from oppression and bondage."[9] Notice that both the Mower and Winstanley imagine man's relationship to the earth in terms of gender and guardianship: Winstanley attributes a natural freedom to the earth, but nevertheless he expects to "labour her in righteousness." According to Winstanley, her enslavement or bondage had been instituted after the Fall of man, as is made clear by the pamphlet titled *A declaration from the poor oppressed people of England, directed to all that call themselves,*

*or are called lords of manors . . . that . . . do intend to cut down the woods and
trees that grow upon the commons and waste Land*" (1649). These self-
proclaimed "Lords of Manors, and Lords of the Land" are told "That
the earth was not made purposely for you, to be Lords of it, and we to
be your Slaves, Servants, and Beggers; but it was made to be a common
Livelihood to all, without respect of persons: And that your buying and
selling of Land, and the Fruits of it, one to another, is *The cursed thing*"
(269). According to Winstanley, both the commercial practice of "buying and selling" and the institution of class differences were the effects
of the Fall, not the work of God. The Mower, like Winstanley, defines
man as "that sov'raign thing and proud" (l. 20). For the Mower, man's
belief in his superiority over nature leads him to use the earth and its
fruits to create his own inventions: red-streaked tulips, hybrid fruits,
and lordships, domains, and estates.[10] Titles of the nobility and the
gentry, according to the Diggers, are as inauthentic to man-"kind" and
as inappropriate to the purposes of the earth as the double bloom is to
the pink or the carnation (l. 9). The Mower's outrage over man's enslavement of the earth stems in part from the earth's apparent willingness to participate in these "unnatural" acts of fertility. That two kinds
of fruit could actually produce a third, that generation occurs outside
of each "kind," disturbs the Mower as much as the unnatural fertility of
man's imagination.

The Mower, like Winstanley, also attacks the commercial system
and profit motives which have turned the fruits of the earth into
commodities:

> The Tulip, white, did for complexion seek,
>   And learn'd to interline its cheek:
> Its Onion root they then so high did hold,
>   That one was for a Meadow sold.
>   (ll. 13–16)

The Mower refers not only to the complex process of hybridization
which resulted in white tulips with red streaks, but also to the phenomenon of "tulipomania," one of the more bizarre but telling chapters in
the history of commercial speculation. In the late 1630s tulips became
a valuable commodity not for any practical use but simply as an object
for investment. Fortunes were made and destroyed through their purchase. According to one source: "For a bulb of the variety of Vice-roy,
one dutchman paid 36 bushels of wheat, 72 of rice, 4 oxen, 12 sheep,
8 pigs, 2 barrels of wine and 4 of beer, 2 tons of butter, a thousand
pounds of cheese, a bed, clothes, and a silver cup; a thousand pounds
of cheese, a bed, clothes, and a silver cup; altogether making a total

value of 2500 Dutch florins. For a single bulb another gave a new carriage and 12 horses, while another gave 12 acres of land."[11] As the Mower remarks: "Its Onion root they then so high did hold, / That one was for a Meadow sold." Winstanley and the Mower contrast the free abundance of Mother Earth and the fruitful meadow to the corrupt human systems of "buying and selling" which make one exotic plant more valuable than the ground from which whole communities can be fed.

Such a perversion of "natural" value is also evident in the worldwide pursuit of rare plants undertaken by upper-class estate owners who sought to announce their wealth and their worldliness through the foreign fruits and flowers in their gardens: "Another World was search'd, through Oceans new, / To find the *Marvel of Peru*" (l. 17).[12] Marvell is quite right in his history of horticulture; the Marvel or Wonder of Peru had been brought to Europe by 1540, where it was domesticated into the English "four o'clock." But the author's use of a plant that includes his own name links him with these excessively priced commodities, and disrupts the Mower's otherwise quite powerful demystification of the role of the market in determining value.[13] The poem suggests that its author, unlike its speaker, does not associate himself with what is natural or plain and pure at all; rather, his status is as artificially derived as the value of these exotic plants. Perhaps Marvell's relationship to his patron is like that of the foreign plant to the gardening aristocrat: both poet and plant announce the wealth and position of their "owner." Marvell suggests that he is a member of his patron's "seraglio," and reminds us that few social estates or social identities are derived from nature; that most are the result of nurture, effort, and history, which necessarily separate society from what is plain and pure. The use of the poet's name, like the use of the Mower's name, reminds us that cultivation is necessarily unnatural but nevertheless inevitable, that the artifice of poetry may be most like exotic flowers, but it includes the same human structuring, the same process of culture that impels the mowing of the fields. Poetry, like the land, is inherently implicated in the monetary and commercial practices of society.

Marvell's poem points out the fallacy in the thought of Winstanley and the Mower, who reject gardens and property as "mans Inventions" but nonetheless reinvent land into "Mother Earth." The outspoken enemies of the Levellers and Diggers are not so subtle in their critique: they take the analogy between female sexuality and land so literally that they assume that advocating the community of goods implies advocating the community of women. The violent implication of the name Levellers was stressed in every way by their enemies, although neither the Levellers nor the Diggers called for the state to abolish private property. In their earlier proposals the Levellers urged Parliament to end base tenures so that copyholders could buy their land; the Diggers called for a "Common Treasury of the Earth," but Winstanley felt that this could never be accomplished through state law or military means, since, if done properly, it had to be the work of the Spirit.[14] Yet the Levellers' campaign for democratic government and the Digger ideal of communal goods threatened many with the complete disruption of the framework of English society, and these fears of disorder manifested themselves in the charge of licentiousness. A pamphlet called *The Remonstrance* satirically represents the Levellers making a proposition to Parliament:

> Yet wee shall not take them to be our cordiall Friends till they appear in our Campes, and renounce both order and rule, and doe as we doe, which is whore, drinke, sweare, roare, deny God, Christ, Holy Ghost, King and Religion. . . . When they have done this we shall take them into our protection, and all their women though they bring thousands with them out of the City. . . . When we have thrust [King and Parliament] out of doores, wee'l have a piece of a thousand Whores; All things are common unto those which doe their God, their King oppose.[15]

Winstanley was quick to counter the claim that the Diggers advocated the community of women by publishing an entire tract on the subject, and desperately trying to distinguish his group from the Ranters, who did practice free love and free divorce, as well as other unusual rites such as the "Californian marriage" (which Christopher Hill enigmatically describes as including "interesting sexual combinations of $1+4$ and $5+1+1$").[16] Winstanley insists, however, that marriage and the family are founded in biblical precedent, and he constantly attempts to rescue the phrase "community of goods" from its association with promiscuity:

> When this universal law of equity rises up in every man and woman, then none shall lay claim to any creature, and say, *This is mine, and that is yours, This is my work, that is yours;* but every one shall put to their hands to till the earth. . . . If it be thus, then saith the scoffer, mens wives shall be common too? or a man may have as many wives as he please?
> I answer, The Law of Righteousnesse and Reason saith no. . . . Reason did not make one man and many women, or one woman and many men to joyn together, to make the Creation perfect, but male and female in singular number, this is enough to encrease seed.[17]

Marriage is still like agriculture for Winstanley, and sexuality like planting the seed, but he works diligently, and finally in vain, to free

his religious vision of shared labor and shared goods from the eroticized sense of disorder that such a vision suggested to those in authority. The minister Thomas Edwards, in his compendium of heretical
errors called *Gangraena*, lists in quick succession first the community of
goods, then that of divorce and polygamy.[18] The connection, of course,
was quite literal: successful inheritance of property within the family
line depended on the lawful observance of the rules of marriage, at
least by women. But the response to the Levellers and Diggers is more
hysterical than carefully calculated: lack of respect for the traditions of
property and class seems to imply lack of respect for all law, and is
imagined as setting free the worst instincts. As the minister Paul Knell
puts it in *A Looking Glasses for Levellers:*

> They are bound therefore to pretend *piety,* like *Absalome* and *Jezebel,* but
> their actions tell the world that they ayme at other ends, even at *libertin-*
> *isme,* that they may be lawlesse, that they may doe what they list, that they
> may roare and whore, yet never be questioned or contraried; for there
> are no men living more given to the flesh, then they that pretend so ex-
> treamly to the spirit; but chiefly, the Inheritance, the Kingdomes wealth
> is that they ayme at, they seek not the kingdom of God, but the riches of
> this kingdome, that the revenue of the Crowne, and the patrimony of the
> Miter, and the Estate of every Loyall Subject may be theirs.[19]

Roaring, whoring, and leveling the wealth of the kingdom seem to be
inextricably linked, as if the loss of the rule of property was indeed a
loss of propriety, a disruption of the ordering principle by which one
made sense out of social experience.[20] To break through bounds in one
sense—the bounds of the enclosed private estate—was to destroy all
bounds, whether those of marriage or of personal discipline. The
fences erected by the class system and attacked by rural laborers in riots, by Winstanley on paper, and the Mower in Marvell's poetry existed
not only in the fields but in the mind; as Mary Douglas argues, the
disruption of these categories resulted in an anxiety about licentious
impurity and danger.[21]

   This anxiety was directed against particular women. As with the Diggers, the response to women was frequently put in terms of unconventional sexual practices and the disruption of marital order, but other,
more political anxieties lay beneath the surface. Just as the Levellers
and Diggers were attacked for their inability to control their appetites
in order to discredit them as political thinkers, so the charge of female
promiscuity was used to discredit the attempts of women to take a more
active role in politics and the church. Women associated with the Leveller cause and radical religion petitioned Parliament several times to

free the imprisoned leaders of their movement, but they were told they
were neglecting their duties as wives, and were urged to return
home.[22] Thomas Edwards argued that the heresies of the religious
sects made them vulnerable to the temptations of licentious behavior,
and represented this danger through the special attraction that such
sects had for women, but what disturbed him most was the state
church's loss of control over the mind:

> Hence then from all that libertinisme and looseness of life in our Secta-
> ries, we may see what unsound and corrupt Doctrine will produce and
> bring forth sooner or later . . . and indeed upon pretences of holinesse
> and greater strictnesse many well meaning and weake people, especially
> women fall to them. . . . The Apostle Paul showes the reason how those
> who creep into houses, prevaile to lead captive silly women, because they
> are *laden with sinnes*, the opinions and errors vented are suitable to lusts
> of their heart, and so carried captive by them.[23]

For the minister John Brindsley, sexual relations between man and
wife, within the sanctified order of marriage, expressed the health and
power of society's larger institutions, including the church: "So as they
who lie in the same bed and in the eye both of God's law and man's are
one, should yet be of *two Churches*, it is such a solecisme, such an *absur-
dity in Christianity*, as I thinke the world never saw practiced much less
heard *pleaded* for, untill this last Age."[24] Lawfulness in marriage represented lawfulness in religion and obedience to the church; sexuality
within marriage was imagined as one link in the great chain by which
social authorities bound individuals together. The charge of sexual lib-
ertinism therefore became a way to focus and organize other, more dis-
tressing challenges to authority. The responses to Mrs. Attaway are well
known: taking Milton's writing on divorce quite seriously, she decided
to end her marriage through her own initiative and take a lover. This
is reported by Thomas Edwards with a kind of lurid pleasure, as he
prints what he represents as the couple's love letters. But the interest of
scholars in Mrs. Attaway's unusual sexual practices is very much like
that of Edwards: it tends to ignore the more significant accounts of her
work as an independent preacher. She interpreted the Bible before
several groups of people with a notable confidence, and after each
meeting turned to the assembly and asked for their questions and comments; she defended the right of women to preach in public. To know
her only as the woman whose reading of Milton led her to leave her
husband and run off with another man is to respond to her as did the
church authorities: that is, to obscure her genuinely radical ideas about
women and church government through a fascination with her sexual
practices. The significant social laws that she broke were not sexual at

all but political: instead of accepting her position within marriage and the church as the object of government and education, she instead attempted to govern and educate others.[25]

In "Upon Appleton House" Andrew Marvell defends the rights of property owners such as his patron Lord General Fairfax against the radical claims of the Levellers and Diggers.[26] He does this by celebrating Fairfax as a successful guardian of his land and an enlightened father to his daughter. The poem emphasizes Fairfax's respect for the principles of hierarchy in the political and the domestic sphere. The link between property and women is quite explicit in the poem, since the estate will eventually be inherited by Maria, the only child of Fairfax and his wife, Anne Vere. Marvell assures his readers that both Maria and the estate will clearly bear the marks of the father's authority:

> This 'tis to have been from the first
> In a *Domestick Heaven* nurst,
> Under the *Discipline* severe
> Of *Fairfax,* and the starry *Vere;*
> Where not one object can come nigh
> But pure, and spotless as the Eye;
> And *Goodness* doth itself intail
> On *Females,* if there want a *Male.*
> (ll. 721–28)

Maria's purity is associated with her ability to control her passions as well as those of prospective lovers; her capacity as the future owner of the Fairfax estates, potentially disruptive to the principles of hierarchy, is certified by "the *Discipline* severe" she has learned from her parents. Such discipline protects her from the radical ideas about property and women which fill the air as Marvell writes this poem in the 1650s, and it ensures that she will inherit a respect for the class system and the traditional role of women along with the land. The educative process originating in the father but carried out by Marvell, Maria's tutor, insulates her from the threatening model of the disruptive woman who uses her education for her own purposes, or in order to call into question the fundamental tenets of seventeenth-century society. The poem considers such a woman in the passage on the meadows of the estate, where the narrator confronts the leveling principles of Winstanley and others, as Marvell does in "The Mower against Gardens," through the figure of the rural laborer who has powerful ideas about the nature of government, but who does not have sufficient understanding of their consequences. For Marvell, mowing represents both the necessity of cultivation and the excessive violence that would occur if the theologically and ideologically unsophisticated thinker were allowed to put his

political ideas into effect; that is, if seventeenth-century society was leveled like the grass on Fairfax's estate. Through the poetic, political hi-
eroglyph of the Mower, Marvell expresses his own sophisticated
ideology: the cultivation of the country, like the cultivation of the land,
must occur under the auspices of enlightened property owners, who
can construct the state while protecting it against those who do not understand the violent implications of their leveling ideas.[27]

The disorder that would be produced by such ideas is represented in
stanza 51 of the poem, when "Bloody Thestylis" overhears the narrator's description of the mowers as "Israelites" as she callously makes
supper out of the birds killed by the mowers' scythes:

> But bloody *Thestylis*, that waites
> To bring the mowing Camp their Cates,
> Greedy as Kites has trussed it up,
> And forthwith means on it to sup:
> When on another quick She lights
> And cryes, he call'd us *Israelites;*
> But now, to make his saying true,
> Rails rain for Quails, for Manna Dew.
>   (ll. 401–8)

Thestylis' callousness is nothing to her real disruptive power: to justify
her actions by quoting Scripture. She turns the narrator's reference to
the Israelites into a justification of the violence in the field. Like the
quails and the manna, the rails have been provided by a God who allows them to be killed for the good of his chosen people. Such a biblical
sanction for violence is more threatening because it is a woman who
constructs it. The wit of "man's inventions," as Thomas Randolph puts
it, becomes deeply disturbing when women wield the tools of language
and scholarship, and use them to construct their own cultural and religious models.[28]

Though Thestylis' name evokes the literary world of pastoral, she is
also akin to the women of the religious sects during the Civil War period who outspokenly used their knowledge of the Bible to counter traditional models of the church.[29] Katherine Chidley, separatist and
Leveller, published a pamphlet in 1641 called *The Justification of the Independent Churches of Christ,* in which she answered a tract by Thomas
Edwards. Such a response from a woman may have been as disturbing
to Edwards as it was to Marvell's narrator:

> Your Question is, *Whether it be fitting, that well meaning Christians should be
> suffered to goe to make Churches?* To this I Answer, It is fitter for well-

meaning Christians than for ill-meaning Christians, for well-meaning Christians be the fittest on earth to make Churches, and to choose their Officers; whether they be Taylors, Felt-makers, Button-makers, Tentmakers, Shepherds, or Ploughmen, or what honest Trade soever, if they are well-meaning Christians; but ill-meaning Priests are very unfit men to make Churches; because what they build up with one hand, they pull downe with the other. . . . *The fourth thing to be minded is (that you say) liberty, the power of government, and rule, to be in the people, are mighty pleasing to flesh and blood, especially in meane persons, and such as have been kept under.* To which I answer, that they that have been kept under, have been kept under by the tyranny of the Man of Sinne; this [those who have been kept under] you confesse to be especially the poore, upon whom these Taskemasters have laid the greatest burthens. Therefore for them to affect liberty is no wonder. . . . *Now in the beginning of your sixth Reason, you say, that liberty will be an undoubted means and way of* [the Independents'] *infinite multiplication and increase, even to thirtie fould.* Truely I think you are afraid, as *Pharaoh* was, least the Lords people should grow mightier than you.[30]

Thomas Edwards would never call the separatists "Israelites," but Katherine Chidley does, as she insists on the link between the growing numbers of Pharaoh's enslaved race in Egypt and the potential power of independent churchgoers freed from the tyranny of the Church of England. Chidley's comments urge us to ask whether there isn't more at stake in Thestylis' reinvention of the narrator's analogy in Marvell's poem: she suggests not only that the mowers are God's chosen people but that God sends them quails and manna, rails and dew, to support their progress toward liberty. If Thestylis thinks the mowers are the chosen people, from which taskmasters are they being freed? From the bishops, the king, and the presbyters? Or from the estate owners upon whose land they work, such as Lord General Fairfax?

It is this question that lies uneasily behind the stanzas that follow, which suggest indirectly but persistently that those "meane persons" who seek to reshape society during the Interregnum use their knowledge of the Bible to sanction the appropriation of property and to justify the violence and carnage that might result:

> The Mower now commands the field;
> In whose new Traverse seemeth wrought
> A Camp of Battail newly fought:
> Where, as the Meads with Hay, the Plain
> Lyes quilted ore with Bodies slain;
> The Women that with forks it fling,
> Do represent the Pillaging.
>
> (ll. 418–24)

Marvell evokes "the careless Victors" of the Civil War (l. 425), and suggests that this carelessness is made most evident in the visible role played by the women in the group. The narrator's association of women with pillaging may point out his fanciful metaphoric powers, but more serious issues are at stake: when the cultural laws that bind land to the upper classes are questioned, the politically active women who call for a reconstruction of society might seem like thieves or pillagers, stealing the property of those traditionally entrusted with society's goods, whether material or intellectual.

The relationship between the mowers and the radical sects of the Civil War coalesces in stanza 57:

> For to this naked equal Flat,
> Which *Levellers* take Pattern at,
> The Villagers in common chase
> Their Cattle, which it closer rase. . . .
>   (ll. 449–52)

Levellers, who proposed that nearly all men should be allowed to vote, and Diggers, who insisted on their customary title to the common and the extinction of all property rights, are evoked here in order to demonize or, worse, display as unsophisticated, their belief that God impels their work of reforming the pattern of society into its "natural" shape. Such a reconstruction is linked by the poem not with the work of nature or of God but with extreme artifice: the engines that turn the "Scene" in the masque or the canvases of painters:

> This *Scene* again withdrawing brings
> A new and empty Face of things;
> A levell'd space, as smooth and plain,
> As Clothes for *Lilly* strecht to stain.
> The World when first created sure
> Was such a Table rase and pure.
> Or rather such is the *Toril*
> Ere the Bulls enter at Madril.
>   (ll. 441–48)

Marvell's poem suggests that models of a primitive or natural order are just as much an "invention" as the painting that will emerge on the canvas, and that the attempt to establish such imaginative inventions in society, whether by man or by woman, will finally bring violent chaos. Those who promise to return society to its original pure form in church or state offer a sense of peace that will last as long as the silence that precedes the bloody bullfight; they ignore the enormous violence that such a process of leveling would entail, and they obscure the murderous chaos that might result.[31]

The threat of armed combat that the mowers, the Levellers, and the Digger-villagers might use to seize the land they work but do not own is silenced in the poem by the flood let loose in stanza 59, meant poetically to represent the biblical flood, but which finally on this estate demonstrates the power of its owner. Fairfax uses one of the new modes of agricultural technology called the floating of the meadows, an aristocratically authorized "invention," akin to enclosure, which promised to increase dramatically the production of grass on the land, and the profits of its owner.[32] In the poem this flooding establishes Fairfax's absolute jurisdiction over the meadow through which the mowers and villagers may make their livelihood, but to which they can never lay a final claim. Marvell affirms the principles of upper-class estate ownership and puts Levellers, Diggers, mowers, and villagers in their proper place, dependent on a fair-minded aristocrat who controls the land according to his more enlightened understanding of agriculture, politics, and society. Like God, Fairfax sends his flood to cleanse the land of these alarming and obnoxious errors; unlike the Levellers and the mowers in Marvell's poems, Fairfax can exercise this godly power to cultivate society because he understands when and how artifice is necessity.

The poem assures us in stanza 89 that the errors of socially inventive women, like "Bloody Thestylis," will never be the work of Maria Fairfax, prospective owner of the estate:

> For *She*, to higher Beauties rais'd,
> Disdains to be for lesser prais'd.
> *She* counts her Beauty to converse
> In all the Languages as *hers;*
> Nor yet in those *her self* imployes
> But for the *Wisdome*, not the *Noyse;*
> Nor yet that *Wisdome* would affect,
> But as 'tis *Heavens Dialect.*
>   (ll. 705–12)

Maria uses her knowledge of languages and her study of religion in a pursuit of *"Wisdome"* that is *"Heavens Dialect"* since it remains contemplative, unworldly, and apolitical. Therefore it cannot turn into the *"Noyse,"* or the disruptive harangue of the unruly woman who threatens the harmony of the social order. Maria's dialect is unlike that of Katherine Chidley, who, along with other Leveller women, presented several petitions calling for the liberty of Leveller leaders to an unreceptive Parliament:

> That since we are assured of our Creation in the image of God, and of an interest in Christ, equal unto men, as also of a proportionable share in the Freedoms of this Commonwealth, we cannot but wonder and grieve that we should appear so despicable in your eyes, as to be thought unworthy to Petition or represent our Grievances to this Honourable House.
>
> Have we not an equal interest with the men of this Nation, in those liberties and securities, contained in the Petition of Right, and other the good Laws of the Land?[33]

Such a voice would indeed call into question Cavalier and Parliamentarian certainties. It is significant that Maria never speaks in "Upon Appleton House," although "Bloody Thestylis" does; when Eve speaks in *Paradise Lost*, she will set in motion the cultural strategies that now allow for the education of women and the cultivation of the land, but only under the "*Discipline* severe" of certain men.

NOTES

I thank Lynda Boose, Richard Burt, Jonathan Crewe, John Rogers, and the members of the English department at Bates College for their very helpful comments and suggestions on this essay.

1. Frank Kermode discusses the Mower and the Cavaliers in "Two Notes on Marvell," *Notes and Queries* 29 (1952), 137; Bruce King's remarks appear in " 'The Mower against Gardens' and the Levellers," *Huntington Library Quarterly* 33 (1970), 242. King's essay is particularly helpful in providing evidence that "the Mower's invective against gardens is similar to the Digger's arguments against property and the enclosure of common lands" (p. 239).

2. After this essay was completed, a fine article by Rosemary Kegl on enclosure, gender relations, and Marvell's mower poems was brought to my attention: " 'Joyning My Labour to My Pain': The Politics of Labor in Marvell's Mower Poems," in *Soliciting Interpretation: Literary Theory and Seventeenth-Century English Poetry,* ed. Elizabeth D. Harvey and Katherine Eisaman Maus (Chicago: University of Chicago Press, 1990), pp. 89–118. I agree with her that Marvell's poetry "reinforces England's new economy and its form of exploitation" (p. 102). Unlike Kegl, I focus on how this issue influenced Marvell's response to the radical sects in the English Civil War, including those with women leaders.

3. Thomas Randolph refers to enclosures as "mans Inventions" in "Upon Love Fondly Refus'd for Conscience Sake," in *English Seventeenth-Century Verse,* ed. Richard S. Sylvester, vol. 2 (New York: Norton, 1974), pp. 419–21, l. 14; subsequent references are to this edition. Thomas Carew, "The Rapture," can also be found in Sylvester, *English Seventeenth-Century Verse,* pp. 374–79, ll. 17–20. George Herbert comments on marriage as enclosure in *The Church-Porch,* in *The Works of George Herbert,* ed. F. E. Hutchinson (Oxford: Clarendon, 1941), p.

7, ll. 19–22. For riots against enclosures in the 1630s, see David Underdown, *Revel, Riot, and Rebellion: Popular Politics and Culture in England, 1603–1660* (Oxford: Oxford University Press, 1987), pp. 106–45; Eric Kerridge, "The Revolts in Wiltshire against Charles I," *Wiltshire Archaelogical and Natural History Magazine* 57 (1958–60), 64–75; and Buchanan Sharpe, *In Contempt of All Authority: Rural Artisans and Riot in the West of England, 1580–1660* (Berkeley: University of California Press, 1980), pp. 170–82, 194–96, 202–12. On enclosure and enclosure riots in the years leading up to and during the Civil War, see H. N. Brailsford, *The Levellers and the English Revolution,* ed. Christopher Hill (London: Cresset, 1961), pp. 426–31.

4. For this point I am indebted to Thomas M. Greene, "The Poetics of Discovery: A Reading of Donne's Elegy 19," *Yale Journal of Criticism* 2, no. 2 (1989), 139.

5. "To His Mistress Going to Bed," in *John Donne: The Complete English Poems,* ed. A. J. Smith (New York: Penguin Books, 1971), pp. 124–26, ll. 27–30.

6. "The real 'powers' he displays in the text are the powers of metaphoric copia." Greene, "The Poetics of Discovery," p. 139.

7. A difficult challenge: I can never tell the difference between the cherry and the berry.

8. Andrew Marvell, "The Mower against Gardens," in *The Poems and Letters of Andrew Marvell,* ed. H. M. Margoliouth, vol. 1 (Oxford: Clarendon Press, 1971), pp. 43–44, l. 31; subsequent citations are to this edition.

9. Gerrard Winstanley, *A Letter to the Lord Fairfax. . .* (London, 1649), in *The Works of Gerrard Winstanley,* ed. George H. Sabine (Ithaca: Cornell University Press, 1941), p. 283; subsequent citations are to this edition. See pp. 71–77 for the full titles of Winstanley's pamphlets.

10. Randolph's poem also explores hierarchic differences in terms of slavery and sovereignty, although the poem advocates such superiority. Randolph suggests that man can demonstrate his higher nature only by rising above his "slaves," the animals, not only in enjoying sexual freedom, but also in developing as many generative pairs of lovers as possible, "lest our Paradise perfection want" (ll. 37–38).

11. Ippolito Pizzetti, *Flowers: A Guide for Your Garden* (New York: H. N. Abrams, 1975), p. 1313. Ivan Fox informed me about "tulipomania." See also Wilfred Blunt, *Tulipomania* (Harmondsworth: Penguin Books, 1950).

12. See Mea Allen, *The Tradescants: Their Plants, Gardens, and Museum, 1570–1662* (London: Michael Joseph, 1964). Allen quotes Francis Thynne's comments on the gardens at Cobham, "in which no varietie of strange flowers and trees doo want, which praise or price maie obtaine from the farthest part of Europe or from other strange countries" (p. 30).

13. I am indebted to my student Steven Tindall, who pointed out Marvell's use of his own name in the poem. Rosemary Kegl also makes this point in "Joyning My Labour," p. 109.

14. The name Leveller was used indiscriminately by the opponents of the radical movements, and at times it was used by the Royalists to refer to the Parliamentarian forces as a whole. John Lilburne and his group, now officially called Levellers, repudiated the name as inappropriate in *A Manifestation* (1649). For the group's political platform and plans for land reform, see Brailsford, *The Levellers,* pp. 431–43, 449, 524–36. Brailsford does assert that the group's plan to end base tenures would have broken "the ascendancy of the squirearchy"(p. 442). The Levellers' proposal to give the vote to every man except servants, receivers of alms, and Royalists might have done so as well. On the Diggers, see Sabine's introduction to Winstanley's *Works,* esp. p. 49 and 51–

60. Winstanley did call for all landless men to work the waste land, and all hired laborers to withdraw from service and work the common for themselves.

15. *The Remonstrance or, Declaration of Mr. Henry Martin; And all the whole Society of Levellers* (n.p., 1648), pp. 3, 5.

16. Christopher Hill, *The World Turned Upside Down: Radical Ideas during the English Revolution* (Harmondsworth: Penguin Books, 1975), p. 314. For Winstanley's distinction between his group and the Ranters, see *A Vindication of those, whose Endeavors is only to make the earth a common treasury, called Diggers. Or, some reasons given by them against the immoderate use of creatures, or the excessive community of women, called ranting; or rather renting.* (1650), in *Works*, pp. 399–403.

17. Gerrard Winstanley, *The New Law of Righteousness* (1649), in *Works*, pp. 184–85.

18. Thomas Edwards, *Gangraena* (London, 1646), 1:34.

19. Paul Knell, *A Looking Glasse for Levellers* (London, 1648), p. 15.

20. See James Turner, *The Politics of Landscape: Rural Scenery and Society in English Poetry, 1630–1660* (Cambridge: Harvard University Press, 1979), pp. 5–6.

21. Mary Douglas, *Purity and Danger: An Analysis of the Concepts of Pollution and Taboo* (London: Routledge & Kegan Paul, 1966).

22. See especially Patricia Higgins, "The Reactions of Women, with Special Reference to Women Petitioners," in *Politics, Religion, and the English Civil War,* ed. Brian Manning (London: Edward Arnold, 1973), p. 213. Also useful is Hill, *The World Turned Upside Down,* pp. 310–11, and Keith Thomas, "Women and the Civil War Sects," *Past and Present* 13 (1958), 42–62.

23. Edwards, *Gangraena*, 3:258, 260.

24. John Brindsley, *A Looking-Glasse for Good Women* (London, 1645), p. 41.

25. Edwards, *Gangraena*, 1:116–223, 2:10–11. Keith Thomas refers to Mrs. Attaway only as "the most celebrated instance" of "sectary women casting off the old husbands and taking new, allegedly for reasons of conscience" ("Women and the Civil War Sects," p. 50). Christopher Hill calls attention to how Mrs. Attaway "has been treated rather flippantly by male historians," and refers to her religious views and innovative management of religious meetings throughout his works; see Christopher Hill, *Milton and the English Revolution* (New York: Viking, 1977), pp. 131–32, 135, 274, 308, 312, 318. See also Hill, *World Turned Upside Down,* pp. 105, 175.

26. This claim is made quite persuasively by Michael Wilding in his discussion of the poem in *The Dragon's Teeth: Literature in the English Revolution* (Oxford: Clarendon Press, 1987), chap. 6. My comments on the poem have been strongly influenced by his, although he says little about the relationship of the poem to the women in the Civil War sects.

27. Leah Marcus uses the term "political hieroglyphs" in her enlightening discussion of "Upon Appleton House" in *The Politics of Mirth: Jonson, Herrick, Milton, Marvell, and the Defense of Old Holiday Pastimes* (Chicago: University of Chicago Press, 1986), p. 247. I found her comments on Thestylis' relation to the Civil War sects and their use of the Bible most helpful, although Marcus does not discuss Thestylis as particularly representative of women in the sects.

28. See Jonathan Crewe's essay "The Garden State: Marvell's Poetics of Enclosure" in this collection for another interpretation of this stanza. Crewe's analysis seems to me brilliant in its explication of the role of the metaphor of "Mother Earth" in the history of economics, and Marvell's response to it; my essay examines the implication of the metaphor for representations of gender

and particular women, as well for property relations. I think it also needs to be pointed out that the power of the analogy between the female body and land did not end *for women* with the coming of capitalism.

29. See Higgins, "The Reactions of Women"; Hill, *The World Turned Upside Down*," pp. *310–11*; and Thomas, "Women and the Civil War Sects," pp. 42–62.

30. Katherine Chidley, *The Justification of the Independent Churches of Christ* (London, 1641), pp. 22–24, 28. See also Katherine Chidley, *A New Yeares Gift, or A Brief Exhortation to Mr. Thomas Edwards* (n.p. 1645), and *Good Councell, to the Petitioners for Presbyterian Government, that they may declare their Faith before they build their Church* (1645). Mrs. Chidley was the mother of one of the treasurers of the Levellers, Samuel Chidley; according to Brailsford, Edwards called her "a brazen-faced, audacious old woman" and reported that she and her son had set up a Brownist church at Bury in Suffolk. See Brailsford, *The Levellers*, pp. 38, 317–18, and Higgins, "The Reactions of Women," pp. 207, 211, 218.

31. Wilding's discussion in *Dragon's Teeth* is particularly helpful on this stanza (pp. 155–56). His comments suggest that the bulls as well as the "Universal Heard" (l. 456) refer to the "bestial" nature of these commoner-activists.

32. See Eric Kerridge, "The Floating of the Wiltshire Water Meadows," *Wiltshire Archaeological and Natural History Magazine* 199 (1953), 105ff.; Eric Kerridge, "The Sheepfold in Wiltshire and the Floating of the Water Meadows," *Economic History Review*, 2d ser., 6 (1954), 286–89; Rowland Vaughan, *Most Approved, and Long experienced Water-workes* (London, 1610).

33. *To the Supreme Authority of England . . . The Humble Petition of divers well-affected Women . . . September 11, 1648* (n.p. 1649). According to Brailsford, the author of the petition was "most likely" Katherine Chidley (*The Levellers*, pp. 317–18). See also Higgins, "The Reactions of Women," p. 218.

13. The Garden State:
Marvell's Poetics of Enclosure

JONATHAN CREWE

In 1970 Rosalie Colie published a book subtitled "Andrew Marvell's Poetry of Criticism."[1] She may thus have been the first to draw attention to the strongly critical and self-critical impulse in Marvell's lyric poetry. One way this impulse manifests itself is in a certain epigrammatic abstraction, impersonality, and crystallizing lucidity in Marvell's writing. Another is the tendency of Marvell's poems to keep on rigorously staging the formal impasses of Renaissance pastoral. Still another is Marvell's production of a sustained metapoetic commentary on his own lyric enterprise and its poetic antecedents. It is partly to this impulse that I owe the term "garden state" in the title of this essay. The phrase comes from the lyric titled "The Garden," and it is embedded, as many will recall, in a wittily misogynistic stanza:

> Such was that happy garden—state,
> While man there walked without a mate:
> After a place so pure, and sweet,
> What other help could yet be meet!
> But 'twas beyond a mortal's share
> To wander solitary there:
> Two paradises 'twere in one
> To live in paradise alone.[2]

The phrase "garden state" captures the tendency of Renaissance pastoral to originate itself in a lost paradise, often specifically Eden, but then insofar as that paradise *is* Eden, to originate itself misogynistically as well, since to recall Eden is also to recall Eve's role in its loss. The phrase performs more than this act of allusive recall, however. In it a problematic relationship between a pastoral and a historico-political condition remains unresolved. The phrase can imply a unified or total condition of pastoral well-being (*otium*) from which the political is virtually excluded, or it can be taken to project a merger of two still antithetical realms: garden and state. It can implicitly oppose the *garden* state as a scene of cultivation to the political state as one of disruptive ambition, violence, and waste; and it can also posit a virtually ecological reconstruction of the political state which desirably approximates the condition of the enclosed, cultivated garden (*hortus conclusus*). These are traditional pastoral concerns which lend themselves to a certain formal abstraction, yet the peculiar conjunctions and dislocations of Marvell's poems are additionally those of a neoclassical pastoral tradition understood to be in historic crisis, and thus thrown back in confusion on many of its own most basic assumptions and resources. Among the well-recognized precipitating factors are the advent of the Civil War and popular revolt, the deposition of Charles I and Cromwell's rise to power, the ongoing construction during the seventeenth century of the early modern political state, and the vexed political economy of land enclosure.[3]

It can of course be argued that this "timeless" poetic tradition is always in historical crisis, and can never be otherwise since it embodies a poetic formalism continuously at odds with historical actuality. This possibility is represented, for example, by the invasive figure of Time in Spenser's Gardens of Adonis or in Shakespeare's pastoral sonnets to the Young Man. Yet this abstract personification of time is also an oversimplification. For Renaissance poets, the specificity of historical crisis and the self-revising capacities of pastoral are at issue at least from Virgil onward. So is the political encoding of pastoral and the interplay in it between formal and historico-political inscription. For Marvell all these issues are unavoidable, and his poetry of criticism presents an informing commentary on them even in its failures to master them. I accordingly take my cue from Marvell in considering the fortunes of the garden state in his pastoral poems.

Despite my doing so, and despite my emphasis on the historical moment rather than the "always and already," a continuing indebtedness to deconstruction will be apparent throughout this discussion, which accordingly cannot represent itself as an exercise in purely historical poetics. My purpose is not to claim Marvell as a deconstructionist before the letter or to assimilate him, as Jonathan Goldberg has done, to what is now sometimes called the postmodern Renaissance.[4] I am making a connection between Marvell's critical poetics and deconstruction partly because, in deconstruction as in Marvell's poems, the question of enclosure poses complex, general problems of formal and historico-political inscription. This complexity is sometimes belied by deconstructive polemics, as well as antideconstructive ones. Derrida, for example, responds thus to activist critics at both ends of the political spectrum, for whom deconstruction is just another ahistorical formalism: "It is in the interest of one side and the other to represent deconstruction as a turning inward and an enclosure by the limits of language, whereas in fact deconstruction begins . . . by deconstructing this very enclosure."[5]

This programmatic statement and others like it leave unanswered innumerable questions about the nature of linguistic enclosure—a phrase that already connects such enclosure to pastoral—as well as about the political implications of deconstructing it. No consensus exists about what necessarily follows, politically or otherwise, from the undoing of enclosure in which deconstruction begins. Rather than apply deconstruction as a codified method to Marvell's texts, then, I hope to generate a certain interplay between Marvell's critical poetics and the language of deconstruction.

The stanza I have quoted from "The Garden" provides a good starting point. As well as being familiar, the stanza is one in which both the conventionality and the disconcerting peculiarity of Marvellian pastoral have previously been recognized. The conventionality has hardly seemed to need explanation, given Renaissance assumptions about the constitutiveness of convention, genre, and formal imitation in poetic composition. The peculiarity, by contrast, *has* seemed to call for explanation. This fantasy of the lost paradise as a condition of self-sufficient male solitude has often been read as that of an egregiously narcissistic, misogynistic male speaker. In this reading the virtual pathology of a consistent if self-betraying persona is often taken to be at issue. If we extend and shift the terms of this rhetorical reading somewhat, it can further suggest that a widespread cultural fantasy of the supposedly autonomous, originary masculine subject is being exposed in the poem. In other words, the speaker is less egregious and more betrayingly typical than might at first be supposed. In the stanza's revision of Genesis, paradise is the single state of man, while woman is constructed not as man's desired complement but as the belated supernumerary, added on by subtraction from the perfect man.

An overdetermined reading of this cultural fantasy would necessarily take account of its connection to the historical eclipse of monarchy in Marvell's time. Insofar as the masculine subject is increasingly cast in the mold of sovereign absolutism from the Jacobean period onward, the dethroning of Charles I entails imaginative and identificatory as well as political loss.[6] A need both to mourn and to recoup this loss is revealed in "The Garden"; in the wake of political monarchy the only masculine absolutism may well be the displaced, solitary absolutism of the imaginary garden state.

In these readings pastoral retirement is heavily invested with cultural and political meanings, but deep pastoral disturbance is not yet fully evident. What remains to be noticed is the conscious whimsicality of the stanza, in which Marvell attempts the self-distancing and mastering irony celebrated by the New Criticism. The correlative absence of any master narrative or true originary moment also calls for attention in a poem marked by abrupt shifts rather than by any consistency of narrative, dramatic persona, or pastoral locale. The speaker's Edenic fantasy does not even begin the poem, but seems like a belated and defensive response to more troubling fantasies of pastoral origin.

In "The Garden" the initial movement of worldly relinquishment is also one of return to Ovidian pastoral-poetic origins. Pan and Syrinx are recalled in a conventional mode of Renaissance pastoral, and the return to these pastoral origins as a form of poetic renewal is linked to an equally conventional dialectic of worldly relinquishment and pastoral recompense. Yet to recall these Ovidian origins is to locate the pastoral source in a mythicized state of nature rather than in the cultivated setting of the garden. It is also to reconnect pastoral to a betrayingly violent origin. These disturbing implications are possibly heightened for Marvell by the Spenserian allegory in *The Shepheardes Calender,* in which Pan and Syrinx are identified with Henry VIII and Anne Boleyn. Not only does pastoral tend to become a decorous mask for political brutality in this allegory, but, as Louis Montrose has argued, the outcome of thwarted male desire is not masculine poetic triumph as usual but the practically virgin birth of Elizabeth I as the disconcerting and displacing sovereign figure of the woman.[7]

In attempting to deallegorize this narrative and simultaneously purge it of violence, Marvell makes a pure love of trees into the original pastoral motive. The inflammatory violence of sexual desire is displaced onto human lovers, who wantonly carve their names on the bark. Implicitly, sexual desire is foreign to the first pastoral world, and is in effect overwritten on it. Yet an impasse is evident here insofar as the overwriting seems to be the only possible writing. Trees do not constitute a legible pastoral text; such a text can seemingly be produced only by defacing them. The discontinuity between pastoral motive and inscription seems unbridgeable in this Ovidian context, while the pure love of trees remains an eccentric reaction formation that might enable "arborophilia" to be listed among the sophisticated perversions.

After this failed Ovidian opening, the return to origins and the dialectic of relinquishment and recompense are restaged in a series of garden settings in which, in keeping with a poem such as "Bermudas," Old and New World elements as well as wild and cultivated ones merge. The enabling condition of the garden fantasy is now a certain categorical breakdown, through which binary impasses are circumvented.

> What wondrous life is this I lead!
> Ripe apples drop about my head;
> The luscious clusters of the vine
> Upon my mouth do crush their wine:
> The nectarene, and curious peach,
> Into my hands themselves do reach;
> Stumbling on melons, as I pass,
> Ensnared with flowers, I fall on grass.
>
> (ll. 33–40)

This moment of full bodily replenishment is succeeded, dialectically as it might now seem, by one of ecstatic bodily divestment:

> Casting the body's vest aside,
> My soul into the boughs does glide:
> There like a bird it sits, and sings
> Then whets, and combs its silver wings.
>
> (ll. 51–54)

The paradise of oral gratification in the "wondrous life" stanza implies a limitless abundance, yet, although the speaker's "fall" may successfully be divorced from any negative biblical implication, it entails his own "passivization" and a corresponding transfer of agency to the virtually force-feeding landscape, of which his body becomes the object. Insofar as a fantasy of "original" maternal bounty informs this stanza, that condition of *otium* can seemingly be recovered only in a mode of suffocating excess, and vegetative incorporation.

The dialectical shift to the next stanza is accordingly an escape from the body through which masculine agency can be reclaimed and a different economy of gratification can be posited, namely, that of the omnipotent mind "Annihilating all that's made / To a green thought in a green shade" (ll. 47–48). In this pleasurable moment of decreation, in which the mind displays its ultimate power (or aspiration) to reduce everything to its own "coloration," all excess, including poetic excess, is to be reduced to zero, thereby restoring perfect equilibrium (green = green). Now, it is through a strong economy of radical impoverishment and imaginative negation that pastoral *otium* is to be reclaimed, and specifically to be reclaimed as an effect of masculine intellectual agency.[8] Yet this movement in the poem is self-negating. Not only is the liberated masculine soul an exotic figure of "feminine" narcissism—the bird of paradise that "whets and combs its silver wings"—but the zero-economy of decreation is tantamount to one of death, with the pastoral subject reduced to a thought-possessed "shade."

Under whatever aspect the garden state as man's estate is reconceived in the poem, it turns out to have consequences at least as disagreeable as gratifying, while the poem's dialectic produces no moment of sublation. The powerfully self-centering if discontinuous "I" of the poem (an "I" whose sole continuity is evidently that of its self-centering desire) is finally dethroned when the speaker finds himself wandering in someone else's formal garden, not one of his own imagining. The garden text (or *florilegium*) is not the poet's but the anonymous gardener's; it is one of microcosmic imitation and limitation, not of creative freedom:

> How well the skilful gardener drew
> Of flowers and herbs this dial new,
> Where from above the milder sun
> Does through a fragrant zodiac run;
> And, as it works, the industrious bee
> Computes its time as well as we.
>
> (ll. 65–70)

The dethroning of the speaker in this poem is connected to his failure to situate himself centrally in a coherent, timeless discourse of pastoral. Thus, insofar as "The Garden" bids to be the definitive Marvell garden poem as well as the one in which the poetic imagination is most fully licensed to create "far other worlds and other seas," this anticlimactic outcome, as well as the poem's belated attempt at ironic mastery, constitutes an imperfect paradigm—all the more so in that the poem is written in the *propria persona* of the pastoral poet. The numerous Marvellian pastorals scripted for such alternative, diminished, or impaired personae as the nymph complaining or the Mower can be read in the light of this failed *propria persona* attempt.

It is the nymph complaining who, perhaps more successfully than any represented masculine speaker, becomes the self-constituting inhabitant of her garden state, capable of delivering the punch line "I have a garden of my own" (l. 71). Her evident capacity to succeed where the masculine garden subject has failed, and to succeed *him* as the Adamic garden subject, makes her at once a displacing and identificatory figure for the male garden poet. She constitutes "her" gar-

den state as one of continuing impenetrability by disabling the
mastering and penetrating gaze of the viewer:

> I have a garden of my own
> But so with roses overgrown,
> And lilies, that you would it guess
> To be a little wilderness.
>
> (ll. 71–74)

What is an enclosed garden to the feminine "I" of the poem is an
alien wilderness to the eye of the objectified beholder ("you"), who can
only look on from the outside. This impenetrable enclosure is the secret garden into which access is possible only on the nymph's terms; to
inhabit it is to inhabit her language—space only, and to become fully
identified with her position.

This is the poem Jonathan Goldberg has plausibly identified as the
canonical Marvell garden poem, in which the entire rhetorical repertoire of Renaissance pastoral is rehearsed.[9] If so, one might add, it is a
radically displaced and highly defensive version of pastoral in extremis.
"Nymph" is a pastoral signifier of the feminine which situates this figure indeterminably on a threshold between the human and the non-
human, nature and culture. The position of the nymph is thus virtually
uninhabitable. At the same time, "nymph" is the signifier of an intense
but virtually unpossessible female sexuality. Marvell's projection of
pastoral innocence as the condition of the nymph thus entails a simultaneous denial of her sexuality and a desire to release or possess it.
Moreover, since desire *for* the nymph as other is entailed in this pastoral
configuration, the innocence of pastoral is tainted not just with a certain knowingness but with what an age more given to naming perversions might have called "nympholepsy."[10] Not only can the pastoral
project not purify itself, but it becomes implicated in an exploitative
sexual politics of masculine impotence. As we shall see, this rule applies
to Marvell's represented tutorial relation to Maria Fairfax in "Upon
Appleton House."

Before turning to "Upon Appleton House," in which these contradictory lyric scenarios are elaborated, let us briefly consider some further attempts by Marvell to envisage a good economy of the garden
state. Ideally, this should mean a good general economy, the political,
material, and psychic aspects of which positively coincide; yet any such
condition seems unrepresentable in the lyrics. In them, the relation between material, political, and psychic formations generally seems negative, contradictory, or noncoincident.[11] So much is already apparent
in one of Marvell's early pastoral lyrics, "Thyrsis and Dorinda." In this

poem Marvell can be said to repeat a widespread Elizabethan critique of Theocritan pastoral, that is to say, of the idyllic pastoral mode representing the lives of shepherds and shepherdesses. Under the historical pressures of land enclosure, the lethal antipastoral consequences of which were already represented in Thomas More's *Utopia*, pastoral idyll could be sustained only with an increasing sense of irony or contradiction. In Marvell's poem the pastoral privation and discontent of the shepherd and shepherdess are virtual givens. The shepherd world is one not of idyllic pastoral but of lack, inequality, and labor, and it is from within that world that idyllic pastoral is projected by the speakers into an Elysian afterlife. The shepherdess, who is already a Marvellian woman in the making, says:

> Oh sweet! Oh sweet! How I my future state
> By silent thinking antedate:
> I prithee let us spend our time to come
> In talking of Elysium.
>
> (ll. 27–30)

The shepherd obliges by doing just that, producing an Elysian fantasy: Shepherds there bear equal sway, / And every nymph's a Queen of May (ll. 37–38). The pastoral idyll is no longer coextensive with the poem but has become embedded in it, while, of necessity, the pastoral personae become do-it-yourself pastoral poets. In the historical present of the poem, pastoral idyll is explicitly a pleasurable verbal artifice, a form of sweet talk (*dulce*) that seems mainly compensatory and wish fulfilling.

A significant difference does, however, emerge between the two speakers. Whereas the shepherd Thyrsis seems content to settle for deferred gratification and the endless elaboration of Elysian fantasy, the shepherdess wishes to inhabit that anticipated future in the present. She hopes that through the power of "silent thinking" her "future state" can be anticipated, in the sense not of being foreseen but of being fully possessed ahead of time. She also hopes that "talking of Elysium" will be fully equivalent to inhabiting a "time to come" that does not unambiguously refer to an afterlife. What the shepherdess demands, in effect, is strong pastoral, in which powers of mind and language can constitute an immediate political reality. The shepherd can produce only weak pastoral of deferral and wish fulfilment. Insisting on realization, the shepherdess ups the ante: "I'm sick, I'm sick, and fain would die, / Convince me now that this is true / By bidding with me all adieu" (ll. 40–42).

What follows this demand for verification is tantamount to a suicide pact. The shepherd consents, not because he believes in the veracity of his own fictions, but because he cannot bear to be parted from the shepherdess. She, despite having found pastoral artifice wanting, remains sufficiently captivated by it to make it subject to suicidal validation. Yet her wish to make pastoral come true seems to have been superinduced on a prior wish to die, and when the voices of the two speakers unite in the last choral stanza, their common language is one of pastoral melancholia. Elysian prospects have given way to a final retrospect on the world of pastoral *negotium* the shepherds are about to leave:

> Then let us give Corillo charge o'the sheep,
> And thou and I'll pick poppies, and them steep
> In wine, and drink on't even till we weep,
> So shall we smoothly pass away in sleep.
>
> (ll. 45–48)

It is not without radical irony that Marvell concludes this shepherd poem with melancholia and suicide. Yet what complicates the outcome is that a surprisingly exotic remedy for pastoral discontents is to be found in the Theocritan landscape. Not only are poppies grown, but the pastoral innocents have evidently stumbled on the recipe for laudanum: opium dissolved in alcohol. I hesitate to say that Marvell here anticipates the Romantic displacement of pastoral idyll into the exotic realm of the opium eater, but the surprising turn taken by the poem is nevertheless prophetic.

In later Marvellian poems pastoral renovation comes to depend, however problematically, on exotic, hypernatural forms of abundance indistinguishable from artifice, or on hyperinflationary economies. New World superabundance in "Bermudas," with its "priceless" apples and naturally occurring "golden lamps," deconstructs the nature-culture oppositions of traditional European pastoral, and the speculative hyperinflation of Dutch tulipomania in "The Mower against Gardens" figures an economy of radical disequilibrium rather than natural equilibrium. These are troublingly excessive, alien forms of renewal to which Marvell stages a deeply implicated resistance through the figure of the Mower.

In "The Mower against Gardens," the Mower identifies ostensibly unnatural economies as bad ones, and proves to be no mean critic of their "perversion" of natural kind.[12] Yet the condition of the Mower's critique is that of being simply *against* gardens, a position in which he is at once a displaced and oppositional figure. From his vantage point the story of gardens gets retold from the beginning as one of bad masculine origin. Excessive male desire as primordial "luxury" (the archaic English term for "lechery") transforms the world into an international bazaar of "luxury" objects, including human ones:

> Luxurious man, to bring his vice in use,
> Did after him the world seduce,
> And from the fields the flowers and plants allure,
> Where nature was most plain and pure.
>
> (ll. 1–4)

The history of gardens accordingly becomes one of endless uprooting and transplantation, in which the breakdown of natural categories or "kinds" allows artificial hybrids such as fancy tulips to be produced for the luxury market.[13] By implication the prolific language of pastoral is subject to the same rootless, debilitating artifice, constitutively so inasmuch as its figures are by definition removed from literal or natural meanings, and its flowers are always artificial. The implication of pastoral poets in this long history of denaturalization can hardly be denied, given the Renaissance understanding of figurative language as an uprooting and displacement of natural language. Yet the situation approaches crisis when the natural grounding of *all* identities and distinctions seems about to be eroded. When this happens in the poem, the English pastoral poet is threatened with imminent metamorphosis into a luxurious exotic. The "Marvel of Peru," an exotic New World import otherwise known as *Jalapa mirabilis,* finds it way into the poem's flower catalogue (l. 18); it represents the new version of himself by which the domestic English Marvell is at once seduced and threatened.[14]

An alternative scene of divine presence, cultivation, and innocent gratification must therefore be constructed. This the Mower proceeds to do by placing himself as well as the authentic scene of cultivation not just against but outside the garden. The true scene of cultivation is now paradoxically an outside inhabited by a decentered figure, not a richly cultivated inside opposed to a wilderness without. The divinely sanctioned community the Mower claims to inhabit as well as the abundant agricultural economy he claims to represent is definitively post-Theocritan; it is also represented as self-sustaining, despite the politics of pastoral enclosure:

> What, though the piping shepherd stock
> The plains with an unnumbered flock,
> This scythe of mine discovers wide

> More ground than all his sheep do hide.
> With this the golden fleece I shear
> Of all these closes every year.
>
> (ll. 49–54)

For the Mower, the meadow evidently sustains a golden-age economy in which the mythical wealth of antiquity materializes in a nonalienated and deallegorized form as golden harvest. It is for this productive rather than consuming economy that the Mower wants to take credit, identifying his own shearing of the meadows with their power of renewal. Yet the meadow is a curious open-closed, outside-inside space which can be conceived only in terms of a rather sophisticated topology. It is increasingly difficult to locate or conceptualize, and the encroachment of sheep runs is defeated only by the creation of this new kind of virtual space. It is not surprising that the "grounds" of his critique—the meadows on which he takes his stand—become an "abyss" in "Upon Appleton House." Moreover, his identification of productivity with mowing—that is to say, with cutting down rather than propagating—entails a complicated, resentful gender politics of female displacement and emulation, represented in his fantasy relations with the shepherdess Juliana. (One apparent outcome of these relations of emulous productive rivalry is the "accident" in which Damon the Mower accomplishes his own downfall by cutting his foot with his scythe. His aggressive yet self-mutilating impulse seems thereby gratified).

The limited and contradictory economies represented in the poems discussed so far are typically articulated by solitary, eccentric speakers. No general economy of the garden state or subject is adumbrated. If these economies can be dialectically subsumed in any general economy, perhaps it is the revolutionary one identified by Goldberg as that of "creative annihilation."[15] It is only in terms of this posited general economy that a number of dispersed moments in Marvell's writings come together: that of the poetic mind in "The Garden" "annihilating all that's made / To a green thought in a green shade" (ll. 7–8); of Cromwell, who "ruin[ed] the great work of time / And cast the kingdoms old / Into another mould" (ll. 34–36); of the decapitation of Charles I, in which the English "state," like the Roman in a comparable moment, "foresaw its happy fate" (l. 72); of the destruction of the fawn in which the nymph's monumental complaint originates. This dialectical mode is a revolutionary one that may seem to incorporate and supersede the more static or nostalgic modes of traditional pastoral while rupturing its forms of containment. The Cromwell of the "Horatian Ode," for example, who explodes out of his garden "plot" and into political history is the dynamic alter ego of the pastoral dreamer who can only *reverse* creation by "annihilating all that's made." Yet Cromwell as historical man of destiny is to end up diminished and haunted in the "Horatian Ode" by "the spirits of the shady night," including his own dead, who have not fully succumbed to his revolutionary dynamism. In "Upon Appleton House" he may further be identified with the death-dealing mower who "commands the field" (l. 418) after the retirement of General Fairfax. Thus the critically abstracted dynamic of creative annihilation seems no less prone to historical reversal and debilitating oxymoron than the poetic discourse from which it is abstracted.

With these preliminaries in mind, I now turn to "Upon Appleton House" as a poem in which Marvell's pastoral poetics are recentered on the great estate. It is true that the poem is often assigned to the so-called country-house genre, founded in English by Jonson's "To Penshurst," and many of the considerations that apply to Jonson's poem are pertinent to Marvell's as well.[16] Yet it is the landed estate rather than the house that constitutes the unit of representation in the poem, and the critical tendency just to assimilate Marvell's poem to Jonson's oversimplifies both poems as well as the relationship between them. This relationship is one of radical disjunction, and the notoriously strange or "marvellous" effects of "Upon Appleton House" are ones of pastoral displacement and decomposition. In Marvell's poem, stress and even breakdown are strongly marked; enclosure spectacularly fails; and powers of masterly poetic composition are overwhelmed. The nation as garden state, to which an expanded pastoral-poetic vocation might correspond, has apparently succumbed to its own internal violence:

> O thou, that dear and happy isle
> The garden of the world ere while. . . .
> What luckless apple did we taste,
> To make us mortal, and thee waste?
> (ll. 321–22, 327–28)

When enclosure is figured later in the poem, it is no longer that of the garden but of the bull ring in Madrid, as if enclosure produces violence instead of excluding it.[17]

The country-house passage at the beginning of the poem, parallel to the one at the beginning of "To Penshurst," sets up the English country house as a model of feudal stability, organic growth and succession, domesticity, and resistance to invasion, including aesthetic invasion:

> Within this sober frame expect
> Work of no foreign architect,

> That unto caves the quarries drew,
> And forests did to pastures hew.
>
> (ll. 1–4)

As in "Penshurst," again, the poem opens with a series of negations, yet here the negations generate no "positive" sense of bounty. As the parallel with Penshurst is extended, forms of natural or domestic enclosure, as well as more abstract powers of geometric circumscription, come under pressure. "Birds contrive an equal nest; / [And] low-roofed tortoises do dwell, / In cases fit of tortoise shell" (ll. 12–14). The General Fairfax of the poem, however, master of Appleton House, is a troubingly restless and oversized figure at whose coming "the laden house does sweat / And scarce endures the Master great" (ll. 49–50). Although the modest architecture of the country house embodies ideal ratios which draw from the speaker the assertion that "these holy mathematics can / In every figure equal man" (ll. 47–48), this assumption is radically undermined rather than confirmed as the poem unfolds.

In all these respects, "Upon Appleton House" seems disjunctively connected to Jonson's "Penshurst," and the disjunction becomes even more marked through the conspicuous absence of a *magna mater*, with whom both the magical bountifulness of the estate *and* efficient domestic management area associated in "To Penshurst." The matrilocal construction of the Penshurst estate in the Jonson poem is the implied condition of its magical bounty, while the domestic confinement of the housewife enables this bounty to be economized and appropriated for a larger political order of sovereignty and patronage, in which poet and king exchange their gifts.[18] In "Appleton House," however, an oppressive inequality and disconnection seemingly defines the relationship between patron and poet. The place of the poet has to be renegotiated. In fact, the possibility of pastoral and poetic *displacement* is figured by the fate of the nuns who once occupied Appleton House as a convent.

Readers of Marvell will recall that the Appleton House referred to in the poem was originally a Cistercian priory called Nun Appleton, which came into the possession of the Fairfax family at the time of the dissolution of the monasteries. Shortly before the dissolution, the heiress Isabel Thwaites, betrothed to William Fairfax of Steeton, had been confined to the monastery by her guardian, the prioress. Fairfax obtained an order for her release, and then seized her from the convent by force. In Marvell's poem this story is retold, but a speech in which the nun tries to persuade the heiress of the attractions of convent life is also quoted at length. The nun's scheme is thwarted when the great Fairfax ancestor breaks into the convent, virtually abducts the heiress for marriage, and founds the heroic Fairfax dynasty. In this moment of founding violence, Providence supposedly announces itself in the triumph of a strongly masculinized, dynastic, nationalistic Protestantism. The nuns are said to dissolve like false enchanters, with no further place in the ongoing historical narrative, while the term "nun" is deleted from "Nun Appleton House." Attempting to situate himself in this providential script, the narrator delivers a belated rebuke to the nuns who attempted to resist this Fairfax invasion: "Ill-counselled women, do you know, / Whom you resist, or what you do?" (ll. 239–40). In terms of the providential script, the convent represents not only the false value of a cloistral chastity which would be famously denounced again in Milton's *Areopagitica,* but also the scandal of an antiprocreative (thus implicitly lesbian) women's community.[19]

Despite the speaker's editorial intervention, Marvell's identification with the historically displaced figure of the prioress is apparent in the (uncensored) speech she addresses to the heiress. In that speech the nun produces a counterscenario to that of dynastic marriage, procreative self-immolation, and feminine disempowerment:

> Each night among us to your side
> Appoint a fresh and virgin bride;
> Whom if Our Lord at midnight find,
> Yet neither should be left behind.
>   (ll. 185–88)

Chastity is here identified not with abstinence but with immunity to masculine violation. Deconstructing many of the constitutive oppositions of pastoral, including those between nature and art, *dulce* and *utile,* economy and luxury, the nun reconstitutes the cloistral interior as an enclosed "feminine" garden state:

> For such indeed are all our arts,
> Still handling Nature's finest parts.
> Flowers dress the altars; for the clothes,
> The sea borne amber we compose;
> Balms for the grieved we draw; and pastes
> We mold, as baits for curious tastes.
>   (ll. 177–82)

The convent as a scene of epicurean innocence incorporates a good deal of Marvell's pastoral itinerary, while the exclusionary discourse of the prioress makes her a political avatar of the nymph complaining. In our own terms, this poem within the poem might be identified as a site of continuing resistance to the dominant sexual ideology, or, better still, as a deliciously subversive closet poem embedded in the obligatory recital of Fairfax succession. Yet in the context of "Appleton House" it figures the exclusion of the pastoral poet from history and his reduction to a state of "feminine" inconsequence. The lesbian nun as poet—conversely the poet as lesbian nun—is a powerful figure only in her self-enclosing text, the historical displacement of which in the poem leaves it exposed to prurient Protestant interpretation. In this context the language of the nun, however innocently uttered, will be heard not just as "subtle" but as a language of endlessly titillating and betraying double entendre. The would-be chaste text of the prioress is no more immune than that of the nymph to the historical violence of interpretation.

Yet if on the one hand his relation to Fairfax as patron threatens the poet with displacement and historical "disappearance," on the other it allows him to interpellate himself in a dynastic and providential history of the Fairfax family. This interpellation logically excludes the poet from being the producer of the Fairfax narrative, but not from being an editorial commentator empowered to reconstitute historical hindsight as providential foresight. This is a strong position, ideologically speaking, but one embarrassingly undermined, as is the poem's providentialism, the premature retirement of Fairfax. As one who seemed providentially scripted to restore the English garden state after a mere violent interlude, and to project English power abroad, Fairfax has stepped out of his part and abandoned the field to the "mower." Instead of carrying history forward, he appears to have turned it adrift.[20] The English garden state shrinks to the proportions of his own fortified garden, while on the boundless meadows outside history transpires in ways that seem to defy all powers of pastoral enclosure. In this scene figures proliferate uncontrollably without natural grounding since the meadow is now an "abyss" where strange mutations of pastoral personae also occur. The mowers, numerous enough to congregate in "camps," are indeterminably laborers or soldiers who "command the field." Despite her Theocritan name, Thestylis, onetime shepherdess, has become a "bloody" figure (l. 401) on the Appleton meadows. She is evidently a figure of the woman turned militant, if not revolutionary, and is thus no longer playing her subjected part. Even more disconcertingly, Thestylis has acquired a voice of her own in which she talks back to her author, not just to a scripted pastoral interlocutor. She does so when he tries to take control of the meadow scene by reconstructing it as one of Mosaic deliverance and hence of providential meaning. "He called us Israelites!" (l. 406), she cries in a celebrated outburst, and then dismantles the forced correspondences through which he tries "to make his saying true" (l. 407).

The insubordinate speech of Thestylis is a crucial marker of the poet's loss of control over gendered pastoral representation in a correlative space of formal enclosure. The counterpart to this powerlessness is the speaker's shift into a spectatorial position from which an increasingly alienated and theatricalized landscape comes into view. More precisely, following the undoing of the pastoral author and the displacement of the omniscient editor, a series of world-historical scenes produced by "engines strange" passes over the stage: Alexander's army; Memphis and the pyramids; the Roman camps. History dissolves into spectacle, and the multiplication of scenes implies a loss of interpretative as well as authorial control.

It is partly in response to this world turned strange that the speaker flees to the woodland as a virtual refugee. In an attempt to reclaim poetic agency and pastoral identity, he must attempt to displace not just the world but a poetic language turned strange:

> Let others tell the paradox,
> How eels now bellow in the ox;
> How horses at their tails do kick,
> Turned as they hang to leeches quick;
> How boats can over bridges sail;
> And fishes do the stables scale.
>
> (ll. 473–78)

These outlandish paradoxes threaten all discursive "reason." The world "scale," for example, has evidently shifted in this context from being a noun that properly names the epidermal covering of a fish to being an active verb that improperly enables the fish to get out of its element and climb up stables, where horses belong. Moreover, in a wild parody of country-house architecture, "scale" reduces the stables to the proportions of the upstart fish. Everything in language and (hence) in the natural world appears to be out of place or functioning improperly. This fluidity and categorical instability of language might be expected to empower the poet-user above all, yet the empowerment is void insofar as language itself appears to have acquired an uncontrollable agency by which the putative "user" is victimized. The hyper-poetic is no poetic at all.

Recovering self-possession and transferring this unmanageable language to unspecified "others" necessitates not only a withdrawal and repositioning of the poetic self but another return to primitive lyric origins, now construed as the birdsong imitated by the pastoral poet:

> The nightingale does here make choice
> To sing the trials of her voice.
> Low shrubs she sits in, and adorns,
> With music high the squatted thorns.
>
> (ll. 513–16)

The belatedly rediscovered lyric vocation of the failing garden-state
poet is a fugitive one, and the voice of the nightingale is also that of
Philomel, the feminine persona in a now avowedly violated and speech-
less guise. This reoriginating song of the nightingale is also one of
darkness, pathos, and continuing pain, not lyric immunity. In short,
the lyric vocation can be renewed only as one of loss, wounding, and
incapacity, and for the male poet only in a mode of self-consciously bizarre ("antic") eccentricity. It is a vocation that entails a high risk of
civil discomfort, and still higher risk of (re)investing "nature" with its
"original" power of suffocating enclosure and vegetative entrapment:

> The oak leaves me embroider all,
> Between which caterpillars crawl:
> The ivy, with familiar trails,
> Me licks, and clasps, and curls, and hales.
> Under this antic cope I move
> Like some great prelate of the grove.
> (ll. 587–92)

The "I" who moves under what one reader has called his poetic "cara-
pace" looks less like nature's high priest than a parodic realization of
the emblematic tortoise of the poem's early stanzas.[21]

What is ultimately threatened in the poem seems to be a radical decomposition of the garden state and a general crisis of representation,
both pastoral and historical. It is under these extreme conditions that
the poem is problematically recentered on the figure of Maria Fairfax,
the heiress of Appleton as nymph uncomplaining. This recentering is
circumstantial insofar as Maria Fairfax was the heir to the Appleton estate in the absence of a Fairfax son, and it also seems like one more
repetition of the Marvellian attempt to recenter the garden-state poem
on the figure of the nymph.[22] Yet here the attempt seems at last, more
historically consequential than it does in any previous poems I have
considered. The displacement of Fairfax in the poem by his daughter
and the continuation of the family line her raises the radical possibility
of a counterideological and counterdynastic lineage of the garden state
as well as of its dynastic continuation through the daughter. In keeping
with this double possibility, the figure of the virgin-nymph, which is
also one of withheld sexuality and maternity, is sustaining and threatening to patriarchal inscription. She is sustaining inasmuch as she is
overcoded in the poem—one might say hysterically so—with providential, apocalyptic, and redemptive meanings that cannot otherwise be
supported or made to cohere. The implication of nearly all pertinent
critical commentary is that the Appleton House nymph is being made

the bearer of patriarchal meanings incapable of being sustained by the figure of the patriarch.[23] She is thus doing double duty as the feminine "other" *and* as the key placeholder in patriarchal representation. In this double guise she is, however, a difficult, contradictory figure. It is within her power as virgin to thwart as well as excite masculine desire, thus rendering Nature "benumb" and "viscous;" it is also within her power to manifest a sexuality intense enough to incinerate the pastoral landscape, leaving it "wholly vitrified" (l. 688). This figure of the nymph is not a feminist one but an apocalpytic one of the feminine in patriarchal representation. She prefigures the end of history as patriarchal narrative, but also figures a repressed "other" history awaiting its annunciation. Such is the true history of the garden state, still unwritten, and still to be written.

NOTES

1. Rosalie Colie, *"My Ecchoing Song:" Andrew Marvell's Poetry of Criticism* (Princeton: Princeton University Press, 1970).

2. Andrew Marvell, "The Garden," in *The Complete Poems*, ed. Elizabeth Story Donno (Harmondsworth: Penguin Books, 1987), p. 100, ll. 57–65. I have cited this responsible modernizing edition, here and throughout this essay, on account of its accessibility and wide use.

3. I am indebted to a number of historical readings of Marvell, among which I would single out John M. Wallace, *Destiny His Choice: The Loyalism of Andrew Marvell* (Princeton: Princeton University Press, 1968); Annabel Patterson, *Marvell and the Civic Crown* (Princeton: Princeton University Press, 1978); and Margarita Stocker, *Apocalyptic Marvell* (Athens: Ohio University Press, 1986).

4. Jonathan Goldberg, "Marvell's Nymph," in *Voice Terminal Echo* (London: Methuen, 1986), pp. 15–37.

5. Jacques Derrida, "But, Beyond . . . (Open Letter to Anne McClintock and Rob Nixon)," in *Race, Writing, and Difference*, ed. Henry Louis Gates (Chicago: University of Chicago Press, 1986), p. 367. For a rhetorical reading that considers relations between formal and historico-political inscription, see Marshall Grossman, "Authoring the Boundary: Allegory, Irony, and the Rebus in 'Upon Appleton House,'" in *"The Muses Common-Weale": Poetry and Politics in the Seventeenth Century*, ed. Claude J. Summers and Ted-Larry Pebworth (Columbia: University of Missouri Press, 1988), pp. 191–206.

6. On the absolutist construction of the Jacobean poetic subject, see especially Jonathan Goldberg, *James I and the Politics of Literature* (Baltimore: Johns Hopkins University Press, 1983).

7. Louis Adrian Montrose, " 'Eliza, Queene of the Shepheardes' and the Pastoral of Power," *English Literary History* 10 (1980): 153–82.

8. This reduction runs counter to the widespread tradition in Renaissance poetics according to which the prolific poetic mind is empowered by its likeness to that of the creator. In English, Sidney's *Apology for Poetry* is the locus classicus for this argument. A "hidden" gender plot is also involved inasmuch as the

male poetic mind asserts itself against female procreativity. This gender aspect is fully evident in the *Apology* when the creative masculine imagination supersedes prolific (albeit "brazen") maternal Nature, with which it goes "hand in hand" only in prepoetic infancy. See Philip Sidney, *An Apology for Poetry*, ed. Geoffrey Shepherd (London: Nelson, 1967), pp. 100–101.

9. Goldberg, "Marvell's Nymph," pp. 14–15.

10. On "nympholepsy" in Marvell's poems, see William Kerrigan, "Marvell and Nymphets," *Greyfriar* 27 (1986), 3–21.

11. The question of material economy as such has been pursued with reference to English pastoral at least since *The Country and the City* by Raymond Williams. Ben Jonson's "To Penshurst," from which "Upon Appleton House" partly derives, has been a leading text for this discussion, both on its own terms and as an implicit critique of Elizabethan pastoral. "To Penshurst" represents a significant departure from the predominantly Theocritan model of Elizabethan pastoral, the represented sheep-herding economy of which is one not of idyllic equilibrium but rather, as Goldberg has argued, of bankrupt excess and privation. See Jonathan Goldberg, "Consuming Texts: Spenser and the Poet's Economy," in *Voice Terminal Echo*, pp. 39–67.

12. See Rosemary Kegl, "Joyning My Labour to My Pain: The Politics of Labor in Marvell's Mower Poems," in *Soliciting Interpretation: Literary Theory and Seventeenth-Century English Poetry*, ed. Elizabeth D. Harvey and Katharine Eisaman Maus (Chicago: University of Chicago Press, 1990), pp. 89–118.

13. The historico-economic discourse of luxury, including its ontological and Edenic inscription, is reviewed in John Sekora, *Luxury: The Concept in Western Thought, Eden to Smollett* (Baltimore: Johns Hopkins University Press, 1987). See also Werner Sombart, *Luxury and Capitalism*, trans. W. R. Dittman (Ann Arbor: University of Michigan Press, 1967).

14. Cristina Malcolmson draws attention to this pun in her contribution to this volume, "The Garden Enclosed / The Woman Enclosed." *Mirabilis Jalapa*, also known as the False Jalap, is identified by Claudia Lazzaro in *The Italian Renaissance Garden* (New Haven: Yale University Press, 1990) as one of the exotics introduced into Renaissance gardens in the late sixteenth century.

15. Goldberg, "Marvell's Nymph," pp. 14–15.

16. See Raymond Williams, *The Country and the City* (New York: Oxford University Press, 1973); Don Wayne, *Penshurst: The Semiotics of Place and the Poetics of History* (Madison: University of Wisconsin Press, 1984), pp. 71–75; and Christopher Kendrick, "The Manor Bound and Unbound: Symbolic Responses to Mid-Seventeenth-Century Crisis" (in press).

17. Rivalry between the ambitions of the poet and the political conqueror within the same national "enclosure" may be implied by the somewhat mysterious lines "And with such to enclose, / Is more than to oppose" (ll. 19–20) in the "Horatian Ode." Both men—or both versions of the ambitious man— can share the Renaissance goal of making the state their great work of art: Cromwell's brazen way is to "cast the kingdoms old, / Into another mould" (ll. 35–36).

18. The unnamed *magna mater* of Penshurst is identified in Wayne, *Penshurst*, pp. 71–75, as Barbara Gamage, the conspicuously fertile wife of Sir Robert Sidney. Wayne cites a classically Erasmian letter from Sidney to his wife in which, while praising her maternal excellence, he pleads with her to relinquish the children for their own advancement in the world of masculine self-formation and patronage. See also Coppélia Kahn, " 'Magic of Bounty': Jaco-

bean Patronage and Maternal Power," *Shakespeare Quarterly* 38 (1987) 34–57; and Goldberg, *James I and the Politics of Literature*, pp. 223–28.

19. The lesbian pastoral of "Upon Appleton House" is discussed in James Holstun, " 'Will You Rent Our Ancient Love Asunder?': Lesbian Elegy in Donne, Marvell, and Milton," *English Literary History* 54 (1987), 835–67. I differ somewhat in my reading of this episode, and especially from Holstun's conclusion that "movement from lesbian to nongay sexuality is . . . seamless" in Marvell's poem (p. 845).

20. Annabel Patterson, *Marvell and the Civic Crown*, wittily sees Fairfax in his military flower garden as an Uncle Toby in the making. She and later readers have divined a rebuke to Fairfax in "Upon Appleton House." The connection to Sterne again raises the issue of masculine impotence, and a psychoanalytic reading of Marvell's thematics of castration would clearly be possible.

21. Stocker, *Apocalyptic Marvell*, p. 163.

22. Lee Erickson, "Marvell's 'Upon Appleton House' and the Fairfax Family," *English Literary Renaissance* 9 (1979), 158–68, has shown that Fairfax's entailment of the estate on his daughter caused anxiety in the family about the continuation of the line.

23. Stocker, *Apocalyptic Marvell*, discloses the saturation of Marvell's texts with the apocalyptic and controversial discourses of the seventeenth century (especially those regarding the world turned upside down, or in which high and low have become confused). Stocker reads these sections of "Upon Appleton House" in ways from which I have profited. She also establishes common ground between Marvell and Milton; my approach would however, tend to separate Marvell from Milton.

14. Dictionary English and the Female Tongue

JULIET FLEMING

> I am supposing that in every society the production of discourse is at once controlled, selected, organised and redistributed according to a certain number of procedures, whose role is to avert its powers and its dangers, to cope with chance events, to evade its ponderous, awesome materiality.
> —Michel Foucault, "The Discourse on Language"

> There is one expression which continually comes to my mind whenever I think of the English language and compare it to others: it seems to me to be positively and expressly *masculine*. It is the language of a grown up man and has very little childish or feminine about it.
> —Otto Jespersen, *Growth and Structure of the English Language*

What is arguably the first dictionary of vernacular English was published by Robert Cawdrey as *A Table Alphabeticall, conteyning and teaching the true writing and understanding of hard usuall English wordes, borrowed from the Hebrew, Greeke, Latine, or French, &. With the interpretation therof by plaine English words, gathered for the benefit and helpe of Ladies, Gentle-women, or any other unskilful persons* (London: Edmund Weaver, 1604).[1] The three dictionaries that followed it, John Bullokar's *English Expositor* (1616), Henry Cockeram's *English Dictionarie* (1623), and Thomas Blount's *Glossographia* (1656), were also directed at least in part to women. This essay investigates the configurations of the relationship between the feminine and the vernacular at the inception of the English dictionary and argues for the importance of this association in the creation of the national "standard."

For it is a curious fact that female difference is regularly evoked in the early history of English lexicography, first through the production of dictionaries "for women," and then through subsequent proposals, some serious and some not, that lexicographers cater to the special needs of women.[2] In what follows I suggest first that the "manliness" that Jespersen found to be the enduring hallmark of English (a quality that is used to mystify the precise nature of its claims to national and international authority) has been produced by an ostentatious departure from what is represented as an erroneous femininity; and second that femininity was rendered unspeakable within "standard" English as the grounds out of which that standard is produced.

I

> Speech is not merely the medium which manifests—or dissembles—desire; it is also the object of desire. Similarly . . . speech is no mere verbalisation of conflicts and systems of domination, but . . . is the very object of man's conflicts.
> —Michel Foucault, "The Discourse on Language"

In England the emergence of the vernacular as a prestige language and its concomitant representation in a fairly standard printed form coincided with and reflected the beginnings of national capitalism. One might therefore expect early prescriptions of English to address themselves in the first instance to those class divisions out of which seventeenth-century Britain was produced—divisions that have certainly determined all subsequent descriptions of standard English.[3] Cawdrey's *Table Alphabeticall* does after all claim to have been "gathered for the benefit . . . of Ladies, Gentlewomen, *or any other unskilful persons*" (emphasis added), while succeeding dictionaries accord an ever diminishing importance to women among those "unskilful" people whose existence justifies the lexicographic project. But it is not until the publication in 1658 of Edward Phillips's *New World of English Words* that the English dictionary falls, for the first time, completely silent on the subject of women; and even after this the ladies' dictionary continues its uncanny irruption into the field of English lexicography, appearing now as a joke, now as a threat, and now as an intimation of the chaos that lies beyond the pale of national linguistic regulation. There may then be something to be gained in following the inclination of the earliest English dictionary and according primacy to the difference made by sex.[4]

Commenting on the importance, to the project of nationalism, of developing a common language and a literature based on it, Max Weber pointed to one typical, but typically overlooked, resource, namely, women. They contributed specifically to the formation of national sentiment linked to language. An erotic lyric addressed to a woman can hardly be written in a foreign language, because then it would be unintelligible to the addressee. The courtly and chivalrous lyric was neither singular, nor always the first literature to displace Latin by the national language, as happened in France, Italy, Germany, or to displace Chinese, as happened in Japan. Nevertheless, the courtly lyric has frequently and permanently done so, and has sublimated national languages into literary languages.[5]

Weber's suggestion that women have acted as catalysts in the development of national vernaculars may not have received the attention it deserves. Its attractive assumption that the national literatures of Europe were written in the first instance "for" women should perhaps be qualified by the observation that to write "to" or about is not necessarily to write "for." That being said, we have yet to account in the field of English literature both for the importance of gender in determining what might be called the literary effect and for the ways in which our literature reflects the institutional practice of a national language.[6] The adequate elaboration of these two narratives would surely entail—if it did not of itself produce—some comprehension of the role played by gender in the construction of the national vernacular.

The fact that it is women who assist at the birth of the English dictionary may also confirm Foucault's intuition that the procedures according to which discourse is controlled are most in evidence around the topics of politics and sex: "It is as though discussion, far from being a transparent, neutral element, allowing us to disarm sexuality and to pacify politics, were one of those privileged areas in which they exercised some of their more awesome powers. In appearance, speech may well be of little account, but the prohibitions surrounding it soon reveal its links with desire and power."[7] A slight reinflection of this formulation opens room for the possibility that, at least in the case of the early English dictionary, it is not so much that politics and sexuality replicate the constraints of the discourses that have produced them, but that the production of the constraints of discourse have required—and may still require—exigent sexual and political formations. That is, although the legislation of standard English may have permitted misogynist stereotypes to be both elaborated outside and firmly fixed inside the realm of language, gender difference played a still more fundamental role in the production of that set of linguistic assumptions and practices that we now call standard English, for it seems to have provided a conceptual grid within which the English vernacular came of age as an authoritative tongue.[8]

Weighing the coincidence of language and gender in four texts produced in England in the first half of the seventeenth century, this essay may appear to privilege, if not "history," then something that corresponds to the appearance of "historicity," within which, according to Foucault, the modern discipline of philology was born. But the engagement of the early English lexicon with gender difference is a story that can be told in more than one register; and among these the Lacanian theory of language acquisition deserves special consideration. Lacan holds that a child's severance from a pre-Oedipal union with its mother is the condition, and reward, for its entrance into the symbolic order. This order (which Lacan calls the Law of the Father, and which is based on and enacts the prohibition of mother-child incest) constitutes a sign system that depends on difference and the absence of the referent. Importantly, the absence that structures difference is the absence of the mother; and women are thus identified with the literal—the absent referent that makes possible the signifying systems of western culture. According to Margaret Homans's summary of Lacan's theory, "The symbolic order, both the legal system and language, depends on the identification of the woman with the literal, and then on the denial that the literal has any connection with masculine figurations."[9]

The early English dictionary, which stages the suppression of the literality of the letter (a literality that in this instance can be thought of as a materiality that threatens, but whose suppression makes possible, the figurative structures of language) thus seems to recapitulate, at the level of a specific culture, Lacan's account of language acquisition in the individual subject. Homans's warning that "the Lacanian view of language is not a universal truth, but the psychoanalytic retelling of a myth to which our culture has long subscribed" offers one way of understanding this unnerving coincidence, for theory and history can then be read as two versions of the same myth. It is, however, a myth that not only structures all accounts of the development of English (including, necessarily, my own), but also represents a retelling of "the master narrative that specifically literary language always tells about its own figurality."[10] So while the association of femininity with literality may be in some crucial sense mistaken, it is a mistake which has constituted our culture and will doubtless continue to govern our analysis of it.

II

I am not yet so lost in lexicography, as to forget that words are the daughters of the earth, and that things are the sons of heaven. . . .

> I wish, however, that the instrument might be less apt to decay, and
> that signs might be made permanent, like the things they denote.
> —Samuel Johnson, *Preface to the Dictionary* (1755)

Johnson's lexicographic concern that female words provide an inadequately permanent vehicle for the male "things" they denote may be
taken to demonstrate that the concept of standard English, which
Johnson's *Dictionary* is now held to have both epitomized and advanced,
is far from gender-neutral.[11] Indeed, in a pair of essays written for *The
World* in 1754, Lord Chesterfield, Johnson's despised patron, had already playfully proposed that articulation of the "rules" of standard
English might provide an opportunity for the official extension of gender norms into the realm of language.

Claiming that he himself had "long lamented that we have no lawful
standard of our language set up, for those to repair to, who might
chuse to speak and write it grammatically and correctly," Chesterfield
congratulated Johnson on having put himself forward as the linguistic
"dictator" of English, and professed his own readiness to be instructed
in its proper use.[12] The flippancy that characterizes Chesterfield's approval (and doubtless contributed to Johnson's sense of having been ill
served by it) constructs Johnson's project as a work of menial seriousness in contrast to Chesterfield's more aristocratic levity. What interests
me here, however, is that Chesterfield's arrogation of a politesse that
will, after all, not be able to take Johnson too seriously finds its fullest
expression in his concern for the ladies. Pretending to hold that language is "indisputably the more immediate province of the fair sex,"
Chesterfield represents women as talking more, coining words at need,
extending established words "to various and very different significations," and finally eschewing the "dry crabbed rules of etymology and
grammar" in favour of a polite, "auricular" spelling that relies on "the
justness and delicacy of the ear." The problem that Chesterfield then
poses for Johnson is where to contain within his dictionary "those
words and phrases which, hastily begot, owe their birth to the incontinence of female eloquence."[13]

Chesterfield's "serious" advice to Johnson in this imaginary dilemma
is to publish "by way of appendix to his great work, a genteel Neological dictionary, containing those polite, though perhaps not strictly
grammatical words and phrases" affected by women. He claims two ad-
vantages for this course. First, by affording space to their words,
Johnson might contain the threat that women pose to the lexicographer: "By such an act of toleration, who knows but he may, in time,
bring them within the pale of the English Language?" Second, by com-
piling a woman's supplement, the lexicographer provides himself with
a key to polite society:

I must also hint to Mr. Johnson, that such a small supplemental dictionary will contribute infinitely to the sale of the great one; and I make no question, but that under the protection of that little work, the great one will be received in the genteelest houses. We shall frequently meet with it in ladies dressing rooms, lying upon the harpsicord, together with the knotting bag, and signor Di Giardino's incomparable concertos; and even sometimes in the powder-rooms of our young nobility, upon the same shelf with their German flute, their powder-mask, and their four-horse whip.[14]

Implying that there is something "ungenteel" about Johnson's project as it stands, Chesterfield proposes a modification that has a curious series of effects. For the "neological appendix" would mark Johnson as an oversexed drudge who looms dangerously close to the wives and daughters of his aristocratic patrons, while giving the dictionary itself the status of a common thing, frequently met with as it circulates in the market or lies undistinguished among other attributes of female or dandaical pleasure. Nonetheless, the humiliation of Johnson which is Chesterfield's joke is not supposed to be absolute: indeed, its humor resides in the assumption that the lexicographer exposes himself to the dangers of the marketplace (both class derogation and an effeminizing contact with women) only to triumph over them. For just as a "proper" man may be produced out of and in contradistinction to his immersion in the company of women, so too the ladies' appendix constitutes a secondary term (here a profusion of "polite" words) out of which a primary term—"Johnsonian English"—may be born.[15]

It is my assumption that women were interpellated as users of hard word lists not because they cared to ascertain the correct use of English but because they could be used to represent its problems. The early English dictionary is a type of colonialist discourse, one that proceeds by the full exhibition of that which is to be effaced or repressed.[16] The choice of woman to represent the lexical extravagance that would justify regulation is facilitated in early modern England both by the ancient misogynist stereotype of the loquacious woman, and by the traditional association of maleness with form and femaleness with matter which informs Johnson's later comment. It may also, however, have had a more local determinant. In western Europe the standardization of a national language was usually proceeded by a *questione della lingua,* in which rival dialects competed to become the basis for the standard. But South East Midlands, the dialect associated with London and its environs, had reigned more or less unchallenged as the prestige dialect of England since its adoption as the language of Chancery by Henry V.[17] In the absence of regional contests, and within a linguistic community that had not yet officially attached the question of language to that of class, sexual difference may have appeared to be the obvious place in which to erect those distinctions that would make possible the division of English into its standard, and consequently nonstandard, forms.[18]

III

> No language . . . is capable of speaking (the) truth without submitting to the common or proper terms that mould it into adequate, that is to say *essential* terms.
> —Luce Irigaray, "The Language of Men"

In his structural analysis of language standardization in Western Europe, John E. Joseph argues that whereas language standards (that is, linguistic value judgments) exist in every linguistic community, "standard languages" represent a specifically European concept, whose defining criteria (including the presence of nonstandard dialects against which the norm can be articulated, the codification of standard norms in written forms such as dictionaries and grammars, and the use of the standard language in prestige functions) are based on the attributes of the European languages and European cultural values. Joseph developed a typical trajectory for standardization of the west European languages, beginning with the breakdown of the stable functional division between a superposed Latin and a native vernacular. The development of the vernacular into a language that could take over the official functions of Latin then proceeds according to two phases, which may overlap in time but which are functionally and ideologically distinct. In the first phase, attention to the perceived "inadequacy" of a native tongue gives rise to a period of rapid elaboration, during which structural or lexical elements are added to make the language "adequate" to new needs. In the second or restrictive phase of standardization, regulations are introduced to stop unsupervised elaboration and make variation less a matter of choice than of fixed rules.[19] It is this second phase, during which an apparently random variation is replaced with one that is hierarchically organized, that produces the standard language as a terrain on which linguistic and social distinctions may be drawn.[20]

Applying Joseph's model to the case of English, we could say that the second half of the sixteenth century witnessed the elaborative phase of standardization—a phase that is most memorably manifest in the production of the national literature that was its aim and sign—while the second or restrictive phase of standardization occupied the seventeenth century. Consequently, when Cawdrey published his *Table Al-*

phabeticall in 1604, English may not yet have been the patriarchal monolith against which some modern feminisms have tilted. According to Richard Foster Jones, whose *Triumph of the English Language* summarizes and replicates contemporary opinions about English, in the first half of the sixteenth century it had been overshadowed by Latin (and, to a more limited extent, by French) and had suffered a reputation as a rude, inadequate, and unpolished tongue, best fit for instruction of the unlearned. Translations and other vernacular works offered prefatory apologies for the inadequacy of their medium, and thereby asserted the superiority of Latin, French, and those who could speak them, even while marking the beginning of the end of their domination.

According to Jones, the middle of the sixteenth century then witnessed an extraordinary period of elaboration, at the end of which the lexicon had been nearly doubled through the addition of words borrowed, coined, and revived, and the old anxiety that there are "moe things, then there are wordes to expresse things by" had apparently been quieted.[21] By the end of Elizabeth's reign the vernacular success of her poets had proved that English was, after all, an "eloquent" tongue, whose geographic and social marginality was coming to an end.[22] It was, however, still "unruled," lacking a grammar, a lexicon, and a standardized spelling; and whereas Sidney, who lived and died while the elaborative stage of English was at its height, considered it one of the strengths of the vernacular that it was not subject to grammatical regulation, at the beginning of the seventeenth century England seems to have felt the need for a vernacular that could operate as a stable register of the authority and the distinctions that were to define the Stuart age. The slow movement of English into the second or restrictive stage of standardization can be plotted by the gradual yielding of sixteenth-century works on rhetoric to the grammars, orthographies, and dictionaries of the seventeenth century.[23]

William Bullokar was perhaps the first person to call for an English grammar and dictionary and predict their stabilizing effect, in his *Booke at Large, for the Amendment of Orthographie for English Speech* (1580). His appeal was seconded two years later in Richard Mulcaster's *Firste Part of the Elementarie* (1582):

> It were a thing verie praiseworthy in my opinion, and no less profitable than praiseworthie, if som one well learned and as laborious a man, wold gather all the words which we use in our English tung, whether naturall or incorporate, out of all professions, as well learned as not, into one dictionarie, and besides the right writing, which is incident to the Alphabete, wold open unto us therin, both their naturall force, and their proper use: that by his honest travell we might be as able to judge of our

own tung, which we have by rote, as we are of others, which we learn by
rule. The want thereof, is the onelie cause why, that verie manie men,
being excellentlie well learned in foreign speche, can hardlie discern
what theie have at home, still shooting fair, but oft missing far, hard censors over other, ill executors themselves.

The dictionary Mulcaster imagines is our own authoritative handbook
to explain the "proper use" of "all the words . . . which we use in our
English tung."[24] Mulcaster displays the same readiness to be told the
"right" use of English by one "well learned and laborious man" that
accounts for the authority enjoyed by Johnson 150 years later. In *The
Defence of Rime* (1603), sounding rather Johnsonian himself, Samuel
Daniel linked linguistic elaboration to the upheavals of a new age and
reign:

> And I cannot but wonder at the strange presumption of some men, that
> dare so audaciously adventure to introduce any whatsoever forraine
> wordes, be they never so strange, and out of themselves, as it were, with-
> out a Parlaiment, without any consent or allowance, establish themselves
> as Free-denizens in our language. But this is but a Character of that per-
> petuall revolution which wee see to be in all things that never remaine
> the same: and we must heerin be content to submit our selves to the law
> of time, which in a few yeeres will make al that for which we now contend
> *Nothing.*[25]

Appeals to encourage the king, the court, Parliament, the universities,
or a specially created academy to ascertain and legislate the "correct"
use of English were heard throughout the seventeenth century, but the
language continued to lack an external or absolute authority until
Johnson, who himself opposed the idea of an academy as counter to
"the spirit of English liberty," established his dictionary on that unthe-
orized and unexamined notion of consensus according to which it still
operates.[26]

    That the consensus producing the list of words of "common" use has
always operated according to a highly restricted franchise is demonstrated by John Cheke's letter to Sir Thomas Hoby concerning his 1557
translation of Castiglione's *Book of Courtier*. Cheke, whose stated pre-
scriptive aim was an English "cleane and pure, unmixt and un-
mangeled with borrowing of other tunges," offered Hoby suggestions
for changing some of the words, "which might verie well be let alone,
but that I am verie curious in mi freendes matters, not to determin, but
to debaat what is best."[27] This image of the lexicon as a small matter
between Cheke and his friends anticipates Johnson's validation of
words as they are used by himself and his literary and social peers; in

such contexts standard English is necessarily registered as that dialect which is common among the "best" speakers, and not among the "ladies, gentlewomen, or other unskilful persons," for whose benefit it is written down. And here we may begin to understand the function of women as people who are not, and may never be, full members of the language community: that it is precisely at the scene of their instruction that the "rules" of English may be articulated.[28]

Experimental works, the early English dictionaries provide a forum within which the conditions and possibilities for a linguistic "consensus" are first noticed and debated. Each is consequently directed to a double audience: first to the lexicographer's political peers, who are invited to join him in discussing "what is best," and then to those "unskilfull persons" whose uncritical belief is necessary to validate a term's "currency."[29] The woman's lexicon is the proving ground for male words and, more important, for the whole male project of lexicography. But while women (and foreigners) may be permitted to lend their assent to the new authoritative functions of English, they are not expected to use it authoritatively themselves; indeed, the adequately "ruled" English turns out to be the exclusive possession of men. The early English dictionary is thus marked by an irony that is characteristic of conduct literature, in that it functions to exclude from a general franchise precisely those people to whom it is addressed.

IV

Language is indisputably the more immediate province of the fair sex.

—Lord Chesterfield (1754)

A Table Alphabeticall was dedicated to five sisters, "the right honourable, Worshipfull, vertuous, and godlie Ladies, the Lady Hastings, the Lady Dudley, the Lady Mountague, the Ladie Wingfield, and the Lady Leigh." The Harington sisters were second cousins both to the translator of Ariosto and, through their mother, Lucie Harington, to Sir Philip Sidney. Cawdrey had apparently enjoyed the friendship and patronage of Lucie Harington since "your Ladyships brother was my scholler, (and now my singuler benefactor) when I taught the Grammer schoole at Okeham"; and it is in consideration of this debt, "and also for that I acknowledge my selfe much beholding and indebted to the most of you, since this time," that Cawdrey ventured to make the Harington sisters "all joyntly patrons . . . and under your names to publish this simple worke."

Since dictionaries are texts that are always heavily dependent on those that precede them, it could be argued that the address to women which characterizes the first four English word lists is merely conventional, Blount having copied it from Cockeram, Cockeram from Bullokar, and Bullokar from Cawdrey.[30] But Cawdrey himself had the idea from John Florio, whose recent translation of the *Essais* of Montaigne had been dedicated to six women in three separate prefaces: Anne Harington and her daughter Lucie, the Countess of Bedford; Elizabeth, Countess of Rutland, and Penelope Rich (the daughter of the first Earl of Essex); and Mary Neville (daughter of Thomas Sackville, Lord Buckhurst) and Elizabeth Grey. In Florio's case the address to women was not coincidental but part of the stance that characterized his long and successful career.

An accomplished courtier and language tutor (whose *Worlde of Wordes, Or, most copious and exact dictionarie in Italian and English* was the last dictionary published in English before the appearance of *A Table Alphabeticall*), Florio worked throughout his career to associate himself with the interests of women, and to link those interests with the status and practice of the European vernaculars. Dedicating his translation of the essays of Montaigne to six women of the Bedford-Harington family (five of whom he had tutored in French and Italian), he had extravagant praise for the linguistic facility of women:

> French hath long time beene termed the language of Ladies: So doth it grace your tongues; so doe your tongues grace it; as if written by men it may have a good garbe, spoken by you it hath a double grace: for so have I heard some of you speake it, as no man, few women, could come near their sweete-relisht ayre of it. That as *Tullie* averred of his Roman Ladies for Latine, so not onely for our mother-tongue, but also for the principall, Italian and French, not onely our princely Mother of Majestie, Magnificence, omnisufficiencie, but (for instance) I avowe, you my first honoured Schollers (whom as ever in heart, so would I honor now by these my laboures) are the purest, finest, and clearest speakers.

Uncoupling speech from writing, Florio here opens the possibility that a language "written by men" may be differently (and in this case better) realized in the mouths of women. Florio's assertion that women make the best vernacular speakers had been inherited by the English humanists from Cicero, who noted with approval that the comparative isolation of women at home allowed them to retain the pronunciation of their ancestors.[31] During the sixteenth century, when the prestige activities of English culture were carried out in Latin or French, the claim that women guard the wellspring of vernacular purity may have appeared to be beside the point of the reproduction of that culture. The rise in the status of English which characterized the turn of the seventeenth century, however, made Cicero's remark newly problematic, and gives added piquancy to Florio's reminder that the vernacular spoken by Cicero's mother-in-law was, after all, Latin.

The year 1603 was a propitious one for the extravagant compliment to women constituted by Florio's translation of Montaigne, for the Bedford-Harington women were chosen by Queen Anne to form her own inner circle after the accession.[32] Florio himself went on to become Italian instructor to the queen, after whom he renamed his dictionary.[33] Cawdrey's dedication of *A Table Alphabeticall* to the five Harington daughters, nieces of Florio's dedicatee Anne Harington, in the year of the accession was then a particularly happy thought, for in following Florio through the mazy politics of patronage, Cawdrey was able to draw on and appear to strengthen that connection between women and the vernacular from which Florio's career had so considerably profited. It is a connection further exploited by John Bullokar, author of the second English dictionary, whose *English Expositor* is once again dedicated to one of the five Harington sisters, the "Singular Good Ladie, the Ladie Jane Vicountesse Mountague."

Published during the early years of James's reign, when the flowering of the European arts in England was being overseen by Queen Anne, these two earliest English dictionaries speak of a particular and newly privileged association between women and vernacular English. It is an association with a history, for fifteenth- and sixteenth-century disdain for the vernacular seems to have left room for women as the patrons and audience for English texts.[34] Walter J. Ong, for example, has suggested that the learning of Latin in early modern England functioned as a male puberty rite that marked the adolescent's entry into the adult world, dividing him from that of his mother and sisters.[35] The "natural speach, which together with their Nources milk they sucked," and the right to define it, was of course later to become an object of desire to the denizens of English culture; but it is tempting to imagine that an early masculine disregard for the "mother tongue" left space for a female-specific vernacular activity—albeit one that left no better record than that which is recorded in the hard word lists that men produced, after the fact, "for women."[36]

But the dream of a time or place beyond the pale of linguistic regulation requires qualification. For language does not exist *except* as a set of rules; it can appear "unruled" only if the validity of the techniques according to which it is regulated are denied. In the sixteenth century English appears to have been not unruled, but ruled differently—perhaps in accordance with a rhetorical rather than grammatical, lexical, and orthographic order; and perhaps according to a system that was not yet structured on the grid of gender difference. But the identification of this "other" order as a period of misrule, and its concomitant association with women, is I think largely the work of that impulse toward a reorganized vernacular that forms part of the project of seventeenth-century English nationalism. That is, it is a chimera that is produced and thrown into the past—and into the domain of women— by precisely that lexical regime whose origins I am interested to chart.[37] The male-authored representations of women speaking differently—gossiping, telling old wives' tales, or speaking euphuism— which appear toward the end of the sixteenth century are then best understood as attempts to *produce* a vernacular that is "in need of" rules; and the female-specific linguistic practices to which they attest may have little historical basis.[38]

The claim that women speak or have spoken differently from men is a peculiarly unreliable index of social practices. Nevertheless, it may be that during the elevation of the vernacular at the beginning of the seventeenth century, women were able to locate themselves at the center of the nation's new cultural enterprise by briefly holding on to the rumor of their special relationship with English. It was, of course, a promotion that was circumscribed in scope, and of brief duration. Anne was not involved in the preparation of the 1611 King James Bible, and was quickly replaced as leading patron of the arts by her two sons. At the same time, the distinction between masculine and feminine which had once corresponded to that between Latin and English was moved inside the vernacular pale: English could now be spoken either in a "manly" or in an "effeminate" way, but its virtues were understood to be "masculine," and its best speakers consequently men.[39] But this is a coincidence that may lead us to suspect that the masculinity that became a hallmark of British high culture was in part designed to contain, and in part produced itself in the act of containing, the epiphenomenon of Queen Anne's influence on the arts.

V

All words, good and bad, are there jumbled indiscriminately together, insomuch that the judicious reader may speak, and write as inelegantly, improperly, and vulgarly as he pleases, by and with the authority of one or other of our WORD BOOKS.
    —Chesterfield, describing the early English dictionary (1754)

A Table Alphabeticall announced itself as a collection of "hard usuall English wordes," gathered out of Hebrew, Greek, Latin, and French. In this context "usual" denotes not words of common use but those terms that are specific to a certain practice or customary among a certain group. Usual words are terms of art, and it is these, together with the strange, marvelous, and sometimes bitterly disputed words that had recently been imported from other languages to supplement the perceived paucity of the vernacular, which constitute the word store of the earliest English dictionaries; capitalizing on and making articulate that association of women with the elaborative principle of language that Chesterfield was to elevate into the Achilles heel of the polite lexicographer.[40] It is notable, however, that this association is made in English somewhat after the fact, as the language enters its restrictive phase, and elaboration consequently acquires a negative value. As a hard word list "for women," the early English dictionary stages itself as representing at once the problem of and a solution to the unregulated vernacular, so that at the very point where it is first "officially" made, the association of women with the principle of elaboration is cast as an aspersion. The proverbial facility of the female tongue had of course long been a cause for anxiety and complaint; from this point, however, it becomes easier to say exactly what is wrong with it, and in what it is wrong. The early alliance of women and hard word lists is then remembered in such Restoration works as the bitterly misogynist and self-parodic *Fop Dictionary: OR, An Alphabetical Catalogue of the Hard and Foreign Names and Terms of the Art Cosmetick, etc. Together with their interpretation, for Instruction of the Unlearned* (London, c. 1680). Designed to display the aberrance of women's vocabulary, *The Fop Dictionary* marks the triumphant emergence of a restrictive standard associated with the linguistic practices of men: the fact that it was written by Mary Evelyn is a reminder of the cultural gymnastics that a woman would now have to perform in order to align herself with the interests and practices of standard English.[41]

Cawdrey's promise to teach his female readers to "better understand many hard English wordes, which they shall heare or read in Scriptures, Sermons, or elsewhere, and also be made to use the same aptly themselves" is reiterated in his offer to teach the "true writing" of such words.[42] But the generosity of this offer requires scrutiny. For while it is true that correct spelling empowers those who know it, Cawdrey's publication of a list of words he says women do not know *creates* the gap it ostensibly tries to bridge—a gap that is in future experienced as a distinction between those who already know how to spell and those who must learn. Thus in 1623, dedicating *The English Dictionarie* to the Earl of Cork, Henry Cockeram is careful to assure the earl that it is "intended only to serve you, not to instruct you." Cockeram's work, which offers to teach "the speedy attaining of an elegant perfection of the English tongue," divides its audience into those whose speech is already elegant and those who will use the text to aspire to be like them. And here the usefulness of the address to women may be the consolation that inheres in the fact that even if she successfully acquires the attributes of class distinction, a woman is still not a man.

The words on Cawdrey's list are certainly "hard" enough, 40 percent of them appearing in only slightly different form in Thomas Thomas's popular Latin-English dictionary, the *Dictionarium Linguae Latinae et Anglicanae* (1588). The *Table Alphabeticall* includes many words for which it is the first English source; and though some (e.g., *agnition* [knowledge], *calliditie* [craftiness], and *obnibulate* [to make dark] enjoyed only a brief and limited currency, others such as *agglutinate, hemisphere,* and *horizon* are still current—a fact that may cast doubt on the attractive suggestion that Cawdrey, Bullokar, and Cockeram willfully coined hard "English" words by anglicizing the lemmas of Latin-English dictionaries.[43] Because of the extraordinary linguistic crisis within which they were composed, it is impossible to recover the precise status of the individual terms that make up the early English hard word lists; but whatever the provenance and status of Cawdrey's "hard words," it is impossible to square his lexicographic practice with his letter "To the reader." There, borrowing heavily from Thomas Wilson's *Art of Rhetorique* (1553), and pointedly refusing to sanction class division as the model for standard English, Cawdrey inveighs against "over fine or curious" speech, the affectation of "strange inkhorne termes," and those who "pouder their talke with over-sea language," and advocates "the plainest and best kind of speech," "such words as are commonlie received," and a "plaine manner": "Do we not speak, because we would have other to understand us? or is not the tongue given for this end, that one might know what another meaneth? Therefore, either wee must make a difference of English, and say, some is learned English, and othersome is rude English, or the one is Court talke, the other is Country-speech, or els we must of necessitie banish all affected Rhetorique, and use altogether one manner of language."[44] Actually, it is the legislation of "one manner of language" that permits not only the distinction of court from country speech, but also the production of a far more intricate range of social differences within a single national language. But what is particularly interesting, because puzzling, about Cawdrey's advice to "banish all affected Rhetorique" is its obviation of the reasons for which the female reader was ostensibly offered the dictionary—that she might understand and use hard English words.[45]

Cawdrey continues his advocacy of a speech that is both uniform and "common" with an appeal to an authority that has become curiously

bifurcated between female and male: "Some men seek so far for outlandish English, that they forget altogether their mothers language, so
that if some of their mothers were alive, they were not able to tell, or
understand what they say, and yet these fine English Clearkes, will say
they speak in their mother tongue; but one might as well charge them,
for counterfeyting the King's English." Reinflecting the passage from
Cicero of which Florio had made recent use, Cawdrey implies that
women, once the guardians of pure and traditional English, have now
lost control, either of their language or of their sons (who speak any
"outlandish" phrase and call it English). Cawdrey recommends recourse to the protection of the monarch when he activates the traditional claim that "the king . . . is lord of this language."[46] Published in
1604, Cawdrey's assertion that English is the *king's* is at least topical, for
the accession of James I had brought to an end a half century of female
rule during which English had been under the nominal aegis of the
queen.[47] Combined with his suggestion that women are no longer fit
guardians of English but are themselves implicated in its elaboration
and corruption, Cawdrey's record of a historical fact speaks also of a
wish that in future English might be secured within the province of
men. His service to women thus involves him in that logic of supple-
mentarity that repeatedly overturns the diachronic account of the role
played by gender in the history of the English lexicon, for at the moment that he asserts the involvement of women with the vernacular,
Cawdrey produces the image of an English from which women have
been and will be excluded.

The second monolingual English dictionary announced itself as *An
English Expositor: Teaching the Interpretation of the Hardest words used in our
Language. With Sundry Explications, Descriptions, and Discourses, by J.B.
Doctor of Physicke* (London: John Legatt, 1616). In two prefatory letters
(which draw both on Florio's representation of a text as an "inknown
infant" seeking godparents, and on his justification of the democratiz-
ing effects of translation), Bullokar represents the publication of his
work, its translation from manuscript to print, as corresponding to a
movement from a private male space to the wider sphere of women.
For as he tells the Viscountess Mountague, its dedicatee:

> Being perswaded (Right Noble Ladie) by some friends, for publike ben-
> efit to make this Collection of words common, which at first was in-
> tended onely for private use, (as written in my youth, at the request of a
> worthy Gentleman, one whose love prevailed much with me) . . . I am
> emboldened to present this little Pamphlet unto your Honour, with hope
> that by your Patronage it shall not only bee protected from injuries, but

also finde favourable entertainment, and perhaps gracefully [be] admitted among greatest Ladies and studious Gentlewomen, to whose reading (I am made beleeve) it will not proove altogether ungratefull.

Representing a circle that is both restricted and common, the company of aristocratic women provides a forum within which the particular combination of humility and arrogance that characterizes Bullokar's publication of his text is recast, allowing him to register his decision to serve a market economy as a decision to serve women—to give them, as he reminds the Viscountess Mountague, something that they will soon find they "want."

Bullokar searched not only for hard, but as he says, "the hardest words used in our language," and he seems to have intended his word list, compiled through years of "observation, reading, study, and charge," as a guide to contemporary vernacular literature. The list is characterized by its ready embrace of the exotic and by its long, anecdotal definitions. It includes, as he says, neologisms from Latin, Greek, Hebrew, and the European vernaculars; "sundry old words now grown out of use," which are marked with an asterisk; "divers termes of art," marked with the field of knowledge to which they belong, such as logic, philosophy, law, medicine, divinity, and astronomy; and the terms of an unnatural natural history, for which Bullokar cites authorities such as Pliny and Avicenna. A shadowy delineation of the dictionary of common use makes its appearance in Bullokar's own description of what his text is not, for in his "Instruction to the Reader" he warns, "If a word bee of different signification, the one easie, the other more difficult, I onely speake of interpretation of the hardest, as in the wordes *Tenne, Girle, Garter*, may appear." According to Bullokar's text a *girle* is a roe buck of two years, while *tenne* and *garter* are terms of heraldry—an anecdote that demonstrates how dictionaries for women provide for the arrogation (and profitable realization) of male knowledge.

The dictionary that followed was published in 1623 (London: Edmund Weaver) with this title page:

The English Dictionarie: or *An Interpreter* of hard English Words. Enabling as well Ladies and Gentlewomen, young Schollers, Clarkes, Merchants, as also Strangers of any Nation, to the understanding of the more difficult Authors already printed in our Language, and the more speedy attaining to an elegant perfection of the English tongue, both in reading, speaking, and writing. Being a Collection of the choicest words contained in the Table Alphabeticall and English Expositor, and of some thousand words never published by any heretofore. By H[enry] C[ockeram] Gent.

Like Bullokar before him, Cockeram is interested to facilitate the reading of "authors already printed in our language," a reminder that English lexicography began, as it has since developed, in tandem with the project of a national literature.[48] Cawdrey's book is divided into three parts. The first is the by now familiar hard word list, comprising "the choicest words themselves now in use, wherin our language is inriched and become so copious, to which words the common sense is annexed." Part 2, however, is a thesaurus where "vulgar" words are glossed by the terms of a "more refined and elegant speech," including "the mocke-wordes which are ridiculously used in our language . . . by too many who study rather to be heard speake, than to understand themselves." Part 3, which continues the humanist practice of providing compilations of adages from which a student could draw to make her style copious, is an encyclopedia of "severall persons, Gods and Goddesses, Giants and Devils, Monsters and Serpents, Birds and Beasts, Rivers, Fishes, Herbs, Stones, Trees and the like," included so that "the diligent learner may not pretend the defect of any helpe which may informe his discourse or practice." Following the earlier suggestion of Cawdrey, Cockeram is here offering a guide to a "speedy attaining of an elegant perfection of the English tongue"—that is, a book of self-help.

The importance that the dictionary was later to assume in patrolling the channels of social mobility is suggested in Cockeram's dedicatory letter to Richard Boyle, Earl of Cork, who was unknown to him. Cockeram justified his dedication with a curious non sequitur: "As I have done my best to accommodate discourse with the choicest language, so I desire that my ambition of being knowne unto your Lordship may not be imputed unto an error of impudence, or an impudence in erring." This can be glossed either as a claim that linguistic decorum may replace other forms of social observance or, more simply, as the statement, "As I am trying hard, so am I not impudent." In either case it functions as a comment on Cockeram's own social ambition, lodging his text within a paradoxical terrain of class difference where to try hard is, precisely, to be impudent.[49]

The English Dictionarie is prefaced by seven poems which are divided over the nature of Cockeram's achievement. John Ford, Bartholomew Hore[?], and John Webster are of the opinion (expressed perhaps with some irony) that Cockeram's text is of value because it adds to the store of "hard" English words. Thus Ford suggests that continental travel will no longer be necessary for gallants seeking "new fashions of complementall phrases"; Webster assures Cockeram that his text will be read "while Words for paiment passe at court"; and Hore underlines the connection between linguistic elaboration and women by associating neologisms with luxury goods as he tells Cockeram's reader, "The *Adage* is far sought, deare bought, please ladies, / You must yield to this Maxime or prove babies."[50] Nicholas Smith, Thomas Spicer, and John Day, however, are prepared to credit Cockeram with having begun the legislation that was to make English not only a "refined" but also a restricted language. Smith attributes to Cockeram's legislative function the future avoidance of "critical disasters"; Spicer congratulates him on having naturalized the neologisms that his work contains; and Day believes that Cockeram has "taught us all good language," reduced "a rude pile / Of barbarous sillables into a stile / Gentle and smooth," and from a "rough speech / taught us all to speake / A perfect language." The seventh and final poem, by John Crugge, is itself divided. Crediting *The English Dictionarie* with having contributed to both the elaboration and the restriction of English, Crugge's poem begins that conflation of the categories "choice" and "common" that determine the later political operations of the English dictionary.

Cockeram's own "Premonition from the Author to the Reader" is characterized by an extraordinary confidence. Acknowledging that the "praise-worthy labours" of others laid the foundation for his own work, he holds that his endeavors may still "bee truly termed rather a necessity . . . than an arrogancie in doing. For . . . what any before me in this kinde have begun, I have not onely fully finished, but thoroughly perfected." Cockeram summarizes his own achievement in terms that demonstrate ambitions beyond the compilation of a hard word list: "I might insist upon the generall use of this worke, especially for Ladies and Gentlewomen, Clarkes, Merchants, young Schollers, Strangers, Travellers, and all such as desire to know the plenty of the English; but I am confident, that experience will be the truest herauld to publish to the world on my behalfe, how my debt to my Countrie is to bee challenged, so my Country shall not altogether boast of any impunity from being indebted to my Studies." Unlike Cawdrey, Cockeram does not pretend that his work was only "gathered for the benefit . . . of Ladies, Gentlewomen, or any other unskilful persons"; indeed, as its function becomes more overtly legislative, the English dictionary displays increasing indifference to those pedagogic needs of women which had been its earliest justification.

The final dictionary in the unbroken chain of works making reference to the needs of women is Thomas Blount's *Glossographia: or, a Dictionary, Interpreting all such Hard Words, Whether Hebrew, Greek, Latin, Italian, Spanish, French, Teutonick, Belgick, British, or Saxon; as are now used in our refined English Tongue. Also the Terms of Divinity, Law, Physick, Mathematics, Heraldry, Anatomy, War, Musick, Architecture; and of several other Arts and Sciences Explicated. With Etymologies, Definitions, and Histor-*

ical Observations on the same. Very useful for all such as desire to understand what they read (London: Thomas Newcomb, 1656). Like *The English Dictionarie*, the *Glossographia* claims for itself a variety of motivations and effects. Blount portrays himself as a plain, representative Englishman who has been "gravelled" in his reading both by an "affected novelty of speech" (of which he disapproves), and by the quantity of foreign and specialist words with which "our best modern Authors . . . have both infinitely enriched and enobled our Language . . . I beleeved myself not singular in this ignorance, and that few, without help of a Dictionary, would be able to understand our ordinary English books." It is this supplemental function that is celebrated in the dictionary's prefatory poem, which asks what is due to Blount for his "industrious observation":

> And re-acquainting our self-stranger *Nation*
> With its disguised self; what's merited
> By rendring our hard *English* Englished;
> What, when our Tongue grew gibbrish, to be then
> National *Interpreter* to Books and Men;
> What ever praise does such deserts attend,
> Know, *Reader,* 'tis thy debt unto my friend.

According to this honorific by J.S. Blount reduced the horrid confusion of English ("our *Tongue,* grown *Labyrinth,* and *Monster* too") to an order correspondent to that of the British nation. Thus, Blount emphasizes the consensus from and for which he speaks; the written works he consulted; "the Enclopeadie of knowledge and concurrence of many learned heads"; and the help of "some very learned and noble my friends" necessary to the completion of his project.

It is interesting, then, that Blount's second and perhaps more overt purpose is the compilation of those terms that it befits a gentleman to know.[51] His ideal reader is the man of leisure whose interests are encyclopedic, shallow, and disinterested; someone who has no need for the detailed knowledge of specialist terms that would suggest an intelligence mired in a particular trade or business. Instead, the *Glossographia* provides

> such and so many of the most useful law terms as I thought necessary for every Gentleman of Estate to understand, not intending anything for the studied Professors of that noble Science . . . as also the names and qualities of at least ordinary Diseases. . . . I held it no less necessary for every Gentleman to be so far seen in Heraldry, as to know (at least) the most usual Terms . . . that he may by consequence be able to least to blazon his own Coat . . . and the terms of many Sciences unfolded; as of Logicke,

Astrology, Geometry, Musick, Architecture, Navigation, etc., with those
of our most ingenious Arts and Exercises, as Printing, Painting, Jewel-
ling, Riding, Hunting, Hawking, etc. . . . I will not say I have met with all
that might require Explication. . . . But I have inserted such as are of
most use, and best worth knowledge.

Encompassing in this "wide survey" that which is now "best worth
knowledge," Blount is frankly catering to "Gentlemen of Estate": men
whose wealth elevates them above the serious details of labor and trade
and makes them fit members of a linguistic as well as a political
franchise.[52] This, however, is a project that may easily represent itself
as having democratic credentials. In Blount's final direction, educated
women, insouciant men, and the ignorant, meet, if not on equal terms,
at least in the same volume with "scholars": "It chiefly intended for the
more-knowing women, and the less-knowing men; or indeed for all
such of the unlearned, who can but finde in an Alphabet, the word
they understand not; yet I think I may modestly say, the best of Schollers may in some part or other be obliged by it." But if Blount's dictionary groups together the members of the nation it serves, producing
an apparent unity out of the disparate interests whose terms it glosses,
this is a grouping that allows old distinctions to be redrawn. By multiplying the available choice among apparently synonymous terms, the
extension and regulation of the lexicon creates opportunities for new
social as well as linguistic discriminations; and an increasingly complicated set of rules for its "correct" use will function to produce exclusion
clauses within the general franchise that the national standard seems
to offer.[53] And finally, the dictionary becomes the ground on which
this new inequality may be staged: for *how* one uses it can now function
as an index of status.

VI

There is, I believe, a third group of rules serving to control discourse. Here, we are no longer dealing with the mastery of the
powers contained within discourse, nor with averting the hazards
of its appearance; it is more a question of determining the conditions under which it may be employed, of imposing a certain number of rules upon those individuals who employ it, thus denying
access to everyone else.
                    —Michel Foucault, "The Discourse on Language"

With the exception of texts such as the parodic *Fop Dictionary* and *The
Lady's Dictionary* (London: John Dunton, 1694), a sort of encyclopedia

for women "in all relations, Companies, conditions and states of life," Blount's *Glossographia* was the last dictionary to mention the needs of women until the publication of J[ohn?] K[ersey?]'s *New English Dictionary* (London, 1702). Announcing itself as a "Compleat Collection Of the Most Proper and Significant Words, Commonly used in the Language," this work marks a watershed in the history of English lexicography since it represents the first attempt to list "all the most proper and significant *English* Words, that are now commonly us'd either in Speech, or in the Familiar way of Writing Letters &c; omitting at the same time such as are obsolete, barbarous, foreign or peculiar to the several Counties of *England;* as also many difficult, abstruse and uncouth Terms of Art." J. K. is aware that "no other book of the same nature, is as yet extant"; though he mentions "a little Tract first set forth by John Bullokar . . . under the title of *An English Expositor*" as one of two works that pretend "to come near our present Design," while in fact "abound[ing] with difficult terms" and containing "few of the genuine and common significant Words of the *English* Tongue" that comprise his own enterprise. For *The New English Dictionary* is a dictionary of "common" use, which offers to "explain such *English* Words as are genuine and used by persons of clear Judgment and good Style."

That such words are chosen on political grounds, as representing the diction already in use among those people who have authority to legislate a desire for its continuance, is indicated by *The New English Dictionary's* description of its intended audience: "The usefulness of this Manual to all Persons not perfectly Masters of the *English* Tongue, and the assistance it gives to young Scholars, Tradesmen, Artificers and others, and particularly, the more ingenious Practitioners of the Female Sex; in attaining to the true manner of Spelling of such Words, as from time to time they have occasion to make use of, will, we hope procure it a favourable Reception." Reinflecting Blount's notion that the audience for a dictionary comprises "the more-knowing women and the less-knowing men," J.K. suggests that women and the unskillful have a weak grasp not of the "hard" but rather of "the genuine Words of their own Mother-tongue." It is telling that at this moment of disjunction, when the lexicographic tradition is adapting itself to a new practical and ideological function, the ignorance of women is reevoked to form the ground on which that function may be justified. It is, however, a strictly vestigial evocation, surviving here only under the pressure of lexicography's new turn. For as English has become coterminous with a "common" national good, the special status of women has been dispersed through the more powerful register of class difference as that now appears on the field of a common language; and here, at last, the English dictionary falls silent on the subject of women.

It is a silence that puzzled James Murray, founding editor of the *Oxford English Dictionary* and the first to remark English lexicography's early appeal to women: "It is noticeable that all these references to the needs of women disappear from the later editions, and are wanting in later dictionaries after 1660; whether this was owing to the fact that the less-knowing women had now come upsides with the more-knowing men, or that with the Restoration, female education went out of fashion, and women sank back again into elegant illiteracy, I leave to the historian to discover." Assuming that the early English dictionary's marked interpellation of a female audience was motivated "largely [by] a consideration of the educational wants of women," Murray interprets its later indifference to women as reflecting either the fulfilment, or the abandonment, of this pedagogical aim.[54] It is important to note, however, that the shift in audience for the English dictionary can be read as a symptom or instance of the larger epistemological shift which Foucault has wrestled to describe.

Localized within the subject of discourse itself, this shift corresponds to a movement away from the "awesome materiality" of language, to a concern with a new "will to verifiable and useful knowledge."[55] The anxiety that once concerned itself with language per se is thus rearticulated as anxiety concerning the division of the social goods generated by its *use*. Although the historical status of language, and in particular the possibility that it once functioned differently, both needs to be asserted and is extraordinarily difficult to ascertain, the appearance of the early English dictionaries can be made to speak of such a shift. For the first page of Cawdrey's *Table Alphabeticall* stages, at least for our criticism, both its own control procedures and the escape of matter from under them, even while it reminds us that lexical regulation was accompanied by and made possible within new standards of typographic and orthographic regularity. For as if to enact the concept they define, the terms *abbreviat* and *abbridge* are bracketed together and glossed by a single explanation "to shorten, or make short," while the lemma *abberation*, "a going a stray, or wandering," appears twice, once near the top and again, out of alphabetical order, at the bottom of the page.

At the place where these two signs enact what they signify, figuring their own figurality, we encounter what seems to be an instance of materiality itself. Especially since within the lexical regime instituted by the dictionary, a regime which must insist on the transparency of the signifier, materiality may show itself as *excess* (as a multiplication that needs to be abridged or curtailed), or again as something that calls attention to itself because it is *out of place*. All language systems are driven both to deny and to reenact their dependence on material (graphic or phonetic) forms; but Cawdrey's wandering lemmas, appearing in a text that will later turn out to have instituted a lexical order that depends, if not on the intangibility, at least on the docility of words, seems to be a particularly obsessional instance of the same. It is, moreover, an instance that asks to be read as representing a particular point in time— that moment in which the materiality of the English lexicon first encountered, and fiercely resisted, the order that was to repress it.

Although such formulations are themselves allegorical—relying on figures that are too obviously figural to invite belief in what, other than themselves, they represent—allegory itself is, after all, nothing more than a missed encounter with that which in another register may be perfectly clear. The development of the dictionary of common use out of lists of hard words may then be understood as the production of one of the culture's most authoritative works from a set of texts that had originally *represented* the problem to which they addressed themselves; the problem that Foucault summarized as the simple fact "that people speak, and that their speech proliferates."[56] But now I hope we can add to this the observation that while in early modern England anxieties concerning the materiality of discourse were articulated through the register of gender, those concerning a will to knowledge were expressed (and expressed later) through the register of class.

N O T E S

Thanks to Andrew Garrett, Stephen Greenblatt, Gwynne Kennedy, Maureen Quilligan, Matthew Rowlinson, Seth Schwartz, and Peter Stallybrass, who all commented on earlier versions of this essay, and to Margreta de Grazia, who read it first and last. The essay is indebted to the work of Derek Attridge, John Barrell, and Patricia Parker in ways that the notes cannot adequately acknowledge.

1. For a description of the fifteenth- and sixteenth-century bilingual lexicographic activity that preceded Cawdrey, see Gertrude Stein, *The English Dictionary before Cawdrey* (Tübingen: Niemeyer, 1986); and Jürgen Schäfer, *Early Modern English Lexicography: A Survey of Monolingual Printed Glossaries and Dictionaries, 1475–1640* (Oxford: Clarendon Press, 1989).

2. For a brilliant and provocative essay on the politics of early lexicography and its present effects, see Allon White, "The Dismal Sacred Word: Academic Language and the Social Reproduction of Seriousness," *LTP: Journal of Literature, Teaching, Politics* 2 (1983), 4–15. Although I concur with White in crediting the early English dictionary with a stern and serious cultural *effect*, I argue that at a local level—the level at which it is addressed to women—its intention is, precisely, less than serious.

3. Tony Crawley cautions that the term "standard language" is itself a precipitate of the problems encountered by nineteenth-century British linguists, for whom a historically validated current norm represented both a solution to

the difficulties of linguistic "description" and permission for the reemergence of prescriptivism within histories of the language; see Tony Crowley, *Standard English and the Politics of Language* (Urbana: University of Illinois Press, 1989), chap. 3. I use the term "standard" to indicate a high-prestige dialect in which a nation's business is conducted, its children are educated, and its literature is ostensibly written: "Standard English" is then at once an idealized norm and a flexible but easily read sign system determining the distribution of real cultural goods. For a comprehensive overview of the social history of the English standard, see Richard Bailey, *Images of English: A Cultural History of the Language* (Ann Arbor: University of Michigan Press, 1991).

4. I am concerned here primarily with the English lexicon, the histories of its orthography, pronunciation, grammar, and handwriting are also entangled—though entangled somewhat differently—in the meshes of gender difference. For an exploration of gender difference in grammar, see Dennis Baron, *Grammar and Gender* (New Haven: Yale University Press, 1986); for a description of a writing hand held "proper" to women, see Jonathan Goldberg, *Writing Matter: From the Hands of the English Renaissance* (Stanford: Stanford University Press, 1990), pp. 137–55.

5. Max Weber, *Essays in Sociology*, trans. and ed. H. H. Gerth and C. Wright Mills (New York: Oxford University Press, 1958), p. 178.

6. The two omissions have been noted by Derek Attridge in *Peculiar Language: Literature as Difference from the Renaissance to James Joyce* (Ithaca: Cornell University Press, 1988), p. 18; and René Balibar in "National Language, Education, Literature" in *Literature Politics and Theory: Papers from the Essex Conference, 1976–84,* ed. Francis Barker et al. (New York: Methuen, 1986), pp. 126–47.

7. Michel Foucault, *Archaeology of Knowledge and the Discourse on Language,* trans. A. M. Sheridan Smith (New York: Pantheon Books, 1972), p. 216.

8. The procedures and the effects of language standardization vary from instance to instance. Formally they depend on whether the standard is derived from a local dialect or from another, superposed language; on the relative developments of the systems of spelling and pronunciation; and on the degree of correspondence between the spoken standard and its written counterpart. For discussion of the different structural configurations according to which standard languages may arise, see William Haas, *Standard Languages, Spoken and Written* (Manchester: Manchester University Press, 1982); James Milroy and Leslie Milroy, *Authority in Language: Investigating Language Prescription and Standardisation* (London: Routledge, 1985); and J. D. Burnley, "Sources of Standardisation in Later Middle English," in *Standardizing English: Essays in the History of Language Change,* ed. Joseph B. Trahern, Jr. (Knoxville: University of Tennessee Press, 1989). The ideals of national unity, racial purity, and cultural elitism that provide the ideological impulses for language standardization are also potentially in conflict. Both the overt and covert politics of standardization may then vary widely, each reflecting, while not coterminous with, the history of the nation-state to which it is bound.

9. Margaret Homans, *Bearing the Word* (Chicago: University of Chicago Press, 1986), p. 10.

10. Ibid., p. 10. See Joel Fineman, " 'The Pas de Calais': Freud, the Transference, and the Sense of Woman's Humor," in *On Puns: The Foundation of Letters,* ed. Jonathan Culler (Oxford: Basil Blackwell, 1988), pp. 100–114. Fineman observes that in psychoanalytic practice transference implies a recursive

repetition that can be transformed into a patient's conscious memory only through the introduction of metaphor: he then remarks that Freud's story of the "pas de Calais," a story told to explain interpretation's purchase on the unconscious, "is a narrative of a metaphor that recounts the master narrative that specifically literary language always tells about its own figurality" (p. 112). Crucially, especially for my purposes, it is a tale that is told, overtly in Freud's version, in the presence of a skeptical woman.

11. For another formulation of this trope, see John Florio, preface to *Worlde of Words, Or most copious and exact dictionarie in Italian and English* (London: Edward Blount, 1598), a work its author chose to consider "masculine": "Some perhaps will except against the sexe, and not allow it for a male broode, sithens as our Italians saie, *Le parole sono femine, & I fatti sono maschy*, Wordes they are women, and deeds they are men. But let such know that *Detti* and *fatti*, wordes and deeds with me are all one gender. And though they were commonly feminine, why might not I by strong imagination (which Physicians give so much power unto) alter their sexe?" Florio, the first English translator of Montaigne, alludes here to his famous essay "Of the Force of the Imagination." Having told the story of a girl whose strenuous jump caused "masculine organs [to come] forth," Montaigne observes, "It is no great wonder, that such accidents doe often happen, for if imagination have power in such things, it is so continually annexed, and so forcibly fastened upon the subject, that lest she [*sic*] should so often fall into the relaps of the same thought, and sharpnesse of desire, it is better one time for all, to incorporate this vile part into wenches." See *The Essays on Morall, Politicke, and Millitarie Discourse of Lord Michaell de Montaigne. First Written by him in French, and now done into English*, 3 vols. (1603; reprint London: J. M. Dent and Sons, 1928), 1:94. For a discussion of this passage and the "one sex" model of human biology it suggests, see Thomas Laqueur, *Making Sex: Body and Gender from the Greeks to Freud* (Cambridge: Harvard University Press, 1990), pp. 126–30. Johnson knew Florio's *Montaigne*, and may be citing it here; his refusal to sustain its playful suggestion that the two sexes are versions of each other may reinforce Laqueur's claim that human sexual nature was reconceptualized during the eighteenth century to accommodate the proposal that the two sexes were incommensurable (p. 5). For a brief discussion of other Renaissance instances of the trope "Women are words, men deeds," see Patricia Parker, *Literary Fat Ladies: Rhetoric, Gender, Property* (London: Methuen, 1987), pp. 22–23, and her essay "On the Tongue: Cross-Gendering, Effeminacy, and the Art of Words," *Style* 23 (1989), 445–65.

12. *The World* (Dublin, 1756), 2:250. Chesterfield continued: "Toleration, adoption, and naturalization have run their lengths. Good order and authority are now necessary. But where shall we find them, and, at the same time, the obedience due to them? We must have recourse to the old Roman expedient in times of confusion, and choose a dictator. Upon this principle, I give my vote for Mr. Johnson to fill that great and arduous post. And I hereby declare, that I make a total surrender of all my rights and privileges in the English language, as a free-born British subject to the said Mr. Johnson during the term of his dictatorship." *The World*, p. 252.

13. Ibid., pp. 256, 258, 255. Chesterfield's sarcastic admiration for women's failure to comply with the rules of written English was anticipated, for example, by Richard Steele, who represents himself as having interrupted a friend in her reading, and easily determined the sex of her correspondent: "I found by some peculiar Modes in Spelling, and a certain Negligence in Grammar,

that it was a female sonnet." Richard Steele, *The Guardian*, March 28, 1713, quoted in Susie I. Tucker, *English Examined* (Cambridge: Cambridge University Press, 1961), p. 69.

14. *The World*, pp. 259, 260. Chesterfield's metaphor of "the pale," one that is extremely common in discussions of the English lexicon, was extant in the eighteenth century largely in the context of the English attempt to "settle" Ireland. It is one instance of a regularly evoked analogy between the lexicographic practice and the internal politics of colonial Britain. For other examples, see Chesterfield's claim that he has "rights and privileges in the English language as a free-born British subject" (see note 12); and Johnson's famous admonition in his *Preface to the Dictionary* (1755): "Tongues, like governments, have a natural tendency to degeneration; we have long preserved our constitution, let us make some struggles for our language." *Johnson's Dictionary: A Modern Selection*, ed. E. L. McAdam, Jr., and George Milne (New York: Pantheon, 1963), p. 27. Chesterfield's claim that "toleration" will eventually bring women "within the pale" of standard English may appear to have some descriptive power, for within the history of the English dictionary female difference is first "specially" catered to and then assimilated, disappearing from the field of serious lexicography by the beginning of the eighteenth century, so that Chesterfield's evocation of it here is, officially at least, a joke. That this assimilation is not tied in any serious way to the real position of women should remind us that, although as an arena within which social discriminations are enforced, language serves as a particularly powerful metaphor for social organization, to assert a *necessary* connection between the linguistic and the political spheres is always to be arguing from within the very heart of national politics.

15. Chesterfield's joke—the introduction of the serious, laboring Johnson to a circle of frivolous women who would value him inappropriately—has been regularly reproduced. Thus "a Johnson's Dictionary" is the leaving present given to each girl on her graduation from Miss Pinkerton's Academy in Thackeray's *Vanity Fair* (1847–48): "On the cover was inserted a copy of 'Lines addressed to a young lady on quitting Miss Pinkerton's school, at the Mall; by the late Revered Dr Samuel Johnson.' In fact the lexicographer's name was always on the lips of this majestic woman, and a visit he had paid to her was the cause of her reputation and fortune." William Thackeray, *Vanity Fair* (London: Dent, 1979), p. 7. Ironically, Miss Pinkerton's model pupil Amelia writes in an attractively slipshod way: "Her letters *were* full of repetition. She wrote rather doubtful grammar sometimes, and in her verses took all sorts of liberties with the metre" (p. 110), whereas Becky Sharp is able to write letters in her husband's name which betray her hand only because they are too well composed to be his (and this in spite of the fact that she throws away her dictionary at Miss Pinkerton's gates). The incongruity of Johnson's presence in a school for girls thus depends on and underlines what Thackeray holds to be the incommensurableness of true femininity with a mastery of standard English. The joke reappears in Elizabeth Gaskell's *Cranford* (1853); (reprint London: Oxford University Press, 1979), where it again structures the difference between two women, for whereas Miss Matty Jenkyns confirms her shy good nature in letters characterized by "bad spelling" (p. 13), her sister Miss Jenkyns, who wears a cravat and holds women the superiors of men, has formed her own "rolling three-piled sentence" on Johnson's letters, and continues to insist that they are "a model for young beginners" (p. 19). The covert assumption that at some level women should not, after all, speak standard English doubtless structures re-

cent perceptions among sociolinguists that women have a tendency to "hyper-correct." It can also be traced in the work of Luce Irigaray, where "the language of men" is opposed to a female speech (or mother tongue) that resists the tyranny of the "proper." Her formulation thus reproduces—without his simple irony—that of Lord Chesterfield. See Luce Irigaray, "The Language of Men," *Cultural Critique* 13 (1989), 191–202. See also W.H. Craig, *Dr Johnson and the Fair Sex* (London: Sampson, Low, Marston, and Co., 1895): "Johnson was petted and fondled and flattered by the women of his time to an extent that probably mortal man never was before or since. . . . He would forgo classics, criticism, philosophy, *belles-lettres*, to talk of caps and manteaux and other female gear with the gentle creatures to whom they were the main business of life" (pp. 2–8).

16. For a description of this process of exhibition followed by exclusion, and a brief discussion of its functioning in the linguistic community of early modern England, see Steven Mullaney, *The Place of the Stage: License, Play, and Power in Renaissance England* (Chicago: University of Chicago Press, 1988), chap. 2. Patricia Parker has already suggested that "the dilation and control of a copiousness figured as female might be seen as the gendered counterpart" of this process of containment through rehearsal (*Literary Fat Ladies*, p. 31).

17. See John Earl Joseph, *Eloquence and Power: The Rise of Language Standards and Standard Languages* (London: Frances Pinter, 1987), pp. 58–60; for a more detailed discussion of the creation of Chancery English and its status as a written standard, see Burnley, "Sources of Standardisation," pp. 23–41; C. Paul Christiansen, "Chancery Standards and the Records of Old London Bridge," in Trahern, *Standardizing English*, pp. 82–112; and John H. Fisher's seminal essay, "Chancery and the Emergence of Standard Written English in the Fifteenth Century," *Speculum* 52 (1977), 870–99.

18. See, however, George Puttenham's brief essay "Of Language" (1589), which has become the locus classicus of English discussions concerning the "best" Renaissance vernacular. Recommending "the usuall speach of the Court, and that of London with 1x myles," and advising the poet to avoid the speech both of "poore rusticall or uncivill people" and of those of the "inferiour sort" who dwell in cities, Puttenham positioned standard English against those intersecting grids of class and region to which it is still tied: I am suggesting only that this positioning was not always as inevitable as it has since appeared to be. George Puttenham, *The Arte of English Poesie* (Kent, Ohio: Kent State University Press, *1970*), pp. 156–57; all subsequent references are to this edition, a facsimile reproduction of the 1906 reprint, edited by Edward Arber.

19. Joseph, *Eloquence and Power*, p. 45–56.

20. Joseph thus connects elaboration and restriction in a diachronic sequence, with restriction following and responding to elaboration. A different, synchronic model for standardization could also be evoked, one in which regulation *produced* elaboration, and in so doing produced itself. For a brief description of the attempt to institute grammatical control of linguistic "abundance" in early modern England which relies on this synchronic model, see Parker, *Literary Fat Ladies*, p. 114. My account relies on both models since I hold first, that English as it standardized produced and thrived on the threat that women and the principles of linguistic elaboration could be assumed to pose to it; and second, that there was a brief moment in the early modern period when English was felt to be—and therefore for some purposes was—beyond the pale of the newly born impulse toward grammatical and lexical regulation.

21. See, for example, Richard Carew, who compares the new English word stock to a healthy mercantilist economy: "For our owne partes, we imploye the borrowed ware soe far to our advantage that we raise a profit of new woordes from the same stock which yeat in their owne countrey are not merchantable," in "The Excellence of the English Tongue," in William Camden *Remaines of a Greater Worke, Concerning Britaine*, 2d ed. (London, 1614). For the source of "moe things," see n. 23.

22. See, for example, John Hoskyns, *Directions for Speech and Style* (1599), in Louise Brown Osborn, *The Life, Letters, and Writings of John Hoskyns, 1566–1638* (New Haven: Yale University Press, 1937), pp. 103–66, which advertised itself as containing "all the Figures of Rhetorick and the Art of the Best English, ex-empyfyed . . . out of *Arcadia*"; and Dennis Kay's comment on Sidney's impor-tance: "Sidney . . . appears to have created the taste by which he was enjoyed. . . . His works were taken to exemplify aesthetic excellence much as the greatest foreign or ancient texts had traditionally been held to do." *Sir Philip Sidney: An Anthology of Modern Criticism*, ed. Dennis Kay (Oxford: Clar-endon, 1987), pp. 3–41. For a famous, and belated, assertion of the adequacy of Elizabethan English—one that has doubtless influenced subsequent histo-ries of the language—see Johnson's *Preface:* "I have fixed Sidney's work for the boundary beyond which I make few excursions. From the authors which rose in the time of Elizabeth, a speech might be formed adequate to all the purposes of use and elegance. If the language of theology were extracted from Hooker and the translation of the Bible; the terms of natural knowledge from Bacon; the phrases of policy, war, and navigation from Raleigh; and the diction of common life from Shakespeare, few ideas would be lost to mankind for want of English words in which they might be expressed" (pp. 18–19).

23. This description is largely a summary of Richard Foster Jones, *The Tri-umph of the English Language: A Survey of Opinions Concerning the Vernacular from the Introduction of Printing to the Restoration* (Stanford: Stanford University Press, 1953). For an example of sixteenth-century distrust of English, see Roger As-cham's *Toxophilus* (London, 1545): "And as for the Latin or Greke tongue, ev-erything is so excellently done in them that none can do better: In the English tongue, contrary, every thinge in a manner so meanly, both for the matter and handelynge that no man can do worse," quoted in Jones, *Triumph*, p. 14. For the anxiety that there are "moe things, than there are words to expresse things by," see Ralph Lever, *The Art of Reason* (London, 1573), quoted in Jones, *Tri-umph*, p. 126; for witness that the vocabulary is being expanded, see John Hors-fal, *The Preacher, or Methode of Preachinge, written in Latin by Nicholas Heminge* (London, 1574), quoted in Jones, *Triumph*, p. 74: "The example of other wise and learned men (who before me have brought into our tongue the artes of Grammar, Logicke, Rhetoricke, Astronomie, Geographie, etc.) did not a little encourage and embolden me"; and for Sidney's opinion of the unruled ver-nacular, see Jones, *Triumph*, p. 198. On the standardizing effect of "poets," see Thomas Nashe (1592): "They have cleansed our language from barbarisme and made the vulgar sort here in *London* (which is the fountaine whose rivers flow round about *England*) to aspire to a richer puritie of speach, than is com-municated with the Comminaltie of any Nation under heaven," in *The Works of Thomas Nashe*, ed. Ronald B. McKerrow and F. P. Wilson (Oxford: Basil Black-well, 1966), 1:193; and for the claim that the newly elaborated English lacked regulation, see Edmund Waller: "We write in sand, our language grows / And like the tide, our work o'erflows," quoted in Bailey, *Images of English*, p. 55.

24. Richard Mulcaster, *Firste Part of the Elementarie* (London, 1582), p. 187. For a brilliant discussion of Mulcaster's attempt to invest "right" writing with some kind of originary status, see Goldberg, *Writing Matter*, pp. 15–55.

25. Samuel Daniel, *The Defence of Rime*, quoted in part in Jones, *Triumph*, p. 203.

26. See Samuel Johnson, *Lives of the Poets* (London, 1779), 3, 16, 1: "In absolute governments there is, sometimes, a general reverence paid to all that has the sanction of power, and the countenance of greatness. How little this is the state of our country needs not to be told. We live in an age in which it is a kind of publick sport to refuse all respect that cannot be enforced. The edicts of an English academy would, probably, be read by many, only that they might be sure to disobey them." In *The Quarterly Review* 109 (January and April 1861), 355, Henry Morley, developing Johnson's suggestion that the English had come to consider linguistic legislation an infringement of their political rights, described the English lexicon's contempt for containment in terms of a simple equation between gender and national politics: "French refinements tended to a tight-lacing of the language in a dictionary carefully designed as stays, which are to this day supposed to give it a fine figure and material support. Broad-chested English has allowed its lungs free-play, and will be strapped up in the leather coverings of no man's dictionary." In 1582, the year in which Mulcaster published *The Elementarie*, the Italian Academia della Crusca was established; the Académie Française was founded in 1635. For an account of the founding of the Acadèmie Française, and its role in both the centralization of the French arts and the production of the certain *je ne sais quoi* used to characterize the official "genius" of the French writer, see Timothy Murray, "The Académie Française," in *A New History of French Literature*, ed. Denis Hollier (Cambridge: Harvard University Press, 1989), pp. 267–73. For an example of the *desire* for an authoritarian ratification of English, see George Snell, *The Right Teaching of Useful Knowledge* (London, 1649), quoted in Jones, *Triumph*, p. 296. Snell called for education in the vernacular, a grammar, and a dictionary of words "in use among the English" to be secured by an act of Parliament or royal edict "Everie word henceforth to be used, by any native of *England*, contrariant to the edict for the English language, [will] bee adjudged and condemned for non-English, barbarous, non-significant, and of none effect, and void to all intent and purpose" (p. 296).

27. Sir John Cheke, letter to Sir Thomas Hoby, July 24, 1557; quoted in Jones, *Triumph* p. 102. See also the conclusion of John Bullokar's prefatory letter to his *An English Expositor* (London, 1616; rpt. Menston, Yorkshire: Scolar Press, 1967): "But as for you (judiciall or courteous reader) whose favour I desire, and whose counsell or friendly correction I will not refuse, if to you (I say) any thing herein shall occurre, which seemeth by me omitted, mistaken, or not fully satisfactory to your expectation . . . I promise that upon warning hereof given to me or the Printer, at a second Impression it shall be amended " (p. A4). This could be argued to be an instance of the characteristic defensiveness of the Jacobean writer going to press. But see also the entry for *crampe* in Richard Huloet's English-Latin dictionary, the *Abecedarium Anglo-Latinum* (London, 1552): "a defecte of the synnowes and muscles, wherby somtyme the whole bodye, and sometyme parte therof is stretched, if it be in parte of the bodye, then it is Englyshed, crampe: if it be in the entier body (which is rare) the name therof in our mother tongue is not known. Conuultio, onis, Spasmus. . . . Some learned man maye Englyshe it."

28. For the use of a female audience as pretext for the explanation of a rule that is otherwise alleged to be common practice, see Puttenham's description of the figure of "Parenthesis or the Insertour": "The figure is so common that it needeth none example, neverthelesse because we are to teache Ladies and Gentlewomen to know their schoole points and termes appertaining to the Art, we may not refuse to yeeld examples even in the plainest cases." Puttenham, *Arte of English Poesie*, p. 180.

29. See, in this context, Patricia Parker's description of Wilson's *Rule of Reason* as being characterized by "a contradiction within the conception of order itself: that it is both legitimated as a representation of something existing and "natural," and, in the anxious as well as the more confident passages of such texts, presented as a form of construction, one that institutes rather than simply reflects." Parker, *Literary Fat Ladies*, p. 118. I am arguing that early English lexicographic texts disguise this contradiction by relating it to the simple "fact" that men and women have different pedagogical needs.

30. The mutual involvement of *The English Dictionarie* and *An English Expositor* provides another example of the interrelatedness of lexicographic texts. The first edition of *The English Dictionarie* (1623) contained extensive borrowings from *An English Expositor* (1616), and later editions of the *Expositor* borrowed in turn from the *Dictionarie*. The last edition of the *Dictionarie* (1670) then took over the new features and the old name of its rival, announcing itself as "The English Dictionary; or an EXPOSITOR of Hard English Words." For an account of the interrelatedness of these and the other early English dictionaries, see the seminal work on early English lexicography, De Witt T. Starnes and Gertrude Noyes, *The English Dictionary from Cawdrey to Johnson, 1604–1755* (Chapel Hill: University of North Carolina Press, 1946).

31. "When I hear my wife's mother Laelia—since it is easier for women to keep the old pronunciation unspoiled, as they do not converse with a number of people and so always retain the accents they heard first—well, I listen to her with the feeling that I am listening to Plautus or Naevius: the actual sound of her voice is so unaffected and natural, that she seems to introduce no trace of display or affectation; and I consequently infer that that was how her father and her ancestors used to speak." Cicero, *De oratore*, trans. H. Rackham (Cambridge: Loeb Classical Library, 1982), p. 37. Of course, even in the sixteenth century not everyone agreed that the purest form of English was that spoken by women. See, for example, Thomas Elyot, who proposed that young men of rank should be exposed only to Latin "or at the leste way that they speake none Englisshe but that whiche is cleane polite perfectly and articulately pronounced omittinge no lettre or sillable as folisshe women often times do of a wantonness wherby diverse noble men and gentilmennes chyldren (as I do at this daye knowe) have attained corrupte and foule pronunciation." Thomas Elyot, *The Boke Named the Gouvernour* (1531), quoted in Bailey, *Images of English*, pp. 35, 252.

32. See Leeds Barroll, "The Court of the First Stuart Queen," in *The Mental World of the Jacobean Court*, ed. Linda Levy Peck (Cambridge: Cambridge University Press, 1992), pp. 191–208.

33. The dictionary was reissued as *Queen Anna's World of Words* (London: Edward Blount, 1611). Florio's attitude to his female readers may be usefully compared with that of Montaigne, which is in considerably less good faith: "It vexeth me, that my Essayes serve Ladies in lieu of common ware and stuff for their hall: this Chap. wil preferre me to their cabinet: I love their society somewhat private; their publicke familiarity wants favor and savor" (*Essays of Montaigne*, 3:70).

34. Again, though, it is impossible to know whether women were granted access to English texts because of their derogated status or whether women's engagement with the vernacular was used to *produce* the inadequacy of English.

35. Walter J. Ong, S.J., "Latin Language Study as a Renaissance Puberty Rite," in *Rhetoric, Romance, and Technology* (Ithaca: Cornell University Press, 1971). Ong's investigation begins with his observation that in early modern England, Latin enjoyed a currency and prestige far in excess of its function. Actually, the authority exercised by a prestige dialect is always in excess of that which can be explained by its ostensible linguistic and social functions; but puberty rites, which function to produce the adult male within a particular group, are a good example of that apportionment of cultural capital which operates behind the scene of linguistic hierarchies to produce such apparent overvaluations. For an illustration of the pedagogical production of this diversion between Latin and English, male and female, see Will Page's Latin lesson in *The Merry Wives of Windsor* 4.1., a scene that is discussed in Parker, *Literary Fat Ladies*, p. 27.

36. The quotation is from E.K.'s letter to Gabriel Harvey in commendation of "the new Poete" which stands as preface to Spenser's *Shepheardes Calender* (London: Hugh Singleton, 1579). This letter, which was probably written by Harvey himself, praises Spenser for his commitment to the vernacular, and in particular for his having "laboured to restore, as to theyr rightfull heritage, such good and naturall English words, as have been long time out of use and almost clear disinherited." *The Shorter Poems of Edmund Spenser*, ed. William A. Oram et al. (New Haven: Yale University Press, 1989), p. 16. Harvey is obviously aligned here with those who invest their cultural ambitions in the vernacular and are prepared to mobilize, rather than deny, its ostensibly domestic origin.

37. Thus, in 1589, when writing the first appraisal of English vernacular poetry, George Puttenham became suddenly and significantly anxious about his commitment to rhetorical ornament. His solution was to claim somewhat belatedly that while ornament is "not unnecessarie to all such as be willing themselves to become good makers in the vulgar, or to be able to judge of other men's makings . . . our chiefe purpose herein is for the learning of Ladies and young Gentlewomen, or idle Courtiers, desirous to become skilful in their owne mother tongue, and for their private recreation to make now and then ditties of pleasure" (Puttenham, *Arte of English Poesie*, pp. 170–71). Compare Montaigne's 1580 essay "Of the Vanitie of Words," in which Montaigne dissociates himself from at least the terms of rhetoric with the improbable claim that they pertain to the conversation of women: "Doe but heare one pronounce *Metonymia, Metaphore, Allegory, Etimologie*, and other such trash names of Grammar, would you not thinke, they meant some forme of a rare and strange language; they are titles and words that concern your chamber-maids Tittle-Tattle" (*Essays of* Montaigne, 1:348).

38. On gossip, see Samuel Rowlands, *Tis Merry When Gossips Greet* (London: W.W., 1602), a work Rowlands describes as a female supplement to *The Canterbury Tales;* and the Clown's description of "tittle-tattling . . . among maids" in *The Winter's Tale* (4.4.). For old wives' tales, see John Aubrey's nostalgic remark in *Miscellanies* (1696): "When I was a child, the fashion was for old women and maids to tell fabulous stories nighttimes of sprights and walking ghosts. This was derived down from mother to daughter." On the vogue for euphuism and its reputation as a woman's dialect, see the printer's preface to John Lyly's *Six Court Comedies* (London: Edward Blount, 1623).

39. The assertion of the masculine qualities of the vernacular was aided by the discovery of and insistence on the Teutonic origins of English, which was the product of the antiquarian movement of the early years of James I's reign. See Jones, *Triumph*, pp. 214–71; Bailey, *Images of English*, pp. 37–57.

40. It is this meaning that is employed by Thomas Blount in *Glossographia* when he glosses the word "embargo" as "an usual word among our Merchants, when their ships or Merchandizes are arrested." But for a reading of Cawdrey that understands his term "usual" to mean "common," see Gertrude E. Noyes, "The First Dictionary: Cawdrey's *Table Alphabeticall*," *Modern Language Notes* 63 (1948), 600–605. See also Derek Attridge's comment on Puttenham's claim that the language spoken in the environs of London was "naturall, pure, and the most usuall of all his countrey" (Puttenham, *Arte of English Poesie*, p. 34). Attridge comments, " 'Usual,' which is clearly nonsense in statistical terms, suggests that Puttenham is able to assimilate the notion of universality to a politically less troublesome notion of cultural superiority" (p. 34). For other examples of association between women and linguistic elaboration, see Puttenham, *Arte of English Poesie*, pp. 166–67; and Humphrey Moseley, *The Academy of Compliments, Wherein Ladyes Gentlewomen, Schollers, and Strangers may accomodate their courtly practice with most Curious Ceremonies, Complementall, Amorous, High Expressions, and forms of speaking and writing. With the Additions of witty Amorous Poems. And a* TABLE *expounding that hard* ENGLISH *words* (London: T. Badger, 1639). A brilliant and extended exploration of the phenomenon can be found in Parker, *Literary Fat Ladies*, pp. 8–35.

41. *The Fop Dictionary* appeared as an appendix to a pamphlet whose full title runs *Mundus Muliebris: or the ladies' dressing-room unlock'd and her toilette spread. Together with the fop-dictionarie compiled for the use of the fair sex*, 2d ed. (London: Richard Bentley, 1690). Mary was the daughter of the diarist John Evelyn. When she died in 1685, her bereaved father attributed the pamphlet to her in his diary, noting that "she could not indure that which they call courtship, among the Gallants," and herself "writ not onely most correct orthography, but with that maturitie of judgement, and exactnesse of the periods, choice expressions, and familiarity of style, that some letters of hers have astonish'd me." *The Diary of John Evelyn*, ed. John Bowle (Oxford: Oxford University Press, 1985), pp. 324–25.

42. Much of Cawdrey's prefatory material, including this promise, is taken almost verbatim from Edmund Coote's *English Schoole-maister*, which the author claimed would teach "a direct course, how any unskilful person may easily both understand any hard English words, which they shal in Scriptures, Sermons, or elsewhere heare or reade: and also be made able to use the same aptly themselves." To this end, Coote "set downe a Table contayning and teaching the true writing and understanding of any hard English word, borrowed from the Greek, Latin, or French"; quoted in Starnes and Noyes, *The English Dictionary*, p. 14.

43. The suggestion was first made by Starnes and Noyes when they discovered the extensive debt that Cawdrey, Bullokar, Cockeram, and Blount owed to Thomas, to Cooper's *Thesaurus Linguae Romanae et Britannicae*, and to John Rider's *Bibliotheca Scholastica* (1589). See Starnes and Noyes, *The English Dictionary*, pp. 13–47. A second explanation for the presence of scarcely naturalized Latin words in the early English dictionary is that even as it yielded its prestige functions to English, Latin remained a powerful source and companion for the standardizing tongue, so that compilers of the hard word lists turned to the

Latin lexicon to check the definitions of words that were, as they claimed, newly current in English (on this see Schäfer, *Early Modern English Lexicography*, p. 2). But the assertion of Thomas Blount that he was citing contemporary authorities for the use of words "that I might not be thought to be the innovator of them" (*Glossographia* [1656]) suggests that the early hard word lists encountered contemporary accusations that they had been willfully padded. See also the elaborated accusation of Elisha Coles in J.K.'s introduction to the *New English Dictionary* (London: Henry Bonwicke, 1702): "In his elaborate Work [he has] inserted several Words purely Latin, without any alteration, as *Dimidietas* for a half; *Sufflamen*, for a Trigger, and some hundreds only vary'd with an *English* Termination, which are scarce ever us'd by any." There is, then, some evidence that the earliest English lexicographers taught as "hard English" words terms they had themselves newly coined out of Latin.

44. For a discussion of another occurrence of the contradictory injunction that women speak both naturally and in a refined and elegant manner, see Ann Rosalind Jones, "Nets and Bridles: Early Modern Conduct Books and Sixteenth-Century Women's Lyrics," in *The Ideology of Conduct: Essays in Literature and the History of Sexuality*, ed. Nancy Armstrong and Leonard Tennenhouse (New York: Methuen, 1987), pp. 42–48.

45. The apparent inconsistencies in Cawdrey's lexicographic theory result in part from his heavy dependence on Cicero's *De oratore*. For Cicero's speaker is able to assume that the orator is in full possession of a correct and adequate Latin "imparted in education by boyhood and fostered by a more intensive and systematic study of literature, or else by the habit of daily conversation in the family circle, and confirmed by books and by reading the old orators and poets" (3.48.) It is precisely this confidence—and the insouciance possessed by the practitioners of a "standard"—that eludes Cawdrey, who is involved in the task of insisting on those qualifications for English.

46. As first recorded in the preface to Chaucer's *Treatise on the Astrolabe* (1391), a work on astronomy compiled and translated from Latin into "light Englissh" for Chaucer's son Lewis. See *The Complete Works of Geoffrey Chaucer*, ed. F. N. Robinson (Oxford: Oxford University Press, 1957), p. 546.

47. See, for example, Thomas Nashe's invective against Gabriel Harvey (1592): "It is not enough that he bepist his credite, about twelve yeeres ago, with *Three proper and wittie familiar letters*, but he must still be running on the *letter*, and abusing the Queenes English without pittie or mercy" (Nashe, *Works*, 1:261).

48. See Jones, *Triumph:* "Literature was considered instrumental to language, not language to literature. Writers are more frequently praised for what they have done for the medium of their expression than for the intrinsic view of their compositions" (p. 183). For an illuminating discussion of the concomitant development of the disciplines of English and the specific type of historical linguistics that informed preparation of the *Oxford English Dictionary*, see Crowley, *Standard English:* "In a precise sense, literature had to come before the language since without written records there could be no history of the language" (p. 120). The citation of authorities to validate the definition of a word did not originate with Cockeram, for Latin glosses had regularly adduced verses or sentences from reputable authors; see Stein, *The English Dictionary*, p. 129.

49. See, for example, H. C. Wyld, who coined the term Received Standard English: "It is characteristic of R[eceived] S[tandard] that it is easy, unstudied,

and natural. The 'best' speakers do not need to take thought for their utterance; they have no theories as to how their native tongue should be pronounced, nor do they reflect upon the sounds they utter. They have perfect confidence in themselves, in their speech, and in their manners. For both bearing and utterance spring from a firm and gracious tradition. 'Their fathers told them'—that suffices." H. C. Wyld, "The Best English: A Claim for the Superiority of Received Standard English" *SPE*, tract 34 (1934), 603–17, 605; quoted in part in Bailey, *Images of English*, p. 8.

50. For other examples of this proverb, see Barnaby Rich, *Faultes, faults, and Nothing else but Faults* (London, 1606): "Farre fet, and deare bought (they say) is fit for Ladies" (p. 28); and Puttenham's example of the figure of metalepsis: "As when we had rather fetch a word a great way off then use one nearer at hand to expresse the matter aswel and plainer. And it seemeth the deviser of this figure, had a desire to please women rather than men: for we use to say by manner of Proverbe: things farrefet and deare bought are good for Ladies" (Puttenham, *Arte of English Poesie*, p. 193). Joseph Swetnam, in *The Arraignment of Lewd, Idle, Froward, and Unconstant Women* (London: Thomas Archer, 1615), draws a further labored connection between female speech and the consumption of delicacies: "There is no women but either she hath a long tongue, or a longing tooth, and they are two ill-neighbours, if they dwell together, for the one will lighten thy purse, if it be still pleased, and the other will waken thee from thy sleep, if it be not charmed." The association of women, neologisms, and an irresponsible taste for luxury goods is regularly evoked during Britain's early definition of its national, linguistic, and economic identities.

51. For a discussion of Blount's inclusion of heraldic terms, and his decision to include, for the first time in the English dictionary, illustrations of those terms, see Michael Hancher, "Bailey and After: Illustrating Meaning," *Word and Image* 8 (Spring 1992), 1–17. Hancher remarks that "it is ironic but not surprising that visual imagery, accommodating the attention of the less literate reader, should encode the ideological interests of a more privileged class" (p. 8).

52. The phrase "wide survey" is from John Barrell's brilliant essay "The Language Properly So-Called: The Authority of Common Usage," in *English Literature in History, 1730–1780: An Equal Wide Survey* (New York: St. Martin's, 1983), pp. 110–75. I am deeply indebted to Barrell's description of the way in which the differentiation of types of knowledge and ways of possessing it was made to reflect class difference in eighteenth-century Britain; I have also profited from his description of how lexical or grammatical regulation confirmed the divisions it pretended to heal: "How the authority of the gentlemen, and of the ruling class, was re-enforced at the level of language; how, that is, a 'correct' English was defined in such a way as to represent it as the natural possession of the gentleman, and to confirm that possession, too, as a source of his political authority" (50).

53. See Raymond Williams's definition of standard English in *Keywords* (New York: Oxford University Press, 1983): "In the mid C19 there arose the curious case of *Standard English*: a selected (class based) use taken as an authoritative example of correctness, which, widely backed by educational institutions, attempted to convict a majority of native speakers of English of speaking their own language 'incorrectly' " (pp. 296–97). Quoted by Bailey, *Images of English*, who notes that "far from a nineteenth-century image, *standard* was applied to prestige varieties of a language as early as 1711, and then the term merely codified a notion already old" (p. 3).

54. James Murray, *The Evolution of English Lexicography* (Oxford: Clarendon Press, 1900), p. 32. Suzanne Hull followed Murray both in noticing that the early English dictionary is addressed to women and in attributing this fact to some real "want" on their part: "Little attention has been given to the fact that these earliest English dictionaries . . . were actually published with women's needs in mind." Suzanne Hull, *Chaste, Silent, and Obedient: English Books for Women, 1450–1640* (San Marino, Calif.: Huntington Library, 1982), p. 64.

55. See Foucault, "The Discourse on Language," p. 216.

56. Ibid., p. 216.

Notes on Contributors

JOHN MICHAEL ARCHER is Associate Professor of English and Comparative Literature at Columbia University. He has written *Sovereignty and Intelligence: Spying and Court Culture in the English Renaissance* (1993).

LYNDA E. BOOSE is Associate Professor of English at Dartmouth College. She is co-editor of *Daughters and Fathers* (1989) and has published on such topics as Shakespeare's daughter-father relations; the politics of Shakespearean criticism; the (unrepresentable) black woman's challenge to patriarchy in early modern English discourse; and shrew-taming, enclosure, and "good-husbandry."

RICHARD BURT is Associate Professor of English at the University of Massachusetts, Amherst. He is the author of *Licensed by Authority: Ben Jonson and the Discourse of Censorship* (Cornell University Press, 1993) and editor of *The Administration of Aesthetics: Censorship, Political Criticism, and the Public Sphere* (forthcoming from the University of Minnesota Press).

WILLIAM C. CARROLL is Professor of English at Boston University. He is the author of *The Great Feast of Language in "Love's Labour's Lost"* and *The Metamorphoses of Shakespearean Comedy* (1985). His essay in this volume is part of a book-in-progress on vagrancy and marginality in early modern England.

THOMAS CARTELLI is Associate Professor of English and Chair of the English Department and Humanities Division of Muhlenberg College. He is the author most recently of *Marlowe, Shakespeare, and the Economy of Theatrical Experience* (1991). The present essay forms part of a book-in-progress titled "Producing Disorder: The Construction of Social Conflict in Early Modern England."

JONATHAN CREWE teaches Renaissance literature and critical theory at Dartmouth College, where he is Professor of English. In addition to numerous articles, he has written *Unredeemed Rhetoric: Thomas Nashe and the Scandal of Authorship* (1982), *Hidden Designs: The Critical Profession and Renaissance Literature* (1986), and *Trials of Authorship: Anterior Forms and Poetic Reconstruction from Wyatt to Shakespeare* (1989).

JULIET FLEMING is Assistant Professor at the University of Southern California. She is completing a book titled *Ladies' Men, the Ladies Text, and the English Renaissance* (forthcoming from Routledge).

JUDITH HABER is Assistant Professor of English at Tufts University. She is the author of *Pastoral and the Poetics of Self-Contradiction,* a study of Renaissance and classical pastoral (forthcoming from Cambridge University Press).

JONATHAN GIL HARRIS is Assistant Professor of English at Ithaca College. He has written articles on Marlowe and Shakespeare and is currently finishing his book "The Incontinent Body Politic: Containment and the Limits of Organic Metaphor in Early Modern England."

CRISTINA MALCOLMSON is an Assistant Professor at Bates College in Lewiston, Maine. Her published articles on gender and society include " 'What You Will': Social Mobility and Gender in *Twelfth Night,*" in *The Matter of Difference,* ed. Valerie Wayne (Cornell University Press, 1991), and " 'As Tame as the Ladies': Politics and Gender in *The Changeling,*" *English Literary Renaissance* (Winter 1990). She is completing a book on George Herbert and vocation.

PHYLLIS RACKIN is Professor of English in General Honors at the University of Pennsylvania and President of the Shakespeare Association of America (1993–1994). Her articles on Shakespeare and related topics have appeared in numerous journals and anthologies. Her most recent book is *Stages of History: Shakespeare's English Chronicles* (Cornell University Press, 1990, and Routledge, 1991). She is presently working with Jean E. Howard on a feminist study of Shakespeare's English history plays.

JOHN ROGERS, an Assistant Professor of English at Yale University, has published articles on Milton and Marvell. He has just completed a book titled "The Matter of Revolution: The Poetics of Materialism in the Age of Milton."

MICHAEL C. SCHOENFELDT is Associate Professor of English and Associate Chair of the Department of English at the University of Michigan, Ann Arbor. He is the author of *Prayer and Power: George Herbert and Renaissance Courtship* (1991), and has published essays on Donne, Herbert, Jonson, Herrick, Milton, and Marvell. He is currently working on a book tentatively titled "The Conduct of Desire in the Renaissance."

JAMES R. SIEMON is Associate Professor of English at Boston University. His publications include *Shakespearean Iconoclasm* (1985), the forthcoming New Mermaids edition of Marlowe's *Jew of Malta,* and various articles on Renaissance drama and culture.

DEBORAH WILLIS is Assistant Professor of English at the University of California, Riverside, where she teaches Shakespeare and Renaissance drama. She is currently completing a book on Shakespeare and witch-hunting, tentatively titled "Notorious Defamations: Gender, Cultural Practice, and the Rise of Witch-Hunting in Early Modern England."

RICHARD WILSON is Lecturer in English at the University of Lancaster and a Visiting Fellow of the Shakespeare Institute, Stratford-upon-Avon. He is the author of numerous essays on Shakespeare and popular culture, a selection of which has been published as *Will Power: Essays on Shakespearean Authority* (1993). He has edited *New Historicism and Renaissance Drama* (1992) and is currently completing a book titled "Gothic Shakespeare: The Theatre of English Violence."

Index